THE
BEER
BOOK

EDITOR-IN-CHIEF
TIM HAMPSON

FOREWORD BY SAM CALAGIONE

THE
BEER
BOOK

WITH CONTRIBUTIONS FROM

TIM HAMPSON • STAN HIERONYMUS • WERNER OBALSKI • ALASTAIR GILMOUR • JORIS PATTYN

LORENZO DABOVE • GILBERT DELOS • CONRAD SEIDL • RON PATTINSON • LAURA STADLER-JENSEN

BRYAN HARRELL • WILLIE SIMPSON • GEOFF GRIGGS • ADRIAN TIERNEY-JONES

LONDON • NEW YORK
MELBOURNE • MUNICH • DELHI

Produced for Dorling Kindersley by
Blue Island Publishing

Publishing Director Rosalyn Ellis
Editorial Director Michael Ellis
Art Director Stephen Bere
Editor Fay Franklin
Designers Marisa Renzullo, Ian Midson
Researchers Rebecca Carman,
Jürgen Scheunemann, Katerina Cerna

For Dorling Kindersley
Project Editor Laura Nickoll
Senior Art Editor Isabel de Cordova
Senior Jacket Creative Nicola Powling
US Editors Shannon Beatty, Jenny Siklós
Managing Editor Dawn Henderson
Managing Art Editor Christine Keilty
Senior Production Editor Jenny Woodcock
Senior Production Controller Wendy Penn

First American Edition, 2008
Published in the United States by DK Publishing
375 Hudson Street
New York, New York 10014

09 10 11   10 9 8 7 6 5 4 3 2
TD398—Sept/2008

Published in Great Britain by Dorling Kindersley Limited.

A catalog record for this book is available from the Library of Congress.

ISBN 978-0-7566-3982-2

DK books are available at special discounts when purchased in bulk for sales
promotions, premiums, fund-raising, or educational use. For details, contact:
DK Publishing Special Markets, 375 Hudson Street, New York, New York
10014 or SpecialSales@dk.com.

Color reproduction by Colourscan, Singapore
Printed and bound in China by Hung Hing

Discover more at
www.dk.com

CONTENTS

FOREWORD BY SAM CALAGIONE

I believe that all beer is good. I also believe some beers are better than others. But my list of top beers would hopefully look very different from yours. The Beer Book is the ultimate toolbox for constructing and expanding your own list of favorites.

This is not a book for beer snobs: folks who want to impress their friends with fancy terminology. It is a book for beer lovers and beer geeks: people who want to learn more about beer because they love to drink it and share it with friends and loved ones.

My biggest hope is that this book will give you the courage and conviction to cheat on your go-to beer. That's right: being a hardcore beer lover means not being afraid to be promiscuous. Experiment. Go nuts. Step outside your comfort zone. Every person's palate is unique, which means we won't all love the same beers, and that is a beautiful thing. Within these pages you will likely find long-lost loves and new flames. With beer, there is nothing immoral about playing the field. Or as the folks at Wasatch Brewery in Utah say in an advertisement for their Polygamy Porter: "Why have just one?"

If we all had the same taste in beer there would only be one kind of beer available. I know—it sounds like the apocalypse. But it really almost happened in the United States not so long ago. Before Prohibition almost every major town had its own local brewery that made beers that reflected the background of the local people. After Prohibition came the mass consolidation and expansion of national breweries that made the light lager style ubiquitous and nearly wiped out the diversity of the local brewing scenes. At our low point in 1978, the United States had a mere 89 breweries (owned by 41 companies); before Prohibition, America had more than 1,500.

Today such a barren beer landscape seems almost unimaginable. There are more than 1,400 breweries in America and our country is not alone in the renaissance of great beer. As the owner of Dogfish Head, I've been lucky enough to travel, speak, and brew abroad in countries such as Denmark, Italy, Canada, The Czech Republic, Norway, and Belgium. Vibrant brewing scenes are thriving in these countries and many more. The passion, pride, and enthusiasm of today's commercial brewers, big and small, are boundless and infectious. I love talking shop and knocking back pints with brewers from other parts of the world. Of course, our native tongues are different, but we all speak the same language when it comes to beer.

Breweries around the world are pushing the envelope, looking backward to indigenous, historical recipes. At the same time many are looking forward and creating their own styles as they follow their brewing muse. Others are putting their own unique thumbprints on traditional styles. World-class examples of all three of these brewing philosophies are well-represented throughout this book.

There is no better time in history to be a beer lover than at this very moment. The breadth of high-quality choices is at an all time high.

The best part about this renaissance (aside from the glorious beer itself, of course) is that it wasn't funded by the half-billion dollar advertising campaigns of a few giant breweries. It was fueled by you: the beer lover. This has truly been an international, grassroots movement where the consumers voted with their wallets for more choice, more diversity, and more flavor. Friends, family members, and neighbors introduced one another to their favorite stouts, pilsners, lambics, IPAs, bocks, extreme beers, and tripel—expanding the international beer appreciation community one member at a time. The word has spread through the work of advocacy groups such as CAMRA, Beer Advocate, Rate Beer, and The Brewers Association. Beer bars, brewpubs, and better restaurants with broad beer lists drew us in and allowed us to further our experience. And now *The Beer Book* has arrived as an encyclopedic roadmap to our ever-expanding beer world.

Experts in the beer world believe in conveying pertinent information to consumers so that they can make up their own minds about what they want to drink. *The Beer Book* was written in this tradition: it gets right to the point, telling you about the beer, how and where it is made, and what the label looks like so you can actually find it in the store. It doesn't tell you if the beer is good or bad – it doesn't score the beer. It respectfully presents the beer, clearly and concisely, for you to score for yourself.

I remember taking part in a tasting at New Belgium Brewery in Colorado a few years ago. A group of brewers were presenting a few of their more exotic beers for the beer press and connoisseurs. Michael Jackson, the recently departed Bard of Beer and patriarch of beer journalism, was leading the tasting. He spoke about La Folie, a great wood-aged sour beer from New Belgium, for a moment, then took questions. The first question was "What do you think of the beer?" Michael answered, "Well I like it, but we have many beer writers and experts in the room, what do YOU think of the beer?" This kicked off a 20-minute open forum where beer lovers shared their personal thoughts and impressions of the beer. To my mind this was the quintessential beer experience: a bunch of beer lovers gathered around the object of their affection, sharing enthusiastic opinions in a welcoming environment.

I get the same warm and fuzzy feeling when I read *The Beer Book*. This is especially true if I am enjoying an IPA or an Imperial Stout as I thumb the pages and make notes next to the interesting beers I have yet to try. Whether you are a novice beer lover or a seasoned brewmaster, there are sure to be some rewarding discoveries within these pages. Every beer in here isn't for everybody. That's why there are so many amazing beers to choose from. Beautiful beers are in the eyes of their beholders. Cheers.

Sam Calagione
President and founder, Dogfish Head Craft Brewery

Author of *Brewing Up A Business*, *Extreme Brewing*, and *He Said Beer, She Said Wine*.

INTRODUCTION

This is a book all about beer—the best long drink in the world. It is a drink that has changed and civilized us, yet too often we think that a beer is just a beer—a standard product of our industrial society. Beer is a product of the land, however, made with wonderful natural ingredients. It is the art, craft, and science of the brewer that turns these ingredients into beer.

This book is an adventure—a journey through a fascinating world of flavors, colors, and aromas. On this expedition into the world of beer, we spend time in the new world of brewing in the United States, then travel through the great brewing nations of Europe—Germany, the British Isles, Belgium, and the Czech Republic. We also visit countries more often associated with their viniculture, such as Italy and France.

For a beer enthusiast, trying to imagine a world without beer is like trying to imagine a world without a sky or the stars above. It is a normal part of human life for so many of us that it can all too easily be taken for granted. But we shouldn't do so. Beer is one of the oldest and most popular drinks known to man. It is thought that about 10,000 years ago, in the Middle East, nomadic peoples began to grow and harvest grain and set up settlements near the fields. Some archeologists believe the reason man did this was to make beer.

EARLY BREWING

The first records of brewing are in the Middle East in Mesopotamia with the Sumerians 6,000 years ago. At least 3,000 years before the Christian era, an intoxicating drink, made from grains, was providing nutrition to people in Egypt. The writings of the Roman historian Pliny record that a fermented drink made from corn and water was drunk regularly across much of northern Europe. As well as enjoyment, there was a religious side to early brewing, and around the world today in tribal communities there are still ceremonies where an ancient form of beer is drunk.

BEER TODAY

The beer industry has two faces, one traditional, the other young and vibrant. Both can be found within this book. We should not decry the older industry—it has helped shape

Sparkling copper brewing kettles on display at the Heineken brewery's visitor center in Amsterdam

Portland Brewing, where the MacTarnahan's beer range is brewed

the way it is today. The older industry gave us refrigeration, science, and marketing—which is why we celebrate here the beers from breweries such as Carlsberg, Anheuser-Busch, and Heineken. They have elevated brewing from serendipity to an art and a science, and their creations are rightly found within this book. The young brewing world is a fascinating and dynamic one, and gets due attention here, too.

THE UNITED STATES

The US is the new world of beer. From Alaska to the Mexican border, American brewers are pushing at boundaries as never before. They brew darker beers, bitterer beers, and hoppier beers than can be found anywhere else.

At the Dogfish Head Brewery in Delaware, founder Sam Calagione is brewing "off centered ales for off centered people." His beers use unusual ingredients or "extreme" amounts of traditional ingredients. White

Muscat grapes, honey, saffron, liquorice, chicory, and coffee have all been added to the kettles.

At the Alaskan Brewery in Juneau, each of the beers emphasizes its regional roots. Its Smoked Porter uses malt smoked with alder at the local fishery. And Samuel Adams in Boston, Massachusetts, continues to push at the boundaries of strength. Utopias, at 26.5% ABV, just keeps getting stronger.

Brooklyn Brewery's brewmaster, Garrett Oliver, has also taken the pairing of beer with food to new heights. He wants every restaurant to have a beer list to stand proudly alongside its wine list.

EUROPE

The great brewing nations of Europe still stand tall, with glorious tradition coupled with intriguing innovation. All across Germany, wonderful beer gardens are to be found. Here, brimming liter steins, booming oompah bands, and exuberant celebrations help make the country a beer paradise. In the main, the country's brewing tastes remains very traditional, with even new brewpubs producing pilsner-style beers rather than being innovative. However, the country has more than 15 classic beer styles, ranging from the rauchbier of Bamberg and Nurnberg to Cologne's soft kölsch, served by the blue-aproned köbes, and the acidic weissbier of Berlin.

In the British Isles, Thornbridge is one of a new wave of small breweries. It has rapidly gained a reputation for innovative beers, with an emphasis on extracting exciting flavors from a wide range of ingredients and methods. Flavor is also key to Alastair Hook, brewmaster at London's Meantime Brewery. His Coffee Porter, which is rich with roasted cappuccino flavors, is brewed with fair-trade coffee beans from Rwanda.

Beer drinkers in Belgium probably have more choice about which beer to drink than in any other country in the world. From Flanders come pale ales and sour red ales. Add to this the gueuze, lambic, and krieks of Brussels, the country's abbey ales and *saisons*, and not forgetting its witbier, and the drinker in Belgium is spoilt for choice.

The town of Pilzeň in the Czech Republic plays an important part in the history of beer. Here, in 1842, brewer Josef Groll mastered the art of triple decoction mashing, which created a golden, clear beer. And, as they say, the rest is history, as pilsner is now the world's dominant beer style.

The traditional winemaking country of Italy has more than its fair share of brewing tyros. Indeed, it is not uncommon to find American brewers touring the country's more innovative new breweries, looking for inspiration.

Teo Musso lives in a part of Italy renowned for its Barolo and Barbera wines. At his Le Baladin brewery he produces "his raptures" using wine and whiskey yeasts. One beer, Xyauyu, is oxidized for a year to produce mouth-tingling, sherrylike flavors.

Former homebrewer Agostino Arioli saw the light after a visit to Grenville Island Brewery in Vancouver, Canada. Today, production at his Birrificio Italiano includes

A fruit beer lambic (wild beer) from Belgium's Cantillon

Fleurette, a beer brewed with barley, wheat, and rye, and flavored with rose petals. His Tipopils, which is hopped with four hop varieties (Hallertauer Magnum, Perle, Herbsucker, and Saaz), was recently voted the world's best pilsner by Ratebeer.com.

PACIFIC RIM

In Japan, the Isekaddoya Brewery uses soybean paste and the juice from a native aromatic citrus fruit called yuzu. Even Cabernet grapes can be found in some Japanese brewers' mash tuns and kettles. And Hakuseikan uses wild, airborne yeasts to make a distinctive, Japanese-style lambic.

In Australia there are more than 100 brewers producing an exciting array of beer styles. The family owned Coopers Brewery, which opened in 1862, continues with its exquisite range of cloudy, bottle-conditioned beers, while relative newcomer Little Creatures, in Fremantle, has introduced US-style, hoppy pale ales to the local market.

BEER VERSUS WINE

Wine and beer should have equal billing in the pantheon of alcoholic drinks. Yet, wine is treated by many as a cultured drink, while beer is not. The brewer has a trickier task than that of the winemaker, too, for the brewer must extract sweet fermentable sugars from cereal rather than resinous grapes. The brewer garners and unleashes the magic of yeast, which converts the sugar into alcohol, and it is the brewer who adds the fragile hops, with their bouquet of aromas, flavors, and cleansing qualities. The result of all this is that drinkers today can choose from more than 100 different styles of beer, covering

Boulevard Brewing, in Kansas City, Missouri

every imaginable flavor and color. From the simple notes of grain, yeast, hops, and water, brewers create a symphony of tastes, colors.

We should drink with our eyes and noses before we take a sip to experience the spectrum of colors and burst of aromas. Then, and only then, take a sip and let the beer unleash its flavors on your tongue.

KNOWLEDGE IS POWER

With copious tasting notes and features that explain beer styles and the role of key ingredients, this book provides the information to understand what creates the complexity of vivid colors, aromas, and flavors in beer. Within these pages are the brewing innovators and creators of some of the world's greatest beers. Beers from many countries are listed, along with information on their alcoholic strength (ABV) and style. It is a companion to a wonderful world in which beer is much

more than just a beer. It should encourage you never to ask just for a beer without first considering its style—pilsner or wheat, fruit or an American IPA, Belgian ale or a gueuze?

In 10,000 years we have changed from hunter gatherers to civilized people with rich cultures. Beer was there right at the beginning and has changed with us from "liquid bread" to a sophisticated drink. Whatever the next 10,000 years bring, we can be pretty sure that beer will still be a vital component of the human experience. For there can be few better pleasures—when returning home after a long day at work or just sitting in a favorite bar—than the pleasure of a great beer. But which one? The choice is yours—enjoy the experience.

Tim Hampson

BEERS TO TRAVEL FOR

KEY NATIONS

USA • GERMANY • BRITISH ISLES • BELGIUM • CZECH REPUBLIC

WASHINGTON, OREGON

Boundary Bay
Diamond Knot
Redhook
Seattle
Mac & Jack's
Fish
WASHINGTON

Pelican
Portland Full Sail
Rogue
Terminal Gravity
Deschutes
OREGON
Caldera

Seattle
Elysian
Georgetown
Hale's
Pike
Pyramid

Portland, Oregon
Bridgeport
Hair of the Dog
Hopworks
Mactarnahan's
Widmer

ALASKA

ALASKA
Midnight Sun
Alaskan

MINNESOTA,

Surly Summit
Leinenkuge
August Schell
MINNESOTA
IOWA
Millstream

NORTHERN CALIFORNIA

Lost Coast Mad River
Eel River
North Coast
Butte Creek/
Sierra Nevada
Anderson Valley Mendocino
Bear Republic Moonlight
Russian River Sacramento
Lagunitas Sudwerk
Marin Trumer
San Francisco
Drake's

San Francisco
Anchor
Shmaltz
Speakeasy

SOUTHERN CALIFORNIA

Green Flash Lost Abbey
Stone
Alesmith/ Alpine
Ballast Point

HAWAII

HAWAII
Kona

COLORADO

New Belgium/
Odell
Oskar Blues Left Hand
Avery/
Coors Boulder
Tommyknocker
Denver
COLORADO
Bristol

Denver
Breckenridge
Flying Dog
Great Divide
Wynkoop

Seattle
WASHINGTON
Portland
OREGON
Bayern/
Big Sky MONTANA NORTH DAKOTA
MINNESOTA
IDAHO
Grand Teton Snake River
WYOMING SOUTH DAKOTA
IOW
San Francisco
Uinta/
Utah Brewers
NEVADA
NEBRASKA
Upstream
UTAH
Denver
COLORADO
Boulevard
Firestone Walker
CALIFORNIA
KANSAS
MISSOURI
Ska/
Steamworks
ARIZONA Marble
OKLAHOMA
Four Peaks NEW MEXICO Choc
Nimbus
TEXAS

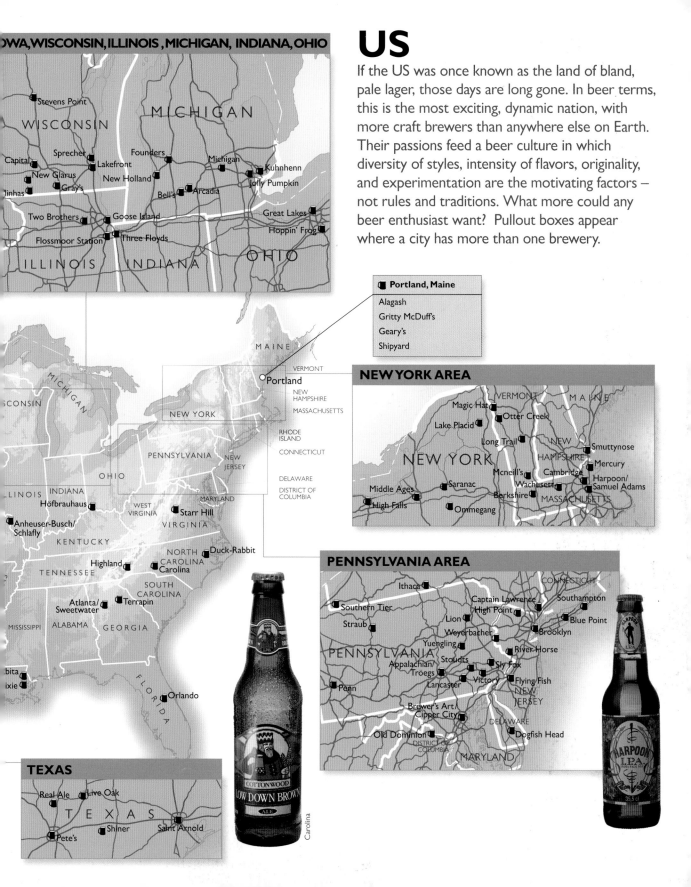

US

If the US was once known as the land of bland, pale lager, those days are long gone. In beer terms, this is the most exciting, dynamic nation, with more craft brewers than anywhere else on Earth. Their passions feed a beer culture in which diversity of styles, intensity of flavors, originality, and experimentation are the motivating factors – not rules and traditions. What more could any beer enthusiast want? Pullout boxes appear where a city has more than one brewery.

IOWA, WISCONSIN, ILLINOIS, MICHIGAN, INDIANA, OHIO

MICHIGAN

WISCONSIN
- Stevens Point
- Sprecher
- Capital
- New Glarus
- Minhas
- Gray's
- Lakefront
- Founders
- New Holland
- Bell's
- Arcadia
- Michigan
- Kuhnhenn
- Jolly Pumpkin
- Two Brothers
- Goose Island
- Great Lakes
- Flossmoor Station
- Three Floyds
- Hoppin' Frog

ILLINOIS   INDIANA   OHIO

Portland, Maine
- Alagash
- Gritty McDuff's
- Geary's
- Shipyard

MAINE

- Portland

VERMONT
NEW HAMPSHIRE
MASSACHUSETTS
RHODE ISLAND
CONNECTICUT
DELAWARE
DISTRICT OF COLUMBIA

NEW YORK
PENNSYLVANIA
NEW JERSEY
MARYLAND

WISCONSIN
MICHIGAN
OHIO
INDIANA
ILLINOIS
KENTUCKY
TENNESSEE
WEST VIRGINIA
VIRGINIA
- Höfbrauhaus
- Anheuser-Busch/Schlafly
- Starr Hill
- Highland
- Carolina
- Duck-Rabbit

NORTH CAROLINA
SOUTH CAROLINA
- Atlanta/Sweetwater
- Terrapin

GEORGIA
ALABAMA
MISSISSIPPI
- bita
- ixie

FLORIDA
- Orlando

NEW YORK AREA

VERMONT   MAINE
- Magic Hat
- Otter Creek
- Lake Placid
- Long Trail
- Smuttynose
- Mercury

NEW YORK
NEW HAMPSHIRE
- Mcneill's
- Cambridge
- Harpoon/Samuel Adams
- Middle Ages
- Saranac
- Wachusett
- Berkshire
- High Falls
- Ommegang

MASSACHUSETTS

PENNSYLVANIA AREA

- Ithaca
- Southern Tier
- Straub

CONNECTICUT
- Captain Lawrence
- Southampton
- High Point
- Lion
- Blue Point
- Weyerbacher
- Brooklyn
- Yuengling
- River Horse

PENNSYLVANIA
- Stoudts
- Sly Fox
- Appalachian/Tröegs
- Victory
- Lancaster
- Flying Fish
- Penn
- Brewer's Art/Cipper City
- Old Dominion
- Dogfish Head

NEW JERSEY
DELAWARE
DISTRICT OF COLUMBIA
MARYLAND

TEXAS

- Real Ale
- Live Oak
- Pete's
- Shiner
- Saint Arnold

T E X A S

Carolina

BREWERY

ABITA

P.O. Box 1510
Abita Springs, LA 70420
www.abita.com

A sleepy town in the pinewoods north of Lake Pontchartrain, Abita Springs was best known for the healing powers of its mineral waters before Abita Brewing opened as a brewpub in 1986. Today Abita operates a fast-growing, thoroughly modern brewery, the largest specialty producer south of the Mason-Dixon line.

ALASKAN

5429 Shaune Drive
Juneau, AK 99801
www.alaskanbeer.com

Although it is located in a coastal community without roads connecting it to the rest of the United States, Alaskan Brewing has grown into a regional force, selling its beer over much of the nation west of the Rockies. Founders Geoff and Marcy Larson focused on native ingredients and recipes from the outset. Alaskan's first and flagship brew, Amber Ale, is based on a beer made across the channel from Juneau back at the turn of the 20th century.

BREWING SECRET Alaskan's Smoked Porter, a beer that typifies what's new in American brewing, is made with malt smoked at a local fishery.

ALESMITH

9368 Cabot Drive
San Diego, CA 92126
www.alesmith.com

One of several San Diego breweries that has pushed Southern California to the forefront of national brewing. It has a wide following for its mostly strong and often esoteric beers, many barrel-aged and vintage-dated.

BREWING SECRET Every employee is an award-winning home brewer.

BEER

PURPLE HAZE
FRUIT BEER 4.75% ABV
Wheat ale infused with raspberry purée. Mildly sweet; a refreshing remedy for southern humidity.

TURBODOG
BROWN ALE 6.1% ABV
Dark, with a rich chocolate nose, and toffee emerging on the palate; a bitter-coffee finish.

AMBER
ALTBIER 5% ABV
Clean caramel on the nose, brightened by spicy hops. Smooth and malty, with balanced bitterness.

BARLEY WINE ALE
BARLEY WINE 10.4% ABV
Cellared in a former gold mine. Rich and smooth, with dark caramel, cherries, and plums. Nicely balanced.

SMOKED PORTER
SMOKED BEER 6.5% ABV
Alder-smoked. Flavors of chocolate and burnt fruit; luscious and oily on the palate. Smoky from the beginning through to a satisfying finish.

WINTER ALE
WINTER BEER 6.4% ABV
Spruce intermingles with fruit at the start. Modestly rich on the palate, woody at the finish.

SPEEDWAY STOUT
IMPERIAL STOUT 12% ABV
It's coffee-infused, complementing a broad imperial palate of chocolate, toffee, currants, and oily nuts.

IPA
INDIA PALE ALE 7.3% ABV
Brimming with hops and fruit salad aromas, including notes of ripe mango and pineapple.

ALLAGASH

100 Industrial Way
Portland, ME 04103
www.allagash.com

Focusing on Belgian-inspired beers, Allagash draws on tradition but does not shy away from innovation. In 2007 it became the first American brewery to build a traditional "coolship" (a huge, open, shallow pan) for spontaneous fermentation by wild yeasts.

BREWING SECRET Some specialty beers are aged in oak bourbon barrels.

ALLAGASH WHITE

WITBIER 6.2% ABV
Appropriately cloudy, fruity, and refreshing. Brightened by subtle coriander and Curaçao orange peel.

CURIEUX

TRIPLE 10% ABV
Allagash Tripel ale, aged in Jim Beam barrels. Orchard fruits and honey meet bourbon, vanilla, and wood.

ALPINE

2351 Alpine Boulevard
Alpine, CA 91901
www.alpinebeerco.com

This brewery is known first for beers whose names describe their hoppy nature, such as Pure Hoppiness and Exponential Hoppiness ("double dry-hopped" and not always available). It also produces beers with unusual ingredients, including a honey ale with orange zest and coriander, and a wheat beer infused with vanilla pods.

PURE HOPPINESS

INDIA PALE ALE 8% ABV
A balance of German hops for spiciness and American Northwest varieties for piney and citrus flavors.

MCILHENNEY'S IRISH RED

IRISH RED 6% ABV
Brewed with 11 malts, including rye. Complex aromas, with caramel and toffee emerging on the palate. A spicy, medium-dry finish.

ANCHOR

705 Mariposa St.
San Francisco, CA 94107
www.anchorbrewing.com

Fritz Maytag saved Anchor Brewing from closing in 1965, introduced US drinkers to many classic styles, and launched a microbrewery revolution.

BREWING SECRET Maytag is known for preserving the indigenous "steam style," which involves using bottom-fermenting yeast at high temperatures in wide, shallow, open pans.

LIBERTY ALE

PALE ALE 6% ABV
A benchmark American pale ale. Fruity and floral on the nose; crisp bitterness on the palate.

ANCHOR STEAM

STEAM BEER 4.9% ABV
A signature woody, minty nose. Well-rounded caramel flavors yield to a firm, crisp finish.

THE BEST-KNOWN BEERS OF THE USA

Over the last 30 years, the US has undergone a sea change in the world of beer. While it now offers great variety, the mass market is packed with pale light beers.

Just a few decades ago, the US was a country with one basic style choice when it came to beer—a pale lager, generally light in body and lacking in hop flavor or aroma. Today, there are more than 1,400 breweries, producing a wider range of beers than has ever been available anywhere in the world before. However, despite this dramatic change, the overall market is still dominated by Anheuser-Busch InBev (who produce Budweiser, Coors, and Miller. The market is led by light beers. In fact, six of the top seven selling domestically produced beers are low-calorie lagers. America's brewing past can still be glimpsed on faded advertisements along the back roads, promoting brands from breweries long gone. But many of those brands are still produced under contract—such as Pabst, Schlitz, and Lone Star—and have avid fans. All are pale lagers that taste much alike.

BUD LITE (LAGER 4.2% ABV)
BUDWEISER (LAGER 5% ABV) *left*
COORS LIGHT (LAGER 4.2% ABV)
center
MILLER LITE (LAGER 4.2% ABV)
BUSCH LIGHT (LAGER 4.2% ABV)
MICHELOB LIGHT (LAGER 4.2% ABV) *right*
PABST (LAGER 5% ABV)
SCHLITZ (LAGER 4.7% ABV)
LONE STAR (LAGER 4.7% ABV)

BREWERY

ANDERSON VALLEY
17700 Highway 253
Boonville, CA 95415
www.avbc.com

Set in Mendocino County's picturesque Anderson Valley, this solar-powered brewery mixes local and international styles and techniques. Some beer names are those of local landmarks, others are in Boontling, a regional dialect.

BREWING SECRET The copper brew kettles were rescued from a closed-down German brewery.

ANHEUSER-BUSCH
One Busch Plaza
St. Louis, MO 63119
www.anheuser-busch.com

Anheuser-Busch brews half the beer sold in the United States, including Budweiser and Bud Light, two of the world's best-selling brands. With its Michelob line, seasonal specialties, and beers produced by its regional breweries for local consumers, the company has significantly broadened the range of its beers.

APPALACHIAN
50 N. Cameron Street
Harrisburg, PA 17101
www.abcbrew.com

There's room in this cavernous facility, rich in bricks and timber, for the brewery, a restaurant, and a separate specialty beer bar. It took two years to restore the century-old building. Founded in Harrisburg in 1997, the Appalachian Brewing Company has two other brewpubs, at Camp Hill and Gettysberg.

ARCADIA
103 West Michigan Avenue
Battle Creek, MI 49017
www.arcadiabrewingcompany.com

Using the British Peter Austin system more common in the Northeast, and brewing with British malts, Arcadia leans toward UK-inspired ales, but made with citrussy and piney Pacific Northwest hops. Ringwood yeast gives the beers a fresh character, and they work particularly well on cask.

BEER

BOONT ESB
EXTRA SPECIAL BITTER 6.8% ABV
Citrussy hops layer fruit on top of bready malt. Tangy in the middle; a long and mildly bitter finish.

MICHELOB
MALT LAGER 5% ABV
Returned to its all-malt roots in 2007. Delicate, with a spicy nose, clean malt middle and crisp, dry finish.

HINTERLAND HEFE WEIZEN
HEFEWEIZEN 5.2% ABV
Banana, orchard fruits, and bubble gum aromas. Fresh, tart wheat on the tongue, and a light clove finish.

LONDON PORTER
PORTER 7.2% ABV
Rich on the nose, flavors of coffee beans, chocolate, and dark fruit, with a lingering, dessertlike finish.

BARNEY FLATS OATMEAL STOUT
OATMEAL STOUT 5.7% ABV
Impression of coffee and cream, sweetness balanced by roasted grains, the complexity heightened by earthy undertones.

STONE MILL ORGANIC PALE ALE
PALE ALE 5.5% ABV
Organic beer under the Green Valley Brewing label. This ale is lightly bready with earthy hop character.

JOLLY SCOT SCOTTISH ALE
SCOTTISH ALE 5.2% ABV
A straightforward session beer. Hints of rich caramel, a touch of smokiness, and a final impression of sweetness.

SCOTCH ALE
SCOTTISH ALE 7.5% ABV
Nuttiness and piney hops don't totally balance here. The final impression is of sweet caramel.

ATLANTA

2323 Defoor Hills Road, NW
Atlanta, GA 30318
www.atlantabrewing.com

Founded in 1993, Atlanta Brewing was recently forced to abandon the iconic red-brick brewery, after which its beers are named, to make way for a highway. New owners have boosted capacity and expanded distribution, building on the southeast's growing reputation for specialty beers.

AUGUST SCHELL

1860 Schell Road
New Ulm, MN 56073
www.schellsbrewery.com

Family-owned since August Schell founded it in 1860, this brewery has perhaps the most beautiful setting in the US, with ornamental gardens and a former carriage house converted into a museum. In 2002 the company took over production of the legendary Grain Belt Premium beer, when that brewery failed, to save a Minnesota icon from extinction.

AVERY

5763 Arapahoe Avenue
Boulder, CO 80803
www.averybrewing.com

Located near the Rocky Mountains, though in a nondescript industrial park, this brewery has earned a reputation for its hoppy beers and its astonishingly strong beers (sometimes they are both). These include a threesome nicknamed the "Demons of Ale," in which the beers average 15 percent ABV apiece.

BALLAST POINT

5401 Linda Vista Road
San Diego, CA 92110
www.ballastpoint.com

This brewery started in the back of a homebrew shop, offering a dizzying variety of beers, including the hop-centric kinds for which San Diego has become known.

BREWING SECRET Their Kölsch has proved so popular that a separate production brewery has been built to keep up with demand.

RED BRICK ALE

BROWN ALE 6.5% ABV
Surprisingly strong. Caramel and toffee throughout, with underlying notes of chocolate and coffee.

RED BRICK WINTER BREW

WINTER BEER 7.5% ABV
A "double chocolate oatmeal porter" relying on barley malt for a range of rich and bitter chocolate flavors.

CARAMEL BOCK

BOCK 5.6% ABV
Rich caramel on the nose, turning rummy on the palate. Sweetness lingers after a not-quite dry finish.

SCHMALTZ ALT

ALTBIER 5% ABV
Subtle combination of biscuit and chocolate balanced by mild, slightly spicy hop flavors and bitterness.

INDIA PALE ALE

INDIA PALE ALE 6.3% ABV
Piney, oily nose, with grapefruit and orange from the aroma to the palate. Unapologetically bitter.

SALVATION

BELGIAN STRONG GOLDEN ALE 9% ABV
Fleshy fruits, particularly apricots, mingle with sweet, spicy aromas and flavors, and a surprising hint of honey.

YELLOWTAIL PALE ALE

KÖLSCH 4.6% ABV
Soft and sweet on the nose with a hint of spices. Dry cracker flavors yield to a floral, but still dry finish.

DORADO DOUBLE IPA

IMPERIAL INDIA PALE ALE 9.6% ABV
Flavors of pine and grapefruit throughout. Hop oils on the palate blend with a solid malt structure. Long, bitter finish.

Anheuser-Busch InBev

One Busch Place,
St Louis, Missouri 63118

Anheuser-Busch InBev is a potent image of America, and it remains so even though the company was taken over by InBev in 2008.

In the 1850s St Louis, in America's Midwest, bustled with German immigrants who had fled revolution in Europe, bringing with them their language, culture, and a love of beer. By 1870 the city had 50 breweries. St Louis is built over limestone caves; today most are sealed up but, at the time, they were natural cold stores, where beer could be kept and conditioned (lagered) until ready for sale. In 1852, George Schneider opened the Bavarian Brewery. Sadly, he wasn't much of a businessman and soon went bust, but this was the beginning of a company that today brews America's best-known beer brand, Budweiser.

The company had a couple more owners before Eberhard Anheuser acquired it in 1860. A German who had emigrated to America in 1843, he made his fortune by making and selling soap. But the brewery owed him money and he took shares in it to clear the debt. He believed he could make money from the beer suds. But it was the involvement of his son-in-law Adolphus Busch in 1864 that sparked the transformation from local brewery into national icon. The company was renamed the Anheuser-Busch Brewing Association in 1879 and, a year later, when Eberhard died, Adolphus became its president. His great-great-grandson August Busch IV is a member of the Anheuser-Busch InBev board.

◄ A NATURAL SALESMAN The biggest asset that Adolphus Busch brought to the business was his exceptional skill as a salesman. He could have sold ice to the Eskimos and coals to Newcastle—instead, he sold a beer to America. Adolphus became the merchant prince of the "king of beers".

▼ DRAY HORSES Anheuser-Busch InBev used shire horses for its beer deliveries in St Louis in the early days, and the horses are still trotted out today on special occasions.

▲ COLD BEER AND FAST TRAINS It was a combination of railways, refrigeration, and pasteurization that meant the beers of St Louis knew no frontiers. Refrigerated railcars saw beer, which might otherwise spoil in days, carried across the country. Over the Rockies to the West Coast, up to the wind-chilled shores of the Great Lakes, across to the hot, humid, burgeoning cities on the East Coast, bottled beer was guaranteed to keep fresh in any climate thanks to pasteurization.

▼ THE ART OF ADVERTISING

It was the marriage of brewing and the new industry of advertising that proved the real key to capturing a mass market. From the use of the American eagle icon to the use of beautiful women in advertising campaigns, Adolphus Busch knew how to market beer. Over the course of 35 years, Adolphus grew a brewery with a production of 4,000 barrels per annum into one turning out more than one million barrels by 1901.

▼ AN AMERICAN SUCCESS

It is hard to imagine the scale of Anheuser-Busch InBev, but, as befits a company that brews nearly one in every two beers drunk in America, it is huge. The new owners have retained its current brewery and offices in St Louis, making it the North American headquarters for the combined company.

▲ BUDWEISER

It was in 1876 that Anheuser first sold a beer called Budweiser. It didn't catch on immediately, though; for a time the locals stuck faithfully with the company's now long-gone St Louis Lager Beer.

▶ MICHELOB

Another popular Anheuser-Busch brand name, Michelob was first sold 1896, with a tiny output aimed at "connoisseurs."

BREWERY

BAYERN

1507 Montana Street
Missoula, MT 59801
www.bayernbrewery.com

Bayern Brewing focuses solely on
the beers of Bavaria, where owner-
brewer Jürgen Knöller was born.
He is a German Diploma Master
Brewer, who started brewing when
he was 16 and joined Bayern when
it opened in 1987, buying the brewery
four years later.

BEAR REPUBLIC

345 Healdsburg Avenue
Healdsburg, CA 95448
www.bearrepublic.com

With a brewpub located amidst the
Sonoma County wine-tasting rooms
and a brewery north of town, Bear
Republic presents a decidedly different
break for wine tourists. Founding
brewmaster (and fireman and race-
car-driver) Richard Norgrove is just
as skilled as any wine blender when
merging hops flavors and aromas.

BELL'S

8938 Krum Avenue
Galesburg, MI 49053
www.bellsbeer.com

The oldest surviving microbrewery
west of Colorado, Bell's (formerly
Kalamazoo Brewing) has grown nearly
700-fold since its first sales in 1985.
Founder Larry Bell has earned a
reputation as something of a maverick.
In 2006 he withdrew his beer from
sale in Illinois, one of the brewery's
top markets, in a distribution dispute.
However, in late 2007 he launched a

range of Kalamazoo (not Bell's) beers
back into the Chicago area. Bell's has
built a new brewing facility outside
Kalamazoo, but the original brewery
remains, along with its appropriately
named Eccentric Café. Bell's beers are
famous for their intensity, although
the brewery flagship is wheat-based.

BEER

BAYERN PILSENER

PILSNER 5% ABV
Flowery to start, with not-quite-
sweet malt flavors quickly followed
by a hoppy bitterness.

BAYERN AMBER

VIENNA LAGER 5.3% ABV
Created when the brewery opened,
blending a rich Oktoberfest malt
profile with Czech Pilsner hops.

RACER 5

INDIA PALE ALE 7% ABV
Delightfully fresh grapefruit and
thick piney aromas, built on a
resinous, malty-sweet middle.

HOP ROD RYE

IMPERIAL INDIA PALE ALE 8% ABV
Bright, citrussy nose with spicy
alcohols. A subtle blend of biscuit
and clean rye. Incessant hops.

EXPEDITION STOUT

IMPERIAL STOUT 11.5% ABV
Begins with an intense blast of dark
fruit (figs and plums) that turns into
chocolate, roasted coffee, and port.

TWO HEARTED ALE

INDIA PALE ALE 7% ABV
Amplified hops, with an initial rush
of grapefruit and orange mingling
with fresh floral notes. Perfectly
balanced, with persistent bitterness.

OBERON ALE

WHEAT BEER 5.8% ABV
A summer refresher. Zesty, with
orange rind in the aroma, and
delicate spiciness behind that.
A crisp, sharp finish.

BEST BROWN ALE

BROWN ALE 5.8% ABV
Brimming with rich flavors such as
caramel and chocolate, subtly
balanced by rustic hops.

BERKSHIRE

12 Rail Road Street South
Deerfield, MA 01373
www.berkshirebrewingcompany.com

Western Massachusetts' local brewery (although its beers are increasingly easy to find in Boston). BBC handles almost all its own distribution, guaranteeing that its beer will be fresh and retain a subtle, balanced complexity that begins with open fermentation.

BREWING SECRET These pure, unfiltered beers must be kept refrigerated.

BIG SKY

5417 Trumpeter Way
Missoula, MT 59808
www.bigskybrew.com

Three partners successfully combined a quality ale with a clever name (albeit one it had to defend in lawsuits lodged by Canadian brewer Moosehead) and an attractive label. Big Sky has grown quickly into a regional brewery selling beer from Alaska to Minnesota, three-quarters of it their flagship brown ale.

BJ'S

Various locations
www.bjsbrewhouse.com

BJ's operates restaurants in more than a dozen states, each selling a line-up of seven regular beers, some brewed on premises and some at other BJ's or at the production brewery in Reno, Nevada. Most locations offer seasonal or special beers, some of them exceptional, such as Nit Wit, a Belgian-style white beer. Many of the beers have won awards.

BLUE POINT

161 River Avenue
Patchogue, NY 11772
www.bluepointbrewing.com

This microbrewery was founded in 1998 in a former ice factory. Its draft beer, brewed here, is on tap across Long Island and in Manhattan; its bottled beer is now outsourced.

BREWING SECRET Blue Point's draft beer is brewed in a direct-fire kettle that comes from Marylands' former Wild Goose Brewery.

DRAYMAN'S PORTER
PORTER 6.2% ABV
Coffeelike aromas, a complex middle (chocolate and toffee), and a pleasantly bitter finish.

RASPBERRY STRONG ALE
FRUIT BEER 9% ABV
Brewed with fresh berries and released for Valentine's Day. Scarily nicknamed "Truth Serum."

MOOSE DROOL
BROWN ALE 5.3% ABV
Dark fruits and nuts mingle with chocolate; sweetness moderated by earthy hop notes. Chocolate-brown with a medium body.

SCAPE GOAT PALE ALE
PALE ALE 4.7% ABV
Biscuity, fruity, and spicy on the palate, balanced by moderate bitterness. Short but dry finish.

JEREMIAH'S RED ALE
STRONG ALE 7.3% ABV
A cross between an Irish red and an English strong ale, with rich, clean caramel-toffee malt. Dry finish.

HARVEST HEFEWEIZEN
HEFEWEIZEN 4.9% ABV
Genuinely Bavarian, cloudy, with substantial banana notes on the nose. Fruity on the palate.

TOASTED LAGER
VIENNA LAGER 5.2% ABV
The direct-fire kettling produces toasted-nut aromas and flavors. A firm, medium-dry finish.

EXTRA SPECIAL BITTER
EXTRA SPECIAL BITTER 5% ABV
Full body, rich caramel flavors balanced by earthy British hops. Best on cask at the brewery.

BREWERY

BOSCOS

Various locations
www.boscosbeer.com

Since 1992 this brewpub chain has been a leader in promoting greater knowledge of beer in the mid-south. Its pubs feature English-inspired cask-conditioned ales, with customers invited to participate as cellermen.

BREWING SECRET Flaming Stone's brewing process involves red-hot chunks of granite being plunged into the wort to caramelize the sugars.

BOULDER

2880 Wilderness Place
Boulder, CO 80301
www.boulderbeer.com

The first US microbrewery outside of California, Boulder has been something of a poster child for the "movement" because its partners began brewing in a goat shed and it relied on the largesse of domestic giant Coors to acquire ingredients. Boulder Beer is available in much of the US, and emphasizes its Colorado roots.

BOULEVARD

2501 Southwest Boulevard
Kansas City, MO 64108
www.blvdbeer.com

Boulevard is all about Midwestern hospitality, starting with friendly tours of its smokestack-topped brewery, and including a range of beers well suited to Heartland dining such as Kansas City's famous barbecue.

BREWING SECRET The brewery's Smokestack Series is a range of Champagne-bottle-conditioned beers.

BOUNDARY BAY

1107 Railroad Avenue
Bellingham, WA 98225
www.bbaybrewery.com

Three brewpubs opened in this town on Bellingham Bay during the beer boom of the 1990s. Boundary Bay is the survivor, and has become one of the nation's most productive brewpubs. Further expansion, both in production and in distribution, is planned. At the brewhouse, a new cask is tapped every Thursday at 4 p.m.

BEER

FLAMING STONE BEER

STEINBEER 4.8% ABV
Brewed in the manner of German stein beers. Caramel, toffee, and nuts throughout. Smoky, dry finish.

HEFEWEIZEN

HEFEWEIZEN 4.8% ABV
Classic bubblegum and banana nose; softer fruity (more banana) and creamy flavors, with underlying spices including light clove notes.

PLANET PORTER

PORTER 5.1% ABV
The brewery's original beer. Dark fruit aromas and flavors. Subdued roasted malts and bitterness.

HAZED & INFUSED

PALE ALE 4.85% ABV
As hazy as promised—hops in suspension—supported by a bouquet of citrus, flowers, and spices.

UNFILTERED WHEAT

US WHEAT BEER 4.5% ABV
A remedy for Missouri humidity, cloudy and lightly grainy, with refreshing citrus throughout.

BULLY PORTER

PORTER 5.4% ABV
Roasted coffee on the nose, with chocolate emerging on the palate. Slightly sweet, rich, with subtle, balancing hop flavors and finish.

IPA

INDIA PALE ALE 6.4% ABV
Rich with Northwest hop flavors and aromas—orange, and grapefruit. Malt sweetness yields to resiny, bitter finish.

IMPERIAL IPA

IMPERIAL INDIA PALE ALE 9% ABV
Thick with rich malts and hops. A blast of oranges, grapefruit, and pineapple, and a long, bitter finish.

BRECKENRIDGE

471 Kalamath Street
Denver, CO 80204
www.breckbrew.com

This was founded as a brewpub in the ski resort of Breckenridge, where a pub still operates, before expanding with the Denver-based brewery, which also has an attached pub. Breckenridge briefly ran a chain of pubs across several states, but only those in Colorado remain.

BREWER'S ART

1106 N. Charles Street
Baltimore, MD 21201
www.thebrewersart.com

Housed in a grand 1902 townhouse in the Mount Vernon area, The Brewer's Art serves Belgian-inspired house beers and an outstanding selection of continental (primarily Belgian) beers in a comfortable dining atmosphere. It recently began brewing and bottling some of its beer under contract in Pennsylvania.

BRIDGEPORT

1313 Northwest Marshall Street
Portland, OR 97209
www.bridgeportbrew.com

BridgePort Brewing holds the trademark of Oregon's Oldest Craft Brewery, and its India Pale Ale has come to define the Northwest's beer character. Despite several expansions, it remains Portland-oriented. It dedicates each release of Old Knucklehead, its seasonal barley wine, to a different local personality.

BRISTOL

1647 South Tejon
Colorado Springs, CO 80906
www.bristolbrewing.com

Since opening in 1994, Bristol Brewing has been the beer hub in Colorado Springs, as others have come and gone. It ventured into experimenting with barrels ahead of many US breweries.

BREWING SECRET It has won awards with a beer made using wild yeast and lactic acid bacteria from raspberries picked in nearby Cheyenne Canyon.

AVALANCHE ALE
AMBER ALE 5.4% ABV
Flagship ale, fruity and tart but balanced with sweetness, including caramel and honey on the palate.

OATMEAL STOUT
OATMEAL STOUT 4.95% ABV
Rich with roasted chocolate and a very creamy texture. Complex, hints of smoke, pleasingly bitter at the end.

GREEN PEPPERCORN TRIPEL
TRIPLE 10% ABV
Effervescent and full of life. Fruity and spicy, a bit of candy sweetness, subdued pepper, and a dryish finish.

RESURRECTION
DOUBLE 7% ABV
Caramel, dark fruits on the palate, and surprising citrus notes. The yeast in the first batch "died" and was "resurrected," hence the name.

INDIA PALE ALE
INDIA PALE ALE 5.5% ABV
Citrussy from the outset. Solid malt backbone, delicate fruits (peaches and apples). Complex hoppy finish.

BLACK STRAP STOUT
STOUT 6% ABV
A rich blend of black strap molasses, chocolate and coffee, finishing with roasted bitterness.

WINTER WARLOCK
OATMEAL STOUT 6.5% ABV
Toasted marshmallows and chocolate up front, creamy chocolate and roasted flavors on the palate.

LAUGHING LAB
SCOTTISH ALE 5.3% ABV
Medium-bodied, with sweet notes of caramel and toffee and a lingering impression of smoke. Best on tap.

BROOKLYN

1 Brewers Row
79 North
11th Street Brooklyn, NY 11211
www.brooklynbrewery.com

While Brooklyn Brewery pays homage to New York's rich brewing history, it is very much a 21st-century business, and occupies New York's first commercial building to derive all of its electricity from wind power. The brewery's bottled beers are made under contract in upstate New York, while brewmaster and well-respected industry spokesperson Garrett Oliver regularly produces seasonals and a reserve series at the brewery, sold on draft throughout the region.

BREWING SECRET The brewery has installed a bottling line for 750 ml Champagne-style corked bottles, creating a line of Belgian-inspired ales.

BUTTE CREEK

945 West 2nd Street
Chico, CA 95928
www.buttecreek.com

Founded in 1996, this brewery was inspired by a neighboring organic winery to begin making organic beers. Golden West Brewing now sells the Butte Creek brand in 24 states and recently launched a second line, Blue Marble Organic, targeting a nationwide audience with lighter-bodied beers.

CALDERA

540 Clover Lane
Ashland, OR 97520
www.calderabrewing.com

Although it's been around since 1997, Caldera has enjoyed increased visibility and distribution since 2005, when it became the first microbrewery in Oregon to install a small-run line for its distinctively packaged canned beers.

BREWING SECRET Caldera sets itself apart by continuing to use whole hop flowers in all its beers.

BROOKLYNER WEISSE

HEFEWEIZEN 5.1% ABV
Effervescent and banana-fruity from the start, backed up with spices, hops and gentle clove notes.

BROWN

BROWN ALE 5.6% ABV
Caramel, chocolate and ripe plums throughout, with minerally undertones and a hint of smoke. A coffee-dry finish.

LOCAL 1

BELGIAN STRONG GOLDEN ALE 9% ABV
An explosion of aromas and flavors of fruits and spices, and a complex texture, all brought together with a chalky-dry finish.

BLACK CHOCOLATE STOUT

IMPERIAL STOUT 10.6% ABV
Pitch black, with a viscous mixture of dark fruits, port, and, of course, bitter chocolate.

ORGANIC PORTER

PORTER 5.5% ABV
Tastes as rich as it looks, with roasted malts balancing chocolate and liquorice flavors.

MATEVEZA YERBA MATE ALE

PALE ALE 5% ABV
Brewed with yerba mate, a South American herbal tea, for a separate marketing company. Citric hops, earthy, and understandably herbal.

IPA

INDIA PALE ALE 6.7% ABV
Makes a large hop impression without being heavy-handed. Citrus, pine, and grapefruit from start to finish.

PILSENER

PILSNER 5% ABV
Gets eight full weeks of lagering. Floral aroma, with just an initial hint of sulfur, with a crisp, hoppy flavor and finish.

CAMBRIDGE

One Kendall Square
Cambridge, MA 02139
www.cambrew.com

At the Cambridge restaurant, beer
and food form a perfect partnership.
Since opening in 1989, Cambridge
has consistently offered beers on tap
that are outside the ordinary—
perhaps aged in wood in the cellar,
spiced with flowers from the garden,
or made with organic pumpkins that
the brewers chop up themselves.

CAPITAL

7734 Terrace Avenue
Middleton, WI 53562
www.capital-brewery.com

Capital Brewery is known for its
excellent German-inspired beers—
brewed in copper kettles from a
defunct German brewery—though
some are made with a twist. Autumnal
Fire, for instance, is a cross between
a doppelbock and an Oktoberfest.

BREWING SECRET Island Wheat's grain is
grown on an island in Lake Michigan.

CAPTAIN LAWRENCE

99 Castleton Street
Pleasantville, NY 10570
www.captainlawrencebrewing.com

Brewmaster-owner Scott Vaccaro
represents the newest generation of
American brewers, with a formal
education in brewing science, then
on-the-job training in the US and
England. Back in his home state, he
founded this brewery with the support
of his family. He is at the forefront in
experimention with barrel ageing.

CAROLINA

110 Barley Park Lane
Mooresville, NC 28115
www.carolinabeer.com

Lighter beers fueled early success for
Carolina Beer & Beverage, but the
company expanded by acquiring the
well-established Cottonwood brands,
then opening its brewery-restaurant,
Woods on South, in Charlotte.

BREWING SECRET Nikki Koontz is one
of the very few women to hold the
top job of craft brewmaster.

TALL PALE ALE
PALE ALE 5.9% ABV
An aromatic blast of Northwest
hops. Pine and grapefruit flavors on
a solid malt foundation.

CERISE CASSÉE
SOUR ALE 8.5% ABV
"Broken Cherry" begins with a sour
mash, aged on wood. A complex
blend of sweet and sour, cherries
and wood.

MUNICH DARK
5.4% ABV
Malt-accented, with early hints of
caramel and nuts. Building richness
with chocolate-toffee notes.

SPECIAL PILSNER
PILSNER 4.8% ABV
Light on the palate with a note of
honey. Lovely floral hop aromas and
a sturdy hop finish.

XTRA GOLD
TRIPLE 9% ABV
Citrus notes from Northwest hops
blend seamlessly with juicy orchard
fruits and a bit of candy sweetness.

SMOKED PORTER
PORTER 6.4% ABV
Smoky to start, but rich dark fruits,
chocolate, and liquorice quickly
emerge. Luscious palate.

COTTONWOOD
LOW DOWN BROWN
BROWN ALE 5.7% ABV
Distinct impression of nuts from
the outset, blending with chocolate
on the palate, and earthy hops.

CAROLINA BLONDE
GOLDEN ALE 5% ABV
Sweet, grainy, and refreshing. The
light version (Lighthouse, 4% ABV)
has only 81 calories per bottle.

Brooklyn Brewery

79 North 11th Street
Brooklyn, NY 11211

New York was once a vibrant brewing city. Before Prohibition there were around 78 breweries there, nearly 50 of which were in Brooklyn, with its large German community. One area of Brooklyn was known as "Brewers' Row."

All that seemed gone forever when, in 1976, the Schaefer and Liebmann families closed their Brooklyn breweries, the last in the city. They were unable to compete with the rise of light American lagers produced in the Midwest. "What made Milwaukee famous" had put an end to brewing in the Big Apple.

In 1984, journalist Steve Hindy returned from a six-year stint in the Middle East. He had learned much on his travels, including how to home-brew beer in Islamic countries where alcohol was not available to buy. He wanted to develop his passion for brewing great beer so, along with his neighbor, former banker Tom Potter, he set up the Brooklyn Brewery in 1987. His craft beers have since become some of the best-selling draft beers in New York City.

▲ **BROOKLYN LAGER** The original brewmaster was Bill Moeller, who developed his recipe for Brooklyn Lager from the notebooks left to him by his grandfather, who was a brewer in Brooklyn at the turn of the 20th century.

▶ **THE WILLIAMSBURG PLANT** The first Brooklyn brews were produced for them by the Matt Brewery in Utica, and it wasn't until 1996 that Brooklyn had its very own brewery.

BROOKLYN LAGER 5.1% ABV   BROOKLYN PILSNER

BROOKLYN BROWN ALE 5.5% ABV   BROOKLYN Weisse

BROOKLYN PENNANT ALE 5.0%   BROOKLYN SUMMER AL

BREWMASTER RESERVE   BROOKLYN HELLES 5.0%   BROOKLYN BLAST! .8

▼ **A GROWING MARKET** Led by companies such as the Brooklyn Brewery, the US has the most vibrant beer culture in the world, and good beer is an affordable luxury. While Brooklyn cannot match the advertising and marketing spend of its bigger competitors, the beers are sold well beyond New York's five boroughs. Drinkers in South Carolina, Georgia, and Michigan can all sup the brews, as can beer-lovers in places as far afield as Denmark, Japan, and Great Britain.

◄ **EXPANDING HORIZONS**
At the outset, the company's philosophy was quite simple. Hindy wanted a full-bodied, full-flavoured beer reminiscent of those that he believed were made in New York's glory days of brewing. Since then, the outlook has broadened — now, Belgian-inspired, bottle-conditioned brews are produced in corked bottles, and thirsty beer-drinkers can quaff a glass of Brooklyn's effervescent and fruity Brooklyner Weisse.

◄ **STEVE HINDY** In 1994, co-founder Steve Hindy was joined by Garrett Oliver, former brewmaster at the Manhattan Brewery. By the time he joined Brooklyn, Garrett had already developed a reputation for his own interpretations of traditional beer styles, and for his writing and lecturing on beer. Within two years of arriving at Brooklyn, he had opened the company's very own brewery.

BREWERY TOURS
SATURDAYS 12–5PM
COMPANY STORE OPEN
DURING TOUR HOURS
FOR INFORMATION ABOUT
SPECIAL EVENTS CALL
718 486-7122
OR LOOK AT
brooklynbrewery.com
FRIDAY TASTING
PANEL 6–PM

BROOKLYNER SCHNEIDER HOPFEN WEISSE LOT #1148

▲ **GARRETT OLIVER** The ambition of brewmaster Garrett Oliver is for every restaurant to offer a beer list as well as one for wine, in order for people to discover for themselves that beer is an honorable companion to even the finest food.

BREWERY

CHOC
120 Southwest Eighth
Krebs, OK 74554
www.chocbeer.com

Pete's Place is an Italian restaurant
with a long history of brewing and
selling Choc Beer. Choctaw Indians
taught injured ex-miner Pete Pritchard
how to make native beer with wheat,
which he sold illegally during Prohibition
at his restaurant. In 1995, under the
stewardship of his grandson Joe, Choc
Beer at last became a legal brew.

CLIPPER CITY
4615 Hollins Ferry Road, Suite B
Baltimore, MD 21227
www.ccbeer.com

Hugh Sisson sold Baltimore's first brewpub in 1995 to found a microbrewery.
He now produces three distinct lines:
Clipper City; the more assertive
Heavy Seas (7.25% ABV or stronger);
and Oxford, which makes organic ales.
BREWING SECRET Hop³ (cubed) is
hopped three ways—in the kettle,
in the hop back, and dry-hopped.

COORS
311 10th Street
Golden, CO 80401
www.coors.com

Although it merged with Molson, and
that company now partners SABMiller
in the US, Coors has continued to
develop less mainstream beers. Its
Blue Moon line competes with the
largest craft brands, and its SandLot
Brewery, within the Coors Field
baseball stadium in Denver, regularly
offers outstanding traditional lagers.

DESCHUTES
901 Southwest Simpson Avenue, Bend,
Oregon 97702, USA
www.deschutesbrewery.com

What began with a brewpub in 1988
in this outdoor-vacation town quickly
expanded with a separate production
facility that's grown into one of the
nation's largest craft breweries. As
well as selling a full line of beers with
notable hop character throughout the
western US, Deschutes still operates
its original brewpub in downtown
Bend and recently opened another in

BEER

MINER MISHAP
SCHWARZBIER 5.3% ABV
Medium-light body, with roasted
coffee beans on the nose; sweetish
caramel-chocolate flavors.

1919 CHOC
US WHEAT BEER 5% ABV
Descendent of the original Choc.
Pours cloudy, with citrus and yeasty
aromas. Light, refreshing palate.

LOOSE CANNON HOP³
INDIA PALE ALE 7.25% ABV
A well-balanced cocktail of hops,
with flavors of tangerine, grapefruit,
and pine. Amber hues.

SMALL CRAFT WARNING
STRONG LAGER 7.25% ABV
An "uber pils" with strong pale
bock qualities. Sturdy bitterness
complements the malty sweetness.

BLUE MOON BELGIAN WHITE
WITBIER 5.4% ABV
Citrussy sweet nose, spicy with notes
of celery. Some wheat sourness,
finishing on the sweet side.

BARMEN PILSNER
PILSNER 5% ABV
Beautiful billowing head when
poured correctly. Rich with Saaz
hops, floral and spicy. Pleasantly
grainy, with a long, bitter finish.

MIRROR POND
PALE ALE 5.2% ABV
Grapefruit and fresh flowers at the
outset. Light, clean biscuit on the
palate, with generous hop flavor.

BLACK BUTTE PORTER
PORTER 5.2% ABV
Well-balanced and complex, aromas
and flavors blend roasted coffee
beans, chocolate, and dark fruit
with signature acidic notes.

Portland. A Bond Street Series of special beer releases, developed "at the pub", has further widened the brewery's portfolio.

BREWING SECRET Deschutes maintains that the character of its beer is due in part to its use of whole hop flowers.

DIAMOND KNOT
621 Front Street
Mukilteo, WA 98275
www.diamondknot.com

Diamond Knot Brewing has grown substantially since founders Bob Maphet and Brian Sollenberger, two Boeing employees, milled grain at home and hauled it to their brewery tucked in the back of a local bar. They've since bought the alehouse and opened a separate production brewery. The menu features stonegrill cooking.

DIXIE
2401 Tulane Avenue
New Orleans, LA 70119
www.distinguished-brands.com/dixie.php

The 100-year-old Dixie Brewery was the last survivor of New Orleans' once-flourishing brewing tradition, with some of its beers aged in historic cypress barrels. That is, until Hurricane Katrina (and the subsequent looters) devastated it in 2005. It's not clear when it might reopen. Meanwhile its beers are being made at the Minhaus Craft Brewery in Wisconsin.

DOGFISH HEAD
6 Cannery Village Center, Milton, Delaware 19968, USA
www.dogfish.com

Brewing in the spirit of founder Sam Calagione's slogan: "Off-centered ales for off-centered people", Dogfish Head has found a national audience for its "extreme beers". These have included ales developed using research from archaeologists; recipes featuring unusual ingredients, from chicory to chilies; and beers that simply have more of everything. *(Continues overleaf)*

THE ABYSS
IMPERIAL STOUT 11% ABV
Brewed with liquorice and molasses, and partially aged in oak barrels. A cornucopia of intense flavors, held together by wonderful texture.

INVERSION IPA
INDIA PALE ALE 6.8% ABV
A swirl of hop aromas (particularly orange zest). Solid, biscuity malt holds its own against bracing bitterness.

IPA
INDIA PALE ALE 6.2% ABV
Opens with a blast of hops, grapefruit, and pine that lasts through a long, juicy, not-too-bitter finish.

STEAMER GLIDE STOUT
STOUT 4.8% ABV
Careful blends throughout—coffee, cocoa, and bittersweet chocolate offset by sweetness. Irish inspired, with a rich, creamy head.

BLACKENED VOODOO
SCHWARZBIER 5% ABV
In 1991, this dark lager was briefly banned in Texas because of the voodoo references on its label. Smooth and light-bodied for southern drinking, with chocolate and toffee notes throughout.

MIDAS TOUCH
HISTORIC BEER 9% ABV
The ingredients—white Muscat grapes, honey, and saffron—create layers of flavor, melded with subtle acidity.

WORLD WIDE STOUT
IMPERIAL STOUT 18% ABV
Not a classic rendition, but much, much stronger. Port-like, with dark fruits, ripe berries, and a massive dose of alcohol.

BREWERY

(Continued) The brewery recently installed the largest wooden brewing vessels built in America since before Prohibition. Calagione is a tireless promoter, and author of three books, including one in which he and his sommelier co-author debate the merits of beer versus wine. Dogfish still operates a brewpub in Rehoboth Beach, where Calagione started in 1995.

BREWING SECRET Pangaea ale blends ingredients from every continent, including water from Antarctica.

DRAKE'S
1933 Davis Street #177
San Leandro, CA 94577
www.drinkdrakes.com

Since acquiring what was then Lind Brewing in 1999, the owners of San Francisco Bay Coffee have added a bottling line and expanded production almost fivefold. "We've been waking people up for so long, we decided we should help them get to sleep," says company vice president Pete Rogers.

DUCK-RABBIT
4519 W Pine Street
Farmville, NC 27828
www.duckrabbitbrewery.com

Known for darkly intense beers, this is one of several small breweries that have thrived since North Carolina changed its law to allow beer stronger than 6% ABV. Duck-Rabbit's distinctive logo is based on an illustration by philosopher Ludwig Wittgenstein.

BREWING SECRET These quirky brewers say "We sing softly to the yeast."

EEL RIVER
1777 Alamar Way
Fortuna, CA 95540
www.eelriverbrewing.com

Eel River had been around less than five years when, in 2000, it became the first certified organic brewery in the US. The brewpub added a production brewery in nearby Scotia in 2007, moving into an abandoned mill. The new brewery is 100 percent powered by biomass—that is, mill waste such as wood chippings, and spent grain from brewing.

BEER

60 MINUTE IPA
INDIA PALE ALE 6% ABV
Flagship session beer brewed with Warrior, Amarillo, and "Mystery Hop X", and brimming with citrus flavors.

FESTINA PECH
SOUR ALE 4.5% ABV
Labeled a "neo-Berliner Weisse" and fermented with peaches. Fruit sweetness is nicely balanced by tart wheat and slightly sour elements.

EXPEDITION ALE
AMBER ALE 6.8% ABV
Rich in chocolate and sweet caramel, balanced by roasted malts and a lingering hops bitterness.

IPA
INDIA PALE ALE 7.2% ABV
A hops sandwich with caramel and fruity malt at the center. Aromatic at the start and bitter at the end.

BALTIC PORTER
BALTIC PORTER 9% ABV
Caramel, toffee, blackcurrants, and other dark fruits, perfectly blended. Smooth, with restrained bitterness.

MILK STOUT
STOUT 5.7% ABV
A well-integrated combination of roasted coffee beans and chocolate, held together by a creamy palate. Sweet, but not too sweet.

ORGANIC PORTER
PORTER 6.3% ABV
Malty and creamy with chocolate aromas and flavors, and lesser notes of roast coffee beans. Robust.

TRIPLE EXULTATION
OLD ALE 9.7% ABV
Not organic. A complex nose of rich caramel-toffee and fruit, then piney hops assert themselves.

Brooklyn Brewery has developed a wide range of beers, many of which are inspired by traditional Belgian, German, and British styles.

BREWERY

ELYSIAN

1221 East Pike Street
Seattle, WA 98122
www.elysianbrewing.com

Elysian Brewing has three locations in Seattle, with the production facility and a restaurant at the original brewery in the Capitol Hill district. Writer-turned-brewmaster Dick Cantwell keeps an exceptionally wide range of beers available, including a seasonal pumpkin ale that provides an excuse to host a popular fall festival.

FIRESTONE WALKER

1400 Ramada Drive
Paso Robles, CA 93446
www.firestonebeer.com

In rolling out its new Union Jack IPA at the start of 2008, Firestone Walker Brewing Company intensified its focus on pale ales. Each one includes a portion of beer fermented in the patented Firestone Union barrel system, which takes inspiration from the historic Burton Union method originated in Burton-on-Trent,

England. Firestone also blends wood-fermented beer with beer from stainless steel to fashion each of its ales. To celebrate recent anniversaries, the brewers created several strong ales aged in a variety of bourbon, brandy, and untreated oak barrels, then blended them into a single release, using input from regional winemakers.

FISH

515 Jefferson Street Southeast
Olympia, WA 98501
www.fishbrewing.com

Close to bankruptcy in 2000, Fish Brewing has redoubled its efforts in recent years on the core range of Fish Tale Organic beers (a portion of the profits from beers in this line goes to protect aquatic habitats). It has since grown into a regional force, and also now produces German-inspired beer under the Leavenworth label.

BEER

DRAGONSTOOTH STOUT

STOUT 7.2% ABV
Dark fruit, chocolate, molasses, bitter coffee, and liquorice aromas and flavors on a slightly oily palate.

PERSEUS PORTER

PORTER 5.4% ABV
Cocoa and roasted nut flavors, and just-right bitterness. Like toasting marshmallows by the campfire.

DOUBLE BARREL ALE

PALE ALE 5% ABV
Contains 15–20 percent oaked beer. Spicy, rounded fermentation-based fruit, vanilla, and a woody rich-but-not-sweet texture.

PALE 31

CALIFORNIA PALE ALE 4.6% ABV
About three percent oaked beer. Bright and citrussy aromas, with layers of fruit and malt on the palate.

UNION JACK IPA

INDIA PALE ALE 7.5% ABV
Juicy hops arrive in waves of citrus, grapefruit, pine, and mangoes, complementing a solid malt base. Oak and bitterness work in tandem.

FIRESTONE 11

STRONG ALE 11% ABV
Rich, with dozens of flavors held together by its texture, shifting from silky to nicely coarse at the end.

FISH TALE ORGANIC IPA

INDIA PALE ALE 5.5% ABV
Fresh taste of Northwest hops, piney and citrussy. Crisply rich, with hops lingering beyond a bitter finish.

OLD WOODY

OLD ALE 10% ABV
Aged in oak barrels for six months, part of a "Reel Ales" series, with a deep range of caramel and dark fruit. On draft only.

FLOSSMOOR STATION

1035 Sterling Avenue
Flossmoor, IL 60422
www.flossmoorstation.com

Brewers Matt Van Wyk and Andrew
Mason have expanded on what
barrel-ageing pioneer Todd Ashman
started at Flossmoor Station
Brewing. They offer a wide range
of award-winning beers in a pub
housed in a former train station.
The brewery recently launched
a small range of bottled beers.

FLYING DOG

2401 Blake Street
Denver, CO 80205
www.flyingdogales.com

With labels by British illustrator Ralph
Steadman, and the "gonzo" spirit of
the late Hunter S. Thompson (both
friends of founder George Stranahan),
Flying Dog is not your average
brewery. The original brewpub
was founded in Aspen but is now
headquartered in Denver, while the
company moved brewing operations
to Frederick in Maryland in 2008.

FLYING FISH

1940 Olney Avenue
Cherry Hill, NJ 08003
www.flyingfish.com

Flying Fish Brewing began worldwide
and then went local. It started out
as a "virtual brewery" on the Internet
before establishing itself as a distinctly
regional brewery in 1996, now serving
a 100-mile (160-km) radius around
its South Jersey home. The brewery
recently increased capacity, with plans
to widen the range of beers on offer.

FOUNDERS

235 Grandville Avenue SW
Grand Rapids, MI 49503
www.foundersbrewing.com

Founders was just another small
brewery until it jettisoned much of its
portfolio for a more esoteric range of
craft beers with names like Devil
Dancer and Old Curmudgeon.

BREWING SECRET Its Kentucky Breakfast
Stout is brewed with coffee and
vanilla, and aged in bourbon barrels in
mines 100 ft (30 m) underground.

PULLMAN BROWN ALE
BROWN ALE 7% ABV
Brewed with hand-toasted malts
and molasses. A full-bodied blend of
chocolate, toffee, and dark fruit.

DE WILDE ZUIDENTREIN
SOUR ALE 7% ABV
A Flanders brown ale, aged in an
oak wine barrel on fresh raspberries
for a year, dosed with wild yeasts.

GONZO IMPERIAL PORTER
PORTER 9% ABV
Rummy, chocolatey, and almost
sweet before dry cocoa flavors and
solid hop bitterness kick in.

DOGGIE STYLE PALE ALE
PALE ALE 5.3% ABV
A fragrant mixture of fresh fruits to
start. Citrus accentuates fruit in the
middle, well balanced by biscuity
malt. Clean, dry finish.

BELGIAN STYLE DUBBEL
DOUBLE 7% ABV
Chocolate mingled with dark fruit,
and a pleasant whiff of alcohol.
Finishes on the sweet side of dry.

ESB ALE
EXTRA SPECIAL BITTER 5.5% ABV
Malt-accented, rich with caramel
and fruit character, and with an
underlying nuttiness. Hops are
American, but restrained.

BREAKFAST STOUT
IMPERIAL STOUT 8.3% ABV
Espresso coffee dominates, with
complex dark chocolate notes and
a rich texture on the tongue.

BLACK RYE
RYE BEER 7% ABV
Not quite black, but tastes it. Best
described as rye bread dipped in a
well-hopped porter. Flavors and
aromas of chocolate and coffee.

ALL ABOUT ...
TASTING

Beer is best drunk in the company of others, whether in a pub or beer café. Take this sense of conviviality further and invite friends to a tasting session—a joyful celebration of the best of John Barleycorn.

Tasting beer involves all the senses. After all, beer has a rich variety of colors, flavors, and aromas. There are few rules, but think about the beers that you are sampling. Either choose a variety of styles, showcasing the diversity of beer, or serve different variations on a theme—a selection of American IPAs, for example, Czech pilsners perhaps, or British bitters. Whichever course you choose, begin with the most delicate beers and end with the most intensely flavored or strongest beers. Between 6 and 10 beers is best. Too many and the palate becomes dulled.

Use large wine or brandy glasses for beer tasting if you can—the shape of these helps to concentrate aromas. Lay out water and crackers, or plain salted crisps, which help to dry the palate between beers.

Then enjoy!

1 POURING Use a clean tasting glass for each beer. Hold the glass at an angle of about 45 degrees at first, straightening it toward the end of the pour to let the beer acquire a head.

3 AROMA Swirl the beer in the glass to help release the aromas. Malty aromas include cereal, dried fruit, coffee beans, biscuit, Ovaltine, chocolate, toffee, and caramel. Hops produce fruity, fragrant, perfumy, spicy, resiny, peppery, citrussy, herbal, and floral notes. Yeast esters add their own character to stronger beers, with rich fruity notes redolent of tropical fruit, bananas, and ripe apricot skin. Lambic and gueuze have powerfully earthy, sweet-and-sour aromas thanks to the presence of wild yeast.

2 APPEARANCE Look at the beer. It should have a clarity and sparkle to it. Judge the color and condition: does it dance and shimmer in the glass? A tired beer lacks life and actually looks dull. As you drink the beer, a laceworklike trace of foam should be left adhering to the side of the glass—again, a sign of good condition.

4 FLAVOR Taste the beer. The tongue detects sweetness at the tip, salt and sour on the sides, and bitterness at the back. Some beers come bearing lots of fruity gifts, while others—especially dark porters and stouts—produce roast, coffee, caramel, and chocolate flavors. Let the beer roll around the tongue, and work out the order of flavors. How does the beer feel in the mouth: smooth, thin, grainy, acidic (lambics again), oily, or chewy. A great beer is about balance and harmony. The malt and hops should be working with each other. Wine tasters always spit, but beer needs to be swallowed for the finish to be noted. Is it bitter? That's the hops. Dry? That's often the effect of the malt. It might be a long, lingering finish, or it might be short and abrupt.

5 TASTING NOTES Make notes on the beer's key aspects—appearance, aroma, taste, and finish—as you go along. On pages 340–45, you'll find charts for starting your own tasting notes.

BREWERY

FOUR PEAKS

1340 East 8th Steet
Tempe, AZ 85281
www.fourpeaks.com

Little surprise that UK-inspired beers make up a good proportion of the many award-winners here. A retired brewer from Young's in London helped fledgling brewmaster Andy Ingram when Four Peaks opened in 1996. Later, Paul Farnsworth, who began working in the breweries of Burton-on-Trent when he was 16 years old, consulted on quality control.

FULL SAIL

506 Columbia Street
Hood River, OR 97031
www.fullsailbrewing.com

Full Sail represents much that is new in American brewing. Founded in 1987, it became employee-owned in 1999, and its beers reflect an independent nature. Living on the Columbia River with easy access to the mountains, most Full Sail employees are outdoor-oriented. The image frequently used on the brewery's promotional material is

of burly brewmaster John Harris, with a keg slung across his shoulder. The core brands (Amber, IPA, and Pale Ale) reach a wide audience in 15 western states.

BREWING SECRET The brewery also offers seasonals that bear the LTD (Living the Dream) label and a bolder series of Brewmaster's Reserve beers throughout the year.

GEARY'S

38 Evergreen Drive
Portland, ME 04103
www.gearybrewing.com

David Geary has followed a traditional English model since the brewery sold its first beer in 1986, focusing on a core range of beers (originally just two) and serving the New England region. Geary's still makes only five regular and three seasonal beers.

BREWING SECRET Geary's uses yeast from Ringwood Brewery in the UK.

BEER

KILTLIFTER

SCOTTISH ALE 6% ABV
Richly malty, with caramel emerging on the palate. Complex, with just a hint of smokiness.

8TH STREET ALE

BEST BITTER 4.5% ABV
Particularly mellow on cask, with caramel and light fruitiness matched with earthy hops, giving way to a medium-bitter finish.

AMBER

AMBER ALE 5.5% ABV
Citrus and spice, quickly balanced by underlying sweetness. Seamless through to a clean finish.

SESSION LAGER

US LAGER 5.1% ABV
Designed as a throwback to beer produced before Prohibition, with appropriately retro packaging. Clean and malt-accented.

TOP SAIL IMPERIAL PORTER BOURBON

IMPERIAL PORTER 9.85% ABV
Second limited special release of its well-established Imperial porter in bourbon barrels. Simply intense after 10 months on wood: Jack Daniels, chocolate, roasted coffee, oak, and other flavors. Will cellar well for years.

HAMPSHIRE SPECIAL

STRONG ALE 7% ABV
Complex balance of slightly burnt caramel, light fruits, and warming alcohol. Traditional bitter finish.

PALE ALE

PALE ALE 4.8% ABV
A showcase for Ringwood yeast, fruity with some underlying caramel, just a bit slick over the tongue.

GEORGETOWN

5840 Airport Way South, Unit 201
Seattle, WA 98108
www.georgetownbeer.com

Co-founder Manny Chao was the first employee at Mac & Jack's Brewery in Redmond and learned his craft well. Georgetown sells only draft beer and initially focused on just one, Manny's Pale Ale. The brewery is one of many artisan businesses in the former Seattle Brewing and Malting plant, where the iconic Rainier brand was formerly brewed.

GOOSE ISLAND

1800 West Fulton Street
Chicago, IL 60612
www.gooseisland.com

This brewery's extensive range of beers reflects the MBA (Master of Beer Appreciation) Program that it established shortly after opening as a brewpub in 1988. When Goose Island built its production brewery in 1995, brewmaster Greg Hall would launch dozens of styles during the course of a year. Goose Island still operates the original pub on Clybourn as well as another near Wrigley Field, and both still offer an "MBA" (it's actually a kind of loyalty card!).

BREWING SECRET Bourbon County Stout (launched as the brewpub's 1,000th batch, in 1995) arguably kicked off the US revolution of ageing beer in bourbon (and then other spirit) barrels.

GORDON BIERSCH

Various locations
www.gordonbiersch.com

Gordon Biersch began as a single brewpub, grew into a chain, then split into two—a brewery in San Jose, and restaurant-breweries that produce a similar line of beers. The San Jose operation also brews private label brands for Trader Joe's and Costco.

BREWING SECRET Dan Gordon, who runs the stand-alone brewery, trained for five years in Bavaria.

MANNY'S PALE ALE

PALE ALE 5.4% ABV
Begins with notes of grapefruit, then hop flavors blend with fermentation fruitiness on the palate.

CHOPPERS RED ALE

EXTRA SPECIAL BITTER 6.5% ABV
A robust take on the style. Opens with a blast of spicy, citrussy hops, but a restrained bitterness lets the rich palate take charge.

INDIA PALE ALE

INDIA PALE ALE 5.9% ABV
Pineapple and grapefruit, full of hop flavor, with a fruit and malt backbone balancing the bitterness.

312 URBAN WHEAT

US WHEAT BEER 4.2% ABV
Typically unfiltered and hazy, with a citrussy, almost sweet, hop nose that announces it is American. Tart, fruity, with underlying creaminess.

MATILDA

BELGIAN STRONG ALE 7% ABV
Wild, lively hopsack aroma, earthy, with rich fruits and a firm, dry, characterful finish.

BOURBON COUNTY STOUT

IMPERIAL STOUT ABV VARIES
Vintages vary, some flashing more bourbon than others. Always a marriage of rich chocolate, dark fruit, vanilla, and certainly bourbon.

HEFEWEIZEN

HEFEWEIZEN 5.4% ABV
Banana and subdued bubblegum to start, with a pinch of spicy cloves. Refreshing, tart wheat flavors.

MÄRZEN

MÄRZEN/OKTOBERFEST 5.7% ABV
Smooth and malty; notes of crusty bread and caramel. Spice flavors add complexity. Clean, dry finish.

BREWERY

GRAND TETON

430 Old Jackson Highway
Victor, ID 83455
www.grandtetonbrewing.com

Founded in 1988 as Otto Brothers' Brewing—a brewpub which claims a place in American beer history by reintroducing a receptacle called the "growler" (a 64-oz beer jug/1.92-liter). The company took its new name in 2000 after building a production brewery at the base of the Teton Mountains near Yellowstone Park.

GREAT DIVIDE

2201 Arapahoe Street
Denver, CO 80205
www.greatdivide.com

Opened in 1994, Great Divide Brewing quickly earned a reputation for carefully balanced beers. Its ales have grown bigger (in strength and hop character), and the brewery's reputation has grown, but its beers still retain that delicate equilibrium. The brewery is a short walk from Coors Field, home of the Rockies baseball team.

GREAT LAKES

2516 Market Avenue
Cleveland, OH 44113
www.greatlakesbrewing.com

Selling its beer across a growing region surrounding Ohio, this brewery has been an industry leader in tracking the quality of its beer on retailers' shelves. Nonetheless, its brewing complex near the historic West Side Market always merits a visit. The original brewpub, established in 1988, sits across from the production brewery, which came online in 1998. Visitors are directed to the taproom's striking Tiger Mahogany bar and shown bullet holes reputedly made by Eliot Ness. He, of course, was the the "untouchable" Prohibition agent who brought down gangster Al Capone. The beer garden looks onto Ohio City's Market Square.

BEER

BITCH CREEK ESB

BROWN ALE 6.5% ABV
Hybrid, with toasted malts as well as caramel. Plenty of piney and citrussy hops. Big, but balanced.

AU NATURALE

GOLDEN ALE 5.2% ABV
Organic, opening with spicy, grassy Hallertau hops and bready malt. Sweet, grainy texture balanced by light bitterness.

HIBERNATION ALE

OLD ALE 8.1% ABV
A complex, earthy nose packed with chocolate, roasted nuts, and freshly baked molasses cookies—flavors just keep emerging.

TITAN IPA

INDIA PALE ALE 6.8% ABV
Balanced, in a big way, with plenty of caramel-sweet body to match the piney, grapefruity hops throughout.

EDMUND FITZGERALD PORTER

PORTER 5.8% ABV
Perfectly balanced, chocolate-mocha throughout, delightful fresh quality, and a dry coffee finish.

DORTMUNDER GOLD

DORTMUNDER 5.8% ABV
Aromas of fresh grain or new-mown hay blend with bright noble hops. Robust and crisp.

ELIOT NESS

VIENNA LAGER 6.2% ABV
Bold and hoppy in the Vienna style, with creamy, nutty maltiness and brisk hoppiness nicely balanced.

BURNING RIVER PALE ALE

PALE ALE 6% ABV
Borders on an India pale ale, brimming with juicy, piney American hops that last through a long, dry finish.

GREEN FLASH

1430 Vantage Court
Vista, CA 92081
www.greenflashbrew.com

Green Flash refers to a rare light phenomenon that lasts only seconds at sunrise or sunset over water. Green seems appropriate for a brewery gaining a national reputation for its hop-accented beers, although brewer Chuck Silva has proved adept at a wide range of styles.

GRITTY MCDUFF'S

396 Fore Street
Portland, ME 04101
www.grittys.com

Opening in Portland Old Port in 1988, Gritty McDuff's was one of the first brewpubs in the northeast and an early outpost for US cask ale. There are now branches in Freeport and Lewiston.

BREWING SECRET The brewery uses traditional English methods, equipment, yeasts, hops, and range of barley malts.

HAIR OF THE DOG

4509 Southeast 23rd Avenue
Portland, OR 97202
www.hairofthedog.com

Chef-turned-brewer Alan Sprints founded this tiny cult brewery in 1994. His first ale, Adam, was brewed in the Adambier style of Dortmund in Germany, and based on the research of beer writer Fred Eckhardt.

BREWING SECRET Every bottle carries a batch number. Check the website to match it to brewing and bottling dates.

HALE'S

4301 Leary Way Northwest
Seattle, WA 98107
www.halesales.com

First opened in western Washington State in 1983, Hale's Brewery has been a fixture in Seattle since 1995. Its English-inspired pub adjoins a "display production" brewery (visible behind glass, with mirrors on the ceiling to show the foamy fermentation in open-top vessels). Hale's sells 75 percent of its beer within 10 miles (17 km) of its brewery.

WEST COAST IPA
INDIA PALE ALE 7% ABV
Northwest hops balanced on a solid malt base. Earthy, floral, citrussy, piney, grapefruity, and bitter.

NUT BROWN ALE
BROWN ALE 5.5% ABV
Deep brown, with nuts and cocoa from the outset, and more chocolate and caramel on the palate. Subdued, earthy hops.

BLACK FLY STOUT
STOUT 4.1% ABV
Surprising coffee aromas and flavors, mingling with chocolate and toffee, but light and satisfyingly dry.

HALLOWEEN ALE
EXTRA SPECIAL BITTER 6% ABV
An autumn release, brewed stronger, aged longer, and with more East Kent Goldings hops than are used in Gritty's Best Bitter.

ADAM
STRONG ALE 10% ABV
Rich and complex, with dark fruits, bread, chocolate, smoked peat, and more, all cleverly unified.

FRED
STRONG ALE 10% ABV
Named after Eckhardt, this beer defies categorization. Dark fruits and juicy ones, spices and hops—impossible to summarize.

PALE AMERICAN ALE
PALE ALE 5.2% ABV
Nods towards the UK, with rounded biscuit malt. Well-balanced by citric, earthy Northwest hops.

EL JEFE HEFEWEIZEN
HEFEWEIZEN 5.2% ABV
Hale's doesn't only do English styles. This is brewed in the Bavarian manner: cloudy, with banana fruity, yeasty character, and light cloves.

Samuel Adams, made by the Boston Beer Company, is one of the USA's most successful craft brewery brands.

HARPOON

306 Northern Avenue
Boston, MA 02210
www.harpoonbrewery.com

This brewery, with major facilities in Boston and Vermont, has tapped into specialty-beer-drinkers' affection for hops, with its flagship IPA accounting for 60 percent of sales. However, its wheat-based UFO has recently been the fastest-growing brand, and its 100 Barrel Series of one-offs guarantees there's always something new.

HIGH FALLS

445 St. Paul Street
Rochester, NY 14605
www.highfalls.com

High Falls is still brewing old-style Genesee beers on the site where they have been made since 1878. It also makes the J.W. Dundee family of beers for the traditional ale market.

BREWING SECRET High Falls is one of the largest and oldest continuously operating breweries in the US.

HIGH POINT

22 Park Place
Butler, NJ 07405
www.ramsteinbeer.com

High Point founder Greg Zaccardi was an American "hop head" until he discovered the wheat beers of Bavaria. He branded his beers Ramstein, after the German city that's home to the largest US Air Force base in Europe, and began making true-to-style weissbiers at High Point Brewing, even though his brewing system was designed for British-style ales.

HIGHLAND

12 Old Charlotte Highway
Asheville, NC 28802
www.highlandbrewing.com

Having moved into a large new production facility in 2006, Highland Brewing was perfectly positioned for the rise in profile of North Carolina beer after state lawmakers eased the limit on beer strength. Asheville is a fast-growing mountain town, with a beer scene to match, including five breweries.

IPA
INDIA PALE ALE 5.9% ABV
Floral at the outset; zestful citrus aromas. More hops in the flavor, biscuitlike palate, subdued bitterness at the end.

MUNICH DARK
DUNKEL 5.5% ABV
Rich, almost sweet, with hints of toast, then chocolate. Restrained hops and a long, smooth finish.

GENESEE CREAM ALE
CREAM ALE 4.9% ABV
Pale, faintly sweet, with roast corn flavors; smooth and easy to drink.

J.W. DUNDEE'S IPA
INDIA PALE ALE 6.3% ABV
A seasonal summer beer. Relatively sweet caramel character, with more bitterness than flavor from its hops. Crisp finish.

RAMSTEIN CLASSIC
DUNKELWEIZEN 5.5% ABV
Sweet chocolate on the nose and palate. Orchard fruits and banana, balanced by light clove and spicy hops.

MAIBOCK
MAIBOCK 7.5% ABV
A spring seasonal. Surprisingly dark with subtle caramel notes. Clean honey-maltiness, not-so-subtle alcohol, and pleasant, herbal hops.

GAELIC ALE
AMBER ALE 5.8% ABV
Its name and caramel character nod toward Scotland, but the resiny hop finish is distinctly American.

OATMEAL PORTER
PORTER 5.8% ABV
Chocolate to start, with roasted coffee beans emerging, more prominent in the mouth. Coffee and cream impression. Dry and bitter.

BREWERY

HÖFBRAUHAUS

305 Park Avenue
Newport, KY 41071
www.hofbrauhausnewport.com

Höfbrauhaus Newport, across the
river from Cincinnati, was the first
licensed franchise of the state-owned
brewery of the same name in Munich.
Bavarian-style beer is brewed on site
(the Las Vegas Höfbrauhaus serves
beer brewed in Munich). The menu
and decor replicate the original, and
there's a beer garden and quiet dining
room too.

HOPPIN' FROG

1680 E. Waterloo Road (Rte 224)
Akron, OH 44306
www.hoppinfrog.com

Brewermaster/owner Fred Karm
opened this smallish brewery making
big beers in 2006. He established his
reputation for bold products while
directing operations for three Thirsty
Dog brewpubs, before the chain went
bankrupt. Thirsty Dog itself has been
revived as a production-only
microbrewery, also in Akron.

HOPWORKS / HUB

2944 SE Powell Boulevard
Portland, OR 97202
www.hopworksbeer.com

Hopworks Urban Brewery is the
first brewery in Portland to offer only
organic beers, part of its commitment
to "green culture." HUB's founder-
brewmaster Christian Ettinger
made Portland's first organic beers.

BREWING SECRET HUB fires its
brewing kettle with bio-diesel fuel.

IRON HILL

Various locations
www.ironhillbrewery.com

Named after a Revolutionary War
landmark in Delaware, the Iron Hill
Brewery & Restaurant chain continues
to grow throughout Delaware and
Pennsylvania, offering a set line-up
at each location but also a range of
specials. Its brewers also package
an Iron Hill Reserve Line in 750 ml
corked bottles for sale at the pubs.

BEER

MUNICH WEIZEN

HEFEWEIZEN 5.4% ABV
Properly cloudy, with subdued fruit
aromas. Banana on the palate, with
distinct cloves and crisp wheat.

DUNKEL

DUNKEL 5.5% ABV
Rich without being heavy. Surprising
caramel and toasted flavors, mild
hop presence with just enough
bitterness.

BORIS THE CRUSHER

IMPERIAL STOUT 9.4% ABV
As thick as motor oil, with intense
aromas of burnt liquorice, chocolate,
and roasted coffee beans.

BODACIOUS BLACK & TAN

STRONG ALE 7.6% ABV
A blend of IPA and BORIS, creating
a tension between piney hops and
coffee-chocolate richness that
holds the beer together.

VELVET ESB

SPECIAL BITTER 5.2% ABV
A session ale by American
standards; rich in caramel, soft
on the palate, with signature
hop character throughout.

ORGANIC IPA

INDIA PALE ALE 6.6% ABV
Fresh hop aromas—pine, grapefruit,
lemon zest. Hop flavors, bitterness
matched by bright malt character.

RUSSIAN IMPERIAL STOUT

IMPERIAL STOUT 9.5% ABV
Rich, dark-chocolate aroma with
supporting coffee notes. Deep
chocolate flavors, balanced by
roasty bitterness.

PIG IRON PORTER

PORTER 5.4% ABV
One of their first beers. Roasted
and rich, it's a full-flavored blend of
coffee, prunes, and dark cherries.

ITHACA

606 Elmira Road
Elmira, NY 14851
www.ithacabeer.com

Located in New York's Finger Lakes region, already well known among wine drinkers, Ithaca Beer Company has boosted the region's beer's profile since brewing began in 1998.

BREWING SECRET The brewery has led efforts to re-establish New York State as a US center of hop growing.

JOLLY PUMPKIN

3115 Broad Street
Dexter, MI 48130
www.jollypumpkin.com

Not quite like any other brewery in the US, Jolly Pumpkin Artisan Ales allows its beers to develop under the influence of local wild yeast. All beers are aged in barrels, and are often blended and re-fermentated in the bottle to deliver effervescent beer. Though its output is small, the brewery has developed a national following.

KONA

75-5629 Kuakini Highway
Kailua Kona, HI 97640
www.konabrewingco.com

Sales are booming everywhere for Kona Brewing, which offers mainland drinkers "a pint of paradise." The Big Island brewery added capacity to meet growing demand in Hawaii, while sales in 17 mainland states have increased even faster. Beers sold on the mainland are made under contract at Widmer Brothers in Oregon.

KUHNHENN

5919 Chicago Road
Warren, MI 48092
www.kbrewery.com

Brothers Brett and Eric Kuhnhenn turned the hardware store their father ran for 35 years into a small brewery, winery, meadery, and brew-on-premises (where customers can make their own beer). The national reputation of Kuhnhenn shows how word of mouth—and the Internet—can help small breweries develop a cult following.

NUT BROWN
BROWN ALE 5% ABV
A deep, inviting brown pour. Nutty, with caramel and chocolate notes, its underlying sweetness is balanced by herbal hops.

OLD HABIT
RYE BEER 9% ABV
Part of a special Excelsior! series. Made with four rye malts, with a portion aged in rye whiskey barrels.

ORO DE CALABAZA
BELGIAN STRONG GOLDEN ALE 8% ABV
Golden and cloudy, tart and spicy, with orchard fruit and citrus. Develops with age.

BAM BIERE
SAISON 4.5% ABV
The whole exceeds the sum of its parts in this "farmhouse" ale, from the hops (billowing head, dry finish) to the spicy malts.

PIPELINE PORTER
PORTER 5.4% ABV
Brewed with local Kona coffee, its flavor is well-integrated. Roasty malt, oily, with chocolate notes.

FIRE ROCK PALE ALE
PALE ALE 6% ABV
Reddish-orange with slightly sweet caramel aromas and flavor, spicy and citric hops are cleverly integrated and balanced.

RASPBERRY EISBOCK
EISBOCK 10.6% ABV
A small-run beer. Complex, rich with raspberries, chocolate, warming alcohol, and a closing tartness.

PENETRATION PORTER
PORTER 5.9% ABV
Almost black, with roasted coffee, chocolate, and dark fruits like cherry filling the nose and the mouth. Citrussy hop finish.

BREWERY

LAGUNITAS

1280 North McDowell Boulevard
Petaluma, CA 94954
www.lagunitas.com

Always known for its hop-driven beers, Lagunitas launched a new range in 2006, each one commemorating a Frank Zappa album and released 40 years after the album of the same name. Founder Tony Magee obtained the permission of the Zappa Family Trust to use the original album art on the bottle label for these beers.

LAKE PLACID

14 Mirror Lake Drive
Lake Placid, NY 12946
www.ubuale.com

Located in the Adirondack Mountains ski resort, this brewery's flagship Ubu Ale became famous when Bill Clinton had "growlers" (64-ounce refillable jugs) delivered to the White House. The company has built a new brewery near its brewpub, offering tours and tastings every Saturday afternoon.

LAKEFRONT

1872 North Commerce Street,
Milwaukee, WI 53212
www.lakefrontbrewery.com

Lakefront Brewing, known since 1987 for a range of robust beers, recently moved to the fore in brewing New Grist gluten-free beer for celiacs who cannot tolerate the grains traditionally used in making beer.

BREWING SECRET New Grist is brewed from sorghum, hops, water, rice, and gluten-free yeast grown on molasses.

LANCASTER

302 North Plum Street
Lancaster, PA 17602
www.lancasterbrewing.com

Lancaster was once dubbed the "Munich of the United States" and home to 14 breweries, some of which flaunted Prohibition. The last of the originals closed nearly 40 years before Lancaster Brewing opened in 1995. The 19th-century former tobacco warehouse also houses a restaurant serving dishes such as mussels cooked in ale, and beer-battered shrimp.

BEER

INDIA PALE ALE

INDIA PALE ALE 5.7% ABV
Brimming with hop character—orange, grapefruit, peaches, pine—over malty sweetness.

KILL UGLY RADIO

INDIA PALE ALE 7.8% ABV
Only in the US is this an IPA. Caramel and fermentation fruit are balanced by spicy, citrussy, and bitter Northwest hops.

UBU ALE

STRONG ALE 7% ABV
On the sweet side, dominated by malt with chocolate, caramel, and dark fruit flavors.

46'ER IPA

INDIA PALE ALE 6% ABV
Honoring all who have climbed the 46 Adirondack High Peaks, this is a classic crisp, stongly hopped IPA.

NEW GRIST

GLUTEN FREE 5% ABV
A tang of citrus zest to start, then a light palate with hints of fruit. Mildy astringent and tart.

RIVERWEST STEIN

VIENNA LAGER 6% ABV
Lightly toasted aromas with hints of caramel. More caramel in the mouth, and hop citrus fruitiness. Woody undertones.

MILK STOUT

MILK STOUT 5.3% ABV
Lightly roasted coffee notes sit well with the creamy texture. Chocolate, dark fruits, and nuttiness.

HOP HOG IPA

INDIA PALE ALE 7.9% ABV
Considerable caramel-malt character is well balanced by hoppy grapefruit, citrus, and spruce.

LEFT HAND

1265 Boston Avenue
Longmont, CO 80501
www.lefthandbrewing.com

The company takes its name from the Arapahoe Chief Niwot, his name translating as "left hand." Originally brewing English-style ales, the brewery merged in 1998 with Tabernash, known for Bavarian-inspired beers. Those beers have now been phased out, but Left Hand continues to develop a wide range of beer styles and produces many seasonal brews too.

MILK STOUT

Milk Stout 5.3% ABV
Complex and smooth, chocolate and burnt toast in the aroma and flavor constantly balanced by creamy sweetness.

BLACKJACK PORTER

Porter 5.2% ABV
Chocolate and liquorice aromas, medium body, with hints of dark cherries and a smooth, dry finish.

LEINENKUGEL'S

1 Jefferson Avenue
Chippewa Falls, WI 54729
www.leinie.com

Since 1988, when Miller Brewing bought a controlling interest, the Jacob Leinenkugel Brewing Company has grown into one of the largest regional breweries in the country, distributing in almost every state.

BREWING SECRET The brewery, founded in 1867, still offers a range reflecting its German heritage.

CREAMY DARK

US Dark Lager 4.9% ABV
As creamy as promised, chocolate with coffee and cream character and a dryish not-too-bitter finish.

SUNSET WHEAT

US Wheat Beer 4.9% ABV
Light but complex beer, almost a fruit salad of aromas and flavors, with some wheaty tartness and coriander spiciness.

LION

700 North Pennsylvania Avenue
Wilkes-Barre, PA 18705
www.lionbrewery.com

The Lion Brewery, founded in 1905, is a survivor—the last of dozens of breweries that once operated in northeastern Pennsylvania. Most recently the brewery has emphasized this heritage with its Stegmaier brand of good-value traditional beers, the roots of which go back to 1857.

STEG 150

Vienna Lager 5.5% ABV
Created to celebrate the brewery's 150th anniversary. Smells like warm toast, malt-accented, lightly sweet but smooth, not cloying.

STEGMAIER PORTER

Porter 5.5% ABV
Notes of sweet chocolate and ripe fruit matched with toasty malt and a coffee-bitter finish.

LIVE OAK

3301 East Fifth Street
Austin, TX 78702
www.liveoakbrewing.com

Live Oak's brewmaster-owner Chip McElroy successfully merges Austin's hip culture with a traditional brewing regimen. More than ten years after opening, the brewery still sells only draft beer.

BREWING SECRET Their classic Pilz is produced with an old-fashioned method that uses a decoction mash.

PILZ

Pilsner 3.9% ABV
Bright golden, with a flowery nose showcasing Saaz hops. Soft and slightly oily palate; dry, bitter finish.

HEFEWEIZEN

Hefeweizen 4.1% ABV
Yeasty, full of bananas, vanilla, and cloves, with a hint of bubblegum. Lush flavors to start with, but dry at the finish. A spring/summer beer.

THE GIANTS OF BREWING

Walk into any airport bar in the world, five-star hotel, or major supermarket and the chances are that it will sell beer from one of the big four multinational breweries. Anheuser-Busch InBev, SABMiller, Heineken, and Carlsberg stand as behemoths in the world of beer. These mega-companies straddle continents and dominate domestic markets. And while their beers are happily drunk by millions of people every day, they do ruffle the feathers of many serious beer lovers, who accuse them of stifling innovation and local and regional beer traditions.

Around the world, the big four are involved in fierce competition, battling it out for the cream of the market share. For this is no cosy cartel, but a full-bloodied battle royal to be the biggest brewer in the world. They grow their businesses organically and through acquisitions, and, now that beer is drunk worldwide, they are targeting Russia, China, and India—places far beyond their traditional markets.

Big they might be, dominated by marketing personnel and accountants they certainly are, but within each of these giant corporations there somewhere beats the heart of a brewer proud to be producing a beer made with good, natural ingredients.

CARLSBERG

Times have changed since JC Jacobsen first introduced the world to Carlsberg in 1847. Carlsberg's three key markets are Western Europe, Eastern Europe, and Asia. The company has majority holdings in several large European breweries, such as Carlsberg UK, Carlsberg in Sweden, Ringnes in Norway, Feldschlösschen in Switzerland, Sinebrychoff in Finland, and Carlsberg Polska. It now wholly owns the Baltic Beverages Holding, which brews beer in Russia, Ukraine, and the Baltic states. Carlsberg also has significant activities in Asia, which are run by its fully owned subsidiary Carlsberg Asia.

▲ Poster for Carlsberg beer dating from 1958.
◀ Carlsberg's original brewery in Denmark was founded in the mid-19th century in Valby.
▼ Carlsberg's original brewhouse is now used to brew the Jacobsen range of specialty beers.

ANHEUSER-BUSCH INBEV

Anheuser-Busch InBev's heritage is rooted in brewing traditions that originate from the Den Hoorn brewery in Leuven, Belgium, dating back to 1366 and the pioneering spirit of the Anheuser brewery, established in 1860 in St Louis, USA. The company was formed in 2008 when the Belgian-based brewer InBev acquired its US rival Anheuser-Busch. The US$52bn takeover represented the largest deal in brewing history. InBev was formed in 2004 when the Belgian company Interbrew – and the Brazilian Companhia de Bebidas das Américas combined to form a new world force in brewing. Interbrew, which style itself as the world's largest local brewer, was formed in 1987 from the merger of Brasseries Artois, then the second largest brewer in Belgium, and Brasseries Piedboeuf, the brewer of Jupiler.

Anheuser-Busch InBev employs more than 120,000 people in over 30 countries across the world – describing itself as "the Best Beer Company in a Better World."

Anheuser-Busch InBev is the leading global brewer and one of the world's top five consumer products companies. Anheuser-Busch InBev manages a portfolio of brands that includes global, flagship brands Budweiser, Stella Artois and Beck's. Striving to be the world's greatest local brewer, the company also manages a portfolio of over 200 other beer brands that includes, fast growing multi-country brands like Leffe and Hoegaarden, and strong local jewels such as Bud Light, Skol, Brahma, Quilmes, Michelob, Harbin, Sedrin, Cass, Klinskoye, Sibirskaya Korona, Chernigivske, and Jupiler. It also has shares in China's Tsingtao Brewery and CompañíaCervecerías Unidas in Argentina.

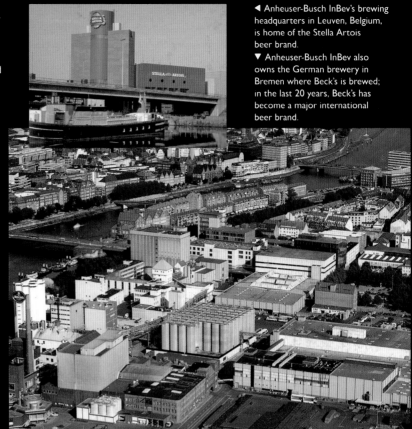

◀ Anheuser-Busch InBev's brewing headquarters in Leuven, Belgium, is home of the Stella Artois beer brand.

▼ Anheuser-Busch InBev also owns the German brewery in Bremen where Beck's is brewed; in the last 20 years, Beck's has become a major international beer brand.

▲ The drayhorses that were once used at Anheuser-Busch have become a symbol of the company's heritage; Budweiser is its most famous brand.

◀ Anheuser-Busch InBev has shares in several other breweries, including a 50 percent stake in Grupo Modelo in Mexico—brewers of Corona beer.

SABMILLER

SABMiller has brewing operations in more than 60 countries across six continents. Its internationally marketed brands include Pilsner Urquell, Peroni Nastro Azzurro, and Miller Genuine Draft; its local brands include Aguila, Miller Lite, Snow, and Tyskie.

SAB (South African Breweries) was founded in 1895 when it launched its first brand, Castle Lager, in its home market of South Africa. The founder, a Swedish entrepreneur called Jacob Letterstedt, intended to provide beer for the thousands of miners and prospectors around Johannesburg.

In 2002, SABMiller was formed after SAB acquired Miller Brewing Company, then the second largest brewery by volume in the USA. The company is growing strongly in China and has recently bought the Dutch company Grolsch, the Netherland's second largest producer of pilsner. In 2007, SABMiller's Russian operation invested $170 million in the construction of a new brewery east of Moscow.

▲ SABMiller's Snow facility has given the company a brewing base in China, where potential is seen for a growing market for SABMiller beers.

▶ ▲ Among the best-known brands that SABMiller owns are Peroni from Italy, Pilsner Urquell from the Czech Republic, Grolsch from the Netherlands, and Miller Lite from the US.

◀ Castle Lager is where it all started for the SAB part of SABMiller; South African Breweries began in 1895, and Castle Lager was its first brew.

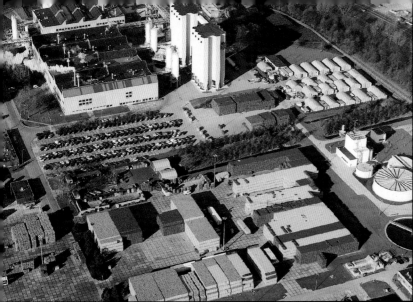

Gerard Heineken, the brewery's founder, set up Heineken in 1864, and immediately began brewing lager.

HEINEKEN

Heineken has its roots in Amsterdam, where Gerard Adriaan Heineken purchased a run-down brewery called the Haystack in 1864. Today, the Heineken brand is the largest beer brand in Europe, and the company claims it is the most valuable beer brand in the world. Heineken also owns Amstel, which is the third largest beer brand in Europe.

Operating in more than 170 countries, through its own breweries and through export and licensing partners, Heineken has the widest global presence of all international brewers. Europe accounts for over half of Heineken's sales. It owns more than 120 breweries in at least 65 countries and employs over 60,000 people. It recently assumed ownership of Scottish and Newcastle breweries in the UK.

▲ Currently Heineken's main brewing facility in the Netherlands, the Zoeterwoude Brewery near Amsterdam was built in 1975.
◄ Heineken is now the largest beer brand in Europe.

HIDDEN GEMS

While the four giants might concentrate most of their marketing strategies and budget on the main brands that they produce, they all also brew gems which beer lovers should certainly seek out.

Carlsberg's Jacobsen Vintage No 1 is said to be the most expensive beer in the world. A 10.5% ABV barley wine, it has been wood aged in Côte d'Or barrels made from Swedish and French oak. It has flavors of vanilla, smoke, caramel, and port.

Anheuser-Busch InBev's Campbell's Scotch Ale (right), at 7.7% ABV, has wonderful spicy and caramel candy aromas. Full of raisin flavors, it has a slightly burnt finish.

In the USA, Anheuser-Busch InBev may be more well known for its classic Budweiser brands, but it also brews a sprightly beer in the style of a Belgian witbier. Shock Top—an unfiltered wheat beer brewed at 5.2% ABV—sports a naturally cloudy consistency and tastes of orange and spices.

Heineken bought the Zywiec Brewery in Poland in the 1990s. At the company's Bracki Brewery in Zamkowy, an aromatic Baltic Porter is brewed in open fermenters. Weighing in at a very hefty 9.5% ABV, it is full of sweet coffee notes.

SABMiller's Castle Milk Stout, at 6% ABV, is a true milk stout, in which lactose sugars have been added to the wort during the brewing process.

► Campbell's Scotch Ale, produced by Anheuser-Busch InBev

BREWERY

LONG TRAIL

Junction Route 4 and 100A
Bridgewater Corners, VT 05035
www.longtrail.com

Long Trail Brewing is a promoter of "EcoBrewing." Among other measures, it uses only two gallons of water for each of beer made (compared to an industry average of 6:1). Although the regional brewery leans heavily on its flagship Long Trail Ale, it continues to broaden its range with seasonal beers.

LOST ABBEY

155 Mata Way
San Marcos, CA 92069
www.lostabbey.com

Lost Abbey beers sometimes pay homage to monastery ales, but some are unlike anything ever brewed in an abbey. Port Brewing, born out of a successful chain of brewpubs in the San Diego area, launched the brand in 2006. Lost Abbey quickly built up a devoted following, with consumers lining up outside to buy its special releases. Brewmaster Tomme Arthur

oversees the ageing room, conjuring up what are best thought of as "Wild American" ales—malt-accented beers enhanced by the barrels in which they are matured.

BREWING SECRET The wooden barrels that once held wines and whiskies now nurture wild yeasts.

LOST COAST

123 West 3rd Street
Eureka, CA 95501
www.lostcoast.com

Set in a historic seaside town amidst Victorian buildings, Lost Coast is itself somewhat historic. The brewery was founded in 1990 by two women, one of them, Barbara Groom, the brewer. "If there's a difference between male and female brewers," Groom has said, "it's that women brewers may make more well-balanced beers, ones with less bitterness."

BEER

LONG TRAIL ALE
ALTBIER 5% ABV
Deep copper, smooth malt aromas, and hop spiciness, but without the hop bitterness of German altbiers.

DOUBLE BAG
STRONG ALE 7.2% ABV
Tastes like a stronger version of Long Trail Ale, particularly rich in caramel and chocolate. Earthy, somewhat pungent, hops.

RED POPPY
SOUR ALE 5.5% ABV
Brown ale with sour cherries, aged in French oak wine barrels for a year. Oaky, with pleasing acidity.

CUVEE DE TOMME
BELGIAN STRONG ALE 11.5% ABV
Flavors of cherries, chocolate, smoke, dark fruits, dried fruits, and vanilla. Balanced by restrained sourness and an acidic finish.

JUDGMENT DAY
BELGIAN STRONG DARK ALE 10.5% ABV
Dark and powerful, with profoundly fruity aromas and palate; chocolate and whisky malt undertones.

ANGEL'S SHARE
BARLEY WINE 11.5% ABV
Some batches are aged in bourbon barrels, some in brandy ones. The result is an intense blend of rich malts and wood character.

DOWNTOWN BROWN
BROWN ALE 5% ABV
Soft and smooth, caramel, nuts, and cocoa throughout, coffee bitterness blending with earthy hops.

8 BALL STOUT
STOUT 5.9% ABV
Creamy, full-bodied, with a balance of bitter chocolate and coffee. Brief sweetness is swept away in the bitter-dry finish.

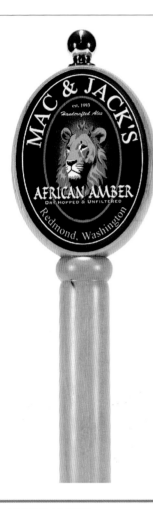

MAC & JACK'S

17825 Northeast 65th Street
Redmond, WA 98025
www.macandjacks.com

Mac and Jack's has grown into a significant regional presence with a tiny range and selling only draft beer. Its African Amber accounts for 90 percent of sales and is the best-selling draft beer in Seattle.

BREWING SECRET Each keg that leaves the brewery contains a mesh bag packed with hops.

MACTARNAHAN'S

2730 Northwest 31st Avenue
Portland, OR 97210
www.macsbeer.com

Portland Brewing, one of Oregon's first breweries, was acquired by Pyramid in 2004. It now brews their beers in Oregon, but also the popular MacTarnahan range, named after Robert "Mac" MacTarnahan, an early investor in Portland Brewing. One of Oregon's most accomplished senior athletes, he was the public face of the brewery until he died in 2004.

MAD RIVER

195 Taylor Way
Blue Lake, CA 95525
www.madriverbrewing.com

Founder Bob Smith built his brewery in 1989 using recycled materials, and has since received many awards for its waste-reduction programs. Mad River reuses 98 percent of its residuals and generates just one yard/ cubic meter of waste a month while brewing about 250,000 gallons of beer per year.

MAGIC HAT

5 Bartlett Road
Burlington, VT 05403
www.magichat.net

Magic Hat's unique and sometimes outrageous packaging and its "non-style" beers have brought double-digit growth year after year. It began in 2008 with construction underway to double capacity, and plans to push distribution into the midwest and south.

BREWING SECRET The Orlio range of beers are certified organic.

AFRICAN AMBER
AMBER 5.4% ABV
Generously dry-hopped and brimming with refreshing citrussy, floral hop aromas and flavors. Caramel on the palate gives way to a medium-dry finish.

MACTARNAHAN'S AMBER ALE
AMBER ALE 5% ABV
Scottish-style caramel and brown sugar sweetness, with citrussy Northwest hops.

BLACKWATCH CREAM PORTER
PORTER 5.3% ABV
Brewed with oatmeal for a creamy mouthfeel. Cocoa and nutty aromas, with richer chocolate and dark fruits on the palate.

JAMAICA RED ALE
AMBER ALE 6.6% ABV
First made for the annual reggae festival. Sweetish nose, with crystal malts and solid, refreshing hops.

STEELHEAD SCOTCH PORTER
PORTER 6.4% ABV
Distinctly a porter, with roasted malt and a touch of sourness. Caramel notes and hints of smoke add complexity.

#9
PALE ALE 4.6% ABV
Apricot-infused. Subtle stone fruits on the palate, sometimes buttery notes. Finishes dry.

ROXY ROLLES
AMBER ALE 5.8% ABV
Brewed for the winter season, rich with caramel and grapefruit aromas and flavors, balanced by closing bitterness.

BREWERY

MARBLE

111 Marble Avenue NW
Albuquerque, NM 87102
www.marblebrewery.com

This new microbrewery has spun out of the award-winning Chama River and Blue Corn brewpubs, both part of the same northern New Mexico restaurant chain. Reflecting shifting beer trends, Marble Brewery's first batch was an assertive India pale ale. Its beers are available throughout the chain.

MARIN

1809 Larkspur Landing Circle
Larkspur, CA 94939
www.marinbrewing.com

Marin Brewing was one of the most honored breweries in early years of Great American Beer Festival awards. It returned to the spotlight in 2007, adding four gold medals to its trophy case. Moylan's, the brewpub Marin brewmaster Brendan Moylan opened in nearby Novato, won gold and silver for its Imperial India Pale Ale.

MCMENAMINS

Various locations
www.mcmenamins.com

The McMenamin brothers seem to have a pub in every Northwestern neighborhood—more than 50 in all—but each one is different, tailored to the location or the premises they inhabit. Some brew on site while others serve McMenamins beer brewed at the Edgefield Brewery, near Portland in Oregon, as well as a range of local beers.

MENDOCINO

South Highway 101
Hopland, CA 13351
www.mendobrew.com

Mendocino Brewing was one of the first success stories among US "boutique" breweries (as they were called at the time). It opened in 1983 as the Hopland Brewery, having acquired equipment, the house yeast, and even a few employees from the groundbreaking, but by then defunct, New Albion Brewery.

BEER

IPA

INDIA PALE ALE 6.2% ABV
West coast oriented, with an opening rush of citrus, particularly grapefruit. Resiny, bitter finish.

KÖLSCH

KÖLSCH 5.5% ABV
A Great American Beer Festival gold medal winner. Fresh but subtle orchard fruits on the nose; light and crisp in the mouth.

SAN QUENTIN'S BREAKOUT STOUT

STOUT 7.1% ABV
Bittersweet chocolate and coffee at the start and end, balanced by sweet molasses in between. Roasty and dry.

STAR BREW TRIPLE WHEAT ALE

US WHEAT BEER 9.5% ABV
A tongue-twister: the juicy, dark fruit of a barley wine, spicy wheat tartness, and intense hop flavors and bitterness.

HAMMERHEAD

PALE ALE 6% ABV
Their bestseller. Abundant caramel sweetness balanced with a large dose of fragrant Northwest hops.

BLACK RABBIT PORTER

PORTER 5.6% ABV
Cocoa and nutty aromas, with sweeter chocolate and roasted nuts in the mouth, as well as a bit of buttery toffee.

RED TAIL ALE

AMBER ALE 6.1% ABV
An earthy nose includes hints of orchard fruits. Layers of creamy malt with notes of liquorice.

BLUE HERON

PALE ALE 6.1% ABV
Orange zest and lemon rind to start, giving way to traditional biscuity malt and a balanced, moderate bitterness.

MERCURY

23 Hayward Street
Ipswich, MA 01938
www.mercurybrewing.com

Founded in 1991 as the Ipswich Brewery, it had sold the rights to its original brands before new owners acquired the brewery in 1999 and renamed it Mercury. Mercury later reacquired the Ipswich brands and has been on a fast growth track, with Ipswich and Stone Cat ales, Mercury old-fashioned soda pop, and even oatmeal stout mustard.

MICHIGAN

1093 Highview Drive
Webberville, MI 48892
www.michiganbrewing.com

Although Michigan Brewing was one of the state's biggest breweries before it bought the defunct Celis brand from international giant Miller, it is now best known for that range of beers. Belgian in style, they were first created by Pierre Celis (brewer of the original Hoegaarden beer) after he moved to Texas. Celis even helped brew the first batches made in Michigan.

MIDDLE AGES

120 Wilkinson Street
Syracuse, NY 13204
www.middleagesbrewing.com

When Mary Rubenstein gave her husband, Marc, a birthday card that read "welcome to the middle ages," she unknowingly named the brewery the two homebrewers would launch in 1995. They've earned a reputation for their cask-conditioned, or "real," ale.

BREWING SECRET Their yeast is descended from an 150-year-old Yorkshire strain.

MIDNIGHT SUN

7329 Arctic Boulevard
Anchorage, AK 99518
www.midnightsunbrewing.com

Midnight Sun has developed a cult following, despite producing only about as much beer as a good-sized brewpub, and distributing only as far as Oregon. A 2007 Seven Deadly Sin series of "excessive" beers is being followed by an "out-of-this-world" range of Nine Planet beers.

IPSWICH ORIGINAL ALE

PALE ALE 5.4% ABV
Lightly bready with tropical fruit on the nose. Pleasing hop flavors meld with a biscuity palate.

IPSWICH DARK ALE

BROWN ALE 6.3% ABV
Bold, with significant citric hops to match a full body of roasted malts, chocolate, brown sugar, and toffee.

CELIS WHITE

WITBIER 4.25% ABV
Cloudy, coriander-spicy, with citrus all the way through, wheat tartness, and a soft finish.

MACKINAC PALE ALE

PALE ALE 5.5% ABV
The brewery flagship, golden-orange, not quite pale, with substantial malt fruitiness. Earthy and citrussy American hops.

GRAIL ALE

PREMIUM BITTER 5.5% ABV
Alive on cask, with a ruby hue and a fresh blend of floral hops and toffee. Notes of plums and dates.

BLACK HEART STOUT

STOUT 6.6% ABV
Fresh coffee and chocolate, with underlying smokiness. Rich yeast character, but a dry finish.

SOCKEYE RED IPA

INDIA PALE ALE 5.7% ABV
Northwest hops upfront, grapefruit and evergreen pine needles later. Complemented by caramel richness.

ARCTIC DEVIL BARLEY WINE

BARLEY WINE 14% ABV
Aged in port, wine, or whiskey barrels, it varies from batch to batch. A malt base, rich with plums and raisins, assures complexity.

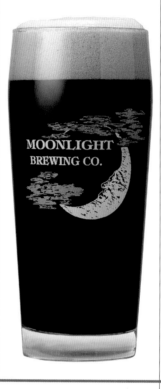

MILLSTREAM

835 48th Avenue
Amana, IA 52203
www.millstreambrewing.com

Millstream is located in the historic Amana Colonies, a region established by German-speaking European settlers before the Civil War. Opening in 1985, it didn't attract the same attention as other microbreweries, but it has an increased presence in the midwest since a change of ownership in 2000.

MINHAS

1208 14th Avenue
Monroe, WI 53566
www.minhasbrewery.com

Ravinder Minhas was just 24 years old when he bought the historic Joseph Huber Brewery in 2006 to produce his popular Mountain Creek brands, already brewed under contract in Monroe for Canadian distribution. Minhas Craft Brewery still makes the Huber brands (dating back to 1843), Berghoff beers, and a line of grocery store house label beers as well.

MOONLIGHT

2218 Laughlin Road
Windsor, CA 95492
www.moonlightbrewing.com

Brian Hunt has run Moonlight Brewing as a one-man operation since 1992, sometimes calling on his family to help deliver beer (available only in kegs). He worked for former brewing giant Schlitz, before founding his farmhouse brewery in Sonoma County.

BREWING SECRET Hunt grows as many as possible of his own hops.

NEW BELGIUM

500 Linden Street
Fort Collins, CO 80524
www.newbelgium.com

New Belgium Brewing's fans praise its beers and the sense of environmental and social responsibility its employees represent. Those beers are particularly coveted east of the Mississippi, where they are nearly impossible to find. Jeff Lebesch and Kim Jordan started out with a system, built to Belgian specifications, in their cellar in 1991.

SCHILD BRAU AMBER
VIENNA LAGER 4.9% ABV
Copper with rich red highlights. A full malt middle that's almost nutty. Floral, spicy hops.

JOHN'S GROCERY GENERATIONS WHITE ALE
WITBIER 5.2% ABV
Cloudy and effervescent. Pepper and coriander spices, fruit character blending with yeast, and finally tart.

LAZY MUTT
GOLDEN ALE 4.8% ABV
The first released under the Minhas brand, billed as a "farmhouse ale" by the brewery but more summer ale than a *saison*.

HUBER BOCK
BOCK 5.4% ABV
Toasty and dry, with caramel notes. Best at Baumgartner's Cheese Store & Tavern near the brewery.

DEATH AND TAXES BLACK
SCHWARZBIER 5% ABV
Very dark, and rich with roasted malt and chocolate flavors, but surprisingly light, clean, and smooth.

REALITY CZECK
PILSNER 4.8% ABV
Almost sweet aromas and flavors of freshly crushed pilsner malt, with new-mown hay and flowery hop notes; splendidly balanced.

FAT TIRE
AMBER ALE 5.3% ABV
Biscuity, malty nose, with toasted caramel in the middle and a balanced finish on the sweet side of dry.

MOTHERSHIP WIT
WITBIER 4.8% ABV
The brewery's first organic beer. Fruity and spicy; a creamy texture and wheat tartness on the tongue. Refreshing acidity at the finish.

They now operate the third largest craft brewery in the US. Best known for Fat Tire Ale, the brewery offers quite a wide range of beers, including its outstanding Blue Paddle Pilsener.

BREWING SECRET New Belgium has more capacity for ageing beer on wood than any brewery other than Rodenbach Brewery in Belgium.

NEW GLARUS

Highway 69
New Glarus, WI 53574
www.newglarusbrewing.com

In 2008, New Glarus Brewing moved into a $21 million plant, just outside a picturesque village settled by Swiss pioneers in 1845. In its rural setting, the attractive complex is designed to look like a Wisconsin dairy farm. In 2002 it was a microbrewery that made 13,700 barrels; by 2007, it had increased this fivefold. The new expansion will allow the brewery to double production and keep pace with soaring sales and the demand for brewmaster Dan Carey's fruit beers and limited-edition "Unplugged" brews. It's an amazing success story given that New Glarus does not ship its beers outside of Wisconsin.

NEW HOLLAND

690 Commerce Court
Holland, MI 49423
www.newhollandbrew.com

New Holland Brewing bottle caps carry the slogan "Art in Fermented Form," which extends from beer to a line of brandy-flavored vodka, gin, rum, and other spirits. To keep up with demand for its assertive beers, the brewery recently put on line a used copper-domed, three-vessel brewhouse acquired from Germany.

LA FOLIE

FLEMISH SOUR 6% ABV
Tart fruits on the nose, then oak and vanilla. Distinct but balanced acidity; a mouth-puckering finish.

ABBEY

DOUBLE 7% ABV
Fruity-spicy aromas of bananas and raisins, with complex chocolate and dark fruit flavors. Rich on the tongue before easing to a dry finish.

SPOTTED COW

CREAM ALE 4.8% ABV
Faintly fruity, tasting of fresh peaches. Pleasantly grainy, light on the tongue, and refreshing.

YOKEL

ZWICKEL 4.7% ABV
Unfiltered lager in the Bavarian tradition. Bready, yeasty, fresh, and dry at finish. The brewery suggests drinkers "Buy Local, Drink Yokel".

FAT SQUIRREL

BROWN ALE 5.5%
Hazelnuts on the nose, blending with chocolate and caramel flavors; nicely balanced by earthy hops.

WISCONSIN CHERRY BEER

FRUIT ALE 5.1% ABV
Packed with Wisconsin-grown Montmorency cherries that dominate the aroma and flavor, balanced by just-right sourness and acidity.

THE POET

OATMEAL STOUT 6.5% ABV
Abundant roast, chocolate, and dark, rummy fruits. Full-bodied and creamy enough to balance the coffee start.

BLACK TULIP

TRIPLE 9% ABV
Floral, with candy and honey sweetness, and fruity notes. Sweet but tart in the mouth, accented by spicy, bitter hops.

NORTH COAST

455 North Main Street
Fort Bragg, CA 95437
www.northcoastbrewing.com

Since opening in 1988, North Coast Brewing has cast a larger shadow than its production levels would suggest. Though small for a regional brewery, it sells beer in 36 states and exports to Europe and the Pacific Rim too. Brewmaster Mark Ruedrich has further extended North Coast's reputation by exploring beer styles before many others, and brewing them well. Most recently the brewery launched an Artisan series, packaged in corked 750 ml bottles. Part of the profits from one, Brother Thelonious, go to the Thelonious Monk Institute of Jazz for music education. That beer has earned the brewery entry into many international jazz clubs.

ODELL

800 East Lincoln Avenue
Fort Collins, CO 80524
www.odellbrewing.com

Odell Brewing opened in 1989 as a gravity-fed brewery housed in a 1915 grain elevator. It has since moved and expanded, but its dedication to traditional brewing hasn't wavered. Like its bigger neighbor, New Belgium, the company is committed to environmentally friendly brewing.

OLD DOMINION

44633 Guilford Drive
Ashburn, VA 20147
www.olddominion.com

The brewery has made highly regarded beers since 1989. Coastal Brewing, a joint venture of Fordham in Maryland and Anheuser-Busch, purchased Old Dominion in 2007, leading to wider availability but a reduction in brands.

BREWING SECRET All Old Dominion beers are strictly kosher.

OLD RASPUTIN

IMPERIAL STOUT 11.6% ABV
Powerful, but subtle enough for flavors to emerge—bitter and sweet chocolate, burnt barley, rum, toffee, dried dark fruits, and espresso.

RED SEAL ALE

PALE ALE 5.5% ABV
Fresh and citrussy. Solid dry malt-caramel character, perfectly balances bracing hoppy bitterness.

BROTHER THELONIOUS

BELGIAN STRONG DARK ALE 9.3% ABV
Spicy and candy-sweet aromas, with dark fruits, notes of banana and caramelized sugar, almost rummy.

PRANQSTER

BELGIAN STRONG GOLDEN ALE 7.6% ABV
Complex, fruity, honeyish aromas. Medium body offers more fruit, a bit of banana candy, and a sweet-smooth finish.

90 SHILLING

SCOTTISH ALE 5.3% ABV
A lighter version of a Scottish ale. Smoothly malty, with some nuttiness and a relatively dry finish.

5 BARREL PALE ALE

PALE ALE 5.2% ABV
Fresh, floral, and fruity (peaches). A hoppy nose, with more hops in the earthy middle, balanced perfectly against rich British malts.

DOMINION LAGER

DORTMUNDER 5.6% ABV
Well-balanced sweet pilsner malt and spicy hops. Bready notes on the palate; clean, and relatively dry.

DOMINION PALE ALE

PALE ALE 5.6% ABV
Pours surprisingly dark, with sweet caramel notes highlighted by citrus and pine from the hops. Almost creamy, and well balanced.

BEER STYLES
US ALES

The huge influx of German-speaking immigrants into the United States in the middle of the 19th century changed more than the ethnic mix of the country. These newcomers brought with them a tradition of beermaking that was to revolutionize the American brewing industry. Lager beers, as well as the odd weissbier, replaced porters and ales. Then, in 1920, began 13 years of Prohibition, which wiped the slate clean as far as brewing heritage was concerned. Those breweries that survived decided that the future lay in a light and neutral-tasting lager-style beer.

However, when a new wave of craft brewers emerged in the late 20th century, its vanguard looked to the beer styles of mainland Europe and the British Isles, and then went on to develop individual versions of amber ales, pale ales, India pale ales, and brown ales. There are approximately 1,500 US breweries today, and many produce ale of some description. After the long reign of pale lager, ale is back with a vengeance.

EXTREME BEERS American ales are big, bold, and inventive, intensely flavored with hops and malt's caramel, biscuity qualities. Exceptional examples of such creativity have led to a coining of the term "extreme beers" to convey a sense of beers that are pushing boundaries and breaking the rules.

CRAFT BREWERS In 1965 Fritz Maytag bought an ailing San Francisco brewery, creating the traditionally brewed Liberty Ale and launching the microbrewery movement. Home brewer and bicycle repairer Ken Grossman is a more recent example of what is now often called the craft brewer—his Sierra Nevada Brewery was founded in 1979. The term pays due tribute to the skill and respect for tradition of this new wave of brewers.

OLD STYLES REVIVED American brewers have been enthusiastic in replicating Old World ales, even those that had become extinct in Europe. Brown ale, somewhat taken for granted in its English homeland, has thus benefited from the magical touch of Brooklyn Brewery's Garrett Oliver, while the long-abandoned hybrid style of Cream Ale is enjoying a renaissance in the form of Honey Cream Ale from Rogue Ales of Oregon.

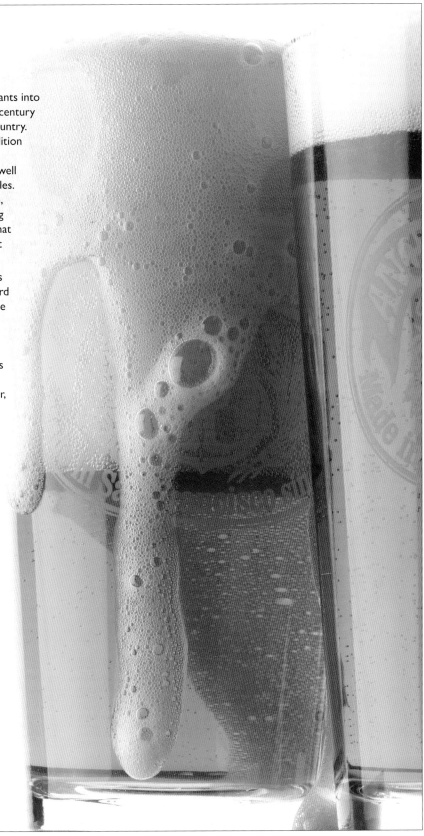

BREWERY

OMMEGANG
656 County Highway 33
Cooperstown, NY 13326
www.ommegang.com

Owned by Belgium's Duvel Moortgat, Brewery Ommegang has brewed ales in the Belgian tradition since 1997, selling limited quantities across much of the US. It hosts one of the nation's most outstanding beer festivals, Belgium Comes to Coopers-town, each summer in the picturesque brewery grounds outside of town.

ORLANDO
1301 Atlanta Avenue
Orlando, FL 32806
www.orlandobrewing.com

Florida's only certified organic brewery, Orlando is trying to find a niche that has so far eluded microbreweries in the state. Forced to relocate because of highway construction, it moved to its new home on April 7, 2006, the anniversary of the end of Prohibition.

OSKAR BLUES
303 Main Street
Lyons, CO 80540
www.oskarblues.com

A small mountain-town brewpub, Oskar Blues sparked a hand-canning revolution among small breweries in the US in 2002, and has grown more than 800 percent as a result. Before owner Dale Katechis won over an audience for Dale's Pale Ale craft beer, drinkers clung to the notion quality beer was not sold in cans.

OTTER CREEK
793 Exchange Street
Middlebury, VT 05753
www.ottercreekbrewing.com

The Wolaver family bought the well-established Otter Creek Brewery in 2002 in order to make its own organic ales, which had previously been made under contract at other breweries. Otter Creek beers are still produced as well, and the "World Tour" series includes Otter Mon (a Jamaican-style stout) and Otteroo (an Australian-style lager).

BEER

HENNEPIN
SAISON 7.7% ABV
Spicy and peppery throughout. Yeasty notes, citrus more apparent on the palate. Tart and dry.

OMMEGANG ABBEY ALE
BELGIAN STRONG DARK ALE 8.5% ABV
The flagship ale, produced in the spirit of a Christmas beer. Rich and chocolatey, with underlying liquorice and festive spices.

BLACKWATER DRY PORTER
PORTER 5.1% ABV
Malt-accented, with roasting coffee beans on the nose, and almost-milky chocolate and caramel flavors.

BLONDE ALE
GOLDEN ALE 4.5% ABV
Pale-straw-colored, light-bodied, with subtle malt aromas turning to apples and peaches on the palate. Dry, but with no bitterness.

DALE'S PALE ALE
PALE ALE 6.5% ABV
Pour it from the can to release a blast of Northwest hops, supported by a rich, malty backbone.

OLD CHUB
SCOTTISH ALE 8% ABV
Malt-accented—even a hint of whiskey malt. Creamy-chewy body carries chocolate and caramel notes well. Powerful and mellow.

OTTER CREEK COPPER ALE
ALTBIER 5.4% ABV
Rich, complex, malty aromas and flavors, with a sneaky bitterness that extends the finish.

WOLAVER'S OATMEAL STOUT
OATMEAL STOUT 5.9% ABV
Chocolate and roasted coffee at the outset, blending with creamy notes in the mouth. Full-bodied, but finishing rather dry.

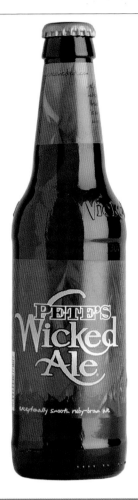

PELICAN

33180 Cape Kiwanda Drive
Pacific City, OR 97135
www.pelicanbrewery.com

Set on the ocean shore, Pelican lies just south of Cape Kiwanda, one of Oregon's most photographed landmarks. Only small quantities are sold outside the pub.

BREWING SECRET Its India Pelican Ale and Doryman's Dark have both been named Grand Champion Beer at the Australian International Beer Awards.

PENN

800 Vinial Street
Pittsburgh, PA 15212
www.pennbrew.com

Operating in the former Eberhardt and Ober Brewery, with lagering caves in the adjoining hillside, the Pennsylvania Brewing Company has brewed in the German tradition since opening in 1986. Its other links with Germany are equally strong, with Teutonic fare on the restaurant menu, a beer garden, and a *rathskeller* (cellar bar).

PETE'S

14800 San Pedro Avenue
San Antonio, TX 78232
www.petes.com

Pete's Brewing was once among the leading new wave of American beer companies. Founder Pete Slosburg sold the business to San Antonio-based Gambrinus in 1988, and the brand has not matched the success of other Gambrinus companies. Brewed under contract in New York, Pete's is less widely available today.

PIKE

1415 1st Avenue
Seattle, WA 98101
www.pikebrewing.com

A stroll through the restaurant side of Pike Brewing is like a trip to a well-kept beer museum. Owners Charles and Rose Ann Finkel have been key figures in reviving interest in traditional beer in the US. In 1978 they founded Merchant du Vin, importing classic European styles, some for the first time, and inspiring a generation of craft brewers.

DORYMAN'S DARK ALE

BROWN ALE 5.8% ABV
Malt qualities—roasted nuts, cocoa, coffee beans, caramel—balanced by Northwest hops.

TSUNAMI STOUT

STOUT 7% ABV
Deep black, with a creamy head. Coffee and chocolate on the nose and palate, rich and almost creamy. Pleasant acidic bite at the end.

PENN WEIZEN

HEFEWEIZEN 5.2% ABV
Bavarian all the way. Banana bubble-gum fruity aromas enlivened by cloves and almost peppery spices.

PENN PILSNER

VIENNA LAGER 5.2% ABV
The flagship, with light, tasty notes that define a Vienna. A true triple-decocted northern German pils.

PETE'S WICKED ALE

BROWN ALE 5.3% ABV
The defining American Brown Ale when brewed to Slosberg's original homebrew recipe lost its bite when the hopping rate was halved.

WICKED STRAWBERRY BLOND

FRUIT ALE 5% ABV
More blonde than strawberry, but berry sweetness begins on the nose and continues through the finish.

PIKE PALE

PALE ALE 5% ABV
Creamy, with juicy hops playing well off a fruity, biscuity medium body, and lingering, nutty dry finish.

PIKE KILT LIFTER

SCOTTISH ALE 6.5% ABV
Caramel-accented, with balancing earthy peat-smoked notes, from the opening aromas through to a just-dry-enough finish.

BREWERY

PYRAMID

st Avenue South
Seattle, WA 98134
www.pyramidbrew.com

Pyramid has developed scores of ales and absorbed other breweries since opening in 1984. Today it emphasizes its wheat beer prowess. It operates several brewpubs on the West coast, with brewing facilities in Washington, Oregon, and California.

BREWING SECRET Magic Hat is in the process of acquiring Pyramid.

REAL ALE

231 San Saba Court
Blanco, TX 78606
www.realalebrewing.com

The brewers at Real Ale Brewing celebrated their 2007 move from a tiny basement brewery to a new facility by doubling their output. As well as using biodiesel for its own trucks, the brewery now sells the fuel (on a not-for-profit basis) to truckers passing through Hill County.

REDHOOK

14300 Northeast 145th Street
Woodinville, WA 98072
www.redhook.com

Redhook has merged with Widmer Brothers, but the two breweries continue to operate separately and sell their own brands. Founded in 1982, Redhook survived despite locals calling its first ale "banana beer." It was not until the introduction of Ballard Bitter in 1984 that it was certain the brewery would succeed.

RIVER HORSE

80 Lambert Lane
Lambertville, NJ 08530
www.riverhorse.com

Founded in 1996, in this historic river town, by three brothers who converted a former oyster cracker plant into a brewery. A Philadelphia investment firm bought control of the brewery in 2007, leaving the brothers in charge of brewing but committing to expand distribution and the product range.

BEER

APRICOT ALE
FRUIT BEER 5.1% ABV
Apricot in color. Apricot on the nose. Apricot and wheaty flavors mingle in the mouth. Clean and light.

HEFEWEIZEN
US HEFEWEIZEN 5.2% ABV
Brewed with 60 percent wheat. Pouring cloudy, slightly grainy, with wheat tartness on the palate.

FULL MOON PALE RYE
PALE RYE 5.6% ABV
Distinctively rye (almost rye bread), balanced with fruitiness in the middle and a lively citrus hop finish.

SISYPHUS
BARLEY WINE 11% ABV
A rich, mahogany-colored beer that varies in strength each vintage. Complex and viscous with toffee notes, it improves with age.

ESB
EXTRA SPECIAL BITTER 5.7% ABV
Caramel on the nose, and a slightly grassy palate, with fruit, honey, and butterscotch notes.

BLACKHOOK PORTER
PORTER 5.2% ABV
The brewery calls this a "London porter." Dark chocolate malts trumped by roasted coffee beans and a pleasant, acrid sour note.

HOP HAZARD
PALE ALE 5.5% ABV
Hop-accented, citric, and grassy aromas, with caramel flavors meeting slightly abrasive hops.

TRIPEL HORSE
TRIPLE 10% ABV
Sweet and spicy nose with vanilla esters, and fresh fruit flavors with satisfying hoppy bitterness. A substantial alcohol bite.

ROCK BOTTOM

Various locations
www.rockbottom.com

The Rock Bottom chain operates more than 30 brewery-restaurants, together producing more than 40,000 barrels annually. They also have over 50 Old Chicago restaurants that offer more than 30 beers each on tap. Each Rock Bottom Brewery Restaurant location usually features similar core beers but the recipes may vary from pub to pub.

ROGUE

2320 OSU Drive, Newport, Oregon 97365, USA
www.rogueales.com

Rogue Ales brewmaster John Maier joined the company a year after it opened in 1988. He has earned an international reputation for brewing envelope-pushing beers by creating a well-structured malt foundation on which to layer massive hop additions. This approach has won hundreds of awards and fostered the growth of the "Rogue Nation"—loyal fans who

eagerly await the release of limited-edition Johns Locker Stock beers. Beyond its home bases of Newport and Portland, Rogue Ales operates brewpubs and restaurants along the west coast, calling them "micro-meeting halls". There's even one at Portland International Airport.

BREWING SECRET Rogue beers are top-fermented using their own PacMan yeast which is well suited for bottle-conditioning.

RUSSIAN RIVER

1812 Ferdinand Court, Santa Rosa, California 95404, USA
www.russianriverbrewing.com

Owner-brewmaster Vinnie Cilurzo's creative use of hops, yeasts, and wine-barrel-ageing make it seem incredible that all his beers come from the same brewery. He was the first to brew an Imperial India Pale Ale commercially, when he was at Blind Pig Brewing. That beer is now called Pliny the Elder and has become the benchmark for the style. (Continues on p68)

TERMINAL STOUT
STOUT ABV VARIABLE
Reflecting local preference, it might be deemed an Imperial Stout at one location, Oatmeal, or Dry elsewhere.

MOLLY'S TITANIC BROWN ALE
BROWN ALE 5.6% ABV
Brown ales vary from pub to pub. This version from Denver is malt-driven. It's an award-winner in the "brown porter" category.

DEAD GUY ALE
HELLER BOCK 6.6% ABV
Complex, clean malt aromas, rich and fruity, becoming toastier on the palate. Bright bitter hops. Dry and spicy.

BRUTAL BITTER
EXTRA SPECIAL BITTER 6.2% ABV
Aromatic and flowery hops become juicier on the palate, braced against fermentation fruit and bready malt. Bitter to the end.

SHAKESPEARE STOUT
STOUT 6% ABV
Dark, roasty, chocolate, and coffee mingle with dark fruits and husky malt. Substantial, balanced hops and an oily/creamy smooth finish.

HAZELNUT BROWN NECTAR
BROWN ALE 6.2% ABV
Inspired by a homebrewer's recipe, with a solid dose of hazelnuts saturating a robust brown ale.

BEATIFICATION
SOUR ALE 6% ABV
A spontaneously fermented blended beer. Complex, tart mix of fruit and wood. Just right acidity at the finish.

PLINY THE ELDER
IMPERIAL INDIA PALE ALE 8% ABV
Hoppy aroma, hoppy flavor, and a hoppy bitterness—all supported by a firm malt base.

BEER TRAIL

OREGON

The term "Beervana" is often used to describe Oregon's culture of craft beer. The state also offers spectacular outdoor recreation from the Pacific Ocean on the west to Hells Canyon on the east, and up and down the Cascade Mountains in the center. Beer touring opportunities abound, and it would be possible to spend weeks traveling and never drink the same beer twice. This three-day trail starts in the seaside town of Newport, which is home to the iconic Rogue Ales brewery. It continues the next day with scenic stops on the way to Portland, then concludes with a full day in the Rose City. For more information visit www.oregonbeer.org.

Rogue's Dead Guy Ale

① DAY 1: NEWPORT AND ROGUE ALES

Rogue Ales Public House is located on OSU Drive, right in the center of the working seaport of Newport. There are plenty of bed and breakfasts to choose from in this friendly town, including Rogue's "Bed and Beer" apartments, above the public house. The public house is also the place to book in for one of the brewery tours, which commence at 3pm daily. *2320 OSU Drive, Newport (www.rogueales.com)*

JOURNEY STATS
3 days
230 km (142 miles)

② DAY 2: PELICAN PUB & BREWERY

The scenic 48-mile (77-km) drive from Newport to Pacific City easily occupies a morning, so you should arrive just in time for lunch at the Pelican Pub & Brewery. The brewery-restaurant is located on the shoreline of Pacific City, where there are outstanding views of the oft-photographed Haystack Rock and Cape Kiwanda. *33180 Cape Kiwanda Drive, Pacific City (www. pelicanbrewery.com)*

DAY 2: GOLDEN VALLEY BREWERY & PUB

The scenic route to McMinnville passes through the Willamette Valley, one of the nation's premier wine-growing regions. The Golden Valley Brewery & Pub offers ales, sometimes aged in wine barrels. *980 East 4th St, McMinnville*

```
0 miles          10 miles
0 km      25 km
```

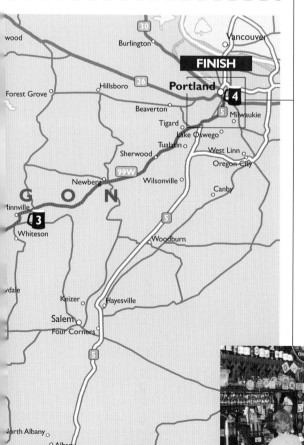

DAY 3: PORTLAND

With more than three dozen breweries in the metropolitan region, it is little wonder residents of Portland like to say they live in "Beervana." Here are some you could visit on Day 3 of this trail.

HAIR OF THE DOG

This tiny brewery uses equipment not originally designed for brewing. Visits by appointment. *4509 SE 23rd Avenue, Portland (www.hairofthedog.com)*

WIDMER (see p78)

Visit the brewery's Gasthaus restaurant to sample the full line-up of beers—including the Alt intended to be the brewery flagship before its Hefeweizen became an American standard. The brewery offers tours on Fridays and Saturdays. *929 North Russell, Portland*

BRIDGEPORT (see p25)

Oregon's oldest surviving brewery helped turn the Pearl District into a hip locale. *1313 Northwest Marshall Street, Portland*

HIGGINS BREWPUB

Greg Higgins uses local produce for his widely praised menu, which pairs well with Oregon beers and wines. *1239 SW Broadway, Portland*

GREEN DRAGON BISTRO AND PUB

This relative newcomer quickly became an instant hit with a trendy crowd. Offers a constantly-changing selection of beers not necessarily found elsewhere, served by a knowledgeable staff. *928 SE 9th Avenue, Portland*

HORSE BRASS PUB

A Portland institution since 1976, the Horse Brass is a sprawling tribute to both the English pub and Oregon beer, offering 52 selections on draft. The pub is especially popular with the late-night crowd. *4534 SE Belmont Street, Portland*

The Flanders Street
Brewpub in Portland, Oregon,
has helped the city gain its
reputation for fine beers.

BEER:
SO MUCH MORE
than just a
Breakfast Drink.

BREWERY

RUSSIAN RIVER

(Continued from p63)
Cilurzo and his wife, Natalie, have built a production brewery separate from their popular downtown brewpub, giving more space for a wider range of barrels and ageing. Each variety (the base beer and barrel type differ) spends at least a year on wood.

BREWING SECRET Cilurzo uses varieties of wild yeast in his beers. They need careful handling by a master brewer, but give great results.

SACRAMENTO

2713 El Paseo Lane
Sacramento, CA 95821
www.sacbrew.com

Although Rubicon, founded in 1987, was Sacramento's first well-known brewery, Sacramento Brewing has grown into the town's largest, since opening in 1995. The company operates two brewery restaurants, distributes packaged beers to a growing market, and is beginning to plan for a separate production facility.

SAINT ARNOLD

2522 Fairway Park Drive
Houston, TX 77092
www.saintarnold.com

The oldest surviving and largest craft brewery in Texas was founded in 1994. Saint Arnold grew out of its "micro" status in 2007, although it continues to sell its beer only within the state borders. Austrian-born St. Arnold is one of the patron saints of beer; the brewery's fermenters are named after other saints.

SAMUEL ADAMS

30 Germania Street, Boston,
Massachusetts 02130, USA
www.samueladams.com

The name Samuel Adams has been synonymous with craft beer since Boston Beer Company was one of just a few specialty beer sellers in the country. The company launched the brand in 1984, when it contracted production to mainstream producers with excess capacity. Boston Beer has since purchased some of those breweries and produces much of its

BEER

TEMPTATION

BELGIAN STRONG ALE 7.2% ABV
Aged in Chardonnay barrels with wild yeast. Complex and vinous. Sharp nose; Chardonnay and oak emerging as it warms.

BLIND PIG IPA

INDIA PALE ALE 6% ABV
Explosive floral, citrus, and pine aromas. Sturdy malt accents the fruit character. Clean tangy finish.

HEFE WEIZEN

HEFEWEIZEN 5.3% ABV
Particularly rich on the palate. Classic aromas and flavors—banana, lemon zest, yeast, wheat, and cloves.

RED HORSE ALE

AMBER ALE 6.2% ABV
Named after the US Air Force R.E.D. H.O.R.S.E. runway repair teams. Deep amber; big across the board with plenty of malt and hops.

AMBER

AMBER ALE 5.5% ABV
Caramel and fermentation fruit, with bright, spicy hops providing balance. Excellent on cask.

ELISSA IPA

INDIA PALE ALE 6.6% ABV
Delightfully hoppy throughout, brimming with grapefruit character. Big and juicy, with rich malt to match the decided bitterness.

BOSTON LAGER

VIENNA LAGER 4.9% ABV
Complex flowery/piney nose. Full-bodied, with caramel in the middle, and a satisfyingly dry finish.

SCOTCH ALE

SCOTTISH ALE 5.4% ABV
Rich with caramel and molasses aromas and flavors. Underlying earthy and smoky notes come from the peat-smoked malt.

own beer. The company holds an employees' homebrew contest each year, with the winner's beer being sold commercially, alongside winning brews from a national amateur competition.

BREWING SECRET Today almost one out of five craft beers sold in the US is a Samuel Adams.

SARANAC
811 Edward Street
Utica, NY 13502
www.saranac.com

Matt Brewing moved the Saranac line to the fore in the 1990s, emphasizing craft beers at the expense of family brands brewed since 1888. Saranac core beers and varietals have thrived, while Matt's historic Utica Club brew remains as a retro favorite.

BREWING SECRET "UC" was the first beer back on sale after Prohibition.

SCHLAFLY
2100 Locust Street
St. Louis, MO 63101
www.schlafly.com

The Saint Louis Brewery makes beers packaged under the Schlafly brand at a suburban location, but the original downtown brewpub, The Taproom, is the location tourists seek out. Co-founder Tom Schlafly wrote a book called *A New Religion in Mecca* about "sharing" the St. Louis market with international giant Anheuser-Busch.

SHINER
603 Brewery Street
Shiner, TX 77984
www.shiner.com

Founded in 1909, the Spoetzl Brewery has ridden the success of Shiner Bock into national prominence. In 2004 it began counting down toward its 100th birthday by releasing a special new beer every year, each one reflecting a German heritage that dates back to the original Shiner Brewing Association.

BLACK LAGER
SCHWARZBIER 4.9% ABV
Roasted but smooth, with caramel and nuts on the palate. Coffee notes throughout, providing a pleasing closing bitterness.

UTOPIAS
STRONG ALE 27% ABV
The strongest beer in the world, aged in brandy and port barrels. Serve and sip like a rare cognac.

BLACK & TAN
BLENDED BEER 5.3% ABV
Blend of Irish stout and German lager. Notes of chocolate and roast barley cut with just a bit of caramel.

PALE ALE
ENGLISH PALE ALE 5.5% ABV
Fruity yeastiness is complemented by crisp, citrussy hops. Building bitterness extends a long, dry finish.

SCHLAFLY PALE ALE
ENGLISH PALE ALE 4.4% ABV
Biscuit and fruit, with a dry, not-too-bitter finish. The brewpubs serve a strong, dry-hopped version.

SCHLAFLY OATMEAL STOUT
OATMEAL STOUT 5.7% ABV
Breakfast in a glass. Coffee and cream are balanced with a slight oiliness from the oatmeal. Smooth, with hints of smoky chocolate.

SHINER HEFEWEIZEN
HEFEWEIZEN 5.3% ABV
Cloudy, brewed in the Bavarian style with a bit of honey added. More wheat character than yeast, with a hint of citrus.

SHINER BOCK
US DARK LAGER 4.4% ABV
A dark lager, rather than a true German bock. Hints of caramel sweetness. Deliberately low on hops.

BREWERY

SHIPYARD

86 Newbury Street
Portland, ME 04101
www.shipyard.com

British-born Shipyard brewmaster Alan Pugsley is one of the best-known figures in craft brewing, having trained under Peter Austin and established breweries around the world, including Geary's in 1984. Shipyard's beers reflect his philosophy of putting drinkability first. While not necessarily drawing huge public attention, this has driven annual double-digit growth.

SHMALTZ

92 Cole Street #338
San Francisco, CA 94117
www.shmaltz.com

Since Jeremy Cowan started selling HE'BREW beer in 1996, the growth of Shmaltz Brewing has increased at an accelerated rate (550 percent from 2003 to 2007). Brewing under contract on both coasts, and selling beer in 25 states, Shmaltz continues to roll out new high-alcohol kosher beers as well as creating the Coney Island Lagers.

SIERRA NEVADA

1075 East 20th Street, Chico, California 95928, USA
www.sierranevada.com

Sierra Nevada Brewing has been introducing beer drinkers to citrussy, piney Northwest hops since former homebrewers Ken Grossman and Paul Camusi launched their flagship Pale Ale in 1981. Although many other more bitter beers have since emerged, the brewery continues to act as a matchmaker between beer drinkers

and hops. Sierra Nevada is also an industry leader in good environmental practice. It has commissioned the first phase of one of the country's largest private solar installations, which will bring it close to its goal of generating 100 percent of its energy needs.

BEER

OLD THUMPER

EXTRA SPECIAL BITTER 5.9% ABV
Brewed under exclusive license from Peter Austin's Ringwood Brewery in England. Richly fruity with well-balanced bitterness.

EXPORT ALE

GOLDEN ALE 5.1% ABV
The flagship ale. Sweet honey and fruit nose continues on the palate.

BITTERSWEET LENNY'S R.I.P.A.

IMPERIAL INDIA PALE ALE 10% ABV
A tribute to Lenny Bruce. Thick with rich malt, long hops; three different rye malts add spiciness.

MESSIAH BOLD

BROWN ALE 5.5% ABV
"The beer you've been waiting for" is complex without being demanding. Coffee, toffee, nuts, and earthy hops in the flavor and aroma.

PALE ALE

PALE ALE 5.6% ABV
Piney, grapefruity Cascade hops play against malt fruitiness on both the nose and the palate.

HARVEST FRESH HOP ALE

INDIA PALE ALE 6.7% ABV
Made with "wet" hops, harvested and brewed on the same day. Oily and aromatic, like picking and using herbs straight from the garden.

BIGFOOT

BARLEY WINE 9.6% ABV
Earthy and chewy, with prominent citric hops and whiskeylike rich malts. Boldly bitter when young.

CELEBRATION ALE

INDIA PALE ALE 6.8% ABV
A winter seasonal, full of citrussy hop flavors, notably of tangerines. A balanced, fruity-caramel malt backbone and persistent bitterness.

SKA

545 Turner Drive
Durango, CO 81301
www.skabrewing.com

Bill Graham and Dave Thibodeau named their brewery for the Jamaican music they played while homebrewing in college, reflecting their motto "it takes characters to brew beer with character." When they founded Ska in 1995, they had day jobs and brewed at night. Now they can't keep up with the demand for their beers and are building a new brewery.

SLY FOX

312 North Lewis Road
Royersford, PA 19468
www.slyfoxbeer.com

Since opening its doors in 1995, Sly Fox Brewing has mirrored many other success stories by bottling special beers in 750 ml bottles, packaging beer in cans, judicious expansion, and distinctive promotions.

BREWING SECRET Come here on Incubus Friday (the first of each month) for the tapping of a new barrel of Triple.

SMUTTYNOSE

225 Heritage Avenue
Portsmouth, NH 03801
www.smuttynose.com

Although Smuttynose Brewing has earned a reputation for its carefully balanced offerings, the brewery was also one of the first to embrace "extreme beers," launching a Big Beer Series in 1998. Succeeding on all fronts, it found itself out of room by 2007, and plans to relocate its brewing, still close to Portsmouth.

SNAKE RIVER

265 S. Millward Street
Jackson, WY 83001
www.snakeriverbrewing.com

Located in central Jackson, with a view of Snow King Mountain and standing but a few miles from the Jackson Hole ski resort, Snake River brewpub occupies an old cinder-block warehouse. It has twice won Small Brewery of the Year at the Great American Beer Festival.

TEN PIN PORTER
PORTER 5.4% ABV
Chocolate and caramel throughout, with roasted coffee stronger in the flavor. Eases into bitterness.

TRUE BLONDE
GOLDEN ALE 4.2% ABV
Brewed with honey made just north of town. Light biscuity malt, hints of honey, and a touch of citric hops.

PIKELAND PILS
PILSNER 4.9% ABV
Fresh and crisp. Delicate pilsner malt is interwoven with grassy, floral hops—spicy, and firmly bitter.

SAISON VOS
SAISON 6.9% ABV
Spicy, fruity, and hoppy nose, very lively on the tongue, tart fruit and bitterness emerging. Satisfyingly dry.

SHOAL'S PALE ALE
PALE ALE 5% ABV
First made at the Portsmouth pub. Pleasant fruity/biscuit palate gives way to a crisp American hop finish.

ROBUST PORTER
PORTER 5.7% ABV
Rich dark fruits and chocolate, well blended throughout. Rich, roasty flavors leave a strong impression for a medium-strength beer.

ZONKER STOUT
STOUT 5.8% ABV
Roasted barley sets a bold tone, with chocolate (almost sweet) underneath. Pleasingly dry finish.

LAGER
VIENNA LAGER 6% ABV
Golden, with a thick white head. Malt-accented, clean toasted and caramel flavors, drying hop finish.

BREWERY

SOUTHAMPTON

40 Bowden Square, Southampton,
New York 11968, USA
www.publick.com

Southampton Publick House's busy brewmaster, Phil Markowski, routinely travels to three breweries in New York State and Pennsylvania to make Southampton-branded beer. As well the eclectic range he's created for the brewery-restaurant on Long Island, he also brews specials, packaged in 750ml corked bottles, and oversees the production of Double White and Secret Ale. Since early 2008, the Southampton range of beers has been marketed by Pabst.

BREWING SECRET Markowski is author of *Farmhouse Ales*, a definitive guide to the *saison* and *bière de garde* styles of Wallonia in Belgium.

SOUTHERN TIER

2051A Stoneman Circle
Lakewood, NY 14750
www.southerntierbrewing.com

When Southern Tier Brewing opened in 2004, it was expected to sell a conservative range of beers. Instead success came with an assertive IPA, followed by other beers that showed an equal ability to deliver great flavor.

BREWING SECRET They continue to push envelopes, as evidenced by a trio of 11 percent imperial stouts.

SPEAKEASY

1195-A Evans Avenue
San Francisco, CA 94124
www.goodbeer.com

Two big eyes peering suspiciously out of the darkness decorate the brewery loading dock at Speakeasy Ales & Lagers, a nod to Prohibition days. Since Speakeasy opened in 1997, local sales have been its core business, and it remains a San Francisco brewery first and foremost. Its Big Daddy IPA is named after venerable local publican David Keene of the Toronado.

BEER

DOUBLE WHITE ALE

WITBIER 6.8% ABV
Bright floral, citric, and sweet notes from the start. Rich textures cut by wheat and orange tartness.

IMPERIAL PORTER

BALTIC PORTER 7.2% ABV
Rich, intoxicating aromas of dark fruit and chocolate, joined by coffee on the palate. Pleasantly bitter finish.

SAISON

SAISON 6.5% ABV
An endorsement for "Farmhouse Ales"—fruity, peppery, slightly tart, earthy, and refreshing.

SECRET ALE

ALTBIER 5.1% ABV
Slightly sweet caramel aromas, with firm bitterness matching rich malt on the palate, lasting beyond the finish.

OAT OATMEAL STOUT

IMPERIAL STOUT 11% ABV (VARIABLE)
Part of a series of Imperial Stouts. Thick and chewy with oatmeal; chocolate-rich, and complexly bitter.

HEAVY WEIZEN

STRONG HEFEWEIZEN 8% ABV
Won't appeal to everybody. Bavarian-inspired, but with more fruity (banana) sweetness, more cloves and spice, and more hops.

BIG DADDY IPA

INDIA PALE ALE 6.5% ABV
Hop driven—juicy citrus and pine. Lightly caramel, enough sturdy malt to stand up to persistent bitterness.

PROHIBITION ALE

AMBER ALE 6.1% ABV
Their flagship, best on draft in San Francisco. Long hop flavors, particularly citrus, playing against a definite caramel sweetness.

SPRECHER

701 West Glendale Avenue
Glendale, WI 53209
www.sprecherbrewery.com

Randy Sprecher started his brewery in downtown Milwaukee in 1985 aiming to do more than brew the German-style beers typical of Milwaukee breweries. He insisted on authenticity, such as using real fruit in fruit beers.

BREWING SECRET Bananas are used in their Mbege African-style beer.

STARR HILL

5391 Three Notched Road
Crozet, VA 22932
www.starrhill.com

Starr Hill Brewing became the second small Virginia brewery in which Anheuser-Busch bought a stake during 2007, when it struck a deal that could lead to national distribution. The brewery has produced well-received, traditional beers since taking over a failed brewpub in 1999 and later adding a production facility.

STEAMWORKS

801 East 2nd Avenue
Durango, CO 81301
www.steamworksbrewing.com

Although Steamworks Brewing sells a full range in its two brewery-restaurants (the other is in Bayfield), it has found the greatest success in an expanding southwestern market with its German-inspired beers. The brewery takes its name from the steam-powered tourist train that runs between Durango and Silverton.

STEVENS POINT

2617 Water Street
Stevens Point, WI 54481
www.pointbeer.com

The Stevens Point Brewery gained a measure of fame when, in 1973 (at a time when American beer choice was at its lowest), *Chicago Daily News* columnist Mike Royko named Point Special as the best beer in the US. Founded in 1857, Stevens Point is the fifth-oldest continuously operating brewery in the country.

BLACK BAVARIAN

SCHWARZBIER 5.9% ABV
Dark sweet molasses nose, with hints of coffee, chocolate, and caramel. Medium-bodied and clean.

HEFE WEISS

HEFEWEIZEN 4.2% ABV
Yeasty, subdued banana and spices on the nose, more banana and honey on a soft palate, brightened by spicy cloves.

DARK STARR STOUT

STOUT 4.75% ABV
Even the nose leaves an impression of dryness. Roasted malt and rich chocolate in a pleasantly light body.

JOMO

VIENNA LAGER 5% ABV
Bready, even toasty to start with. Toastier and full malts in the mouth with a hint of noble hops and clean, balancing bitterness.

STEAM ENGINE LAGER

AMBER LAGER 5.4% ABV
Pours a bright copper, with sweet malt on the nose. More caramel in the flavor, even honey.

COLORADO KÖLSCH

KÖLSCH 4.2% ABV
Not as bright or crisp as you'd find in Cologne, but popular as a light lager with lingering sweetness.

POINT SPECIAL

US LAGER 5.1% ABV
Has a loyal regional following. Pours bright and drinks smooth, with sweet malt and hints of grassy hops.

SPRING BOCK

MAIBOCK 5.8% ABV
A spring seasonal since 1938. Dominated by rich pilsner malt, with a pleasant, light toastiness on the palate. Clean hop bitterness.

BREWERY

STONE

1999 Citracado Parkway
Escondido, CA 92029
www.stonebrew.com

Although some find the "you are not worthy" campaign, used to promote Arrogant Bastard Ale, off putting, CEO Greg Koch's argument in favor of particularly full-flavored beers is the opposite of elitist. He doesn't think beer appreciation takes special skill: "If you want to turn people on to great beer, use great beer to do it," he says. That philosophy has resulted in 30 percent annual growth year after year. After building a larger brewery in 2006, the company added the Stone Brewing World Bistro & Gardens, serving local organic "slow food" dishes and featuring a large, lovely beer garden landscaped with boulders and dry-stone walls, reflecting the brewery's name.

STRAUB

303 Sorg Street
St. Marys, PA 15857
www.straubbeer.com

Straub is a family-run throwback to 1872, when it was founded. The brewery enjoyed record sales in 2007, although its flagship beer is a pale lager brewed with shaved corn. It sells 60 percent of its beer in its home town, and offers visitors an "Eternal Tap" (pour-your-own beer).

SUDWERK

2001 2nd Street
Davis, CA 95616
www.sudwerk.com

Officially Privabrauerei Hübsch, it's understandable that this brewery-restaurant focused on German-style beer and food when it opened in 1990. The restaurant has since been sold, and the menu now features "California cuisine," but beer from the separate Sudwerk Brewery remains old world. The brewery itself has been for up for sale since 2005.

BEER

IPA
INDIA PALE ALE 6.9% ABV
Fruity hop aromas meet firm malt character at the start, developing complexity, finishing bitter but bright.

ARROGANT BASTARD ALE
STRONG ALE 7.2% ABV
Promises to be aggressive and certainly lives up to it. Juicy hops matched throughout by rich malt. Lingering bitter finish.

IMPERIAL RUSSIAN STOUT
IMPERIAL STOUT 9.4% ABV
Intense, full of chocolate, roasted coffee and dark fruits. All balanced by a brooding bitterness.

SMOKED PORTER
PORTER 5.9% ABV
Smoke plays a supporting role, joining roasted coffee beans on the nose, and chocolate on the palate, adding depth throughout.

STRAUB
US LAGER 4.3% ABV
Fresh and grainy, light and clean on the tongue. Minimal hoppiness, the only bitterness is balancing.

PETER STRAUB'S SPECIAL DARK
AMBER LAGER 5% ABV
Based on a bock, but lighter. Sweet malt on the palate, with caramel and a touch of spiciness.

SUDWERK HELLES
HELLES 4.9% ABV
Aromas and flavors of sweet malt. Complex texture on the palate; firm but unimposing hops.

SUDWERK PILSNER
PILSNER 5.2% ABV
Sweet malt brightens the nose, mixed with spicy hops. Full-bodied. Bread-dough yeastiness balanced with lingering bitterness.

SUMMIT

910 Montreal Circle
Saint Paul, MN 55102
www.summitbrewing.com

Focusing on its Twin Cities market and a small core of beers, Summit Brewing has grown into one of the country's largest craft breweries, eventually building Minnesota's first brand new production brewery since the 1930s. It is expanding distribution to 13 states and has begun to offer special release beers.

SURLY

4811 Dusharme Drive
Brooklyn Center, MN 55429
www.surlybrewing.com

Surly Brewing sold its first beer in February of 2006, and by December, the *Minneapolis St. Paul City Pages* had named founder Omar Ansari as one of its "artists of the year." Packaged in cans and sold only in Minnesota, the brewery's often intense, and seldom "to style," beers have developed a national following.

TERMINAL GRAVITY

803 SE School Street
Enterprise, OR 97828
www.terminalgravitybrewing.com

The brewpub that Steve Carper and Dean Duquette literally built themselves in 1997 in Northeast Oregon has expanded into a microbrewery. When it opened, they leased space to a baker and installed a kitchen that turns out great sausages. "We're the brewer, the baker, and the sausage maker," Duquette said at the time.

TERRAPIN

255 Newton Bridge Road
Athens, GA 30607
www.terrapinbeer.com

Spike Buckowski and John Cochran began shipping beer from their own brewhouse early in 2008, almost six years after the Terrapin Beer Company started selling contract-brewed Rye Pale Ale. That beer was an immediate hit, as was the Monster Beer Tour, a series of strong beers released after Georgia raised its 6 percent ABV cap on beer.

EXTRA PALE ALE

PALE ALE 5.3% ABV
Distinctive, but not overpowering, citrus nose, firm, fruity middle and dry finish with a scent of lemon.

GREAT NORTHERN PORTER

PORTER 5.6% ABV
Roast notes and a chocolate bitterness merge well with herbal hops and balance the sweet caramel-toffee flavors.

BENDER

BROWN ALE 5.1% ABV
Brewed with oatmeal, adding creamy texture to a blend of chocolate, dark fruit, and nuts.

FURIOUS

INDIA PALE ALE 6.2% ABV
Only for those favoring the most aggressive of hopping. Piney and oily, only somewhat balanced by caramel. Flat out bitter.

IPA

INDIA PALE ALE 6.7% ABV
Rich malts playing against citrus hops. Thick on the tongue, but cut by grapefruit. Citrus lingers.

EXTRA SPECIAL GOLDEN / ESG

PALE ALE 5.4% ABV
Noteworthy for its peach-tinged fermentation flavor, mingling nicely with light malt sweetness, and citrussy hops.

RYE PALE ALE

PALE ALE 5.3% ABV
Rye blends with bright grapefruit, adds texture to fruit fermentation, and complements late bitterness.

WAKE-N-BAKE COFFEE OATMEAL IMPERIAL STOUT

IMPERIAL STOUT 8.1% ABV
It's all in the name, along with chocolate-covered dark fruits.

BREWERY

THREE FLOYDS

9750 Indiana Parkway
Munster, IN 46321
www.threefloyds.com

Beginning with its flagship Alpha King in 1996, Three Floyds Brewing had lived by the philosophy of brewmaster Nick Floyd: "I love the smell of hops in the morning. It smells like victory."

BREWING SECRET The annual release of Dark Lord Russian Imperial Stout sells out in one day, with customers driving hundreds of miles to buy it.

TRUMER

1404 Fourth Street
Berkeley, CA 94710
www.trumer-international.com

The US Trumer Brauerei is a partnership between Texas-based Gambrinus, which bought and remodeled a closed brewery in 2004, and the Trumer Brauerei in Austria. The Pils is brewed to the same recipe at each brewery.

BREWING SECRET Bottles for taste-testing are regularly exchanged between breweries to ensure consistency.

TWO BROTHERS

30W315 Calumet Avenue
Warrenville, IL 60555
www.twobrothers.com

Brothers Jim and Jason Ebel opened their brewery in 1997 with a brewhouse designed to produce traditional hefeweizen, supplemented with recycled equipment. For instance, their grandfather donated bulk milk tanks from his dairy farm. Recently, a line of stronger beers has fueled the growth of all brands.

UINTA

1722 South Fremont Drive
Salt Lake City, UT 84104
www.uintabrewing.com

Uinta Brewing actively promotes Utah's outdoor culture and the environment, using slogans like "Keeping Utah the way we found it—except with beer." The brewery joined Utah Power's Blue Sky Program in 2002, when it installed a new brewhouse and became 100 percent wind-powered.

BEER

ALPHA KING

PALE ALE 6% ABV
Opens with a rush of citrus fruits. Firm malt backbone, matched by hop oils. Prolonged bitterness.

GUMBALLHEAD

US WHEAT BEER 4.8% ABV
Citrus and orchard fruits on the nose, followed by wheat tartness and hops throughout.

TRUMER PILS

PILSNER 4.9% ABV
Grassy and grainy fresh, a lovely blend of pilsner malt and noble hops. Slightly sweet palate, noble hop flavor, and a lively mouth feel. Refreshing dry finish.

DOMAINE DUPAGE

BIERE DE GARDE 5.9% ABV
Sweet malts, including caramel on the nose. More caramel-toffee on the palate. Clean, smooth finish.

EBELS WEISS BEER

HEFEWEIZEN 4.9% ABV
Banana and cloves, maybe lemon too, from the outset. Bready and wheat-tart in the mouth, moving on to a smooth, light finish.

KING'S PEAK PORTER

PORTER 4% ABV
Coffee and cream sweetness, restrained dark fruit on the palate, with a pepper and cocoa dry finish.

ANNIVERSARY BARLEY WINE

BARLEY WINE 10% ABV
Malt-accented, with notes of molasses and candied fruits. Properly bitter and warming.

UPSTREAM

514 South 11th Street
Omaha, NE 68102
www.upstreambrewing.com

Since opening in 1996 as part of an "unlinked chain" started by Wynkoop Brewery, Upstream (a translation of the Native American name for Omaha) has gained independence, opened a second pub, and brewed varieties of beers not previously found in Nebraska.

BREWING SECRET Developments include barrel-ageing, and the use of wild yeast.

UTAH BREWERS

1763 South 300 West
Salt Lake City, UT 84115
www.utahbeers.com

Schirf Brewing Co. and Squatters Brewing Co. already operated (as they still do) their own brewery-restaurants when, in 2000, they established the Utah Brewers Cooperative as a production and packaging brewery.

BREWING SECRET Utah law limits beers to 4 percent ABV, except for those sold in state stores.

VICTORY

420 Acorn Lane
Downingtown, PA 19335
www.victorybeer.com

Victory Brewing founders Ron Barchet and Bill Covaleski—who met on a school bus in 1973—traveled much of the beer world, apprenticed in Germany, and worked in US micro-breweries before starting their own in 1996. The breadth of their interests is reflected in the range of their beers, and their new brewhouse is designed to produce almost any style in a traditional manner. They earned an early reputation for hoppy American beers, and their Belgian-inspired ales are among their most popular.

BREWING SECRET Victory has long-term contracts with German hop-growers to assure the availability of authentic ingredients for their lagers.

BATCH 1,000 BARLEY WINE
BARLEY WINE 10.2% ABV
Caramel and vinous on the nose and palate, blending with lively fruity esters. Rich, almost chewy, palate.

GRAND CRU
BELGIAN STRONG ALE 9% ABV
Aged for a year in oak wine barrels. Earthy and woody nose, delicate citrus and honey on the palate, ultimately balanced.

SQUATTERS PROVO GIRL PILSNER
PILSNER 4% ABV
Flowery hops freshen a bready nose. A mild sweetness yields to a dry, bracing finish. Light bodied.

WASATCH POLYGAMY PORTER
PORTER 4% ABV
"Why have just one?," the brewery asks. Chocolate dominates, with some roast and a short, dry finish.

PRIMA PILS
PILSNER 5.3% ABV
Fresh flowery aromas, cookielike palate, and a solidly bitter-rough finish. Sturdy yet delicate.

GOLDEN MONKEY
TRIPLE 9.5% ABV
Spicy, with hints of banana followed by light pepper. Candy-sweet on the palate, with a dry finish.

HOPDEVIL IPA
INDIA PALE ALE 6.5% ABV
Spicy hop aromas, hop flavors, and woody bitterness throughout, laid on a firm malt base.

WHIRLWIND WITBIER
WITBIER 5% ABV
Assertive orange, peppery spices, and cloves on the nose. Silky in the mouth, quickly matched by a spicy bite and tart wheat.

BREWERY

WACHUSETT
175 State Road East
Westminster, MA 01473
www.wachusettbrew.com

Wachusett founders Ned, Kevin, and Peter concentrate on delivering fresh beer close to home, and 70 percent of sales are in Worcester County, central Massachusetts. They have set up a program to enable students from their alma mater of Worcester Polytechnic to earn college credit while working at the brewery.

WEYERBACHER
905 Line Street
Easton, PA 18042
www.weyerbacher.com

Since opening in a livery stable, with a nod toward English-inspired ales but using the original spelling of his German name, founder Dan Weirback has changed directions a few times. The company briefly tried the brewpub business, but then moved to a larger facility, and has thrived by making big, bold "New American" beers.

WIDMER
929 North Russell
Portland, OR 97227
www.widmer.com

More than two decades old, the US-centric Hefeweizen (cloudy but accented by yeast rather than hops) that the Widmer brothers basically invented continues to drive double-digit growth. Widmer and Redhook have merged to form a single company called Craft Breweries Alliance, but Widmer maintains its own brewery.

WYNKOOP
1634 18th Street
Denver, CO 80202
www.wynkoop.com

The first brewpub in the Rockies, Wynkoop settled into Denver's "LoDo" area before it was trendy, and co-founder John Hickenlooper later became the city's mayor. A gathering spot after hours during the Great American Beer Festival each fall, the pub sponsors an annual search for America's Beer Drinker of the Year.

BEER

COUNTRY ALE
GOLDEN ALE 5% ABV
The partners' first creation strikes a balance between floral hops and bready, toasted malts.

BLUEBERRY
FRUIT BEER 4.4% ABV
This wheat-based beer plays to mixed reviews, with natural blueberry the dominant note, particularly on the nose.

HOPS INFUSION
INDIA PALE ALE 6.2% ABV
Hops focused, but with a malt backbone to support a blast of citrus, pine, fresh pepper, and more.

IMPERIAL PUMPKIN ALE
SPICED BEER 8% ABV
Seasonal. An alcohol-infused slice of pumpkin pie—loaded with plenty of nutmeg and cinnamon.

HEFEWEIZEN
US HEFEWEIZEN 4.9% ABV
Citrus, particularly lemon zest, is matched against clean, bready-yet-tart wheat. Finale of grapefruit.

SNOW PLOW
MILK STOUT 5.5% ABV
Coffee on the nose becomes creamier on the palate, roasted notes blending with rich chocolate.

WIXA WEISS
HEFEWEIZEN 5.4% ABV
Begins with aromas of bananas, orchard fruits, and bubblegum. Tart wheat on the tongue, while clove lingers in the back of the throat.

PATTY'S CHILE BEER
SPICED BEER 4.5% ABV
A light, German-style beer with a punch delivered by heaps of Anaheim chilies added to every barrel.

MORE BEERS OF
THE US

The US is the home of craft brewing, with more small-batch producers than anywhere else in the world. These are often very regional operations, with their beers traveling no farther than the local and neighboring towns.

GRAY'S

2424 West Court Street, Janesville, Wisconsin 53545, USA
www.graybrewing.com

The Gray family has been brewing in Janesville since 1856, but not always alcoholic beer. The brewery focused on making soda between 1912 (when it quit beer-production just ahead of Prohibition) and 1994, when Gray's was forced to rebuild its plant after an arson attack and decided to return to its beermaking heritage.

OATMEAL STOUT
OATMEAL STOUT 5.6% ABV
Roasted coffee beans and chocolate, with caramel and sweet creaminess. Lightly bitter, dry at the finish.

IRISH RED
AMBER ALE 6.2% ABV
A spring seasonal, with a reddish-amber pour that signals rich, slightly sweet malt flavors, followed by muted earthy hops.

NIMBUS

3850 East 44th Street, Tucson, Arizona 85713, USA
www.nimbusbeer.com

Nimbus has made ales since 1997, first using equipment scavenged from Vermont and later modernizing and expanding. The name comes from founder-brewer Nimbus Couzin.

BREWING SECRET The water profile here is much like that of Burton-on-Trent in England—hard and rich in sulfur.

PALO VERDA PALE ALE
PALE ALE 5.5% ABV
Abundant Northwest hop aroma, and flavors of citrus and pine. Best quaffed close to the brewery.

OLD MONKEYSHINE
OLD ALE 8% ABV
Rich malts and British hops give this beer an old-world feel. Full-bodied, with caramel, chocolate and even Christmas-cake flavors.

MCNEILL'S

90 Elliot Street, Brattleboro, Vermont 05301, USA
www.myspace.com/mcneillsbrewery

Founder Ray McNeill, a classically trained cellist, has prided himself on careful research into traditional styles since opening his brewpub in 1991. The names of his beers, however, are sometimes less than traditional, or even appetizing.

BREWING SECRET McNeill is developing plans for a production brewery.

DEAD HORSE INDIA PALE ALE
INDIA PALE ALE 5.7% ABV
Floral and earthy, East Kent Goldings hops on a sturdy base of rich English malts. Woody, dry finish.

DUCK BREATH BITTER
PREMIUM BITTER 5.5% ABV
Rich with British malts, pleasantly mineral in character, and a sneaky bitterness. Best on cask at the pub.

STOUDTS

2800 North Reading Road, Route 272 Adamstown, PA 19501
www.stoudtsbeer.com

Founders Carol (the brewer) and Ed Stoudt founded their brewery and adjoining steakhouse with a focus on German-inspired beers, and for more than 20 years, they have balanced European tradition and American innovation. The Stoudt's adjoining antiques mall is one of many in the "Antiques Capital of America."

PILS
PILSNER 4.8% ABV
A crisp expression of Saaz hops, flowery up front, spicy in the middle, long and dry at the finish.

FAT DOG STOUT
IMPERIAL STOUT 9% ABV
An oatmeal stout, but brewed to Imperial strength. Thick and rich with molasses, prunes, and bittersweet coffee flavors.

SWEETWATER

195 Ottley Drive
Atlanta, GA 30324
www.sweetwaterbrew.com

This is the dominant craft brewery in the southeast. Its flagship Extra Pale Ale continues to drive strong growth, but, since Georgia has permitted the sale of stronger beer, SweetWater has done well with hefty brews like its 6.4% IPA and Festive Ale.

BREWING SECRET Festive Ale is brewed on only one day of each year.

420 EXTRA PALE ALE
PALE ALE 5.2% ABV
A light-on-the tongue blend of citrussy hops and honeyish malt.

FESTIVE ALE
SPICED BEER 8.6% ABV
A holiday offering, as malt-rich as its mahogany color suggests. Spiced with both cinnamon and mace, but not overdone.

TOMMYKNOCKER

1401 Miner Street
Idaho Springs, CO 80452
www.tommyknocker.com

Tommyknocker Brewing's name stems from the town's mining background—after gold was discovered in 1859, the Argo mine supplied the Denver mint with half its gold needs. The Cornish miners who worked here were firm believers in pixies called Tommyknockers who lived in the mines and could bring good luck and protection.

BUTT HEAD BOCK
DOPPELBOCK 8.2% ABV
Caramel and toasted malts on the nose. Richer on the palate, warming, with surprising berry fruitiness.

PICK AXE PALE ALE
PALE ALE 6.2% ABV
Hop-spicy nose with noticeable malt fruitiness, biscuit on the palate as well as earthy hops.

TRÖEGS

800 Paxton Street
Harrisburg, PA 17104
www.troegs.com

In 2007, just one year after Tröegs Brewing tripled the size of its brewing plant, brother-owners John and Chris Trogner added equipment to double their production capacity. Although its core beers sustain growth, specials such as Mad Elf, brewed with cherries, and a "Scratch" series of one-offs, have created demand well beyond Pennsylvania.

TROGENATOR
DOPPELBOCK 8.2% ABV
Malt driven, with sweet caramel and toffee aromas, and toasted bread crust in a medium body.

HOPBACK AMBER
AMBER ALE 5.6% ABV
Caramel-sweet fruit character with bright, floral-spicy hops. The amped-up version is called Nugget Nectar.

YUENGLING

5th and Mahantongo Streets
Pottsville, PA 17901
www.yuengling.com

The oldest brewing company in the US, operating since 1829, Yuengling brews with adjuncts, but has set itself apart from more mainstream producers. The brewery has thrived right along with craft, all-malt beers. It has built a second brewery (the original is in Pottsville) and bought a large, idle Florida brewery to help keep up with demand.

TRADITIONAL LAGER
US LAGER 4.9% ABV
Amber color and light body. Slightly sweet, floral aromas, and sweet again on the palate. Crisp at the end, with subtle bitterness.

ORIGINAL BLACK & TAN
BLENDED BEER 5.2% ABV
A blend of Yuengling Premium and Porter. Pours quite dark, with chocolate and caramel flavors.

BREWERY

BEER

BREWERY

BEER

Pyramid Breweries,
based in Seattle, is a
characterful brewery
with a bar restaurant.

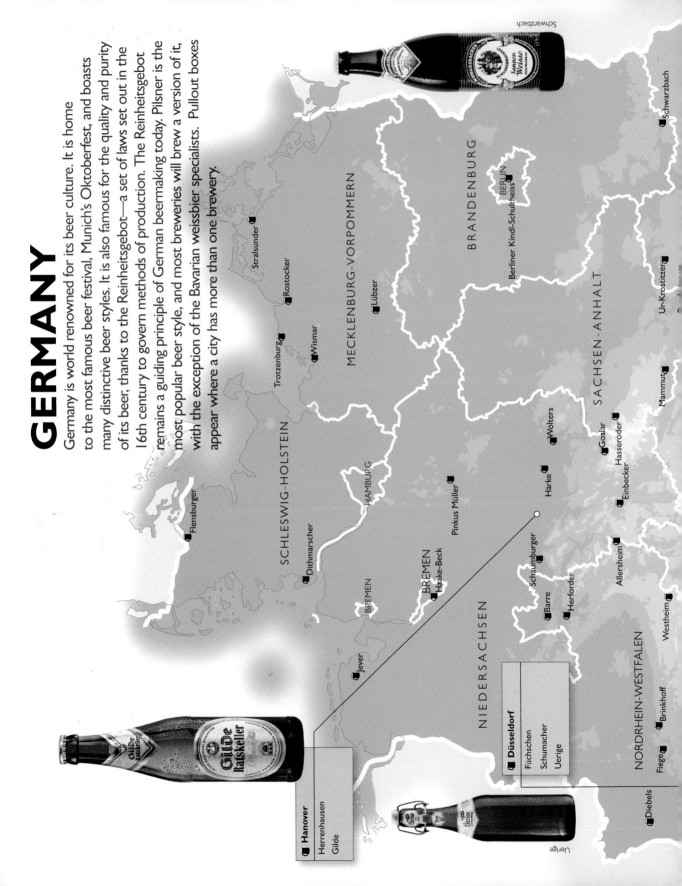

GERMANY

Germany is world renowned for its beer culture. It is home to the most famous beer festival, Munich's Oktoberfest, and boasts many distinctive beer styles. It is also famous for the quality and purity of its beer, thanks to the Reinheitsgebot—a set of laws set out in the 16th century to govern methods of production. The Reinheitsgebot remains a guiding principle of German beermaking today. Pilsner is the most popular beer style, and most breweries will brew a version of it, with the exception of the Bavarian weissbier specialists. Pullout boxes appear where a city has more than one brewery.

Schwarzbach

Schwarzbach

Stralsunder

Rostocker

Wismar

Trotzenburg

Lübzer

BERLIN

Berliner Kindl-Schultheiss

BRANDENBURG

MECKLENBURG-VORPOMMERN

Ur-Krostitzer

SACHSEN-ANHALT

Mammut

Goslar

Hasseröder

Einbecker

Wolters

Härke

SCHLESWIG-HOLSTEIN

Flensburger

Dithmarscher

HAMBURG

Pinkus Müller

BREMEN

BREMEN

Haake-Beck

Schaumburger

Barre

Herforder

Allersheim

NIEDERSACHSEN

Jever

Westheim

NORDRHEIN-WESTFALEN

Fiege

Brinkhoff

Diebels

Düsseldorf		
Füchschen		
Schumacher		
Uerige		

Uerige

Hanover		
Herrenhausen		
Gilde		

Chemnitz
Braustolz
Reichenbrand

Freiberger/
Ganter

Bamberg
Fässla
Schlenkerla

Regensburg
Bischofshof
Kneitinger
Thurn & Taxis
Weltenburg

Jandelsbrunner
Hutthurmer

Altenburg

Rosenbrauerei Pössneck
Sternquell
Gottmannsgrüner
Lang-Bräu

Bucher Bräu
Erl
Röhrl
Arco
Aldersbach
Traunstein

Braugold

Saalfeld
Nailaer Wohng
Kulmbacher
Maisel
Friedenfels

Meininger

Leikeim
Greif
Kitzmann
Tucher

Bruckmüller/
Schloderer

Altöttinger
Jettenbach
Unertl
Maxlrain
Auer

Weihenstephan
Grünbach
Erdinger
Schweiger
Ayinger
Reutberg

Eichhorn
Göller
Kesselring
Kauzen
Dobler
Landwehr-Bräu

B A Y E R N

Schneider
Kuchlbauer
Herrngiersdorf
Felsenbräu Thalmannsfeld

Au In Der Hallertau

Neumarkter Lammsbräu
Fürstlichen Ellingen

Werner
Lohrer
Schlappeseppel

Streck

Weideneder

Scheyern

Fürst Wallerstein
Ankerbräu Nördlingen
Dinkelacker-Schwabenbräu

Riegele

König Ludwig

München
Airbräu
Augustiner
Hacker-Pschorr
Hofbräu München
Löwenbräu

Crailsheimer Engelbräu

Glaab
Michelsbräu
Faust
Distelhäuser

Binding

Lindenbräu

Andechs
Aktien
Dachsbräu Weilheim

Gold Ochsen

Berg

Nesselwang
Zötler

Herborner
Licher

H E S S E N

Schmucker

Bischoff
Weldebräu
Heidelberg Kulturbrauerei

Darmstädter'n

B A D E N - W Ü R T T E M B E R G

Schussenrieder
Leibinger
Krone Tettnang

Weilheim
Schilling

Krombacher

Königsbacher
Maximilians

Kirner

Mettlacher Abteibräu

Bitburger

R H E I N L A N D -
P F A L Z

SAARLAND

Fürstenberg
Alpirsbach

T H Ü R I N G E N

Alpirsbach

BREWERY

AIRBRÄU

Münchner Airportcenter, Terminalstr. Mitte 18, 85356 München, Germany
www.allresto.de

This brewery has a unique location: set between the two terminals of Munich airport. It opened in 2004 at the same time as the airport's new Terminal 2, and it includes a much-frequented restaurant and beer garden. Two brewing kettles are situated right in the middle of the restaurant.

AKTIEN

Hohe Buchleute 3, 87600 Kaufbeuren, Germany
www.aktienbrauerei.de

The origins of brewing at the Aktien brewery in Kaufbeuren can be traced back to the early 14th century. In more recent times, Aktien has taken over the Löwen and Rosen breweries.

BREWING SECRET Aktien still brews its beer strictly according to the Bavarian Purity Law set in 1516.

ALDERSBACH

Freiherr-von-Aretin-Platz 1, 94501 Aldersbach, Germany
www.aldersbach.de

The modern operation seen today grew out of a small brewery attached to a monastery dating from the 13th century. The range of beers has grown over the centuries; white beer started to be brewed in 1928, and today the company produces 13 different styles of beer.

ALLERSHEIM

Allersheim 6, 37603 Holzminden, Germany
www.brauerei-allersheim.de

Founded in 1854, this brewery was, for Otto Baumgarten, merely a sideline to farming. He harvested the grain in his own fields, but had to buy in the hops. Production grew over the years, though, and today the brewery has 40 employees.

BREWING SECRET The beers are brewed to suit discerning local palates.

BEER

FLIEGERQUELL
LAGER 5.2% ABV
Deep golden, finely structured, and classically dry. It is brewed for international palates.

KUMULUS
WHITE BEER 5.4% ABV
Typical yellow color; a sparkling, very fresh white beer, refreshing and full-bodied.

NATURTRÜBES KELLERBIER
KELLERBIER 5.1% ABV
Unfiltered and naturally cloudy out of the cellar. The slightly sweet taste is typical of one of the oldest styles of beer in Bavaria.

FENDT DIESELROSSÖL
MÄRZEN 5.9% ABV
A malty, aromatic structure and a full-bodied, slightly bitter taste. Goes well with venison dishes.

FREIHERRN PILS
PILSNER 4.5% ABV
Mild bitterness in the hopping. The lightly malted grain results in a dry, fine taste.

KLOSTER DUNKEL
DUNKEL 5% ABV
Full-bodied and malty, with a typical dark mahogany color; the roasted flavor is due to the dark malts.

LANDBIER
PILSNER 5% ABV
A pilsner with a mash bill from light and dark malt. Soft in taste, with a typical malty aroma.

BLUE MOON
BEER AND COLA 1.9% ABV
A pleasant mix of dry hops and cola. It's not too sweet, because the mix is produced without sugar.

THE BEST-KNOWN BEERS IN GERMANY

There are about 1,300 breweries in Germany today, mostly in the south. Bavaria alone has 700 breweries.

Internationally, the most famous German beer is Beck's, which is owned by the global drinks giant Anheuser-Busch InBev. Another world-famous German brand is Holsten, which is a subsidiary of the Danish Carlsberg Group. Löwenbräu was the first German export beer to become famous after World War II; it is now part of Anheuser-Busch InBev. However, these international brands are not on the huge scale of Anheuser-Busch InBev's Budweiser in the US, nor are they the top-selling beers in Germany itself. In fact, they are relatively small in comparison with the biggest names on the German domestic market, such as Krombacher, Veltin's, Warsteiner, and Bitburger. Most of the large German breweries produce pilsner as their main product. In terms of specialty beers, the German No.1 is Erdinger Weissbier (wheat beer), and Clausthaler is widely popular for low-alcohol beers. However, the majority of successful German breweries proudly keep themselves relatively very small, limiting their distribution to a regional market; indeed, many are home breweries that have become famous in association with a single village or even a single restaurant.

BECKS (PILSNER 4.8% ABV) *left*
BITBURGER (PILSNER 4.8% ABV)
CLAUSTHALER (LOW ALCOHOL 0.45% ABV)
ERDINGER (WHEAT 5.3% ABV) *center*
HOLSTEN (PILSNER 4.8% ABV) *right*
KROMBACHER (PILSNER 4.8% ABV)
VELTINS (PILSNER 4.8% ABV)

ALPIRSBACH

Alpirsbacher Klosterbräu, Marktplatz 1, 72275 Alpirsbach, Germany
www.alpirsbacher.de

A railroad was constructed through the Black Forest at the end of the 19th century, which brought many visitors to the village of Alpirsbach. Johann Gottfried Glauner helped to cater for them by reopening the old village brewery. Sales were good, and today the beer from Alpirsbach is produced by the fourth generation of the family.

KLEINER MÖNCH
LAGER 5.2% ABV
The golden color promises a fresh, young beer. It is full-bodied with a flavor of caramel from the malt.

SCHWARZES PILS
PILSNER 4.9% ABV
Deep red-black color and a strong taste, with a roasted malt aroma that is unmistakable.

ALTENBURG

Brauereistr. 20, 04600 Altenburg, Germany
www.brauerei-altenburg.de

Founded in 1871, this brewery produced its first beer in 1873 and soon became successful. The company was taken over by the Communists after World War II. Since the 1990 Reunification of Germany, however, the Altenburg story has started anew, and it is again the biggest brewery in the region.

ALTENBURGER SCHWARZE
SCHWARZBIER 4.9% ABV
This mahogany-colored beer has an aromatic, malty taste with an intense note of hops.

FESTBIER
BOCK 6% ABV
Amber-colored beer, full-bodied, with a taste of mild hops. It is brewed specially for local festivals.

ALTÖTTINGER

Altöttinger Hell-Brau, Herrenmühlstr. 15, 84503 Altötting, Germany
www.altoettinger-hellbraeu.de

The Bavarian town of Altötting is home to the Altötting Madonna, a world-famous pilgrimage site. In 1890 Georg Hell expanded production at a local brewery to help cater to thirsty pilgrims. Today the brewery produces eight different beers.

BREWING SECRET The finest hops and best German malts are used.

BAYERISCHE DUNKEL
DUNKEL 5.2% ABV
Roasty and malty taste, but fresh, and with a long finish. A dark specialty with its own character.

FEIN-HERB
LAGER 5% ABV
The best malts, combined with a careful selection of hops, produce an exceptionally dry, fine taste.

BREWERY

ANDECHS

Klosterbaruerei Andechs, Bergstr. 2,
82346 Andechs, Germany
www.andechs.de

The Benedictine monks of Andechs
began to produce beer in 1455. The
monastery updated its brewery in
1972, investing in modern equipment.
Still closely associated with the holy
mountain pilgrimage site southwest of
Munich, Andechs today is a brand
name that's internationally known.

ANKERBRÄU NORDLINGEN

Ankergasse 4, 86720 Nördlingen,
Germany
www.ankerbrauerei.de

The brewery's history can be traced
from 1608, when several beers were
brewed here for a festival. It was
acquired by the Grandel family at the
end of the 19th century.

BREWING SECRET The beers are made
with local malts, mineral water from
the Ries, and hops from Spalt.

ARCO

Schlossallee 1, 94554 Moos, Germany
www.arcobraeu.de

Arco has been owned by the Counts
of Arco-Zinneberg for 450 years. The
castle and brewery belonging to the
family are situated in Moos, a small
town in the heart of Niederbayern
in Bavaria, where the rivers Isar and
Donau converge. The current Count
Arco personally launched the beers in
the US in 2004.

AU IN DER HALLERTAU

Schlossbrauerei Au in der Hallertau,
Schlossbräugasse 2, 84072 Au, Germany
www.auer-bier.de

Au is at the heart of the largest
hop-growing area in the world.
It was linked with the master brewer
Schweiger in 1590 and, since 1846,
has been owned by six generations
of the Earls Beck of Peccoz.
A modern approach is an essential
feature of the management at Au in
der Hallertau.

BEER

BERGBOCK HELL

BOCK 7% ABV
A strong beer, but it tastes mild and
aromatic. Its typical light sweetness
gives it a full body.

DOPPELBOCK DUNKEL

BOCK 7% ABV
This world-famous beer has a really
strong taste. The dark malts give it
an unmistakable character, with a
light aroma of hops in the finish.

LAGER HELL

LAGER 5% ABV
A full-flavored clear, yellow beer;
pleasant and full-bodied, with a fine
aroma at the beginning.

NÖRDLINGER PREMIUM PILS

PILSNER 4.7% ABV
A very flowery hop aroma turns
slightly bitter and a bit sparkling on
the tongue.

SCHLOSS HELL

LAGER 4.9% ABV
With its soft but full-bodied taste
and golden color, Arco's Schloss
Hell typifies Bavarian lager.

URFASS

LAGER 5.2% ABV
Slightly more bitter than the Schloss
Hell, and especially spicy, this is a
real premium lager of Bavaria.

HOPFENGOLD

EXPORT 5% ABV
Golden color, full-bodied taste with
fine bitters of hops and clear malt.
Nice finish, not too sweet.

HOLLEDAUER LEICHTES

WHEAT BEER 3.3% ABV
A cloudy yellow, light wheat beer,
fresh and lightly sparkling; not too
heavy a taste, and with a slightly
bitter finish.

AUER

Münchner Str. 80, 83022 Rosenheim, Germany
www.auerbraeu.de

Between 1887 and 1920, Johann Auer acquired several plots of land and some breweries around the town of Rosenheim, southeast of Munich. Since then, the company has expanded considerably.

BREWING SECRET When it was founded, this was one of the most modern breweries in Bavaria.

AUGUSTINER

Landsberger Str. 31-35, 80339 München, Germany
www.augustiner-braeu.de

Founded in 1328, this is the oldest brewery in Munich and one of only two in the city (along with Hofbräu München) that do not belong to a giant of the global brewing industry. The site as it is today was constructed in 1885. Augustiner beer has become famous around the world even though the brewery does not advertise itself.

AYINGER

Zornedinger Str. 1, 85653 Aying, Germany
www.ayinger.de

Johann Liebhard founded this brewery in Aying in 1876, at a time when there were about 6,000 breweries in Bavaria. That number has dropped to about 700 today, but Ayinger has survived and was renovated by the Inselkammer family in 1999. It has since become more widely known.

BARRE

Berliner Str. 122-124, 32312 Lübbecke, Germany
www.barre.de

Family-owned since 1842, the Barre Privatbrauerei lies in the Westphalian region between the Wester and Rhine rivers. Barre's special beers are well known and loved in the region.

BREWING SECRET The company uses its own spring to supply fresh water for the brewery.

BAJUWARE DUNKEL
DUNKEL 5.5% ABV
Brewed in old-fashioned Bavarian style, this beer has a malty aroma and a full-bodied character.

WEIZENBOCK
WHEAT BOCK 7% ABV
A strong, spicy specialty. A good accompaniment to hearty cheeses or sweet desserts.

EDELSTOFF
EXPORT 5.6% ABV
The unusual dark golden color displays its special character. A sweet and obvious hop taste guides you to a very malty finish.

WEISSBIER
WHEAT BEER 5.4% ABV
Golden and cloudy, this is a full-bodied wheat beer with a citrus taste and light bitters in the finish.

JAHRHUNDERTBIER
EXPORT 5.5% ABV
A honeylike aroma with light flowery hops leads on to a harmonious finish.

CELEBRATOR
DOPPELBOCK 6.7% ABV
The taste of malt dominates this nearly black, strong beer. It is not as sweet as other doppelbocks of the same quality.

BARRE PILSENER
PILSNER 4.8% ABV
The clear golden-yellow color is typical of a pilsner, as is the fine taste of hops and the malty finish. Medium-bodied.

BARRE DUNKEL
DUNKEL 4.8% ABV
Fine aromas of malt, strongly flavored, and with a finish of light bitters.

Revelers clink glasses during Oktoberfest—the world-famous annual 16-day Festival of Beer that has been staged in Munich since 1810.

BREWERY

BERG

Berg Brauerei Ulrich Zimmermann, Brauhausstr. 2, 89548 Ehingen-Berg, Germany
www.bergbier.de

Berg, founded in 1757, is family-owned and one of the smallest breweries in Germany.

BREWING SECRET Berg makes use of corn in brewing, which is supplied by an organic farm nearby.

BERGQUELL

Weststr. 7, Löbau, Germany
www.bergquell-loebau.de

With its long brewing tradition, the Bergquell Brauerei Löbau has played an important role in the Lausitz region since 1846. It is also one of the most advanced breweries in the whole of Germany and is well known for its wide range of special beers.

BREWING SECRET The special beers have an international following.

BERLINER KINDL-SCHULTHEISS

Indira-Ghandi-Str. 66-69, 13053 Berlin, Germany
www.berliner-kindl.de

The union of the Berliner Kindl and Berliner Schultheiss breweries in 2006 was symbolic for Germany, whose breweries had declined through post-War division. The merger has generated a great many new brands, produced in one of the most modern brewing facilities in Germany.

BINDING

Darmstädter Landstrasse 185, 60598 Frankfurt, Germany
www.clausthaler.de

Conrad Binding started in the year 1870 with a small brewery in the ancient city of Frankfurt am Main. The other big brewery of the city, Henninger, was acquired by Binding in 2001. Since 2002 the company has been a member of the Radeberger group. The Clausthaler brands are a low-alcohol specialty of Binding.

BEER

BERG ORIGINAL
LAGER 4.8% ABV
Its smooth, dry taste makes this beer the most popular brand offered by the brewery.

BERG MÄRZEN
MÄRZEN 6.1% ABV
A typical strong beer. The taste is very hearty, not least because of its high dose of hops.

KIRSCH PORTER
PORTER 4.2% ABV
A black beer with a cherry flavor and typical porter qualities. Malty and full-bodied.

LAUSITZER PORTER
PORTER 4.4% ABV
Typical porter with a dry, roasted malt taste. It is full-bodied and not too heavy; dark colored and a little bit sweet.

MÄRKISCHER LANDMANN
SCHWARZBIER 4.9% ABV
Black and highly malty, but without any bitterness. A genuine original of the Märkish region.

BOCKBIER
BOCK 7% ABV
Golden, strong, and not too sweet; pleasant, with a smooth finish—a typical bock.

CLAUSTHALER CLASSIC
LOW ALCOHOL 0.45% ABV
Full-bodied, with a fresh and pleasant taste, and light aromas of fine hops; golden colored.

CLAUSTHALER EXTRA HERB
LOW ALCOHOL 0.45% ABV
A very strong and spicy beer with a pleasant bitterness of hops and a malty finish. A fresh beer with a golden color.

BISCHOFF

Wellerhof, 50321 Brühl, Germany
www.bischoff-koelsch.de

This privately owned brewery was established in farm buildings at the beginning of the 1960s, in an area of Brühl, near Cologne, that has been inhabited since Roman times.

BREWING SECRET The brewery's kölsch is a specialty of the Cologne region and is traditionally served in a tall, narrow glass.

BISCHOFSHOF

Heitzerstr. 2, 93049 Regensburg, Germany
www.bischofshof.de

The Bischofshof brewery started life attached to Regensburg Cathedral. Records show that it was brewing in 1230 for the Bishop. At the beginning of the 20th century, it moved to a new location in order to expand. Nowadays, Bischofshof beer is produced in one of the most modern facilities in the brewing industry.

BITBURGER

Römermauer. 3, 54634 Bitburg/ Eifel, Germany
www.bitburger.de

Founded in 1817, Bitburger is a pilsner specialist. It is well known through international sponsorship of sporting events, and is widely regarded as the best brewery for pilsner on draft.

BREWING SECRET The company always uses two-row summer barley, and its testing brewery is unique in Germany.

BRAUGOLD

Schillerstr. 7, 99096 Erfurt, Germany
www.braugold.de

The brewery was founded in 1822, and acquired other breweries over time—up until 1948, the point at which it was nationalized by the GDR. After Reunification in 1990, Braugold was purchased by the Licher Privatbrauerei.

BREWING SECRET The brewers follow recipes from the famous Thüringer brewery.

BISCHOFF KÖLSCH

KÖLSCH 4.9% ABV
Clear golden color; fresh and sweet, with light notes of hops.

RADLER

BEER BLEND 2.5% ABV
Clear yellow in color, with lemonade-citrus aromas. It is sparkling and very refreshing.

WEISSBIER HELL

WHEAT BEER 5.1% ABV
An old Bavarian specialty: fresh, clear, sparkling, and slightly sweet—in a pleasant way.

BISCHOFSHOF PILS

PILSNER 5.1% ABV
Creamy foam and a light, sparkling start. Good bitter taste; light aromas of fine hops.

PREMIUM PILS

PILSNER 4.8% ABV
A clear, typical pilsner with a light, bitter taste; smooth, but very dry. On draft it is fresh and elegant.

BITBURGER LIGHT

PILSNER 2.8% ABV
The light sister of the premium. Though only 2.8% ABV, it is full-bodied, with a fresh cask taste.

BRAUGOLD SPEZIAL

PILSNER 4.9% ABV
Has the typical golden color and dryness of a pilsner; highly aromatic with a balanced bitterness of hops on the palate.

BRAUGOLD BOCK

BOCK 6.5% ABV
Its balanced, bitter aroma and strong flavor are typical of a bock.

BREWERY

BRAUSTOLZ

Am Feldschlösschen 18, 09116
Chemnitz, Germany
www.braustolz.de

A farmer founded this brewery in
1868. The company was modernized
after World War I, nationalized in
1945, and renovated in 1991. Today it
employs more than 50 people and
produces many different styles of beer.

BREWING SECRET A 1991 investment of
DM40 million for modern equipment
ensured the brewery's future.

BRINKHOFF

Lütgendortmunder Hellweg 242, 44388
Dortmund, Germany
www.brinkhoffs.de

From its humble origins in 1844 as a
small home brewery, Brinkhoff has
had more than 160 years of success,
to become a brand known far beyond
its hometown of Dortmund, one of
the beer capitals of the world.
Brinkhoff's No. 1 is a notable name
for every lover of the special pilsners
from this region.

BUCHER BRÄU

Elsenthaler Str. 5-7, 9441 Grafenau,
Germany
www.bucher-braeu.de

A medium-sized brewery that moved
to the heart of the Bavarian Forest in
1982 after outgrowing its premises in
the center of Grafenau. It has been
owned by the Bucher family since
1863 (now in its fifth generation).

BREWING SECRET The natural cloudiness
of the Hefeweizen comes from the
yeast added at the time of bottling.

CRAILSHEIMER ENGELBRÄU

Haller Str. 29, 74564 Crailsheim, Germany
www.engelbier.de

When this brewery was founded by
Georg Fach in 1738, Crailsheim had
4,000 inhabitants and 13 breweries.
Fach was not to know that his
company would become one of the
most successful in the country.

BREWING SECRET A survey of what
women like in a beer led to the
creation of the First Lady brand.

BEER

BRAUSTOLZ LANDBIER

EXPORT 5.2% ABV
Golden, smooth, malty, and with a
fine aroma of hops—an earthy beer.

BRAUSTOLZ PILS

PILSNER 4.9% ABV
A classic pilsner with a very dry and
fresh taste, accompanied by obvious
aromas of bitter hops.

BRINKHOFF'S NO. 1

PILSNER 5% ABV
Typical bitter aromas of a pilsner.
Smooth, slightly sparkling, with a
golden-yellow color.

BRINKHOFF'S RADLER

BEER BLEND 2.5% ABV
Honey-colored, sparkling, and
pleasant with citrus aromas; very
refreshing and not too sweet.

GRAFENAUER HEFEWEIZEN

WHEAT BEER 5.2% ABV
Fresh and sparkling. The light taste
of yeast is fine and aromatic. There
is a little sweetness.

HELLES

LAGER 4.9% ABV
Clear yellow beer, slightly bitter,
with a reasonable sweetness, and
a taste of the finest hops. A rather
strong but rounded finish.

FIRST LADY

DUNKLER BOCK 5.9% ABV
Mild, lightly bitter, and with
a harmonious malty aroma.

KELLERBIER DUNKEL

DUNKEL 5.3% ABV
Beautiful mahogany color; aromas
of malt and yeast; full-bodied, with
a taste that is both sweet and
pleasantly bitter.

DACHSBRÄU WEILHEIM

Murnauer Str. 5, 82362 Weilheim, Germany
www.dachsbier.de

It was a master brewer from Munich who founded the Dachsbräu on a farm in Weilheim in 1879. Georg Dachs began to produce wheat beer, and the family-owned brewery has since grown ever bigger.

BREWING SECRET The most significant characteristic of the beer is that it is traditionally hand-crafted.

DARMSTÄDTER

Goebelstr. 7, 64293 Darmstadt, Germany
www.darmstaedter.de

The brewery stands next to the train station in Darmstadt—hence the train logo, used since 1847, and the animated steam engine on its website.

BREWING SECRET A revolution in the company's history was the complete change-over of all bottles to clip-tops in the year 2000.

DIEBELS

Brauerei-Diebels-Str. 1, 47661 Issum, Germany
www.diebels.de

Diebels was privately owned from 1878 until 2001, when the brewery was taken over by global drinks giant InBev. The Düsseldorfer Alt is the brewery's most famous brand and is sold all over Germany. Other, newer brands include a pilsner and a cola-blended beer called Dimix.

DINKELACKER-SCHWABENBRÄU

Tübinger Str. 46, 70178 Stuttgart, Germany
www.ds-kg.de

Carl Dinkelacker was the first to brew pilsner in Stuttgart at the end of the 19th century, and his contemporary Robert Leicht was the first to deliver beer by car. Today, their breweries are in partnership and together form the biggest player in Baden-Württemberg.

DUNKLER DOPPELBOCK
DOPPELBOCK 7.5% ABV
Strong and sweet, this typical doppelbock has malt aromas from the start, and is very full-bodied.

URHELL
LAGER 5.5% ABV
A kellerbier—unfiltered, cloudy, and yellow—it tastes very mild at the beginning, has light aromas of fine hops, and is fresh and pleasant.

PILSNER
PILSNER 4.8% ABV
A clear and elegant beer. A large amount of fine hops make this a typical pilsner: fresh and dry with a good bitter aroma.

1847 ZWICKELBIER
LAGER 4.8% ABV
Unfiltered and cloudy with subtle aromas of fine malt and a smooth, yeasty taste.

DIEBELS ALT
ALTBIER 4.9% ABV
Roasted malt aromas harmonize with a sweet caramel taste; the finish is slightly bitter from hops.

DIEBELS PILS
PILSNER 4.9% ABV
The full-body, light bitterness, and malt aromas are typical of a pilsner, as is the dark golden color.

DINKELACKER PRIVAT
LAGER 5.1% ABV
A fine, smooth, and clear golden lager with a mild aroma of hops and a light note of malt.

DINKELACKER CD-PILS
PILSNER 4.9% ABV
Noble dry pilsner with strong aromas of hops and light malts; very harmonious and pleasant.

BREWERY

DISTELHÄUSER

Grünsfelder Str. 3, 97941 Tauberbischofsheim, Germany
www.distelhaeuser.de

The Bauer family has owned this brewery since 1876. It is situated on the famous "Romantic Street" in Tauberbischofsheim, which is closely associated with the German Romantic period. The long-standing success of the brewery is due to its attention to quality over the course of its history.

DITHMARSCHER

Oesterstr. 18, 25709 Marne Holstein, Germany
www.dithmarscher.de

This brewery, on the east coast of Schleswig-Holstein, has been operating for more than 230 years. It started as a small home brewery; today it is bigger, but the beers are still handmade.

BREWING SECRET The sparkle comes from using the charmant method of pressurized fermentation, and the addition of dry, fresh carbonic acid.

DÖBLER

Kornmarkt 6, 91438 Bad Windsheim, Germany
www.brauhaus-doebler.de

Döbler celebrated its 140th anniversary in 2007. Production was traditional until 1950, after which the brewery switched to creating young-styled beers using technologically advanced equipment.

BREWING SECRET The barley has come from sustainable sources since 1986.

EICHHORN

Dörfleinstr. 43, 96103 Hallstadt, Germany
www.brauerei-eichhorn.de

Eichhorn was originally called the Schwarzer Adler (Black Eagle) brewery. The family do nothing other than hand craft their beers, but always using the latest equipment.

BREWING SECRET The beers are given extra time to mature, and their adherence to the Bavarian Purity Law won't be changing in the near future.

BEER

DISTELHÄUSER LANDBIER
EXPORT 5.1% ABV
Malty aroma and a slightly caramel taste; it has a mild sweetness and is rounded at the finish. Sometimes described as a "ladies' beer."

DISTELHÄUSER PILS
PILSNER 4.9% ABV
Topped by a snow-white foam, this beer has a harmonious bitterness and a great aroma of hops.

DITHMARSCHER DUNKEL
DUNKEL 4.9% ABV
This beer has a full-bodied charmant character and a spicy taste with notes of roastiness. A typical color: dark mahogany.

DITHMARSCHER PILS
PILSNER 4.8% ABV
A mild and spicy beer, golden-yellow in color, slightly sparkling.

LAND MÄRZEN
MÄRZEN 5.4% ABV
A very light märzen; dark yellow, with a pleasant taste, not too sweet, but full-bodied with a nice yeast finish.

REICHSSTADTBIER
KELLERBIER 5% ABV
Full-bodied, unfiltered, and cloudy, with a taste of yeast. It is available on draft.

KELLERBIER NATURTRÜB
LAGER 5% ABV
Yellow and naturally cloudy, the kellerbier does not have much carbon acidity, so it has a slight, but well-balanced, hop bitterness.

EICHHORN PILS
PILSNER 5% ABV
Clear golden, dry pilsner, with a fine bitterness of hops accompanying light aromas of malt.

EINBECKER

Papenstr. 4, 37574 Einbeck, Germany
www.einbecker.com

The story goes that, in 1521, Martin
Luther said that Einbecker's beer was
his favorite. In 1612, Bavarian dukes
engaged a master brewer from
Einbeck, whose beer eventually
became known as bock, in a
corruption of the name Einbeck.

ERDINGER

Lange Zeile 1+3, 85435 Erding, Germany
www.erdinger.de

This is the biggest and most famous
specialist wheat beer brewery in the
world. The first mention of a brewery
at Erding was in 1886, but it was not
until 1949 that the name Erdinger
Weissbräu was used.

BREWING SECRET Fresh spring water and
hops from the Hallertau region are
used in brewing.

ERL

Straubinger Str. 10, 94333 Geiselhöring,
Germany
www.erl-braeu.de

The owners, Ludwig IV and his
brother Günter, are the 11th
generation of the Erl family at the
helm of this brewery. Everything
about the family and their beers is
steeped in tradition.

BREWING SECRET The family farm
supplies the finest raw materials for
the beers made here.

FÄSSLA

Obere Königstr. 19-21, 96052 Bamberg,
Germany
www.faessla.de

In 1649, just a year after the end of
the Thirty Years' War, master brewer
Hans Lauer founded this brewery in
Bamberg. In modern times, 1986 was
a turning point, when the Kalb family
took over control. Fässla's specialty
beers are well known in the region.

BREWING SECRET Bambergator is the
strongest beer brewed in Bamberg.

UR-BOCK HELL
BOCK 6.5% ABV
The pale malt and fine hops give
this classic bock a hearty taste.

EINBECKER SPEZIAL
EXPORT 5.2% ABV
Has the typical golden-yellow color
of an export beer. Has a fine,
slightly sweet flavor.

ERDINGER PIKANTUS
DARK WEIZENBOCK 7.3% ABV
Normally a wheat bock is sweet,
but not so Erdinger's. Watch out
for the ABV on this one.

ERDINGER SCHNEEWEISSE
WINTER BEER 5.6% ABV
Darker and heavier bodied than the
normal weizen. It is available
between October and February.

ERL-BOCK
BOCK 7.2% ABV
A clear, elegant bock with a fine
bitter taste and harmonious finish.

ERL DUNKEL
DUNKEL 5.3% ABV
One of Erl's oldest beer styles,
chestnut in color, and with a rather
strong taste. A nice, light bitterness
of hops in the finish.

LAGERBIER
LAGER 5.5% ABV
Strong yellow in color; fine,
compact foam; sparkling. Full-
bodied and slightly malty with
a light bitter taste.

BAMBERGATOR
DOPPELBOCK 8.5% ABV
A dark brown, full-bodied, and very
strong doppelbock, bursting with
harmonious hop bitters.

ALL ABOUT ...
MALT

Beer is an agricultural product that begins its life in a field of golden, swaying grain—usually barley. After the harvest the grains are taken to a malt house, or maltings, where the commencement of the magical journey that ends in the glass takes place. In brewing lore, malt, or malted barley, was known as the "soul" of beer—a raw material that has an alchemical power to provide color and aroma, as well as the rich and distinctive array of flavors. There can be no beer without malt: it provides the sugars essential for yeast to feed on during fermentation, the by-products of which are carbon dioxide and alcohol.

COLOR Though it doesn't tell the whole story, the color of a beer gives an indication of the malts that have been used. Black malt is used in the very darkest beers, such as stouts; amber ales will often contain Brown malt or Crystal malt; pilsner-style beers often use Caramalt for lightness and a sweet note.

BARLEY The barley grown for brewing is either two- or six-row barley. Two-row is common in Europe, while American brewers have traditionally used six-row; this is partly due to cost, but also because it works well with rice or corn, common adjuncts in beers produced by the larger brewers.

SELECTING THE GRAIN There are several strains of barley. In the UK, as well as with some selective American brewers, Maris Otter is the chosen one, while others include Golden Promise and Optic. Just as beer divides into styles, barley has its variations too. In Britain and Belgium, winter-sown barley is used, because of its robust flavor, while German and Czech brewers prefer lighter and sweeter tasting spring-sown barley.

GERMINATION

The first step of the malting process is to kick-start germination in the grains. This helps produce enzymes that break down the starch into the essential soluble malt sugars. This process involves steeping the grains in water and then laying them out to dry. The grains are turned over several times each day to ensure that the emerging rootlets don't link up with each other. The skill of the maltster is to know when to stop the germination—after that it's off to the kiln for drying.

KILNING

Shorter kilning times produce lightly cured malts that give a golden sparkle to ale and lager. Pale malt usually forms the majority of the grain in the mash tun—this is because it has the highest levels of starch and the enzymes that convert starch into fermentable sugars. A longer rest in the kiln means darker malts and a deeper color, body, and flavor.

STORAGE

A visit to a brewery's malt store will unlock the mysteries of this magical grain: expect sacks of Pale malt, Chocolate malt (so-called because it tastes like chocolate), Black malt, Rye malt, Lager malt, Brown malt, and Caramalt. You may also find roasted barley, which is unmalted and a vital constituent of Irish dry stout, such as Guinness or Murphy's. Stewing malt in a way similar to making toffee produces Crystal malt, which adds body and a rich spiciness to beer.

BREWERY

FAUST

Hauptstr. 219, 63897 Miltenberg, Germany
www.faust.de

A typical regional family-run company. The brewery is about 350 years old and changed hands many times in the first 200 years of its history. The Fausts took over in 1895, and still own it today. There are many different styles of beer produced, some of which have won prizes.

FELSENBRÄU THALMANNSFELD

91790 Thalmannsfeld, Germany
www.felsenbraeu-thalmannsfeld.de

These handcrafted beers come from one of the loveliest parts of Bavaria, between the Altmühltal and Franconia. The third generation of the family guides the brewery and uses traditional recipes.

BREWING SECRET The energy for production comes from solar power.

FIEGE

Moritz Fiege, Scharnhorststr. 21-25, 44787 Bochum, Germany
www.moritzfiege.de

"We are a classic regional brewery" says Hugo Fiege, the boss of the company. He sees his brewery as an ambassador for the Ruhr region. It is an institution offering typical local beers—inhabitants of the Ruhr love their beer. There is little chance of a big global player acquiring Fiege....

FLENSBURGER

Munketoft 12, 24937 Flensburg, Germany
www.flensburger.de

Five citizens of Flensburg founded this brewery in 1888. During the 1970s, the brewery's reputation was enhanced when a comedian kept referring to a "Flasch Flens" in his act. The term came to be used for a bottle of Flensburger, which at the time was the only German beer to use clip-top bottles.

BEER

SCHWARZVIERTLER
DUNKEL 5.2% ABV
Dark, roasty, and slightly smoky. There is also caramel and a little bitter-chocolate on the tongue. It is full-bodied and has a dry finish.

FAUST KRÄUSEN
KELLERBIER 5.5% ABV
A mild, full-bodied beer with a light note of honey; it is very fresh.

MÄRZEN
EXPORT 5.4% ABV
A typical märzen: dark-yellow and with a strong taste and aromas of barley-malt. Light scent of hops in the finish.

FELSENTRUNK
LAGER 4.9% ABV
A light, sweet taste; it sparkles a little; very fresh and with a nice bitter aroma in the finish.

MORITZ FIEGE PILS
PILSNER 4.9% ABV
A classic pilsner with bitter aromas of good hops, a light malty taste, and a fine dry structure.

SCHWARZBIER
SCHWARZBIER 4.9% ABV
Elegant and with a malty sweetness, this coffee-colored beer has light bitter aromas of fine hops.

FLENSBURGER PILS
PILSNER 4.8% ABV
A typical golden pilsner—malty, refreshing, and with slightly bitter aromas of hops in the finish.

KELLERBIER
KELLERBIER 4.8% ABV
Amber and cloudy, like all kellerbiers, the Flensburger version is full-bodied and tastes naturally fresh, slightly sweet, and has a dry finish.

FREIBERGER

Am Fürstenwald, 09599 Freiberg, Germany
www.freiberger-bier.de

This brewery was the first in Sachsen to produce a pilsner. Other exclusive beers followed: Freiberger Silberquell (1903) and a wheat beer (1909). The Eichbaum brewery in Mannheim has acquired Freiberger and is focusing on making it one of the most modern beer producers in Germany.

FRIEDENFELS

Schlossbrauerei Friedenfels, Gemmingenstr. 33, 95688 Friedenfels, Germany
www.schlossbrauerei-friedenfels.de

The brewery is situated in the southern part of the largest forest in Europe, between Oberpfälzer Wald and Fichtelgebirge. Friedenfels is the leading brewery of the region.

BREWING SECRET The pure springs of the national park have helped Friedenfels to produce excellent beers for more than 100 years.

FÜCHSCHEN

Ratinger Str. 28, 40213 Düsseldorf, Germany
www.fuechschen.de

Altbier has been a favored brew at Füchschen since 1848. The fourth generation of the family is in charge. There have been some changes since 1995, including the installation of new brewing equipment.

BREWING SECRET The Düsseldorf carnival in February is a good opportunity to sample the altbier.

FÜRSTLICHEN ELLINGEN

Schloss-Strasse 19, 91792 Ellingen, Germany
www.fuerst-carl.de

Owner Carl Friedrich Fürst von Wrede is a direct descendant of Napoleon's field marshal Carl Philipp, Prince of Wrede. The brewery opposite his castle in Ellingen was founded in 1690, but the brewing history of Ellingen is certainly older. The beer has been called Fürst Carl for about 200 years.

JUBILÄUMS-FESTBIER
MÄRZEN 5.8% ABV
With aromas of malt and a very fine taste of hops, this amber-colored beer is pleasant and full-bodied.

SCHWARZES BERGB'ER
SCHWARZBIER 4.7% ABV
Deep black, with fresh, malty aromas. Full-bodied and precisely balanced between malts and hops.

FRIEDENFELSER PILS LEICHT
LIGHT BEER 2.8% ABV
This reduced-alcohol beer is golden and on the dry side, with aromas of fine hops in the finish.

FRIEDENFELSER WEIZEN LEICHT
LIGHT WHEAT BEER 2.7% ABV
This light beer is fermented in the bottle. Its taste is a mixture of bitter hops and sweet barley and wheat—typical of the style.

FÜCHSCHEN ALT
ALTBIER 4.5% ABV
Dark mahogany in color, this typical Düsseldorfer is malty with a very intense aroma of hops. Slightly carbonated, and fresh.

SILBERFÜCHSEN
WHEAT BEER 5.4% ABV
A northern-style wheat beer, less sweet than its Bavarian counterpart. Smooth, fruity, and sparkling.

FÜRST CARL JOSEFI BOCK
BOCK 7% ABV
A creamy, malty, and full-bodied beer, with a velvet and silky texture.

FÜRST CARL URHELL
LAGER 4.6% ABV
The clear yellow color is typical for a lager; the taste is pleasant and not too dry, with very little sweetness.

BREWERY

FÜRST WALLERSTEIN

Berg 78, 86757 Wallerstein, Germany
www.fuerst-wallerstein.de

The success of this brewery spans 400 years under the same family, who have always employed skillful brewers. In 2008 Alexander Jesina was appointed; he started his brewing career in the famous monastery of Andechs.

BREWING SECRET It's a family tradition that consistency is more important than short-term success.

FÜRSTENBERG

Postplatz 1-4, 78166 Donaueschingen, Germany
www.fuerstenberg.de

Count Heinrich I von Fürstenberg was granted the right to brew beer in 1283, but it was not until 300 years later that a proper brewery was built. Fürstenberg was a major brewery by the beginning of the 20th century.

BREWING SECRET The beers are made with water from the Black Forest and yeast from Donaueschingen.

GANTER

Schwarzwaldstr. 43, 79117 Freiburg, Germany
www.ganter.com

Ganter was founded more than 140 years ago and is still family-owned. The brewery buildings were damaged in World War II and had to be rebuilt. The 1950s and '60s were successful, but beer-drinking in the region has since declined. After some years of struggling, however, Ganter is finding a new lease of life in broader markets.

GILDE

Hildesheimer Str. 132, Hanover, Germany
www.gildebrau.de

It was about 500 years ago that Cord Broyhan presented his beer to the people of Hanover. *Broyhan*—a pale style of wheat beer—was popular for centuries in the city. Gilde, Hanover's longest-surviving brewery, now owned by InBev, was founded in 1870.

BREWING SECRET A modern version of *broyhan* is exported to the US.

BEER

ZWICKEL

LAGER 4.7% ABV
The Wallerstein Zwickelbeer is a cloudy golden specialty beer with a really natural quality to it.

WEISSBIERPILS

PILSNER/WHEAT BEER BLEND 5.1% ABV
Sparkling and golden with some cloudiness; yeasty in flavor, with some citrus notes and a dry finish.

FÜRSTENBERG GOLD

LAGER 4.9% ABV
Smooth, with few aromas of hops. This clear golden beer is a bit sweeter than the usual lager.

FÜRSTENBERG HEFE DUNKEL

DUNKEL 5.4% ABV
Chestnut in color, and sparkling; harmonious with a malty aroma and light caramel sweetness, yet strong in the mouth.

WODAN

DOPPELBOCK 7.5% ABV
Roasty aromas; malty-sweet at the start, but the finish is mild and slightly bitter.

GANTER ECHT HEFEWEIZEN DUNKEL

DARK WHEAT BEER 5.4% ABV
Dark malt, a fine yeast, and a full body are the important characteristics of this beer.

RATSKELLER PREMIUM PILS

PILSNER 4.9% ABV
A dry, golden-yellow pilsner; full-bodied, typical bitterness of hops, and a nice finish.

LINDENER SPECIAL

EXPORT 5.1% ABV
The most successful export beer of Niedersachsen has a golden color and tastes pleasant with smooth yeast-flower flavors in the mouth.

GLAAB

Frankfurter Str. 9, 63500 Seligenstadt, Germany
www.glaabsbraeu.de

For more than 250 years this brewery has been owned by the Glaab family. It was founded in 1744 and became known for its wide variety of beers and for Vitamalz, the biggest German brand of pure malt drinks. The company is the only private brewery in the Offenbach region, to the south of Frankfurt.

GOLD OCHSEN

Veitsbrunnenweg 3-8, 89073 Ulm, Germany
www.gold-ochsen.de

It was in 1597 when the brewery-restaurant Zum Goldenen Ochsen was opened in the ancient city of Ulm. The brewery has been in the hands of one family since 1868.

BREWING SECRET The current, fifth generation of owners are moving with the times and employing eco-friendly processes.

GÖLLER

Wildgarten 12, 97475 Zeil am Main, Germany
www.brauerei-goeller.de

Joseph Göller acquired this brewery and restaurant in 1908. Both have grown steadily over the years. In 1998 the renovated restaurant was leased by the Zeiler family.

BREWING SECRET Göller strives to make high-quality beers using modern, environmentally friendly techniques.

GOSLAR

An der Abzucht 1a, 38640 Goslar, Germany
www.brauhaus-goslar.de

Goslar, by the Gose river, has been famous for its beer since 995. Gose beer was popular for centuries, but fell out of favor in the early 20th century. However, Goslar launched "The Gose" again in 2004.

BREWING SECRET Gose contains coriander and salt, and therefore does not follow the Purity Law.

1744
KELLERBIER 5.3% ABV
This cloudy, amber-colored beer is Glaab's youngest product. The taste of fine malt is typical.

DUNKLES
DUNKEL 5.3% ABV
Clear amber-colored beer in which the light bitterness of hops is prominent. A great dunkel with a nice malty finish.

GOLD OCHSEN ORIGINAL
LAGER 5.1% ABV
Light bitterness with the aromas of fine hops. A very rounded and smooth taste, with some sweetness in the finish.

GOLD OCHSEN RADLER
SHANDY 2.5% ABV
The mixture (50 percent beer, 50 percent lemonade) is sparkling and full-bodied, fruity and fresh.

GÖLLER RAUCHBIER
SPECIAL BEER 5.2% ABV
This amber-colored regional specialty has light aromas of fine hops and a smoky, roasted malt taste.

GÖLLER LAGER
LAGER 4.9% ABV
A clear, golden lager with a light, malty taste and fine aromas of hops. The recipe is an ancient one.

HELLE GOSE
WHEAT BEER 4.9% ABV
Naturally cloudy and golden, this beer is pleasant with light bitterness from the hops, and malt aromas.

DUNKLE GOSE
DUNKEL 4.9% ABV
Light reddish-brown color; smoky with malt aromas. The brewers add a third special malt.

The Hofbräuhaus in Munich is arguably Germany's best-known beer hall, offering lots of beer, traditional food, and sometimes live music.

BEER STYLES

GERMAN BEER

Even though pilsner-style beers dominate the German market, the country has a good range of breweries that continue to produce distinctive, traditional types of beer. Altbier *(see p132)* and kölsch *(see p123)* are perhaps the most influential with brewers and beer enthusiasts elsewhere in the world, but the smoky rauchbier, sweet black schwarzbier, and subtle gose testify that there is much more to explore in the world of German beer.

In northern Germany, in the former industrial city of Dortmund, Dortmunder export is a style of lager drier and slightly stronger than the average pils or helles. This golden beer was popular with factory workers but, sadly, it is now becoming less easy to find.

Other hard-to-find variations on the lager theme include kellerbier, steinbier, spezial, roggen (rue beer), and zoigl, which is a communally brewed beer found in northeastern Bavaria. One of the rarest German beer styles is gose, a wheat beer flavoured with a little salt and coriander. It can only be found in Leipzig and the nearby town of Goslar, from whence the name of the beer originated.

SMOKY BEERS In Franconia, a neighbor of Bavaria, the beautiful and ancient town of Bamberg is the center for rauchbier, or smoke beer. Here, malt is kilned over beechwood fires to give the beer its smoky character. Despite their smokiness, these beers are very appealing, dry, and moreish, and go well with robust dishes and smoked foods.

DARK BEERS German dark beers come in two varieties—schwarzbier ("black beer") and dunkel (meaning "dark"). The former was a dying beer style until given a new lease of life in the old East German province of Thuringia. Expect a pitch-black and luscious beer, with mocha coffee, vanilla, and burnt toffee notes.

BAVARIAN DUNKELS Bavarian dunkels are deep reddish-brown in color. One of the best examples of this style is Weltenburger Kloster's Barock Dunkel—a firm, well-bodied beer, with chocolate and cocoa on the palate and nose.

GOTTMANNSGRÜNER

Von-Koch-Str.2, 95180 Berg, Germany
www.gottmannsgruener.de

Gottmannsgrüner was granted the right to brew in 1535. Caroline Freifrau von Waldenfels is the current head—the daughter of Ernst-Albrecht who retired in 2005. The brewery was awarded the silver medal at the European Beer Awards in 2006 for its schwarzbier.

GREIF

Serlbacher Str. 10, 91301 Forchheim, Germany
www.brauerei-greif.de

Kapuzinerwirt, a famous restaurant in Forchheim, was founded in 1848, a year of revolution in Germany. This incarnation of the company lasted for more than 100 years. During the 1990s there was investment in new production equipment, and today the brewery is one of the most technologically advanced in the region.

GRÜNBACH

Kellerberg 2, 85461 Bockhorn, Germany
www.schlossbrauerei-gruenbach.de

Grünbach has had a host of owners, including the famous Paulaner and Erdinger breweries. Alexander Noll is currently at the helm.

BREWING SECRET Grünbach's Benno Scharl wheat beer carries the name of an 18th-century Bavarian master brewer who wrote an influential textbook on brewing techniques.

HAAKE-BECK

Am Deich 18/19, 28365 Bremen, Germany
www.haake-beck.de

Founded in 1826, the Haake-Beck brewery is one of the most famous in northern Germany. Milestones in the company's history include the creation of Haake-Beck Kräusen Pils and the first Maibock in 1950. It is part of the InBev stable today.

BREWING SECRET Haake-Beck's sister is the famous Beck's label, which is exported by InBev around the world.

GOTTMANNSGRÜNER SCHWARZE

SCHWARZBIER 4.8% ABV
A really black, full-bodied beer with malt aromas and a slightly sweet taste.

MOBILATOR

DOPPELBOCK 7.8% ABV
A clear doppelbock with a rounded malty character: fine, dry, and pleasantly flavored. It's available throughout the year.

DUNKLE WEISSE

WHEAT BEER 5.4% ABV
A dark amber, full-flavored wheat beer with some sweetness and light malt in the finish.

ANNAFESTBIER

EXPORT 5.5% ABV
Amber in color and sporting a fine, smooth foam. Sweet, full-bodied, and with delicate aromas of dried fruits and banana.

ALTWEIZEN GOLD

WHEAT BEER 5.3% ABV
Clear golden and finely balanced between yeast and carbonic acid, with a lightly sparkling, dry freshness.

BENNO SCHARL

WHEAT BEER 5.3% ABV
Yellow, and clouded with yeast, Benno Scharl tastes mild and sweet, pleasant and well balanced.

HAAKE-BECK 12

EXPORT 5% ABV
This is a new Haake-Beck. A harmonious, golden beer, with a level of sweetness that is often liked by women drinkers.

EDEL HELL

LAGER 4.7% ABV
A mild alternative to the pilsner: not so dry, a little bit sweet, and golden like a typical lager.

BREWERY

HACKER-PSCHORR

Hochstr. 75, 81541 München, Germany
www.hacker-pschorr.de

Hacker-Pschorr is one of the most traditional breweries in Munich, and its restaurant is a tourist attraction, especially during Oktoberfest. Beer production was mentioned for the first time here in 1417.

BREWING SECRET The Purity Law and principles of long lagering are followed; there are no preservatives or additives.

HÄRKE

Am Werderpark 5, 31224 Peine, Germany
www.haerke-brauerei.de

Härke has been a family-owned brewery since 1890, but the first beer was brewed here much earlier, in 1666. The Härkes constructed a new building for the brewery in 1927, and it has been enlarged and renovated in subsequent decades.

BREWING SECRET Organic produce is used in some beers.

HASSERÖDER

Auerhahnring 1, 38855 Wernigerode, Germany
www.hasseroeder.de

Hasseröder is a name known around the world for sports sponsorship. Production started in 1882 and was an immediate success. It was the best-selling beer in East Germany—and the pilsner lovers in the west did not wait long after Reunification to try it.

BREWING SECRET Water from the Harz mountains imparts a smoothness.

HEIDELBERG KULTURBRAUEREI

Leyergasse 6, 69117 Heidelberg, Germany
www.heidelberger-kulturbrauerei.de

The practice of beermaking was first established here in 1235, but the region was an economic backwater, and the brewery had to struggle through the centuries. Since 1999, however, it has had a rebirth as the Kulturbrauerei in the city of Heidelberg.

BEER

1417
KELLERBIER 5.5% ABV
Naturally cloudy, unfiltered, with a dull golden color. Low carbonic acid makes it very smooth.

SUPERIOR
MÜNCHNER SPECIAL 6% ABV
The clear, amber-colored Superior is based on an old recipe and has a malty, aromatic taste, without too many hops. Highly drinkable.

1890
PILSNER 4.9% ABV
A real lager, but with a pilsner touch. Mild, dry, and influenced by fine aromatic hops and sweet malts.

HÄRKE PILS
PILSNER 4.9% ABV
Nice bitter taste of organic hops and malt. A real pilsner with a dry taste and pleasant finish.

HASSERÖDER PREMIUM EXPORT
EXPORT 5.5% ABV
Smooth, with some sweetness and a harmonious bitter aroma of hops with malty notes; golden color.

HASSERÖDER PREMIUM PILS
PILSNER 4.9% ABV
Full-bodied pilsner taste; well balanced bitter aromas of fine hops, and malty flavors.

KELLERBIER
KELLERBIER 5.6% ABV
This beer is amber colored, naturally cloudy, nicely bitter, full-bodied, and with a fine roasty aroma—like a märzen.

KRÄUSEN
HELLES 5.2% ABV
The Kräusen from Heidelberg is unfiltered, slightly cloudy, and golden. It is mild, and similar to a pilsner.

HERBORNER

Alte Marburger Str. 2-8, 35745 Herborn, Germany
www.herborner-bier.de

In 1871 Adolf Schramm came to Herborn to assist his widowed sister at a small brewery. He later built a new one, and the brewery remained in the family until 1945. Traditional brewing methods continue to be used.

BREWING SECRET The first steam brewery in Herborn, its transition to modern production has been skillfully handled.

HERFORDER

Gebr.-Uekermann-Str. 1, 32120 Hiddenhausen, Germany
www.herforder.de

The brewery was founded in 1878 as Gebrüder Uekermann, Brauerei zum Felsenkeller. Since then there have been many innovations in production, bottling, and styles of beer. The latest chapter began in 2007, following integration within the Warsteiner Group, but Herforder is still a family-run company.

HERRNGIERSDORF

Schlossallee 5, 84097 Herrngiersdorf, Germany
www.schlossbrauerei-herrngiersdorf.de

Herrngiersdorf is situated between Regensburg and Landhut, in the middle of Niederbayern. With more than 875 years of history behind it, this is the oldest private brewery in the world. It has been owned by the Pausinger family since 1899. Since 1995 the sixth generation of the family has been managing it.

HOFBRÄU MÜNCHEN

Hofbräuallee 1, 81829 München, Germany
www.hofbraeuhaus.com

The Hofbräuhaus in Munich is a very famous restaurant, frequented by visitors from around the world. It was founded in 1607 by Maximilian I, Duke of Bavaria. The linked brewery is situated in Riem, outside of the city.

BREWING SECRET The water used to brew Hofbräu is drawn from a depth of 490 ft (150 m).

CLASSIX
DUNKEL 4.5% ABV
This dark amber lager has a mild bitterness of fine hops. Roasted malt dominates the taste, especially in the finish.

EXPORT
EXPORT 4.9% ABV
Malty aromas on the nose, full-bodied, light sweet malty taste, and fine hop bitters.

FELSENKELLER
DARK LAGER 5.2% ABV
A traditional dark beer with a well-balanced, malty aroma and fine bitters of hops.

HERFORDER SCHWARZBIER
SCHWARZBIER 4.9% ABV
Coffee-colored dark beer with a highly aromatic malt, smooth aroma of fine hops, and some sweetness.

SÜNDENBOCK
BOCK 7.3% ABV
A typical dark doppelbock with a light taste of caramel; very full-bodied and sweet in the finish.

PUBLINER
DUNKEL 4.9% ABV
This beer is very dark and has a strong taste, with very roasty malt aromas and light bitters of hops. (The Irish would love it...)

HOFBRÄU ORIGINAL
MÜNCHNER HELLES 5.1% ABV
This clear golden beer is refreshing and dry, with a harmonious balance of malt and hops.

HOFBRÄU DUNKEL
DUNKEL 5.5% ABV
This is the oldest type of Bavarian beer, dark amber in color, and full of fine flavor and enticing malt aromas.

BREWERY

HÜTT

Hütt-Brauerei Bettenhäuser, Knallhütte, 34225 Baunatal, Germany
www.huett.de

Beer has been brewed at this site since 1752, and the family-owned company is now in its ninth generation. The brewery has always been linked with the Knallhütte restaurant here.

BREWING SECRET Hutt brews its beers to suit local tastes, but they also appeal to a much wider market.

HUTTHURMER

Marktplatz 5, 94116 Hutthurm, Germany
www.hutthurmer.de

The beers from the Bavarian Forest are well known far beyond regional borders. The local Raiffeisenbank has been the owner since 1914.

BREWING SECRET Keeping the traditional arts of brewing going consistently since 1577 is the secret of this Bavarian brewery's success.

JANDELSBRUNNER

Hauptstr. 17, 94118 Jandelsbrunn, Germany
www.jandelsbrunner.de

The Langs have owned this brewery since 1810. In the 20th century, there was renewal of equipment such as new filling machines, and the construction of new production plants and maturing cellars.

BREWING SECRET In 2004 photovoltaic equipment was added, to harness the power of the sun for brewing.

JETTENBACH

Am Schlossberg 1, 84555 Jettenbach am Inn, Germany
www.brauerei-jettenbach.de

The history of brewing in Bavaria has been closely associated with the story of Toerring for more than 700 years. The Toerrings fought for the right to found breweries to produce beer for themselves and the local pubs and restaurants. The master brewers of the family have also become famous in their own right.

BEER

SCHWARZES GOLD
DUNKEL 4.9% ABV
Smooth brown color, dry, and very fresh; sweet-tasting and with aromas of malt and fine hops.

LUXUS PILS
PILSNER 4.9% ABV
Bitter aromas of fine hops, very elegant, malty taste, and a clear golden color: a very high-quality pilsner.

TRADITION-EXPORT
EXPORT 5.4% ABV
The gold export beer is full-bodied and not too sweet. A light aroma of hops is significant in the finish.

TRADITION DUNKEL
DUNKEL 5.3% ABV
Dark malt gives this beer its typical color and aroma. The light hoppiness makes a pleasant drink.

DOPPELBOCK
DOPPELBOCK 8% ABV
The color of this doppelbock is mahogany, the taste malty, flowery, and slightly sweet, with a nice bitter note when finishing.

UR-WEIZEN
WHEAT BEER 5.3% ABV
Amber-colored and cloudy from the yeast, this malty beer tastes flowery with a mild, sweet finish.

GRAF IGNAZ PREMIUM
PILSNER 4.9% ABV
A real pilsner—clear, golden, and lightly sparkling; strongly flavored with fine, balanced bitters of hops.

GRAF IGNAZ LAGER
LAGER 4.9% ABV
This golden beer is dry and has nice aromas of fine malt. There is some sweetness on the tongue.

JEVER

Elisabethufer 18, 26441 Jever, Germany
www.jever.de

Jever is one of the top breweries in Germany. Established 160 years ago, the company started producing its export beer in the 1950s. The pilsner as we know it took off during the "pils-wave" of the 1960s. Radeberger bought Jever in 2005.

BREWING SECRET Jever is famous for making one of the driest pilsners in existence.

JEVER FUN
LOW ALCOHOL 0.25% ABV
Almost alcohol-free, but with a similar taste to the pilsner. Hop-bitters and a pilsner taste pervade this golden beer.

JEVER PILSENER
PILSNER 4.8% ABV
The master brewers use a lot of hops at Jever, and their bitterness makes this pilsner very dry.

KAUZEN

Uffenheimer Str. 17, 97199 Ochsenfurt, Germany
www.kauzen.de

The most remarkable time in the history of Kauzen was its survival between 1919 and 1945, and the time after World War II, when it had problems getting hold of equipment, malts, and hops to produce beer. Today, Kauzen is one of the most modern breweries in Bavaria with a good position in the market.

KÄUZLE
LAGER 4.8% ABV
A modern, clear golden beer with sweet, malty aromas, and a light bitter taste of fine hops at the end.

KAUZEN ORIGINAL 1809
LAGER 5.2% ABV
With its golden yellow color, this beer is a typical lager; it tastes less dry than usual—indeed, a bit sweet.

KESSELRING

Leithenbukweg 13, 97342 Marktsteft, Germany
www.kesselring-bier.de

This brewery was founded in the 19th century and became sucessful after 1914, when Adolf Kesselring took over the management. By the early 1960s, Kesselring was producing 650,000 gallons (3 million liters) of beer and 110,000 gallons (half a million liters) of soft drinks each year; the quantities have doubled since then.

URFRÄNKISCHES LANDBIER
LAGER 5.3% ABV
A fresh beer with a clear golden color. The taste is a rounded combination of hops and malt.

KESSELRING SCHLEMMER SCHWARZE
WHEAT BEER 5.3% ABV
Very sparkling and fresh; a light aroma of hops in the finish.

KIRNER

Kallenfelser Str. 2-4, 55606 Kirn, Germany
www.kirner.de

The Andres family became part of the beer world in the mid-17th century, a time when every restaurant in Kirn was brewing its own beer. By the end of the century, however, the Andreses were supplying other restaurants, and this was the beginning of a success story that continues to this day.

KIRNER KYR
PILSNER LIGHT 2.8% ABV
This clear golden-yellow beer has less alcohol than most, but it tastes like a real pilsner. Elegant, dry, with a light touch of fine hops.

KIRNER PUR
PILSNER 4.8% ABV
Cloudy and yellow, this pilsner is natural, unfiltered, and full-bodied, with a light taste of yeast.

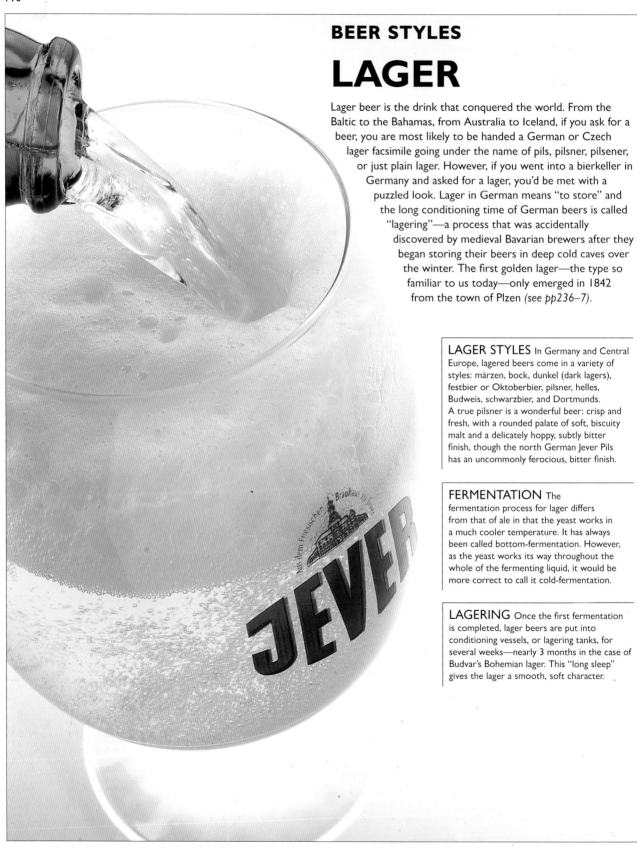

LAGER

Lager beer is the drink that conquered the world. From the Baltic to the Bahamas, from Australia to Iceland, if you ask for a beer, you are most likely to be handed a German or Czech lager facsimile going under the name of pils, pilsner, pilsener, or just plain lager. However, if you went into a bierkeller in Germany and asked for a lager, you'd be met with a puzzled look. Lager in German means "to store" and the long conditioning time of German beers is called "lagering"—a process that was accidentally discovered by medieval Bavarian brewers after they began storing their beers in deep cold caves over the winter. The first golden lager—the type so familiar to us today—only emerged in 1842 from the town of Plzen (see pp236–7).

LAGER STYLES In Germany and Central Europe, lagered beers come in a variety of styles: märzen, bock, dunkel (dark lagers), festbier or Oktoberbier, pilsner, helles, Budweis, schwarzbier, and Dortmunds. A true pilsner is a wonderful beer: crisp and fresh, with a rounded palate of soft, biscuity malt and a delicately hoppy, subtly bitter finish, though the north German Jever Pils has an uncommonly ferocious, bitter finish.

FERMENTATION The fermentation process for lager differs from that of ale in that the yeast works in a much cooler temperature. It has always been called bottom-fermentation. However, as the yeast works its way throughout the whole of the fermenting liquid, it would be more correct to call it cold-fermentation.

LAGERING Once the first fermentation is completed, lager beers are put into conditioning vessels, or lagering tanks, for several weeks—nearly 3 months in the case of Budvar's Bohemian lager. This "long sleep" gives the lager a smooth, soft character.

KITZMANN

Südliche Stadtmauerstr. 25, 91054
Erlangen, Germany
www.kitzmann.de

The Kitzmann brewery in Erlangen
near Nuremberg began brewing beer
in 1733, but it took another 100 years
for the business to really take off.
Subsequent generations have ensured
the loyalty of drinkers by adhering
to the old traditions of this great
brewing city through the years.

KNEITINGER

Kreuzgasse 7, 93047 Regensburg,
Germany
www.kneitinger.de

Kneitinger is one of the best-known
traditional restaurants in the city of
Regensburg. Master brewer Johann
Kneitinger acquired the brewery and
farmland in 1865 to assure the best
raw materials for brewing.

BREWING SECRET Johann Kneitinger
developed the strong bock beer that
the brewery still produces.

KÖNIG LUDWIG

Augsburger Stre. 41, 82256
Fürstenfeldbruck, Germany
www.kaltenberg.de

The history of the Bavarian royal
family, the Wittelsbachers, is closely
connected with the art of beermaking. Today, HRH Luitpold Prince
of Bavaria continues the family
business successfully with his brands
König Ludwig and Kaltenberg. The
latter brand name refers to the
brewery at Kaltenberg Castle.

KÖNIGSBACHER

An der Königsbach 8, 56075 Koblenz,
Germany
www.koenigsbacher.de

Beer has been made here since 1689.
From 1970 it was linked to other
breweries such as Richmondis-Bräu in
Cologne and Hamacher in Aachen,
and it is now in the Carlsberg group.

BREWING SECRET Königsbacher was the
first brewery in Germany to use
automatic filling machines for casks,
starting in 1974.

KITZMANN KELLERBIER
KELLERBIER 4.9% ABV
This is a really old-fashioned beer:
unfiltered, cloudy, with fine aromas
of hops and a malty finish.

KITZMANN URBOCK
BOCK 7.1% ABV
A rounded, fine bock, which is
rather heavy in taste, but well
balanced between hops and malt,
and with a smooth foam.

KNEITINGER BOCK
BOCK 6.8% ABV
Black-brown in color, full-bodied,
with a creamy foam, and tasting of
malt—this is a perfect bock.

KNEITINGER DUNKEL EXPORT
EXPORT 5.5% ABV
This dark, ancient beer is malty
with light hops and a creamy foam
—visitors from all over the world
love this typical beer of Regensburg.

KÖNIG LUDWIG DUNKEL
DUNKEL 5.1% ABV
Amber, with a smooth taste of dark
malt and fine hops, this is the most
popular dunkel in Germany.

KÖNIG LUDWIG WEISSBIER
WHEAT BEER 5.5% ABV
One of the most popular wheat
beers in Bavaria; cloudy yellow, with
fine hops in the finish. A very
traditional, non-filtered specialty.

KÖNIGSBACHER PILSENER
PILSNER 4.8% ABV
Gold, sparkling, and aromatic. The
fine hops contribute to a very thick,
creamy foam and a great finish.

1689
TRADITIONAL LAGER 5.2% ABV
This noble, amber-colored
traditional beer tastes rather
strong and robust; it is dry,
medium-bodied, and pleasant.

BREWERY

BEER

BREWERY

KROMBACHER

Hagener Str. 261, 57223 Kreuztal-Krombach, Germany
www.krombacher.de

The brewery was first mentioned in records in 1803, but it was not until 1908 that the Krombacher brand was truly established. Business flagged between the wars, then began to rise again in the 1990s. Since 2005, Krombacher has become the leading premium brand in Germany, making 100 million gallons (500 million liters) of beer each year.

KRONE TETTNANG

Bärenplatz 7, 88069 Tettnang, Germany
www.krone-tettnang.de

Krone Tettnang is a small craft brewery that has been owned by the Tauscher family for seven generations. It is a member of "Brewers with Body and Soul"—a group of ten small companies who aim to produce beer "in another, but traditional, way...."

BREWING SECRET The first organic beer of the Bodensee region was made here in 1993.

KUCHLBAUER

Römerstr. 5-9, 93326 Abensberg, Germany
www.kuchlbauer.de

Bestowed the right to brew beer in 1300, this is one of the oldest official breweries in the world. The Kuchlbauers were from Regensburg, but in 1751 they acquired a property in Abensberg, where they have been brewing ever since.

BREWING SECRET Their success stems from focusing on brewing wheat beers.

KULMBACHER

Lichtenfelser Str. 9, 95326 Kulmbach, Germany
www.kulmbacher.de

The name of Kulmbach, a city in northern Bavaria, is known to beer-lovers throughout the world. Its fame began with the offerings of beer master Wolfgang Reichel in 1846. Since his time, many other brands have joined the company, and production is now about 70 million gallons (300 million liters) of beer each year.

BEER

KROMBACHER PILS
PILSNER 4.8% ABV
The taste is elegant, fresh and dry, with light bitters of hops in the finish. Golden in color.

KROMBACHER WEIZEN
WHEAT BEER 5.3% ABV
Very new: an unfiltered, naturally cloudy, yellow beer. Sparkling, with a smooth taste, a little bit sweet, fruity, and full-bodied.

KELLERPILS
PILSNER 4.7% ABV
The famous first organic beer of the region. Unfiltered and cloudy, it has the typical pilsner bitterness of hops and some sweetness of malt.

KRONENBIER
LAGER 4.9% ABV
Richly flavored traditional beer with the finest possible malt aroma, and a light finish of fine hops.

KUCHLBAUER WEISSE
WHEAT BEER 5.4% ABV
One of the most famous and typical wheat beers—slightly cloudy, sparkling, and sweet.

ALTE LIEBE DUNKLE WEISSE
WHEAT BEER 5.4% ABV
Dark mahogany and very aromatic with malts. Rather sweet; not much bitterness, but fine hops are present on the tongue.

MÖNCHSHOF SCHWARZBIER
SCHWARZBIER 4.9% ABV
Dark roasted malts and fine hops. The deep, dark color and fine aroma are typical of schwarzbiers.

KAPUZINER WEISSBIER
WHEAT BEER 5.4% ABV
Naturally cloudy, sparkling and with a sweet and fruity taste; this unfiltered beer is typical of the wheat beer style.

LANDSKRON

An der Landskronbrauerei 116, 02826 Görlitz, Germany
www.landskron.de

Founded in 1869, the Landskron brewery in eastern Germany was always one of the most important in the region. Owned by the state under the GDR, it was only after the Reunification in 1990 that the beers were brewed according to the rules of the Purity Law in Germany.

LANDWEHR-BRÄU

Reichelshofen 31, 91628 Steinsfeld, Germany
www.landwehr-braeu.de

The Landwehr brewery is a modern, yet traditionally minded, company. Beer has been produced at this site since 1755, and from 1913 it has been owned by the Wörner family.

BREWING SECRET Brewing and filling technologies are as advanced as possible, important factors in the guarantee of quality.

LANG-BRÄU

Bayreuther Str. 18-19, 95632 Wunsiedel, Germany
www.lang-braeu.de

Schönbrunn, near Wunsiedel, is home to this small brewery, which produces 13 different styles of beer. Production levels are relatively low, yet this company is world famous because of the wide distribution of its Benedikt XVI ("The Pope's beer," 7.5% ABV). Interestingly, they also brew an "Erotic beer" (5.5% ABV).

LEIBINGER

Friedhofstr. 20-36, 88212 Ravensburg, Germany
www.leibinger.de

This brewery was founded in 1894 in Ravensburg by Max Leibinger. Max Leibinger II took over in 1959 and began the modernization of the brewery. Michael Leibinger is now at the helm.

BREWING SECRET 100 percent of the ingredients in Leibinger beers are sourced locally.

LANDSKRON EIN SCHLESIER
EXPORT 5.2% ABV
A traditional dark-golden beer, naturally strong, brewed with a light malty taste and a fine finish of hops.

LANDSKRON LAUSITZER KINDL
PILSNER 4.8% ABV
Clear golden-yellow, this beer has a very fresh and dry taste—a result of using fine hops—and a light, malty finish.

DUNKLER BOCK
BOCK 6.6% ABV
Reminiscent of hazelnuts, this beer is a typical bock with its aromas of malts, and fine bitter taste of hops.

DUNKEL
MÄRZEN 5% ABV
Coffeelike—nearly black in color—this dunkel has a roasted malt aroma and a light bitterness of hops in the finish.

SCHÖNBRUNNER PILS
PILSNER 5% ABV
A clear golden pilsner with harmonious flavors. The finish is spectacular with fine hops.

SCHÖNBRUNNER SPECIAL
EXPORT 5.5% ABV
Clear gold and full-bodied, with a malty finish and notes of fine hops.

MAX
SPECIAL 5.2% ABV
This mix of malts from wheat, barley, and fine hops has a subtle taste. A very successful beer.

EDELPILS
PILSNER 4.9% ABV
The taste is markedly of hops, which is typical for a pilsner. It is sparkling, with delicate hop-flower notes and dryness in the mouth.

BEER TRAIL

BAMBERG

Can there be a better place in the world to drink beer?
This beautiful, baroque island city, on the banks of the River Regnitz
and the Main-Donau Canal is in the Upper Franconia region of Bavaria.
It is built on medieval foundations and is home to 70,000 people and
11 breweries. The city is a base for many US army personnel and their
families—and they have helped, no doubt, to take the fame of this
beer paradise around the world.

Many of Bamberg's beers have a smoky secret. To malt a cereal,
the grain has to begin to germinate, converting complicated sugars
into simpler ones, which then can be broken down even farther in
the mash tun. But the process has to be stopped before it goes too far
and the grain's goodness is lost to the brewer. Heat is normally used
to arrest germination, but, in Franconia, maltsters developed a smoky
technique of stopping the grain's growth. The germinating grain is
heated over beechwood fires, which imparts marvelous wood fire,
peaty aromas, and flavors to the finished beers.

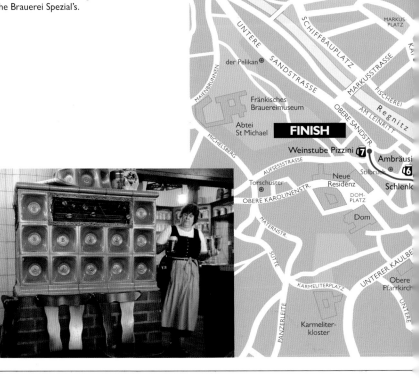

1 KLOSTERBRAU
Beer has been brewed at Klosterbrau since 1533. Down a cobbled
street, time seems to slip away in this fairytale of a brewery tap.
The range includes a schwarzbier, braunbier, weizen, pils, and a bock.
Oberre Muhlbruck 3, Bamberg (www.klosterbraueu.de)

JOURNEY STATS
30 mins, plus drinking time
2 miles (3 km)

2 OLD TOWN HALL
The river is never far away in
Bamberg. The stroll to Brauerei
Spezial's passes the spectacular
medieval stone-and-timbered Old
Town Hall, which seems precariously
balanced on the footings of an
ancient bridge. Take a moment
to admire it before heading on
to the Brauerei Spezial's.

3 THE BRAUEREI SPEZIAL'S
The Brauerei Spezial's is very much
a locals' bar, decorated with laughter and
conversations. Its Specizil Rauchbier has
subtle, soft toffee flavors and even a hint
of burnt straw. Spezial uses smoked malt
in at least four of its other beers. By the
bar is a serving hatch, where locals come
to fill containers with beer for drinking at
home. *Obere Königstrasse 10, Bamberg
(www.brauerei-spezial.de)*

4 BRAUEREI FÄSSLA

Directly opposite Brauerei Spezial's is Brauerei Fässla. Brewing started here in 1649. The brewery tap has a comfortable, wood-paneled, country-style room, and above it is a small hotel. The brewery's logo—a dwarf rolling a barrel of beer—decorates the glasses and dark furniture. Fässla's easy-drinking Lagerbier melds malty flavors with a fresh, soft bitterness. *Obere Königsstrasse 19–21, Bamberg (www.faessla.de)*

5 SCHLENKERLA

Vibrant and friendly, Schlenkerla is Bamberg's best-known bar and restaurant. The warmth of its world-famous rauchbier, with its smoked whiskey and cheese overtones, is as warm as the welcome. Tables are often shared, and the atmosphere is highly convivial. Beer is the social lubricant and the perfect accompaniment to robust Bavarian dishes such as onions stuffed with beery meatballs. *Dominikanerstrasse 6, Bamberg (www.smokebeer.com)*

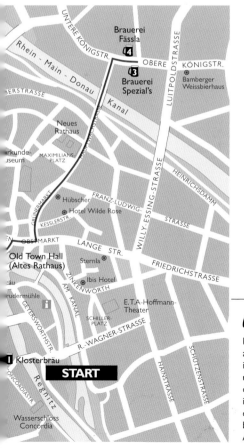

6 AMBRÄUSIANUM

Opposite Schlenkerla is the Ambräusianum. Here, the brewing vessels can be seen, which makes it seem more like a modern brewpub than one of Bamberg's traditional establishments, and it is a relative newcomer, being open only since 2004. Weekend breakfasts comprise a glass of wheat beer with three locally made Bavarian veal sausages and a pretzel. *Dominikanerstrasse 10, Bamberg (www.ambraeusianum.de)*

7 WEINSTUBE PIZZINI

The exterior of the Weinstube Pizzini is somewhat unprepossessing, and do not be deterred by its name— it is neither a wine bar nor a pizza restaurant. Inside this small, brown decorated and time-worn bar, there is a warm-hearted welcome and the opportunity to try Fässla and Spezial beers, as well as a dunkel from Andechser. *Ober Sandstrasse 17, Bamberg*

0 yards 200

0 metres 200

UNTERE KÖNIGSTR.

Brauerei Fässla

4

Rhein - Main - Donau

OBERE KÖNIGSTR.

LUITPOLDSTRASSE

Bamberger Weissbierhaus

3 Brauerei Spezial's

Kanal

BERSTRASSE

Neues Rathaus

MAXIMILIANS-PLATZ

HEINRICHSDAMM

rkunde-jseum

WILLY-LESSING-STRASSE

Hübscher

FRANZ-LUDWIG-

Hotel Wilde Rose

STRASSE

KESSLERSTR.

OBSTMARKT

LANGE STR.

FRIEDRICHSTRASSE

Old Town Hall (Altes Rathaus)

Sternla

Ibis Hotel

ZINKENWORTH

AM KANAL

GEYERSWÖRTHSTR.

SCHILLER-PLATZ

E.T.A-Hoffmann-Theater

R. WAGNER-STRASSE

SCHÜTZENSTRASSE

HAINSTRASSE

rudermühle

1 Klosterbräu

START

Regnitz

CONCORDIAstr.

Wasserschloss Concordia

Rauchbier - Gaststätte ❖Kachelofen❖ - Kellerbier

The bars of Bamberg are known for their rauchbier (smoked beer), which uses beechwood-smoked malt.

BREWERY

LEIKEIM

Langheimer Str. 14, 96264 Altenkunstadt, Germany
www.leikeim.de

About 120 years old, the brewery is still owned by the Leikeim family, now in the fourth generation. Today, after several renovations, the company is the second-largest in Germany selling beer in clip-top bottles. Dieter Leikeim, who runs the operation, has largely been responsible for turning Leikeim into a premium brewery.

LICHER

In den Hardtberggärten, 35423 Lich, Germany
www.licher.de

Tradition is an important concept at this brewery, which has been going since 1854. There is a philosophy of quality at Licher that is obvious when you drink their beers.

BREWING SECRET The basics for making good beer—malt, hops, and water—are all from sustainable sources.

LINDENBRÄU

Stuttgarter Str. 43, 76337 Waldbronn, Germany
www.lindenbraeu-waldbronn.de

Lindenbräu can look back to a history spanning three centuries. In 2000 it had a major renovation, which involved stripping the old buildings back to a shell, then creating a very modern interior. The old barn was turned into a covered beer garden.

LOHRER

Ludwigstr. 3, 97816 Lohr am Main, Germany
www.lohrer-bier.de

The brewery was founded in the late 19th century to produce beer specifically for a restaurant. Lohrer reintroduced clip-top bottles in the early 1980s. It is now a subsidiary of the Würzburger Hofbräu.

BREWING SECRET Lohrer has a history of the judicious introduction of new beers, like its wheat beer in 1982.

BEER

LEIKEIM PREMIUM
PILSNER 4.9% ABV
Dry, and with more fine aromas of hops than most other pilsners. The finish has only light aromas of malt.

LEIKEIM RADLER
BEER BLEND 2.5% ABV
Very clear, yellow beer with a distinct lemon taste and only a few traces of bitterness. Sparkling and very fresh.

LICHER WEIZEN
WHEAT BEER 5.4% ABV
A favorite of the brewery: fine yeast and hops give the beer a special note, while the sweetness gives it a full-bodied taste.

LICHER DOPPELBOCK
DOPPELBOCK 7.6% ABV
Heartiness is the main characteristic of this dark beer. Some sweetness in the finish makes it very pleasant.

PILS
PILSNER 5% ABV
A real pilsner: clear golden and with a strong but smooth taste, and a bitter aroma of fine hops.

ORIGINAL
LAGER 5% ABV
An amber-colored beer with a very aromatic, malty taste and a slightly stronger bitterness than usual. The sweetness is like a märzen.

KEILER WEISSBIER
WHEAT BEER 4.9% ABV
Naturally cloudy, dark amber-colored, and unfiltered, the Keiler is balanced between wheat and barley malts. Slightly sweet, with a fine aroma of hops in the finish.

LOHRER BÖCKLE
BOCK 7% ABV
The strongest Lohrer beer: rather heavy but pleasant and full-bodied.

LÖWENBRÄU

Nymphenburger Str. 7, 80335 München, Germany
www.loewenbraeu.de

Löwenbräu is one of the most famous brands in the world. The company is more than 500 years old. In 1948, only three years after the end of World War II, Löwenbräu began exporting again: first to Switzerland, then further afield. In 1997 there was a marriage between Löwenbräu and Spatenbräu; today both are part of the global player InBev.

LÜBZER

Eisenbeissstr. 1, 19386 Lübz, Germany
www.luebzer.de

Beer has been produced in Lübz for 130 years. Today the brewery is a part of Carlsberg A/S Denmark, and the company has a capacity of 20 million gallons (100 million liters) of beer annually. In eastern Germany, Lübzer Pils is one of the biggest brands and popular, even with beer aficionados.

MAISEL

Hindenburgstr. 9, 95445 Bayreuth, Germany
www.maisel.com

Hans and Eberhardt Maisel founded the brewery in the city of Richard Wagner in 1887. The family decided to concentrate the production on wheat beer in 1955, and Maisel became a trendsetter for this style.

BREWING SECRET Their success is the result of a high level of ability in the hand-crafting of beers.

MAXLRAIN

Schlossbrauerei Maxlrain, Aiblinger Str. 1, 83104 Tuntenhausen/ Maxrain, Germany
www.maxlrain.de

Emperor Karl the Great was the founder of the castle of Maxlrain in the year 804. The current owner of the castle and its attached brewery—Leo, Count of Hohenthal von Bergen—is proud of his tradition and the high quality of his ingredients.

TRIUMPHATOR
DOPPELBOCK 7.6% ABV
Dark brown in color, the Triumphator has a strong flavor of malt, but only a subtle aroma of hops. Sweet.

LÖWENBRAEU URTYP
EXPORT 5.4% ABV
A balanced flavor with fine aromas of malt; full-bodied, pleasant, and fresh; with mild hops in the finish.

LÜBZER URKRAFT
LAGER 6% ABV
This amber-colored beer has a bit more alcohol than usual, a full-bodied taste, and plenty of aroma.

LÜBZER LEMON
PILSNER AND LEMON 2.5% ABV
Fresh lemons, limeade, and only 2.5% ABV give this clear yellow mixture a really refreshing taste.

MAISEL'S WEISSE
WHEAT BEER 5.2% ABV
The color is typical for Maisel: a gleaming red. Fermentation in the bottle gives the beer fruity notes and mild nuttiness in the finish.

MAISEL'S DAMPFBIER
SPECIAL BEER 4.9% ABV
A very old-fashioned beer: the mix of different malts gives it a really special, fine character

JUBILATOR
DOPPELBOCK 7% ABV
A dark-colored beer with a strong but satisfying taste, rounded and smooth with fine roasty malts in the finish.

AIBLINGER SCHWARZE
DARK EXPORT 5% ABV
Mahogany, with a fine, malty aroma and smooth taste. Full-bodied and not too sweet.

BREWERY

MEININGER
Am Bielstein 3, 98617 Meiningen, Germany
www.meininger-privatbrauerei.de

Founded in 1841, this brewery has had a checkered history. When the GDR was established, Meininger was nationalized, like most other companies in East Germany, and it faced difficult trading conditions in the aftermath of Reunification. Today, Meininger produces 1.8 million gallons (8 million liters) of beer each year, for a local and a wider market.

METTLACHER ABTEIBRÄU
Bahnhofstr. 32, 66693 Mettlach, Germany
www.abtei-brauerei.de

Mettlacher specializes in natural, unfiltered beer. Guests can watch the brewing process from the attached restaurant. The brewers promote the beer styles of the region and run courses on beer production.

BREWING SECRET High-quality basic products, modern techniques, and the energy of the brewers ensure success.

MICHELSBRÄU
Fahrstr. 83-85, 64832 Babenhausen, Germany
www.michelsbraeu.de

The brewery is situated in the heart of the small city of Babenhausen. It was founded in 1815 and has been managed by the Schuberts since 1925. The production is handcrafted, and the master brewer uses the best malts and hops available.

BREWING SECRET The water comes from a spring in the vicinity of the brewery.

NESSELWANG
Postbrauerei Nesselwang, Hauptstr. 25, 87484 Nesselwang, Germany
www.post-brauerei-nesselwang.de

In the second half of the 17th century there were five breweries in Nesselwang. For 200 years this one was called the Adler brewery; its incarnation as Nesselwang began in 1883, and it has enjoyed continuous success since World War II.

BEER

MEININGER GOLD URHELL
LAGER 4.7% ABV
Fresh and lightly sparkling; a clear golden beer. It has a light aroma of fine hops.

MEININGER HELLER BOCK
BOCK 6.3% ABV
This amber-yellow bock is available throughout the year. Its taste is pleasant, and there is a delicious aroma of hops.

ABTEI-BOCK
BOCK 6.2% ABV
Strong-roasted bock with obvious roasty aromas and an even more intense flavor of fine hops.

ABTEI-JOSEF-SUD
WHEAT BEER 5.1% ABV
The dark amber-colored wheat beer is sparkling and has typical aromas from the mash of wheat and barley malts.

MICHELSBRÄU HEXE
EXPORT 5.2% ABV
This special beer has a malty aroma and fine bitters of hops. It is amber-yellow and a delight to drink.

MICHELSBRÄU PILS
PILSNER 4.9% ABV
The golden pilsner is fresh with a fine and gleaming foam. It has a balanced aroma of hops, and tastes lightly bitter, dry, and elegant.

DUNKEL
DUNKEL 4.9% ABV
A dark-brown speciality that tastes of roasted malts. It is slightly sweet and finishes with a whisper of hop bitterness.

POSTILLON
WHEAT BEER 4.9% ABV
A typical amber wheat beer: sparkling, with a fresh taste of light hops and malts, and a sweet finish.

NEUMARKTER LAMMSBRÄU

Ehrnsberger e.K.Amberger Str. 1, 92318 Neumarkt, Germany
www.lammsbraeu.de

Family-owned since 1800, the company turned to organic beer production in 1987 and now has about 14 types.

BREWING SECRET Neumarkter Lammsbräu works with about 100 organic farmers to ensure the quality of its ingredients.

PINKUS MÜLLER

Kreuzstr. 4-10, 48143 Münster, Germany
www.pinkus-mueller.de

The story of the Müller family began in 1816 in Münster. The company expanded over the years. Today, Pinkus Müller is the last of about 150 traditional breweries in Münster, and an attraction in the town. Its restaurant serves regional specialities.

BREWING SECRET The raw materials for its unfiltered beers are all organic.

REICHENBRAND

Zwickauer Str. 478, 09117 Chemnitz, Germany
www.brauerei-bergt.de

Reichenbrand is located in the city of Chemnitz. The brewery first opened in 1874, but went bankrupt 21 years later. Joachim Bergt then took over and guided the company through difficult times. The GDR nationalized it; after Reunification, the family took it back. It has been renovated and is now enjoying more prosperous times.

REUTBERG

Klosterbrauerei Reutberg, Am Reutberg 2, 83679 Sachsenkamm, Germany
www.klosterbrauerei-reutberg.de

The monastery at Reutberg started brewing its own beer in the 19th century. In 1901 the Franziskaner monks stopped brewing, but the local people protested. Production started again in 1906, with new machines and cellars. In 1987 a proposed merger with Holzkirchen failed, and Reutberg continues to brew its own beer independently.

URSTOFF
LAGER 4.7% ABV
Brewed with fewer hops than a pilsner, so it tastes less bitter; it is pleasant and has a nice finish.

DINKELBIER
SPECIAL BEER 5.1% ABV
Dinkel is similar to wheat beer but is a much older style. It has balanced basic ingredients and the sparkle of a wheat beer, and tastes strong.

PINKUS PILS
PILSNER 5.2% ABV
A colour like straw; it tastes dry and has a medium aroma of hops in the finish.

ORIGINAL ALT
ALTBIER 5.1% ABV
The wine-like character comes from an extra-long period of maturation. Dark golden, with light bitter aromas in the finish.

HELLES
LAGER 4.2% ABV
This light, golden beer is full-bodied with a rounded bitter aroma from the hops.

PREMIUM
EXPORT 5.5% ABV
Typically dark yellow, this beer is as full-bodied as its sibling, but more aromatic from hops, and it has a fine, dry, and bitter finish.

EXPORT DUNKEL
DUNKEL 5.2% ABV
Dark malt gives the beer its typical dark amber colour. The smell is malty, and the texture full-bodied with a harmonious finish.

JOSEFI BOCK
BOCK 6.9% ABV
This strong, amber beer has a mild taste with a pleasant, malty aroma: a well-balanced beer.

The **Früh brewery tap**, close to Cologne's cathedral, is the perfect place to drink a glass of kölsch.

BEER STYLES
KÖLSCH

Although the appearance of a glass of golden kölsch might suggest the lager method of bottom- or cold-fermentation, the unique beer of Cologne (Köln) is a member of the ale family. It might have the hue of a pilsner, and spend a month in cold maturation (or lagering), but it is a beer made with top- or warm-fermenting yeast. This marks it out as a survivor from the time when Germany was home to all sorts of unusual beers, many of which would qualify as ales. It is also one of those rare beers with its own appellation: since 1985, no brewery outside the city of Cologne or a handful of nearby villages can call its beer a kölsch. It's for this reason that American craft brewers, many of whom are keen supporters of the beers of Cologne, have to call their brews "kölsch-style".

Naturally, the citizens of Cologne are extremely proud of their beer. Sample kölsch at its best in the atmospheric brewery taps of Früh (close to the cathedral) and Dom on the Alteburger Strasse.

LIGHT AND SUBTLE This is not a big bruiser of a beer: expect delicate fruit and malt flavors on the palate, with hints of berry fruit, followed by a subtle sweetness and a quick, clean finish. It's a refreshing style of beer, easily drinkable, and normally around 5% ABV. It makes a wonderful aperitif or social drink, and is also ideal for serving at the dining table with light salads or delicate white fish.

KÖBES OF KÖLN Just like its close rival alt, from the neighboring Rhineland city of Dusseldorf, kölsch is delivered by wandering bands of blue-apron-wearing waiters called köbes. The beer arrives in small, cylindrical glasses called stange; they are carried on round trays, with each glass sitting in its own hole.

BREWERY

RIEGELE

Frölichstr. 26, 86150 Augsburg, Germany
www.riegele.de

The history of brewing here goes back to 1386. Sebastian Riegele bought the small company in 1884, and developed it so well that in 1911, a new brewery was built outside central Augsburg. Today Riegele is still family-owned and operates several restaurants as well as the brewery.

BREWING SECRET Riegele has its own malt-producing company.

RÖHRL

Heerstr. 13, 94315 Straubing, Germany
www.roehrlbraeu.de

Straubing in Niederbayern is home to the brewery that Josef Röhrl founded in 1881. From the beginning, it was family-owned. After difficulties at the end of World War II, the family managed to re-establish it as a very successful company.

BREWING SECRET The introduction of their wheat beer in 1976 brought them widespread recognition.

ROSENBRAUEREI PÖSSNECK

Dr.-Wilhelm-Külz-Str.41, 07381 Pössneck, Germany
www.rosenbrauerei.de

Brewing has been taking place in Pössneck since the 16th century. The company was nationalized in 1951, and had fallen into a state of disrepair by the time of Reunification. By 1994, however, the Rosenbrauerei was back on course for success.

ROSTOCKER

Doberaner Str. 27, 18057 Rostock, Germany
www.rostocker.de

In 1878 the engineers Mahn and Ohlerich acquired the Julius Meyer'sche Bierbrauerei. There followed a highly successful era until the outbreak of World War II. Beck & Co. now own the brewery.

BREWING SECRET Since 1991 the brewery has grown year-on-year, and not only due to the Beck connection.

BEER

COMMERZIENRAT RIEGELE PRIVAT
EXPORT 5.2% ABV
Golden and gleaming, with aromas of malt and hop-flowers; the taste is smooth and mild, with a lovely bitterness of hops.

SEBASTIAN RIEGELE'S WEISSE
WHEAT BEER 5% ABV
Unfiltered, cloudy, and yellow. A yeast-flower taste with fruitiness and fine bitters of hops.

STRAUBINGER WEISSE
WHEAT BEER 5.3% ABV
Full-bodied, fresh, sparkling, and very fruity on the palate, with a mild aroma of hops.

RÖHRL'S GÄUBODEN LANDBIER
LAGER 4.8% ABV
The name comes from the famous beer festival in Straubing. It has a light barley and hops taste with a nice, very slightly bitter finish.

ROSEN KELLERBIER
SPECIAL BEER 4.8% ABV
This traditional beer has a cloudy yellow color; it is full-bodied and aromatic with a light, malty aroma.

SCHWARZE ROSE
SCHWARZBIER 4.9% ABV
Sparkling and almost black, with a nice roasted malt aroma and some bitterness in the finish.

ROSTOCKER BOCK
BOCK 6.9% ABV
More bitter than other bocks. Full-bodied with malt aromas and a rich caramel taste.

ROSTOCKER EXPORT
EXPORT 5.5% ABV
Golden colored, the beer has a fine aroma of hops and a slightly flowery bitterness.

SAALFELD

Bürgerliches Brauhaus Saalfeld, Pössnecker Str. 55, 07318 Saalfeld, Germany
www.brauhaus-saalfeld.de

The tradition of brewing beer is more than 100 years old in Saalfeld. In the 1950s the brewery was partially renovated, but many machines were still old fashioned. New owners have since invested €7 million to modernize the equipment.

SCHAUMBURGER

St. Annen 11, 31655 Stadthagen, Germany
www.schaumburger-brauerei.de

The brewery was founded in 1873 in Stadthagen. Production stopped during World War II, but the beer was on sale again from 1948.

BREWING SECRET The brewery uses water from the Bornan spring, which has similar qualities to water from Pilsen in the Czech Republic—where the original pilsner was made.

SCHEYERN

Klosterbrauerei Sheyern, Schyrenplatz 1, 85298 Scheyern, Germany
www.klosterbrauerei-scheyern.de

The monks of Scheyern started brewing beer in 1119. Later, the brewery was leased to a producer in Augsburg, but the monastery (one of the oldest in Bavaria) has recently started up beer production again. The brewery is in the middle of the famous Hallertau region—the biggest area of hop cultivation in the world.

SCHILLING

Hirschbrauerei Schilling KG, Agilshardter Str. 37, 72587 Römerstein, Germany
www.boehringer-biere.de

From 1826 to the present day, the history of this brewery has been turbulent, with many alterations over the years. It was acquired in 1874 by Johannes Jakob Schilling along with a restaurant called Hirsch, and a farm.

BREWING SECRET The brewery exerts a strong influence over the organic production of its raw ingredients.

UR-SAALFELDER GROTTENPILS
PILSNER 4.8% ABV
A traditional clear golden pilsner, full-bodied, and with a noble bitterness from hops.

UR-SAALFELDER PILS
PILSNER 4.8% ABV
This classic pilsner has a fine, dry taste with a light sparkle at the beginning and a harmonious, bitter aroma at the finish.

SCHAUMBURGER PRIVATBOCK
BOCK 6.5% ABV
Typical bock with a light malt aroma, strong flavor, and a nice finish from fine hops.

SCHAUMBURGER LÜTTJE LAGE
LIGHT BEER 3% ABV
A special light beer that in northern Germany is drunk along with corn schnapps. It is low in alcohol and delightfully light.

KLOSTER GOLD HELL
LAGER 5.4% ABV
Golden in color, and with a mild flavor of hops.

HOPFAZUPFABIER
MÄRZEN 5.6% ABV
Hopfazupfa is Bavarian for "the man who harvests hops," and it was for such men that this golden-colored beer was originally produced. Fine-flavored with light aromas of hops.

BÖHRINGER KELLERPILS
PILSNER 4.8% ABV
Unfiltered, yellow, and cloudy. Pleasant with a light, bitter aroma of hops, not too heavy but elegant.

BÖHRINGER BOCKBIER
BOCK 6.1% ABV
A very full-bodied bock, with a sweet taste and a light bitterness from the hops.

BREWERY

SCHLAPPESEPPEL

Schlossgasse 24, 63739 Aschaffenburg, Germany
www.schlappeseppel-de

When King Gustav Adolf of Sweden conquered the city of Aschaffenburg (south of Frankfurt) in the year 1631, there was not a drop of beer at the castle. The only person available to brew beer was a lame soldier called Shlappe Seppel ("flabby Joseph"). The Schlappeseppel was born...

SCHLENKERLA

Dominikaner Str. 6, 96049 Bamberg, Germany
www.schlenkerla.de

This legendary brewery was known by 1405. Today it is still a relatively small company, run by a family in its sixth generation. The so-called "smoked beer" is a specialty of Bamberg.

BREWING SECRET The distinctive, smoky aroma of Schlenkerla's beers comes from beechwood smoke that pervades the malt as it dries above the oven.

SCHLODERER

Rathausstr. 4, 92224 Amberg, Germany
www.schlodererbraeu.de

The Schloderer Bräu is a typical brewery-restaurant situated in the ancient city of Amberg. While dining, guests can watch the brewing of beer in action. There are standard brands and also seasonal ones such as wedding beer or "the beer of the witches." To accompany the beers is an array of regional dishes and special menus.

SCHMUCKER

Hauptstr. 89, 64756 Mossautal, Germany
www.schmucker-bier.de

Founded in 1780, this brewery is still a private company. The beer is considered as regional, but dealers transport it around the country, and there are even exports to Italy, Spain, France, South Korea, and the US. The brewery has 90 employees.

BREWING SECRET The hardness of the local spring water is a key factor in the character of Schmucker beers.

BEER

SCHLAPPESEPPEL EXPORT
EXPORT 5.5% ABV
A classic, golden export beer with a light aroma of hops and some sweetness on the palate.

SCHLAPPESEPPEL PILSENER
PILSNER 5% ABV
A golden and not-too-light pilsner: the taste is strong but smooth, with a fine aroma of hops and malt.

AECHT SCHLENKERLA RAUCHBIER
MÄRZEN 5.1% ABV
A very dark, dry beer. It has smoky and roasted malt aromas and a finish of light hops. A pure pleasure.

RAUCHBIER URBOCK
BOCK 6.5% ABV
A traditional dark bock with Schlenkerla's trademark smoky and roasty aromas; dry, malty taste and a good sweetness in the finish.

SCHLODI KULT
LAGER 5.2% ABV
Naturally cloudy and yellow, the Kult tastes dry and fine-flavored, it slightly sparkling, and very fresh.

SCHLODERER DUNKEL
DUNKEL 4.9% ABV
Dark amber in color, naturally cloudy, and slightly smoky with malt aromas and some sweetness.

MEISTER PILS
PILSNER 4.8% ABV
Clear yellow and gleaming, this typical full-bodied pilsner has a strong aroma of hops; it is smooth with a strong bitterness.

HEFEWEIZEN
WHEAT BEER 5% ABV
Deep yellow and cloudy, full-bodied; a smooth taste accompanied by a smell of fruits and yeast.

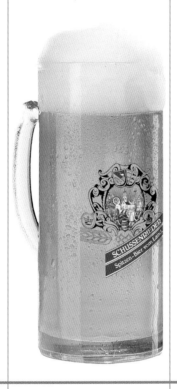

SCHNEIDER

Private Weissbierbrauerei Schneider, Emil-Ott-Str. 1-5, 93309 Kelheim, Germany
www.schneider-weisse.de

The Schneider brewery has been a family-owned company since it was founded. From its original location in Munich, Schneider moved to Kelheim after World War II. The former brewery in central Munich has since become a world-famous restaurant.

SCHNEIDER WEISSE ORIGINAL

WHEAT BEER 5.4% ABV
People call it "liquid amber," and they are right: the amber-mahogany color is beautiful. Fresh, full-bodied, and with a light, bitter finish.

AVENTINUS

STRONG WHEAT BEER 8.2% ABV
Almost black, legendary beer, with chocolate and dried-fruit aromas; full-bodied, very thick, and fresh.

SCHUSSENRIEDER

Wilhelm-Schussen-Str. 12, 88427 Bad Schussenried, Germany
www.schussenrieder.de

The first brewers in the region were monks at a monastery in the 12th century. The modern story started in 1906, when master brewer Josef Ott acquired the brewery. The Ott family are still the owners.

BREWING SECRET The brewery is a traditional one and only uses barley and hops from the region.

ORIGINAL NO.1

LAGER 4.7% ABV
A natural, unfiltered, cloudy yellow beer full of malt aromas and a light finish of fine hops.

KRONEN-PERLE

LAGER 4.7% ABV
The clear golden color is typical of this kind of beer; the pleasant taste is as well. It is a mild beer, considered to be a summer drink.

SCHWARZBACH

Schleisinger Str. 27, 98673 Schwarzbach, Germany
www.schlossbrauerei-schwarzbach.de

The owner of the Schwarzbach restaurant was the first to brew beer on this site—during the occupation of the Würzburg bishop's troops in 1400. During wars and revolutions, the brewery was destroyed and rebuilt. It was nationalized by the GDR in 1949. The story has begun afresh since the Reunification of Germany in 1990.

SONNEN WEISSE

WHEAT BEER 5% ABV
Sparkling-fresh with a typical taste of yeast, sweetness, and fine hops. The appearance is golden-yellow and slightly cloudy.

RAUBRITTER DUNKEL

DUNKEL 5% ABV
Dark and malty, this beer is full-bodied, smooth, and the favorite of more than just the knights....

SCHWEIGER

Ebersberger Str. 25, 85570 Markt Schwaben, Germany
www.schweiger-bier.de

Ludwig Schweiger was by trade a miller but in the 1930s he somehow founded a brewery, which is now managed by his descendants. Their best-known beer today is the Schmankerl-Weisse.

BREWING SECRET The brewery has used its own malt since 1963, and also sold its malt to other brewers.

HELLES EXPORT

EXPORT 5.1% ABV
A classic beer with a light, dry taste. It is pleasant, with a nice bitterness of hops in the finish.

ORIGINAL SCHMANKERL-WEISSE DUNKEL

WHEAT BEER 5.1% ABV
Naturally dark and cloudy, this beer is light and sparkling on the palate.

THE STORY OF ...

Weltenburger Kloster

Asamstrase 32,
93309 Kelheim, Germany

In a courtyard, where giant chestnut trees shade visitors from the sun, the church of the Weltenburg Monastery and the Kloster brewery stand side-by-side. Set on a bend in the Danube, this must be one of the most dramatic and magnificent brewery locations in the world. The beautifully decorated baroque Benedictine abbey is hewn from the 150-million-year-old Jurassic limestone that forms towering cliffs on both sides of the river. Brewery and river usually co-exist harmoniously, but lines and dates on an exterior wall bear witness to the power of the river in full flood. The most recent inundation, in 2005, nearly closed the brewery.

Weltenburg Monastery was founded in the 7th century by two monks, Eustasic and Agilus, followers of St. Columbanus, one of the patron saints of brewing. Manuscripts in the monastery's library show that beer has been brewed here for over 1,000 years, with production only being halted from 1803 to 1846. This makes it the oldest abbey brewery in the world. But, although the ancient site is redolent with tradition, this is a forward-looking, hi-tech, automated brewery.

The Kloster's brewmaster is Anton Miller. In his early twenties, he is looking forward to a long career at the brewery. His predecessor brewed here for 49 years.

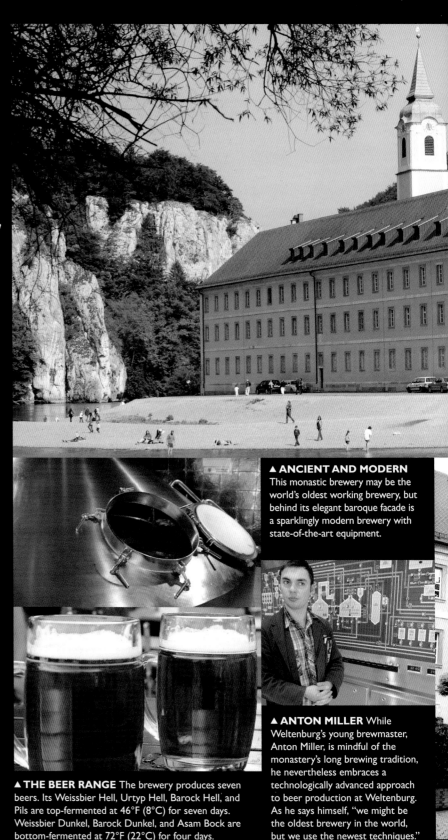

▲ ANCIENT AND MODERN This monastic brewery may be the world's oldest working brewery, but behind its elegant baroque facade is a sparklingly modern brewery with state-of-the-art equipment.

▲ ANTON MILLER While Weltenburg's young brewmaster, Anton Miller, is mindful of the monastery's long brewing tradition, he nevertheless embraces a technologically advanced approach to beer production at Weltenburg. As he says himself, "we might be the oldest brewery in the world, but we use the newest techniques."

▲ THE BEER RANGE The brewery produces seven beers. Its Weissbier Hell, Urtyp Hell, Barock Hell, and Pils are top-fermented at 46°F (8°C) for seven days. Weissbier Dunkel, Barock Dunkel, and Asam Bock are bottom-fermented at 72°F (22°C) for four days.

► **LAGERING** The Weltenburger Kloster lager store is located beneath 130 ft (40 m) of limestone rock. Here, the Dunkel is stored at 32°F (0°C), and sometimes lower, for at least three months. This slowly releases the Barock Dunkel's aromatic, malty flavors and well-balanced richness. The beer was presented with the Gold Medal in the Dark Lagers category at the World Beer Cup 2008 in San Diego.

◄ **QUALITY INGREDIENTS** Miller prides himself on the brewery's close links with local Bavarian farmers. Each June he visits the barley fields to choose the grain, which will then be malted in Bamberg. The sweet and spicy Perle Hallertau hops, used in pellet form at the brewery, come from three farms near Munich.

▲ **THE BEER GARDEN** Visitors should not miss the opportunity of sampling the beer, which is pumped directly to its own bar. The beer garden is open throughout the year and is renowned not only for its beer, but also for its extensive range of traditional Bavarian dishes, including suckling pig, boiled beef, and Klosterwurst, a spicy home-made sausage. The brewery is open to the public on weekends.

BREWERY

STERNQUELL

Dobenauer Str. 83, 08523 Plauen, Germany
www.sternquell.de

The Aktienbrauverein in Plauen was nationalized after World War II and given a new name—Sternquell. After Reunification, the brewery quickly enjoyed success and is now in the top three of the East German territories.

BREWING SECRET A pre-Reunification program of investment was the basis for its future success.

STRALSUNDER

Greifswalder Chaussee 84-85, 18439 Stralsund, Germany
www.stralsunder.de

The art of brewing has been closely connected with the city of Stralsund for centuries. This brewery was founded in 1827. After nationalization it faced increasing difficulties but, since 1997, it has been enjoying success again.

BREWING SECRET When the brewery relaunched in 1997, it reintroduced a well-loved traditional beer from its past.

STRECK

Ludwig-Jahn-Str. 11 9745 Ostheim, Germany
www.streckbier.de

In 1718 Peter Streck started brewing beer mainly for his own family. Soon, though, other people clamored to buy his brews. In 1884 the brewery began to acquire technical equipment. By 2000 the 10th generation was in control of the company. The Strecks are already planning how to celebrate their 300th anniversary in 2018.

THURN & TAXIS

Fürstliche Brauerei Thurn & Taxis Vertriebsgesellschaft, Am Kreuzhof 5, 93055 Regensburg, Germany
www.thurnundtaxisbiere.de

The story of the princes of Thurn and Taxis is closely connected with both the development of the German postal service and the brewing of beer.

BREWING SECRET The family was the first in Germany to promote pilsner, to brew rye beer, and to offer wheat beer on draft.

BEER

STERNQUELL DUNKEL
DUNKEL 5.3% ABV
A dark amber beer with a light aroma of hops and a pleasant, malty taste; smooth and full-bodied.

STERNQUELL PILS
PILSNER 4.9% ABV
The obvious taste of fine hops, creamy foam, and clear golden color make this a true pilsner. Very aromatic and mildly sparkling.

STRALSUNDER LAGER
LAGER 4.7% ABV
Fine malts give a full body. The beer is smooth and mild, with some sweetness in the finish.

STRALSUNDER PILS
PILSNER 4.9% ABV
A typical pilsner—clear golden, full-bodied, pleasant, with the dry aromas of fine hops, and some bitterness.

OSTHEIMER DUNKEL
DUNKEL 4.5% ABV
Dark amber from special malts, this beer has a malty aroma and is full-bodied and pleasant.

WEIZENBOCK
BOCK 7.1% ABV
A naturally cloudy, amber-colored beer, sparkling and fresh, with some sweetness and light bitters of hops.

ST. WOLFGANG DUNKEL
DUNKEL 4.8% ABV
Dark-colored from fine dark malts, this typical, full-bodied dunkel has a roasted aroma and tastes malty.

THURN & TAXIS EXPORT
EXPORT 5.3% ABV
A flavor of mild hops and malts makes this full-bodied, golden beer a favorite.

TRAUNSTEIN

Hofbräuhaus Traunstein, Hofgasse 6-11, 83278 Traunstein, Germany
www.hb-ts.de

From its date of founding in 1612, the brewery had centuries of difficulties, including near-destruction by firestorms. Its luck changed in 1975, when Hofbräuhaus Traunstein was decorated with eight gold medals for its regional beers. Today the company has about 60 employees.

TROTZENBURG

Ostsee Brauhaus AG "Trotzenburg," Strandstr. 41, 18225 Kühlungsborn, Germany
www.brauhaus-trotzenburg.de

In 1839 a certain Herr Moll opened a tavern in an old forester's house, which developed into a brewery-restaurant. The name Trotzenburg was adopted only in 1913. By the end of the 1980s, it had grown dilapidated, and was closed down. It has since reopened, and is part of the Ostsee Brauhaus AG.

TUCHER

Schwabacher Str. 106, 90763 Fürth, Germany
www.tucher.de

The Tucher story began in Nuremberg in 1672, with the production of wheat beer. After the brewery was modernized in 1855, two-thirds of the beers were exported. Today Tucher is a part of the Radeberger Group.

BREWING SECRET This brewery is the most traditional in northern Bavaria.

UERIGE

Bergerstr. 1, 40123 Düsseldorf, Germany
www.uerige.de

The brewery, attached to a famous restaurant in Düsseldorf, is situated in the heart of this historic town, near the Rhine river. Since 1862 it has produced the city's famous beer—altbier. Michael Jackson, the famous beer and whiskey critic, once awarded Uerige's beer four stars—a rare high judgment from the specialist.

FÜRSTEN TRUNK

EXPORT 5.5% ABV
From start to finish, the aroma of hops plays an important role in the structure of this specialty beer.

1612ER ZWICKELBIER

TRADITIONAL EXPORT 5.3% ABV
Unfiltered and straight from the cellar; cloudy, golden, fresh-tasting, and not too sparkling.

TROTZENBURGER SPECIAL

LAGER 4.9% ABV
Copper-colored, full-bodied, and dry enough to exude the aroma of fine hops without being too dry.

TROTZENBURGER ORIGINAL

LAGER 4.9% ABV
Amber-colored, with a light bitterness and a malty finish. Very pleasant because of its fine yeast.

DUNKLES HEFEWEIZEN

WHEAT BEER 5.2% ABV
Dark color and a strong taste with clear malt aromas; a very smooth beer with a little sparkle at the beginning.

HELLES HEFEWEIZEN

WHEAT BEER 5.2% ABV
Cloudy yellow, with a refreshing taste of yeast and some sweetness. A sparkling pleasure.

UERIGE ALT

ALTBIER 4.7% ABV
This nearly black beer has lots of bitter aromas. It is full-bodied with a nice roasty aroma and sweet finish.

UERIGE STICKE

BOCK 6% ABV
Tastes heavy but is nevertheless elegant. The black color signifies a large amount of malts and hops, and the taste bears this out.

Blue-aproned beer waiters known as köbes provide drinkers with a steady supply of altbier in the bars of Düsseldorf.

ALTBIER

"Alt" is the German word for old, and it's an apt term for the altbiers of the Rhineland—not because they are aged (they're drunk fresh) but because the "old" top-fermented style dates back to a period before lagered beers swept all before them. Düsseldorf is the home of altbier, although examples are also found in Hanover, Munster, Holland, and the US. A Düsseldorfer alt is clear copper-bronze in colour, with a bright white head. It's a biscuity, gritty beer, closer to British bitter than to lager, but with its rough edges smoothed out by a period of cold maturation.

Diebels and Frankenheim are the big sellers, but a visit to the old town (Altstadt) of the beer's native city reveals a quartet of small brewpubs considered by connoisseurs to be the beating heart of this venerable beer style: Schumacher, Schlüssel, Füchschen, and Uerige. Within these hallowed halls, waiters called köbes, in blue shirts and aprons, weave their way through the crowds, looking for empty glasses to be replenished. With tray in hand, topping up the thirsty (until asked to stop!), and posing for pictures, they take great pride in their profession and deserve their exalted place in the hierarchy of the pub.

SCHUMACHER AND SCHLÜSSEL
Just as with British bitter, there are subtle differences and nuances that distinguish one alt from another. Schumacher Altbier (4.6% ABV) is light amber in color, with a fruity, nutty palate. Schlüssel Altbier (5% ABV) is delicately fragrant on the nose, biscuity, and has a lingering dry finish.

FÜCHSCHEN AND UERIGE
Füchschen Altbier (4.5% ABV) has a biscuity nose with hints of resiny hops in the background. Uerige Altbier (4.5% ABV) is richly malty on the nose, underpinned by the subtle resin of hops; it is fragrant and fruity, with a dry and bitter finish.

BREWERY

UNERTL

Lerchenberger Str. 6, 83527 Haag, Germany
www.unertl.de

This wheat-beer specialist was established at the beginning of the 20th century. Production levels have remained almost constant over the years. However, the increasing popularity of this style, coupled with special bottlings, have given Unertl a rarity value.

UR-KROSTITZER

Brauereistr. 12, 04509 Krostitz, Germany
www.ur-krostitzer.de

A portrait of the 17th-century Swedish King Gustav II Adolf graces the Ur-Krostitzer labels. The story goes that, in 1631, during the Thirty Years' War, the king came to Krostitz, parched by a hot, dry wind. He was given a glass of the town's festival beer to quench his thirst, and declared it excellent. The brand is now part of the Radeberger Group.

WALDSCHLÖSSCHEN

Am Brauhaus 8b, 01099 Dresden, Germany
www.waldschloesschen.de

In 1836 a group of important Dresden citizens met to discuss the foundation of a brewery to produce "beer of Bavarian style." Two years later the plan became reality at a location named Waldschlösschen.

WEIDENEDER

Marktplatz 43, 84367 Tann, Germany
www.weidener.com

Brewing has been a tradition in Tann since the 14th century. The name Weideneder first appeared in the 15th century. The company currently produces 11 different beers and 16 non-alcoholic beverages.

BREWING SECRET The village produces its own malt, and a spring owned by the brewer's family has been supplying the company's water for 100 years.

BEER

UNERTL WEISSBIER BOCK
WHEAT BEER BOCK 6.7% ABV
A dark color for a white bock, but with a strong and pleasant taste. The alcohol is packed within fine malts and hops.

UNERTL WEISSBIER
WHEAT BEER 4.8% ABV
The flagship wheat beer of this brewery is aromatic with yeast and banana notes.

FEINHERBES PILSENER
PILSNER 5% ABV
A brilliant pilsner with a lightly sparkling attitude, a dry aroma of hops, and a very elegant taste.

SCHWARZES
SCHWARZBIER 4.9% ABV
Ur-Krostitzer's Schwarzes is the most famous black beer in the country. It has a fine malty taste and a nice, light, hoppy finish.

ZWICKELBIER
LAGER 5.5% ABV
A golden, cloudy appearance, as the beer is unfiltered. It is full-bodied and pleasant, with an enticing aroma of hops.

WALDSCHLÖSSCHEN DUNKEL
DUNKEL 5.5% ABV
Malty taste. Light, bitter aromas from fine hops at the finish round off a very harmonious beer.

PRIVAT HELL
LAGER 5.1% ABV
A clear golden classic helles beer, full-bodied and mild, with a light aroma of hops and malt.

HELL EXPORT
EXPORT 5.2% ABV
The favorite of the brewery: golden yellow with a smooth, harmonious taste, and a noble bitterness from fine hops.

WEIHENSTEPHAN

Alte Akademie 2, 85354 Freising, Germany
www.brauerei-weihenstephan.de

This brewery is not only the oldest in existence (dating from 725), it is also the most technologically advanced. Weihenstephan is the world's foremost center for brewing technology, and hundreds of master brewers around the world have trained here. Not surprisingly, the beer offerings are of the highest order.

WEILHEIM

Schillerstr. 3, 78604 Rietheim-Weilheim, Germany
www.lammbrauerei-weilheim.de

Beer has been produced on this site for 360 years—it is one of the oldest and smallest breweries in the area, and has been family-owned since 1882. The brewery has been partly renovated, with new cellars.

BREWING SECRET The Storz family describe their product as a naturally matured beer.

WELTENBURG

Klosterbaruerei Weltenburg, Heitzerstr. 2, 93049 Regensburg, Germany
www.weltenburger.de

The Benedictine abbey of Weltenburg houses the oldest abbey brewery in the world, founded in 1050. The location is delightful, close to the scenic Donau-Durchbruch gorge. The abbey's restaurant is famous.

BREWING SECRET Despite its history, the beer is made with the most advanced equipment, but is long-matured.

WERNER

Hauptstr. 13-15, 97490 Poppenhausen, Germany
www.wernerbraeu.de

In 1840 the Werner family acquired this brewery in Poppenhausen. It was one of the first breweries in Bavaria to produce a pilsner beer. By 1991 it was selling 3.5 million gallons (16 million liters) each year and had about 100 employees. In 1999 it was bought by Würzburger Hofbräu.

ORIGINAL
LAGER 5.1% ABV
The mild and pleasant taste is a result of a longer-than-usual period of storage and maturation.

HEFEWEISSBIER DUNKEL
WHEAT BEER 5.3% ABV
This beer is very well balanced. Its dark color is typical of the style, as is the soft, malty, and full-bodied taste.

WEILHEIMER BOCKBIER
BOCK 9% ABV
Gleaming black with a roasty malt aroma and sweet taste.

SCHWARZES WÄLDLE
SCHWARZBIER 5.8% ABV
Amber-colored from its malt, this beer tastes mild, yet fun on the palate.

ASAM BOCK
BOCK 6.9% ABV
A dark mahogany doppelbock. Very pleasant, it tastes slightly sweet with nice malty aromas in the finish.

ANNO 1050
EXPORT 5.5% ABV
The abbey's anniversary beer has a distinctive mix of malt aromas balanced with hops.

WERNER PILS
PILSNER 4.9% ABV
The clear golden color is typical of pilsner; the taste is elegant, with a fine, dry aroma of hops and malt.

WERNER HEFEWEISSE HELL
WHEAT BEER 5.1% ABV
Carbonated, fresh taste; unfiltered and naturally cloudy with a sweet, malty aroma in the finish.

BREWERY

WESTHEIM

Kasseler Str. 7, 34431 Marsberg-Westheim, Germany
www.brauerei-westheim.de

The first Count of Stolberg bought Westheim in 1840. It was enlarged in 1876 by Count Herman, the great-grandfather of the owner today. The company also owns Westheim farm, but has leased it out since 1994.

BREWING SECRET The water for brewing comes from Westheim's own spring.

WISMAR

Kleine Hohe Str. 15, 23966 Wismar, Germany
www.brauhaus-wismar.de

In the early 15th century, there were about 180 breweries registered in Wismar, and the town was well known all over Europe. The Brauhaus Wismar was opened in 1452. Today it is the last brewery remaining in the city and, since 1995, it has brewed beer in the style of the medieval Hanseatic League breweries of northern Europe.

WOLTERS

Hofbrauhaus Wolters, Wolfenbütteler Strasse 39, 38102 Braunschweig, Germany
www.hofbrauhaus-wolters.de

The brewery was founded in 1627 in Braunschweig. Wolters' beers are well known in the region and much further afield. In 2005, InBev, the owner at the time, tried to put the brewery into liquidation, but a group of former CEOs acquired it instead.

ZÖTLER

Grüntenstr. 2, 87549 Rettenberg, Germany
www.zoetler.de

The oldest family-owned brewery in Germany (founded 1447). After a long period under the Müller family, the name Zötler first appeared in 1919; the descendants of the joint families are still in charge.

BREWING SECRET Zötler's Vollmond Bier is brewed only on nights with a full moon.

BEER

GRAF STOLBERG DUNKEL
DUNKEL 4.8% ABV
Has fine malt aromas from dark, roasted malt. Light bitters of hops are very typical of this amber beer.

WILDSCHÜTZ KLOSTERMANN
LAGER 4.8% ABV
Unfiltered and natural cloudy with a fine taste of malt, this beer is smooth with some bitter aromas.

WISMARER MUMME
LAGER 4.8% ABV
An old-fashioned, golden beer with lovely aromas of malt, light hops on the tongue, and a long, sweet finish.

ROTER ERIC
SPECIAL BEER 4.8% ABV
The light red color comes from the malt; the beer is smooth and aromatic, with a sweet finish.

PRINZEN SUD
LAGER 4.9% ABV
Fresh and lightly sparkling, this beer has light bitter aromas of hops and a fine yeast in the finish.

MÄRZEN
EXPORT 5.4% ABV
Full-bodied märzen with a fine, mild aroma of hops. It is very pleasant and has an attractive clear golden-amber color.

ST. STEPHANS BOCK
DOPPELBOCK 7.1% ABV
A strong and noble beer; the roasted barley-malt exudes wonderful aromas.

VOLLMOND BIER
LAGER 5.1% ABV
This beer has a smooth malt aroma and tastes strong, with a light bitterness in the finish.

MORE BEERS OF
GERMANY

In Germany the tradition of regional brewing is still very strong, and communities are justly proud of their local beers. Many such beers are available only on draft and are seldom seen outside of their home towns.

BRUCKMÜLLER

Vilsstr. 4, 92224 Amberg, Germany
www.bruckmueller.de

Beer has been produced by this company for more than 500 years. The story began with the Franziskaner monks in the year 1490, under the name Prewhaus der Parfusser. The Bruckmüller family has continued the tradition since 1803 and is now in its seventh generation. Soft drinks are produced, too.

HERRENHAUSEN

Herrenhäuser Strasse 83-99, Hanover, Germany
www.herrenhaeuser.de

Herrenhäuser Premium Pilsener is sold in pubs and restaurants throughout the region—guests order a "Herry." This is a traditional but forward-thinking company that has been guided through the last 140 years by five generations of one family.

BREWING SECRET "Herry" uses lots of malt and hops, and mineral water.

MAMMUT

Juri-Gagarin-Str. 33, 06526 Sangerhausen, Germany
www.mammut-brauerei.de

Founded in 1877, the brewery was nationalized by the GDR in its 71st year. It was modernized in 1958. More brands have been produced since the reunification in 1990. Today, Mammut is very successful in the region.

BREWING SECRET Partnership with a local malt producer in 1952 has ensured supplies of the highest quality.

MAXIMILIANS

Didierstr. 25, 56112 Lahnstein, Germany
www.maximilians-brauwiesen.de

A relative baby on the German brewing scene, Maximilians is a restaurant and brewery in Lahnstein that opened in 1995. It is housed in a charming, fairytale pink castle overlooking the Rhine.

BREWING SECRET The beer is brewed with top-quality natural ingredients, according to old recipes.

BREWERY

KNAPPENTRUNK
DUNKEL 5.3% ABV
Malty, but not too sweet, with a clear aroma of hops, which is unusual for a dunkel. Full-bodied.

KELLERBIER
LAGER 5.3% ABV
Unfiltered and naturally cloudy. The taste is strong and full-bodied, with aromas of fine malts and a lightly bitter hop finish.

PREMIUM PILSENER
PILSNER 4.9% ABV
Golden, dry, malty, and with the rather strong, bitter pilsner aroma of fine hops.

WEIZENBIER
WHEAT BEER 5.2% ABV
Unfiltered, yellow, and naturally cloudy. There is a bit of sparkle, and the taste is harmonious, pleasantly sweet, and fresh.

MAMMUT GIANT GOLD
LAGER 4.8% ABV
A fairly new brand, less dry than a normal pilsner, but with a full aroma.

MAMMUT BLACK
SCHWARZBIER 4.9% ABV
A traditional style, black-brown in color. Flavorful and fresh, with a light malty finish.

WIESENWEIZEN
WHEAT BEER 5.1% ABV
A huge dose of wheat-malt gives this beer a smooth and mild taste. It is sparkling and refreshing, with light aromas of hops in the finish.

BRAUWIESEN SPEZIEL
LAGER 5.4% ABV
Caramel-sweet, with typical aromas of malt and bitters of hops. Golden-yellow color.

BEER

NAILAER WOHN

Hofer Str. 21, 95119 Naila, Germany
www.wohn-bier.de

Harking back to a brewing license from 1464, the Privat-Brauerei Bürgerbräu Naila Andreas Wohn was so-named in 1928. Modern technical equipment is used, but there are also hand-crafting techniques to keep more than 20 employees busy.

BREWING SECRET The dunkel was inspired by former master brewer Hans Wohn.

REUDNITZER

Mühlstr. 13, 04317 Leipzig, Germany
www.reudnitzer.de

Founded in 1862, Reudnitzer was badly damaged during World War II. The GDR nationalized the company in 1945 and formed a union with other Saxonian breweries. After the Reunification of Germany, Reudnitzer became part of a conglomerate— 2003 was the most successful year in its history.

SCHUMACHER

Brauerei Ferdinand Schumacher, Oststr. 123, 40210 Düsseldorf, Germany
www.brauerei-schumacher.de

Altbier is the classic beer in Düsseldorf, and the Schumacher brewery, founded in 1838, is one of the most famous producers, serving it in its adjoining restaurant.

BREWING SECRET In the 1980s the brewery was completely renovated with the newest technology.

WELDEBRÄU

Brauereistr. 1, 68723 Plankstadt, Germany
www.welde.de

The brewery dates from 1746, but it was not until 1846, when master brewer Heinrich Seitz took over, that the story started to be one of success. The brewery was reconstructed in 1934, and enlarged in the 1980s. Today, Welde is a modern company with a portfolio of interesting beers.

BREWERY

WOHN ALT NAILAER DUNKEL
DUNKEL 4.8% ABV
A dark-brown, light-bodied beer dominated by fine aromas of hops and malt from start to finish.

WOHN BRAUMEISTER ORIGINAL
LAGER 5% ABV
Clear yellow and pleasant, with a fresh taste dominated by fine basics, especially hops in the finish.

PREMIUM PILSENER
PILSNER 5% ABV
A thin-bodied pilsner with a strong note of hops, an enticing aroma, and a fresh flavor.

REUDNITZER HELLER URBOCK
BOCK 6.9% ABV
A dark-golden bock with a hearty taste. It has some sweetness and fine hops in the finish.

SCHUMACHER ALT
ALTBIER 4.6% ABV
A dark beer with a smooth and sweet, roasted malt taste, and a finish accompanied by fine aromas of hops.

SCHUMACHER LATZEN
ALTBIER 5.5% ABV
A bit stronger than the normal altbier; it is aromatic with malt, but sweet as well.

HEFEWEIZEN
WHEAT BEER 4.9% ABV
The beer has both dryness and sweetness. A fine yeast ensures a balance in the taste.

SHWARZE WONNE
SCHWARZBIER 4.8% ABV
This coffee-colored specialty is very full-bodied and rounded, with a nice sparkle on the palate.

BEER

Paulaner, like so many German breweries, was founded by an order of monks. The company now has franchises around the world.

BRITISH ISLES

In world beer terms, the reputation of the British Isles rests on ales that are packed with flavor, yet only moderately strong. The beer culture is still centered on the pub, though there is a growing trend toward drinking bottled beer at home. Draft beer from cask is seen as a cut above bottled beer in terms of quality and flavor, but most pub chains favor Continental-style lagers in preference to British ales. The good news for beer lovers is that craft brewing is on the up, both in terms of the numbers of micros now actively producing and the kinds of beers being sought out and drunk. Pullout boxes appear where a city has more than one brewery.

Edinburgh
Caledonian
Innis & Gunn

Newcastle
Big Lamp
Hadrian & Border
Newcastle Federation
Mordue
Jarrow
Wylam

Sunderland
Darwin
Double Maxim

Belhaven

Traquair

High House

Orkney

Cairngorm

Inveralmond

Harviestoun

Williams

Broughton

Atlas

Fyne Ales

Traditional Scottish Ales

Black Isle

Isle Of Skye

S C O T L A N D

Isle Of Arran

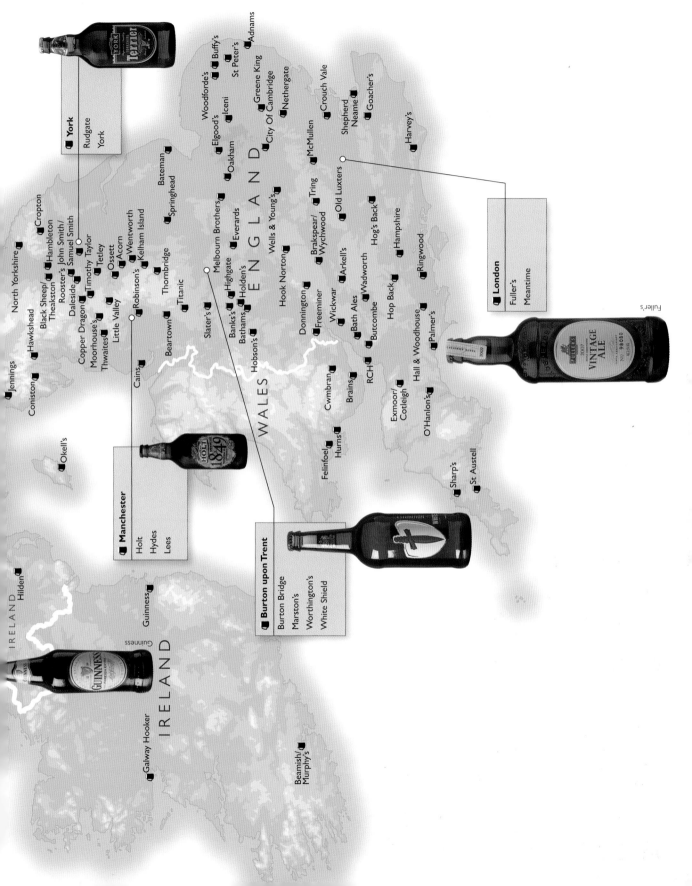

York
Rudgate
York

London
Fuller's
Meantime

Manchester
Holt
Hydes
Lees

Burton upon Trent
Burton Bridge
Marston's
Worthington's
White Shield

IRELAND

Hilden

Guinness

Guinness

IRELAND

Galway Hooker

Beamish/
Murphy's

ENGLAND

WALES

North Yorkshire
Jennings
Coniston
Hawkshead
Black Sheep/
Theakston
Hambleton
Rooster's
Cropton
John Smith/
Samuel Smith
Daleside
Copper Dragon
Moorhouse's
Timothy Taylor
Thwaites
Tetley
Little Valley
Ossett
Acorn
Wentworth
Kelham Island
Okell's
Bateman
Springhead
Thornbridge
Cains
Robinson's
Titanic
Beartown
Slater's
Melbourn Brothers
Banks's
Highgate
Everards
Holden's
Bathams
Hobson's
Wells & Young's
Hook Norton
Donnington
Freeminer
Wickwar
Brakspear/
Wychwood
Tring
McMullen
Old Luxters
Arkell's
Bath Ales
Butcombe
Wadworth
Hop Back
Hall & Woodhouse
Palmer's
Hog's Back
Hampshire
Ringwood
Cwmbran
Brains
RCH
Exmoor/
Cotleigh
O'Hanlon's
Felinfoel
Hurns
Sharp's
St Austell
Woodforde's
Buffy's
St Peter's
Adnams
Elgood's
Iceni
Greene King
City Of Cambridge
Nethergate
Oakham
Crouch Vale
Shepherd
Neame
Goacher's
Harvey's

Fuller's

BREWERY

ACORN

Wombwell, Barnsley,
South Yorkshire, England S73 8HA
www.acornbrewery.net

One of the newer microbreweries in England, Acorn was set up in 2003 and doubled capacity in its first four years. It now produces 40 barrels (6,500 liters) every week.

BREWING SECRET The yeast strain from the 1850s Barnsley Brewery has been reintroduced, coinciding with the company gathering significant awards.

ADNAMS

Southwold, Suffolk, England IP18 6JW
www.adnams.co.uk

Its "Beers from the Coast" have been brewed in the classic English seaside town of Southwold since 1872. In recent years, technological innovation has driven refurbishment, while an emphasis on traditional methods has been studiously maintained. An eco-friendly distribution center—complete with living grass roof—summarizes the dynamic approach.

ARKELL'S

Swindon, Wiltshire, England SN2 7RU
www.arkells.com

John Arkell returned from Ontario, Canada—where he had founded the village of Arkell—to grow barley and to brew beer. The brewery has been owned by family members since its establishment in 1843. The building is Grade II-listed (indicating its historical and cultural importance), and the whole site has been designated an Urban Conservation Area.

ATLAS

Kinlochleven, Argyll, Scotland PH50 4SG
www.atlasbrewery.com

Developed in a former aluminum smelter near Glencoe in the Scottish Highlands, Atlas Brewery completed its conversion with its first brew in 2002. Along with Orkney Brewery, Atlas is now part of Sinclair Breweries Ltd.

BREWING SECRET Direct gas flames heat the copper, a method believed to create sharper beer color and a cleaner flavor "attack."

BEER

BARNSLEY BITTER
BITTER 3.8% ABV
Ripe chestnut in color, with a rounded, rich flavor that lingers in the bitter finish.

BARNSLEY GOLD
STRONG BITTER 4.3% ABV
Beautifully golden, with citrus fruit hop aromas orchestrating the ensemble through to its dry finish.

ADNAMS BROADSIDE
STRONG BITTER 4.7% ABV
Rich, fruitcake aromas dominate initially, giving way to an elegant hop and malt association.

ADNAMS BITTER
BITTER 3.7% ABV
Aromatic hop and biscuit malt fragrances introduce a lingering, dry, and refreshingly bitter flavor.

KINGSDOWN SPECIAL ALE
BEST BITTER 5% ABV
Ripe fruit nose and typical Arkell's hoppiness form a malt and bitter-sweet experience.

ARKELL'S 3B
BITTER 4% ABV
Sweetly scented malt perceptible beneath a distinct hoppy aroma. Delicate, well-balanced nutty flavor.

THREE SISTERS
SPECIAL BITTER 4.2% ABV
Complex, dark, yet refreshing, with dried and fresh fruit balancing toasted barley and liquorice.

LATITUDE CASK PILSNER
PILSNER 3.6% ABV
Straw colored, dominated by crisp citrus hop characteristics. Polled within the world's top 50 beers.

BEST-KNOWN BEERS IN THE BRITISH ISLES

In the multilayered global business that is vast-volume brewing, the Molson Coors Brewing Company owns several British Isles' brands.

Among the well-known brands now owned by Molson Coors are: Worthington, Caffrey's, and Carling, which produces the British Isles' biggest-selling lager. In the high-volume market, huge emphasis and budgets are concentrated on sports sponsorship and promoting chilled beers, served through advanced "extra cold" and "extra fast" bar technology. The global giant Carlsberg is a big player too, and has production plants in Northampton—for its own lagers, such as Carlsberg Export—and Leeds, where it brews the Tetley range of beers. Tetley has been fully owned by Carlsberg since 1998. Britain's largest brewer, Scottish & Newcastle—which produces brands such as Newcastle Brown Ale, John Smith's (the British Isles' biggest-selling bitter), and international brands such as Fosters and Kronenbourg—finally lost its independence in 2008, when it was bought out in a Carlsberg/Heineken joint venture. Closure of its Reading plant by 2010 had already been announced, leaving three UK sites: Newcastle Federation; John Smith's in Tadcaster; and Royal in Manchester; it also retains a small stake in Edinburgh-based Caledonian.

CARLING (LAGER 4.1% ABV) left
NEWCASTLE BROWN
  (BROWN ALE 4.7% ABV) center
JOHN SMITH'S (BITTER 3.8% ABV) right

BANKS'S
Wolverhampton, West Midlands, England WV1 4NY
www.bankssbeer.co.uk

The brewery, built in 1875, occupies a traditional, handsome site in the center of Wolverhampton and has been part of the Marston's Beer Company (formerly Wolverhampton & Dudley) since 2007. More than 50 million pints (24 million liters) are brewed every year. Innovative marketing initiatives include a campaign to protect local dialects from extinction.

BATEMAN
Wainfleet, Lincolnshire, England PE24 4JE
www.bateman.co.uk

One of the country's oldest and most picturesque family breweries—with a windmill towering high above—it has a well-deserved reputation for "good honest ales." A family split almost destroyed the business in the 1980s, but it survived, blossomed, and has developed a new brewhouse and engaging visitor center.

BATH ALES
Warmley, Bristol, England BS30 8XN
www.bathales.com

The founders' brewing backgrounds and insistence on traditional methods operating alongside cutting-edge technology has resulted in Bath Ale's reputation for distinctive, characterful, and flavorsome ales. The success of the business has led to the brewery twice outgrowing its premises since it was established in 1995. A bottling plant and shop continue the growth.

BANKS'S ORIGINAL
BITTER 3.5% ABV
Well-balanced session bitter, full-bodied and malty, with traces of fruit in the flavor.

BANKS'S BITTER
BITTER 3.8% ABV
Full-flavored, with winey, fruit overtones and a malt and hop influence on the palate.

XXXB
STRONG BITTER 4.8% ABV
Classic russet-tan ale, with a well constructed blend of malt, hops, and fruitiness.

XB BITTER
BITTER 3.7% ABV
Finely balanced, with an apple-influenced hop aroma that lingers alongside the malty flavor.

GEM BITTER
BEST BITTER 4.1% ABV
Rich and full-textured, with a malt, fruit, and bitter-sweet hop quality throughout.

SPECIAL PALE ALE (SPA)
PALE ALE 3.7% ABV
A prominent hop aroma and bitter malty touch complement its light-bodied character.

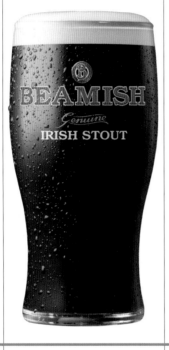

BREWERY

BATHAMS

Brierley Hill, West Midlands,
England DY5 2TN
www.bathams.com

The brewery's frontage—actually the
Vine Inn—is emblazoned with a
quotation from Shakespeare's *Two
Gentlemen of Verona*: "Blessing of you:
You brew good ale." Five generations of
the Batham family have been involved
since the brewery was established in
1877, each nurturing its reputation
for classic Black Country mild ales.

BEAMISH

Cork, Co Cork, Ireland
www.beamish.ie

Originating in 1792 near the medieval
city gates and close to the prison
where the severed heads of executed
criminals used to be put on display,
Beamish is believed to be Ireland's
oldest porter brewery. The brewery
has passed through several
international hands over the years, and
the incumbent, Scottish & Newcastle,
is itself now in foreign ownership.

BEARTOWN

Congleton, Cheshire, England CW12 3RH
www.beartownbrewery.co.uk

Bear baiting was a popular pastime in
Elizabethan Congleton, where the
senior public offices were Mayor,
Aletaster, and Bear Warden. A
traditional song suggests the town
even sold a rare bible in order to pay
for a more aggressive combatant. The
town's brewery today was founded in
1994 and supports charities such as
Asian bear rescue centers.

BELHAVEN

Dunbar, East Lothian,
Scotland EH42 1RS
www.belhaven.co.uk

Records show that 14th-century
Benedictine monks brewed in the
coastal town, and water is still drawn
from the wells they sunk. Austrian
Emperor Francis I favored Belhaven
beers, referring to them in 1827
as "the burgundy of Scotland."
The brewery lost its independence in
2005, when taken over by Greene King.

BEER

BATHAMS BEST BITTER

BEST BITTER 4.5% ABV
Straw-colored ale, with an initial
sweetness, soon overtaken by a
complex, dry, hoppy flavor.

BATHAMS MILD ALE

MILD 3.5% ABV
A fruity, dark brown mild; sweet
and well-balanced, with a hoppy
fruit finish.

BEAMISH IRISH STOUT

STOUT 4.1% ABV
Delicate hop character, chocolate
notes, and relative paleness possibly
places it closer to a porter.

BEAMISH RED ALE

IRISH RED ALE 4.2% ABV
Distinctly red-hued, malt-accented,
and rounded, with soft, sweet fruit
flavors on the palate.

KODIAK GOLD

BITTER 4% ABV
A straw-colored quencher, with a
citrus fruit nose, some biscuit malt
on the palate, and a sharp bitterness.

BLACK BEAR

MILD 5% ABV
A strong, mild ale, dark ruby in
color, with a subtle roast malt
profile rising to a sweet finish.

ST. ANDREWS ALE

STRONG BITTER 4.9% ABV
Alternating in flavor between
roasted malt, caramel, and tart
fruit, with spicy hop aromas.

BELHAVEN 80 SHILLING ALE

SCOTTISH HEAVY 4.2% ABV
Classical Scottish "heavy" with huge
malt profile then some hop and
fruit flavors emerging.

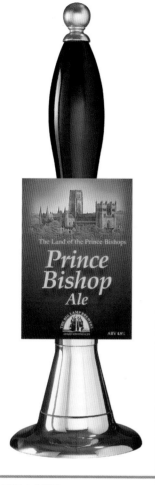

BIG LAMP

Newburn, Newcastle upon Tyne,
England NE15 8NL
www.biglampbrewers.co.uk

Northeast England's oldest
microbrewery was established in
1982. It relocated in 1997 to a listed
Victorian water-pumping station near
the Tyne Riverside Country Park.
There, a popular on-site pub and
restaurant, The Keelman, along with
accommodation in Keelman Lodge,
have won it prestigious tourism awards.

BLACK ISLE

Munlochy, Ross-shire, Scotland IV8 8NZ
www.blackislebrewery.com

The mission of this small independent
operation, which lies in the heart of
the Scottish Highlands, is to produce
a range of top-quality organic beers,
packaged in recycled materials. No
artificial fertilizers or herbicides are
applied to the hops and barley it uses.

BREWING SECRET The beers are bottle-
conditioned, and so undergo a second
fermentation in the bottle.

BLACK SHEEP

Masham, North Yorkshire,
England HG4 4EN
www.blacksheepbrewery.com

The Theakston family has brewed in
Masham, North Yorkshire, for six
generations, but a loss of independence
led to Paul Theakston stepping aside.
Far from leaving brewing though, he
then established Black Sheep in a
former maltings sitting high above the
Ure River. Since 1992, and through
one of the most challenging periods of

British brewing history, Black Sheep
has enjoyed continuous growth,
physically and in reputation, resulting
in a £5m doubling of capacity in 2006
and the installation of an extra
brewhouse, new fermenting vessels,
conditioning tanks, and a cask racking
plant. A magnificent visitor center and
bistro are important attractions too.

BREWING SECRET Generous amounts of
Goldings hops are essential to the
Black Sheep character.

PRINCE BISHOP ALE
STRONG BITTER 4.8% ABV
An easy-drinking, golden bitter
with a full, fruity hop aroma and
a spicy bitterness.

SUMMERHILL STOUT
STOUT 4.4% ABV
A savory, dark stout with a
roasted malt nature and malty,
long-lasting piquancy.

YELLOWHAMMER IPA
INDIA PALE ALE 4% ABV
A pale golden-colored hoppy bitter
with a sharp grapefruit aroma and
refreshing yeasty finish.

ORGANIC BLONDE
PREMIUM LAGER 4.5% ABV
A premium, continental-style lager
beer with a light biscuit palate, and
fresh grassy aroma.

BLACK SHEEP ALE
BITTER 4.4% ABV
Full-flavored, with a rich, fruity
aroma, bitter-sweet malty taste,
and long, dry finish.

BEST BITTER
BEST BITTER 3.8% ABV
This best-seller is well hopped, light
golden in color, with a distinctive
dry, refreshing tang.

RIGGWELTER
PREMIUM BITTER 5.9% ABV
A strong, complex, fruity bitter,
with dashes of pear drops and
hints of liquorice.

EMMERDALE ALE
BITTER 5% ABV
Fruity Goldings hops and Maris
Otter barley progress to a long,
dry, and bitter finish.

BREWERY

BRAINS

Crawshay Street, Cardiff,
Glamorgan, Wales CF10 1SP
www.sabrain.com

A major force in regional brewing, Brains is tremendously proud of its Welsh heritage. Ales are produced in a traditional fashion at the company's landmark Cardiff Brewery, to which it was relocated in 2000 from the nearby Old Brewery, where the famous "pint of Brains" had been produced for more than 100 years.

BRAKSPREAR

Witney, Oxfordshire,
England OX28 4DP
www.brakspear.co.uk

The long-established Brakspear Brewery closed its Henley operation in 2002, but the production of its beers was taken on by Wychwood Brewery.
BREWING SECRET Wychwood uses Brakspear's original equipment to brew these beers, including the unique "double drop" wooden fermenting vessels, and its complex yeast strain.

BROUGHTON

Broughton, Biggar, Peeblesshire,
Scotland ML12 6HQ
www.broughtonales.co.uk

A small, independent brewery situated in the Scottish Borders, Broughton draws heavily on local history and legend for its full range of styles. Production includes 18 cask ales, 11 different bottled beers for the domestic and export markets, two own-label beers for selected supermarkets, and one keg beer.

BUFFY'S

Tivetshall St Mary, Norwich,
Norfolk, England NR15 2DO
www.buffys.co.uk

A 15th-century residence, a home-brewing insurance executive, and a beer-loving piano tuner combined to establish this dynamic enterprise in 1993, when Roger and Julie Abrahams first brewed in outbuildings at Mardle Hall. Various upgradings and expansion have followed, along with local and national awards for their beer.

BEER

BRAINS SA GOLD
BEST BITTER 4.2% ABV
Its spirit aroma blends gentle malt and spiced hop with malt-rich and fruit flavors.

BRAINS BITTER
BITTER 3.7% ABV
Rich amber color, with subtle malt and crisp hop aromas. Well balanced, with some bitterness.

BRAKSPEAR BITTER
BITTER 3.4% ABV
An initial malt and well-hopped bitterness develops into a bitter-sweet and fruity finish.

BRAKSPEAR SPECIAL
STRONG BITTER 4.3% ABV
Full-bodied, with a hint of sweetness and dry hop bitterness before finishing citrus-fruity.

GREENMANTLE ALE
BITTER 3.9% ABV
Dark copper colored, with a rich fruit and bitter-sweet encounter, and hop-bitter finale.

BLACK DOUGLAS
PREMIUM BITTER 5.2% ABV
Dark ruby-red with a rich, full-bodied maltiness and overtones of preserved fruit.

NORWICH TERRIER
BITTER 3.6% ABV
A pale, refreshing ale, with a sturdy body and solid bite—just like the dog after which it is named!

BUFFY'S BITTER
BITTER 3.9% ABV
Best-seller, with a distinct, hoppy nose and traces of roast malt on the palate.

BURTON BRIDGE

Burton upon Trent, Staffordshire, England DE14 1SY
www.burtonbridgebrewery.co.uk

In 1984, a brewery engineer and a technical manager put one and one together to make two—pub and brewhouse. Equipment was sourced from other breweries and a local farmyard, as well as parts that were found languishing in an old garage. As for the pub seating, that was salvaged from a Methodist church.

BUTCOMBE

Wrington, Somerset, England BS40 5PA
www.butcombe.com

The philosophy here is simple: "Beer is a natural product, let's keep it that way." This much-expanded brewery—established in farm buildings in 1978—now produces almost seven million pints annually from its four brands, none of which contains added sugars, colorings, or preservatives. The brewery also operates 15 pubs.

CAINS

Stanhope Street, Liverpool, England L8 5XJ
www.cains.co.uk

The red-brick Victorian building may date to 1850, but under the innovative stewardship of the Dusanj brothers—the first Southeast Asian family to run a British brewery—this is no time-capsule operation. Cains is one of the fastest-growing British breweries, with a £30m turnover, 150 employees, and more than 120 million pints brewed annually.

CAIRNGORM

Aviemore, Highlands, Scotland PH22 1ST
www.cairngormbrewery.com

Scotland's most dramatic scenery forms the backdrop to the brewery, which was established in 2001 within the Cairngorms National Park. Its portfolio of 18 beers has attracted numerous industry awards.

BREWING SECRET Cairngorm makes innovative use of local ingredients, such as the emblematic thistle, which is added for bitterness.

GOLDEN DELICIOUS
BITTER 3.8% ABV
Originally a summer special, this delicately-hopped bitter is evenly tempered, dry, and lingering.

XL BITTER
BEST BITTER 4% ABV
Malty-nosed, enveloped in fruity hops, with a hint of chocolate caramel and an astringent finish.

BUTCOMBE BLOND
BITTER 4.3% ABV
Light and fruity, with a medium bitter finish. Slovenian and Saaz hops create a floral sweetness.

BUTCOMBE BITTER
BITTER 4% ABV
Noticeably bitter, with a citrus hop, slight sulfurous nose; light fruit notes and dry finish.

CAINS WHEAT BEER
WHEAT BEER 4% ABV
Organically-produced, with aromas of banana and vanilla, unripe fruit flavors, and a touch of spiced hop.

CAINS FINEST BITTER
BITTER 4% ABV
A full-bodied yet refreshing bitter, with rich malt flavors and earthy, farmlike aromas.

TRADE WINDS
WHEAT BEER 4.3% ABV
Multi-award winning golden wheat beer, with intense hop and elderflower aromas and fruity palate.

BLACK GOLD
STOUT 4.4% ABV
Silky-bodied, award-winning stout, with subtle bitterness, roast barley assurance, and late sweetness.

ALL ABOUT ...

HOPS

If malt is traditionally known as the soul of beer, charged with the duty of providing color, sweetness, and, last but not least, sugars on which yeast will feast to produce alcohol and CO_2, then hops provide the razzamatazz—the rich, spicy, floral notes that give so much character and pizzazz to beer. Think of a glass of British bitter, with its tangy, fruity, counterpoint to the sweetness of the malt—that's the work of the hops. Even with a glass of delicately hopped golden ale, hops are providing a gentle, breezy hint of summer blossom, while the hop's forthright character is right to the front of a pungent and well-hopped IPA. As well as yielding aroma and bitterness, hops also have preservative qualities, helping to keep beer fresh for longer.

In the British Isles, hopped beer was initially seen as fit only for foreigners such as Flemish merchants. Ironically, it was the latter group who brought their favorite hopped beer over the Channel in the 1400s. It found favor with the locals and, by the late 16th century, it was in the ascendancy.

BEFORE HOPS Prior to hops becoming the common currency of brewing, people drank ale— a strong brew of fermented malted barley flavored with spices and herbs. The Williams Brothers' Alba Scots Pine Ale is a rare example today of an ale brewed without hops, but with pine needles instead.

CULTIVATION Seen in their natural state, hops grow in what looks like a vineyard, with the plants draping themselves downward from 18-ft (6-m) high lines, the bright green hop cones hanging like fruit.

FORM Fresh hops are pale green in color. For use in the brewery, hops come in various guises, including dried cones and small pellets. Occcasionally, hop oil is used to infuse the brew.

DRYING

In England, hops are traditionally grown in Kent, Herefordshire, and Worcestershire, and September's harvest finds the hop yards heavy with the scent of picked hops on their way to the dryer. Drying used to be carried out in oast houses, and those still standing bear witness to the industry of the past. Hops would have been dried in a kiln known as an oast; typically this would have been housed in a building with a conical roof for drawing out the humid air.

VARIETIES If names such as Pinot Noir and Syrah have lovers of the grape cooing with pleasure, then those in the world of beer lick their lips in anticipation at the mention of hop varieties such as Goldings, Fuggles, Cascade, First Gold, and Saaz. The hop is truly a noble creature.

TIMING Bittering hops are added to the wort at the start of the boil, while the more delicate aromatic hops are thrown into the kettle during the middle and end of the boil. The skill of the brewer is to add the right hops at the right time.

CZECH HOPS The Žatec region in Bohemia and the Yakima Valley in Washington in the US are home to notable hop fields. The Yakima Valley used to be dominated by Cluster hops, but today many varieties are grown, including the Saaz or Žatec hops. The Czech town of Žatec gives its name to a region that produces highly prized aromatic hops, the flowery bouquet of which can be found in many great pilsners.

BREWERY

CALEDONIAN

42 Slateford Road, Edinburgh,
Scotland EH11 1PH
www.caledonian-brewery.co.uk

The Caledonian attitude to brewing beer is similar to that of drinking it—the longer you've been doing it, the more quality you demand. It is the sole survivor of some 40 breweries that once resided in Edinburgh.

BREWING SECRET Caledonian is one of the last breweries to use traditional direct-fired coppers to boil the wort.

CAMERONS

Hartlepool, County Durham,
England TS24 7QS
www.cameronsbrewery.co.uk

Camerons has been brewing under various ownerships since 1865. Its brewing hall is remarkable, with magnificent Italian marble walls and fine wrought-iron detailing, while the water is drawn from its own well.

BREWING SECRET A microbrewery for cask ale experimentation and short runs also operates at the site.

CITY OF CAMBRIDGE

Chittering, Cambridge,
England CB5 9PH
www.cambridge-brewery.co.uk

An environmentally conscious brewery, City of Cambridge was set up in 1997 and relocated three years later due to the popularity of its beers. An innovative system copes with brewery waste by filtering out pollutants through a series of reed beds, marsh plants, and ponds. Awards for beer quality and conservation have followed.

CONISTON

Coniston, Cumbria,
England LA21 8HL
www.conistonbrewery.com

The brewery was set up in 1995 behind a 400-year-old coaching inn, residents of which have included artist JMW Turner, poet Samuel Taylor Coleridge, and Donald Campbell. Campbell's ill-fated attempt on the world water speed record on Coniston Water in 1967 is commemorated by the brewery's flagship beer, Bluebird.

BEER

CALEDONIAN 80 SHILLING
SCOTTISH HEAVY 4.2% ABV
Russett-brown and typically malt-led, with an underlay of raspberry and a suggestion of chocolate.

DEUCHARS IPA
INDIA PALE ALE 3.8% ABV
A strident hop aroma, with citrus notes and a degree of maltiness that never wavers.

STRONGARM
STRONG BITTER 4.7% ABV
Well-rounded ruby red ale, with a malt and hop balance, developing a fruity flavor.

NIMMO'S XXXX
BITTER 4.4% ABV
A light golden beer, with a well-weighted malt and hop character and lingering aftertaste.

HOBSON'S CHOICE
BITTER 4.1% ABV
A light golden ale; distinctly hoppy on the nose, and in the refreshingly bitter finish.

BOATHOUSE BITTER
BITTER 3.8% ABV
A rich, chocolatey nose is underpinned by citrus hoppiness and a malt and fruit flavor.

BLUEBIRD BITTER
BITTER 3.6% ABV
Its single varietal hop (Challenger) creates an inviting aroma and influences a light, clean palate.

OLD MAN ALE
BEST BITTER 4.2% ABV
Exuberant in its aroma of fruit, coatings of roasted chocolate malt, and tart hoppiness.

COPPER DRAGON

Skipton, North Yorkshire,
England BD23 2QR
www.copperdragon.uk.com

Two years studying the UK brewing industry preceded the formation of Copper Dragon at the former Skipton Brewery in 2002. A new German-style, steam-powered brewhouse was soon needed, and continued growth has demanded another expansion in 2008, with the commissioning of a 60-barrel (9,800-liter) operation.

COTLEIGH

Wiveliscombe, Somerset,
England TA4 2RE
www.cotleighbrewery.co.uk

Life for Cotleigh began in 1979 in a farmhouse stable block, and the business has changed hands twice since. Each owner has built upon its previous successes and expanded the operation to meet demand.

BREWING SECRET The New Harvest Ale is brewed with Herefordshire hops just a day after picking.

CROPTON

Cropton, North Yorkshire,
England YO18 8HH
www.croptonbrewery.com

Brewing started in 1984, and a purpose-built plant was installed 10 years later, before being greatly expanded in 2006 in order to produce 100 barrels (16,000 liters) a week. Virtually all beers are available bottle-conditioned, all are additive-free, approved by the Vegetarian Society, and are suitable for vegans to boot.

CROUCH VALE

South Woodham Ferrers, Essex,
England CM3 5ZA
www.crouch-vale.co.uk

Crouch Vale is one of the great microbrewing success stories of recent years. The small, independent company has twice won the ultimate cask beer accolade: the Campaign For Real Ale Supreme Champion Beer of Britain (2005 and 2006) for its Brewers Gold. Needless to say, the brewery has expanded into a new site since.

GOLDEN PIPPIN
BITTER 3.9% ABV
Light, refreshing, and blonde, with citrus fruit flavors appealing to ale and lager drinkers alike.

BEST BITTER
BEST BITTER 3.8% ABV
An amber-colored, well-balanced, malty, and hoppy session ale, brewed for the northern palate.

TAWNY OWL PREMIUM BITTER
BEST BITTER 3.8% ABV
Well-balanced, light copper colored, with a subtle hop palate and sweet malt flavor.

BARN OWL PREMIUM ALE
BEST BITTER 4.5% ABV
Dark copper, with hints of toffee and nut that swoop to a smooth, malty, bittersweet finish.

TWO PINTS BITTER
BITTER 4% ABV
A crafty balance of hop flavors, caramel sweetness, and malty aftertaste creates a classic bitter.

MONKMAN'S SLAUGHTER
PREMIUM BITTER 6% ABV
Full-bodied, with distinct malty, chocolate, caramel, and autumn fruit flavors; subtle hoppy bitterness.

BREWERS GOLD
BITTER 4% ABV
Pale, refreshing, and perfumily hoppy, with aromas of sweet, tropical fruits and a bitter finish.

ESSEX BOYS BITTER
BITTER 3.5% ABV
Pale brown, with noticeable malt and citrus hops on the nose and a dry finish.

BREWERY

CWMBRAN

Upper Cwmbran, Torfaen,
Wales NP44 5AS
www.cwmbranbrewery.co.uk

A mountain spring in Gwent's Eastern Valley supplies the brewery, where the original concept was to first establish a single beer—a local ale for local people—before going on to produce a range of beers in the long term. A solid customer base has built up, and bottled beers are now stocked by selected supermarkets.

DALESIDE

Harrogate, North Yorkshire,
England HG1 4PT
www.dalesidebrewery.co.uk

The Victorian spa town of Harrogate is renowned for its restorative waters, so it is no surprise to discover an impressive range of beers brewed there. Heritage-rich recipes have been revived, with a philosophy that demands the highest quality of raw ingredients are allied to the latest methods of production.

DARWIN

Sunderland, Tyne & Wear,
England SR1 2QE
www.darwinbrewery.com

The Darwin set-up is unique in that its commercial operation is complemented by a test brew plant based at the University of Sunderland. There, students on the Brewlab brewing sciences course are able to trial some 40 new beers each year. The best of them are then produced at the award-winning site.

DONNINGTON

Stow-on-the-Wold, Gloucestershire,
England GL54 1EP

Thomas Arkell bought an idyllic 13th-century watermill in 1827, and brewing began on the premises in 1865. The mill passed through direct descendants of Thomas to the redoubtable Claude Arkell, who died in 2007. His cousins took up the challenge to continue and develop the brewery, which still uses the waterwheel for some of its power.

BEER

CROW VALLEY BITTER
BITTER 4.2% ABV
Gentle hop and malt aromas are followed by nicely countered malt, hop, and fruit infusions.

DRAYMAN'S CHOICE
MILD 3.8% ABV
Latent fruit and hop influences are present throughout the malty bittersweetness of this mild ale.

DALESIDE BLONDE
BITTER 3.9% ABV
Distinctively hoppy, with sherbet and citrus flavors culminating in a bitter, but short, finish.

OLD LEG OVER
BITTER 4.1% ABV
An admirable balance of nut and fruit on the palate, and a suggestion of herbs in the aroma.

EVOLUTION ALE
BITTER 4% ABV
Light, clean, and satisfying, with a dry, hoppy character and layers of malt throughout.

GHOST ALE
BITTER 4.1% ABV
Golden and richly hopped, with citrus aromas dominating, followed by a well-balanced fruit piquancy.

DOUBLE DONN
BEST BITTER 4.4% ABV
Dark, well-balanced bitter with a fruit and malt dalliance and dry, malt-hinted finish.

DONNINGTON XXX
BITTER 3.6% ABV
Subtle in profile, but some hop, chocolate, and liquorice appear before a noticeably malty finish.

DOUBLE MAXIM

Hughton-le-Spring,
Sunderland, England
www.dmbc.org.uk

After several years contracting out
the company's eponymous beer, a new
brewery was opened in 2007 to cope
with demand. Bottling facilities are
planned for the near future.

BREWING SECRET Double Maxim uses an
original Vaux Brewery recipe, which
head brewer Jim Murray used when
he worked at Vaux in 1968.

DURHAM BREWERY

Unit 5a, Bowburn North Industrial
Estate, Bowburn, County Durham,
England DH6 5PF
www.durham-brewery.co.uk

A home-brewing hobby evolved into a
business in 1994, when two former
music teachers faced redundancy.
Award after award has followed,
principally through attention to detail
and the production of beers that wring
expressive flavors and aromas out of
every ingredient. Beer names celebrate
Durham's ecclesiastical culture.

ELGOOD'S

Wisbech, Cambridgeshire,
England PE13 1LN
www.elgoods-brewery.co.uk

The Georgian facade of this 1795
brewery may speak of its history, but
significant technical advances lie
behind, and Elgood's is now one of the
UK's most progressive producers. The
fifth generation of the Elgood family
does, however, incorporate traditional
values and time-honored methods
into its forward-looking approach.

EVERARDS

Castle Acres, Narborough,
Leicestershire, England LE19 1BY
www.everards.co.uk

After brewing his first pint in 1849,
William Everard stated his intention,
and one that the fifth-generation family
is proud to uphold: "No effort shall
be found wanting in the production
and supply of genuine ale of first-rate
quality." Integrity remains king today.

BREWING SECRET Fuggles and Goldings
are the key hops here.

DOUBLE MAXIM
BROWN ALE 4.7% ABV
Caramel in the aroma; continues
through bittersweet flavors, then
expands into toffee notes.

SAMSON
BEST BITTER 4.6% ABV
A dependable northeast English
bitter, with a whiff of hop and a
malt-infused body.

EVENSONG
STRONG BITTER 5% ABV
A 1937 recipe. The deep ruby color
unveils luscious toffee notes and a
generous hop bitterness.

MAGUS
BITTER 3.8% ABV
A pale session best-seller, with
aromatically complex continental
lager qualities and citrus undertones.

BLACK DOG
MILD 3.6% ABV
Well-balanced mild, with a roasted
malt integrity, reinforced by a
single hop variety.

GREYHOUND STRONG BITTER
STRONG BITTER 5.2% ABV
Raisin characteristics coerced from
dark sugars and roasted malt
contrast aromatic leafy English hops.

TIGER
BITTER 4.2% ABV
Some spicy hop and caramel on the
nose. Classically bittersweet palate,
with a rounded toffeeness.

ORIGINAL
STRONG BITTER 5.2% ABV
Copper-hued, full-bodied, and a
toasted caramel aroma beckoning
port wine and fruit flavors.

BREWERY

EXMOOR

Wiveliscombe, Somerset,
England TA4 2NY
www.exmoorales.co.uk

Exmoor was among the first wave of microbreweries in the early 1980s. Its fundamentals have never altered from a reliance on skills, investment in innovation, and adherence to the principles of small-batch brewing. Being Somerset's largest brewery positions it as a regional producer, and the potential of its backbone brands is still to be fully capitalized upon.

FELINFOEL

Lanelli, Carmarthenshire,
Wales SA14 8LB
www.felinfoel-brewery.com

Sitting astride the Liedi River and leaning heavily on the industrial traditions of south Wales—and its workers' thirsts—Felinfoel Brewery has been in existence since 1878. It is famed for producing Britain's first canned beer in 1935. Extensive modernization came in the 1970s, but Felinfoel is still family-owned.

FREEMINER

Cinderford, Gloucestershire,
England GL14 3JA
www.freeminer.com

Anyone born in the Forest of Dean who has worked in a coal mine for a year and a day may open his own mine. Few such mines remain, but Freeminer celebrates this heritage with its ales.

BREWING SECRET Freeminer ales are made from traditional malt varieties and whole Worcestershire hops in open-topped fermenters.

FULLER'S

Chiswick Lane South, London,
England W4 2QB
www.fullers.co.uk

London's last remaining traditional family brewer, Fuller's has been based at the historic Griffin Brewery near the Thames River in Chiswick since 1845. Brewing on the site, however, goes back 350 years. Despite its global prominence, Fuller's retains a small company spirit and formidably energetic outlook. Its beers, among

BEER

EXMOOR GOLD
BITTER 4.5% ABV
Powerful earthy hop, lemon, and juicy malt aromas; fruity, butterscotch sweetness, and memorable finish.

EXMOOR ALE
BITTER 3.8% ABV
Medium-bodied, with some malt and hop in the aroma and bitter hop aftertaste.

DOUBLE DRAGON
BITTER 4.2% ABV
Invitingly rich in color, malty and subtly hopped, with an evenly balanced, full-drinking nature.

CAMBRIAN BITTER
BITTER 3.9% ABV
Labeled "a good, honest Welsh bitter," the bitter is full-flavored, with balanced malt and hop aromas.

SPECULATION
STRONG BITTER 4.8% ABV
An initial chocolate sweetness is replaced by a hoppy rush and rich malt flavor layer.

FREEMINER BITTER
STRONG BITTER 4.8% ABV
Distinctly bitter and abundantly hoppy, balanced by a malt character that denotes "no-nonsense" beer.

LONDON PRIDE
BITTER 4.1% ABV
A fruity sweet malt nose and a floral spiced hop presence with marmalade undercurrents.

ESB
EXTRA STRONG BITTER 5.5% ABV
Complex aromas, with the house-style orange fruit complementing tangy hops and roasted malt.

the country's most consistent, have received countless awards, notably the Campaign For Real Ale Champion Beer of Britain, which it has won five times. Although firmly at the forefront of British ale production, Fuller's remains resolutely true to traditional brewing techniques. The company bought Hampshire brewer George Gale in 2005, and its beers are now brewed at Chiswick.

FYNE ALES

Cairndow, Argyll, Scotland PA268BJ
www.fyneales.com

Given that this brewery was set up in a redundant milking parlor as recently as 2001, it seems all the more remarkable that Fyne Ales has already begun winning national brewing awards.

BREWING SECRET Soft water from a burn tumbling into Loch Fyne in the Scottish Highlands is integral to the character and success of Fyne Ales.

GALWAY HOOKER

Roscommon Town, Galway, Ireland
www.galwayhooker.ie

Launched in 2006, Galway Hooker is brewed by two proud "hopoholics" who believe in the joy and variety of experimentation. An online beer-naming competition came up with the Galway Hooker name, which refers to a traditional West Irish sailboat. The philosophy is that beer is like any quality foodstuff—the fresher and less processed, the better.

GOACHER'S

Maidstone, Kent,
England ME15 6TA
www.goachers.com

The plant was purpose-built in 1983 and revived the art of brewing in Maidstone after an 11-year hiatus. It is constructed along classic lines, with full-mash brewing and open fermenters in stainless-steel vessels.

BREWING SECRET Whole Kentish hops and 100 percent malted barley produce ales with a distinct character.

VINTAGE ALE
BARLEY WINE 8.5% ABV (VARIABLE)
Annually produced using different malt and hop varieties. Each vintage is different, all are intriguing.

CHISWICK BITTER
BITTER 3.5% ABV
A fresh citrus hop nature with a touch of malt sweetness on the palate. Pleasingly dry finish.

MAVERICK
BEST BITTER 4.2% ABV
Mahogany colored and fully robust, with warm roasted malt flavors and fruity hop aromas.

HIGHLANDER
SCOTTISH HEAVY 4.8% ABV
A strong traditional Scottish-style ale, with intense malt properties and a citrus hop aroma.

GALWAY HOOKER IRISH PALE ALE
PALE ALE 4.4% ABV
Balanced tangy bitterness and understated biscuit flavors complement a floral aroma and citrus dry finish.

BEST DARK ALE
BEST BITTER 4.1% ABV
The original Goacher's derives its complex, full-bodied nature from a bittersweet malty infusion.

FINE LIGHT ALE
BITTER 3.7% ABV
A consistent and rewarding floral hop tang and moderate malt palate from aroma to aftertaste.

BREWERY

GREENE KING

Bury St. Edmunds, Suffolk,
England IP33 1QT
www.greeneking.co.uk

After more than 200 years, Greene King has developed into a formidable and dynamic force in the highly competitive British brewing industry. All beers are brewed at Bury St. Edmunds, where ale has featured since the 11th century. Benjamin Greene opened his brewery in 1799 and it merged with the rival King

Brewery in 1887. The company has in recent years acquired several of its competitors—namely, Morland, Ruddles, Ridley's, and Hardy & Hanson —and closed them amid some controversy. Belhaven of Dunbar was another recent acquisition, it being bought up in 2005.

BREWING SECRET Greene King's flagship Abbot Ale spends "two sabbaths" under fermentation, as master brewers' ideal practices demand.

GUINNESS

St. James's Gate, Dublin 8, Ireland
www.guinness.com

When you can make a virtue out of the time it takes to pour a pint— 119.5 seconds to be precise—you know you have no ordinary beer in your hands. Guinness defines stout, Ireland, and Irishness, but it is also inextricably linked with innovation in physics, chemistry, packaging, and advertising. The St. James's Gate Brewery—occupying a 62-acre

(25-hectare) prime slice of Dublin— is often likened to a citadel, but it is very much a living, working space and, 250 years after young Arthur Guinness's first mash, it is brewed in 50 countries worldwide and enjoyed in 150.

BREWING SECRET The amount of hops used is instrumental to the dry quality of Guinness Stout; Brettonamyces yeast also contributes to its dry style.

BEER

ABBOT ALE
STRONG BITTER 5% ABV
A biscuit malt and spicy hop aroma, with a tangy and bittersweet fruit and malt palate.

IPA
INDIA PALE ALE 3.6% ABV
Distinctly copper-colored, with a clean, fresh hop savoriness and subtle, sweetish malty nose.

OLD SPECKLED HEN
PREMIUM BITTER 5.2% ABV
Rich and intense, with a savory, spicy malt flavor, allied with a fruity sweetness.

RUDDLES' COUNTY
BEST BITTER 4.3% ABV
A premium ale that displays a fruity sweetness and a definite hoppy, dry finish.

GUINNESS ORIGINAL
STOUT 4.2% ABV
The packaged version's coffee and cream aroma highlights fruit, chocolate, and some late hoppiness.

DRAUGHT GUINNESS
STOUT 4.1% ABV
Some hop aroma apparent, then fruit, cream, and dark toffee flavors develop with liquorice tinges.

FOREIGN EXTRA STOUT
SPECIAL STOUT 7.5% ABV
Leafy hop aroma, with burnt toast, rich malt, bitter coffee, and liquorice flavors ripening effortlessly.

GUINNESS RED
IRISH RED ALE 4.1% ABV
Rather than the familiar black and white, lighter roasted barley gives it a rich red color.

HADRIAN & BORDER

Newcastle upon Tyne,
England NE6 1AS
www.hadrian-border-brewery.co.uk

Born out of a "marriage" between
Border Brewery of Berwick upon
Tweed and Hadrian of Newcastle
upon Tyne, the company continues to
grow, year on year, throughout a
distribution area that reaches from
Edinburgh to North Yorkshire. Its
award-winning ales are brewed in a
20-barrel (3,200-liter) plant.

HALL & WOODHOUSE

Blandford St. Mary, Dorset,
England DT11 9LS
www.hall-woodhouse.co.uk

An independent family firm, Hall &
Woodhouse is owned and run by
fifth-generation Woodhouses,
who remain loyal to the brewery's
dictum: "Dorset ales with real
character." Its visitor center is
a major tourist attraction, and a new,
environmentally friendly brewery
is planned to sit at the heart of the
local community.

HAMBLETON

Holme-on-Swale, North Yorkshire,
England YO7 4JE
www.hambletonales.co.uk

A million-pound investment has
resulted in a completely new brewery
for Hambleton, with state-of-the-art
bottling facilities. Innovation has been
at the heart of the operation since
1991, as evident in the label designs and
bespoke brewing equipment. Several
awards, including one for a gluten-free
range, have been well deserved.

HAMPSHIRE

Romsey, Hampshire, England SO51 0NR
www.hampshirebrewery.com

After five years of steady growth,
Hampshire's small team relocated to
larger premises in 1999, sourcing and
converting vessels from other
breweries. Demand continues due to
a reputation earned for the quality of
Hampshire beers.

BREWING SECRET The wide array of beers
use a medley of different malts and hops
to produce a wealth of flavors.

CENTURION BEST BITTER
BEST BITTER 4.5% ABV
Light in color, with a distinct hop
palate and smooth, clean lacings of
understated fruitiness.

FARNE ISLAND
BITTER 4% ABV
An amber-colored, well-rounded
bitter, with a heightened sense of
malt and a hoppy finale.

BADGER FIRST GOLD
BITTER 4% ABV
An exceptional golden ale, using a
single hop, First Gold, for character
and a distinctive flavor.

TANGLEFOOT
STRONG BITTER 5% ABV
Light golden, with a noticeable
floral dry hop aroma that contrasts
with biscuit and fruit notes.

STALLION
BITTER 4.2% ABV
For some, a true Yorkshire bitter,
with its malty character, nuttiness,
and enhanced hopping rate.

NIGHTMARE
PORTER 5% ABV
An extra-stout porter that uses a
combination of four malts for a
massively complex flavor.

PRIDE OF ROMSEY
STRONG BITTER 5% ABV
Fragrant hops offer citrus—
grapefruit and lemon—bitterness,
complementing an elegant maltiness.

LIONHEART
LIONHEART 4.5% ABV
Golden, with a fresh fruit and malt
fragrance, which introduces a subtle,
hoppy, and refreshing sophistication.

THE STORY OF ...

Guinness

St James's Gate,
Dublin 8, Ireland

Ask for a pint of the "black stuff" wherever you are in the world and the likelihood is you will be served a glass of Guinness. With a body seemingly as dark as the blackest night and topped with a snow white flourish of foam, it is one of the world's most recognizable beers. Guinness is a dry stout, its flavor unerringly roasty, with a hint of smokiness. Its dark hue and distinctive creamy flavor come from the use of an abundance of barley, which is roasted in a giant drum within the St James's Gate Brewery, filling the air around with luscious, burnt coffee aromas.

The Guinness story began more than 240 years ago, when Arthur Guinness built a brewery in Dublin, the keystone of which was decorated with a relief of Ceres, the Roman goddess of grain. By 1900 the brewery's fame and its beer had traveled far and wide, and Guinness had become the biggest brewer in the world, producing more than one million barrels a year.

Today, with a number of variations, Guinness is brewed in more than 40 countries. Drinkers in Britain and Ireland commonly see it sold on draft. However, in many other parts of the world, including Nigeria and Indonesia, it is sold in bottles in a variety of different strengths from 4.1% to 8% ABV.

▼ THE STOREHOUSE The old fermenting room has been transformed into one of Ireland's most successful tourist attractions, with more visitors than the Blarney Stone. Inside the building—which was the first steel-framed multi-story building in the British Isles, and was modeled on a Chicago skyscraper—can be found the story of Guinness.

▲ ROASTED BARLEY Like most beers, Guinness is made from barley, hops, and yeast. But it is the addition of flaked barley and dark roasted barley that gives Guinness its unique color and smooth bitterness. Roasted barley forms part of the mash bill, though additional quantities are added to the wort during the boil (*left*).

▲ POURING GUINNESS To pour the perfect creamy Guinness takes time and perhaps a little patience. It requires a double, slow pour that can take nearly two minutes. It is not unknown for pubs in Ireland to have a line of partially filled glasses on the bar at opening time waiting for customers to arrive, when the final pour is made.

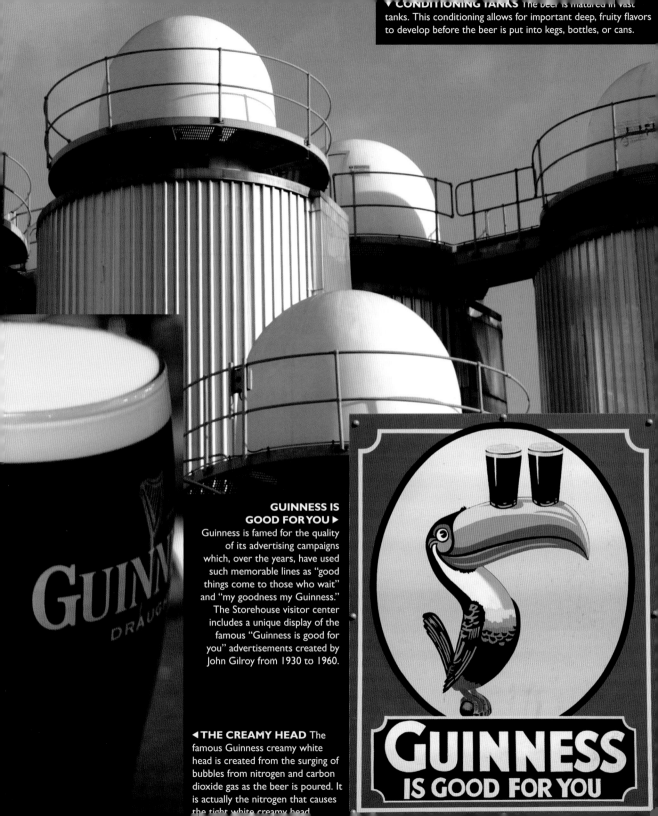

▼ **CONDITIONING TANKS** The beer is matured in vast tanks. This conditioning allows for important deep, fruity flavors to develop before the beer is put into kegs, bottles, or cans.

GUINNESS IS GOOD FOR YOU ▶

Guinness is famed for the quality of its advertising campaigns which, over the years, have used such memorable lines as "good things come to those who wait" and "my goodness my Guinness." The Storehouse visitor center includes a unique display of the famous "Guinness is good for you" advertisements created by John Gilroy from 1930 to 1960.

◀ THE CREAMY HEAD The famous Guinness creamy white head is created from the surging of bubbles from nitrogen and carbon dioxide gas as the beer is poured. It is actually the nitrogen that causes the tight white creamy head

GUINNESS IS GOOD FOR YOU

BREWERY

HARVEY'S

Lewes, East Sussex, England BN7 2AH
www.harveys.org.uk

The seventh generation of John Harvey's descendants are still involved in this prime example of Victorian Gothic-style brewery grandeur. The tower and brewhouse dominate the skyline, and the fermenting rooms and cellars remain structurally unaltered, although they now house a modern plant with equipment that has increased production enormously.

HARVIESTOUN

Alva, Clackmannanshire, England FK12 5DQ
www.harviestoun-brewery.co.uk

The brewers of Harviestoun say they can't pretend it's a job—it's their work, but also their play and their passion. Curiosity toward flavors and aromas wrung from natural ingredients was the brewery's mission in 1985, when the business was originally set up, and a move to a purpose-built plant with fresh investment has resulted in national accolades.

HAWKSHEAD

Staveley, Cumbria, England LA8 9LR
www.hawksheadbrewery.co.uk

The focus at Hawkshead is on traditional beer styles that have been given a modern twist. A new 20-barrel (3,200-liter) brewhouse was fitted out in 2006—an integral feature is a farm gate for leaning on contemplatively. The brewery's public beer hall, where award-winning ales are served, is a magnificent showcase for the beers and their provenance.

HIGHGATE

Walsall, West Midlands, England WS1 3AP
www.highgatebrewery.com

James Fletcher started brewing in 1898 to serve the labor-intensive "workshop of England." It has since passed through several hands — Mitchells & Butler, Bass, Aston Manor, and, today, the Global Star pub company.

BREWERY SECRET Some original Victorian equipment is still used, including coppers topped off by "Chinese hat" funnels.

BEER

BLUE LABEL
PALE ALE 3.6% ABV
Deliciously full-bodied though fairly low in alcohol, with a whiff of leafy hop and sweet malt counterbalance.

ARMADA ALE
BEST BITTER 4.5% ABV
Amber colored, with a well-balanced combination of fruit and hops on the palate.

BITTER & TWISTED
BITTER 3.8% ABV
Ripe grapefruit and lemon-influenced hop aromas are anchored by a distinct maltiness.

SCHIEHALLION
PREMIUM LAGER 4.8% ABV
Cask lager, brewed with Bavarian hops for a delightful nose. A rigid maltiness prevails throughout.

LAKELAND RED
RED ALE 4.2% ABV
A bittersweet red ale, malty and spicy on the palate, with juicy, woody aromas.

LAKELAND GOLD
BEST BITTER 4.4% ABV
Hoppy and uncompromisingly bitter, with complex fruit flavors from its English and American hop blend.

DAVENPORTS ORIGINAL
BEST BITTER 4% ABV
Full-bodied and copper-colored, with ample malt and fruit balanced by a satisfying bitter finish.

DARK MILD
MILD 3.6% ABV
A typical Black Country mild, with complex preserved fruit, chocolate malt, and traces of spicy hops.

HIGH HOUSE

Matfen, Northumberland,
England NE20 0RG
www.highhousefarmbrewery.co.uk

The 2001 foot-and-mouth crisis
persuaded farmer Steven Urwin that
diversification was necessary. Being an
eager home-brewer, he undertook
a course at Sunderland University's
Brewlab. He requistioned listed farm
buildings for brewing, and success
since then has led to national and
regional brewing awards—all displayed
in the visitor center.

HILDEN

Lisburn, County Antrim,
Ireland BT 27 4TY
www.hildenbrewery.co.uk

The family-run microbrewery sparked
something of a revolution when it was
set up in 1981, reintroducing cask-
conditioned beer to Ireland. The
brewhouse—a former stables
belonging to a leading linen
manufacturer—now produces five
ales: a porter, a blonde, a premium
red, and two amber styles.

HOBSON'S

Cleobury Mortimer, Worcestershire,
England DY14 8RD
www.hobsons-brewery.co.uk

Success has evolved out of a hand-to-
mouth existence, a steadily growing
reputation, brewery expansion,
relocation, and a sprinkling of single-
mindedness. At the heart of all this
has been a determination to brew a
mild at a time when the style was
perceived to be in freefall. Yet in 2007
it was judged Supreme Champion
Beer of Britain.

HOG'S BACK

Tongham, Surrey, England GU10 1DE
www.hogsback.co.uk

Established in 1992, the Hog's Back
brewhouse takes up part of an 18th-
century farm. Steady expansion,
extensions to storage facilities, and
re-equipping the fermenting room
have continued since, and many awards
have been gathered along the way.

BREWERY SECRETS "Late hops" are added
at the end of the boil, contributing
additional fragrance to the beer.

NEL'S BEST
BEST BITTER 4.2% ABV
Full-bodied, golden, and easy on the
palate, with a delightful hoppiness
and mantle of malt.

AULD HEMP
BITTER 3.8% ABV
A rewarding, fresh malty aroma
precedes malt and fruit flavors.
Named after a farm sheepdog.

HILDEN ALE
BITTER 4% ABV
Refreshingly sharp on the palate,
with a late pronounced hoppiness
rounding off its full flavor.

MOLLY MALONE ALE
PORTER 4.6% ABV
Dark ruby-red porter, with a
complex structure playing on hop
bitterness and chocolate malt.

TOWN CRIER
BEST BITTER 4.5% ABV
Pale and straw colored, with some
malt sweetness, an earthy hop
impression, and dry finish.

HOBSON'S MILD
MILD 3.2% ABV
Traditional, with a clever wringing
of roasted malt and nutty flavors
from its ingredients.

TRADITIONAL ENGLISH ALE / TEA
BEST BITTER 4.2% ABV
Well-crafted, with delicate, fruity
aromas, some bittersweet malt
flavoring, and a long, dry finish.

HOG'S BACK BITTER
BITTER 3.7% ABV
A biscuit-influenced session bitter,
with a fragrantly aromatic citrus
fruit and light malt afterglow.

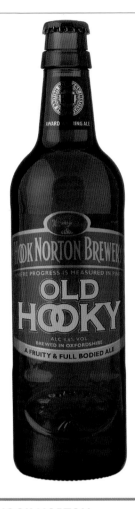

BREWERY

HOLDEN'S

Woodsetton, Dudley, West Midlands,
England DY1 4LW
www.holdensbrewery.co.uk

Third and fourth-generation family
members are very much involved in
the Holden's business, which started
life in the 1920s with a brewpub,
before expanding next door into a
neatly tiled brewery on two floors.

BREWING SECRET The mild uses a mix of
amber malt, caramalt, and black malt,
along with Fuggles hops.

HOLT

Cheetham, Manchester,
England M3 1JD
www.joseph-holt.com

A family business survivor in an
increasingly corporate sector, Holt's
admits—with some pride—to being
unashamedly old-fashioned. That does
not mean backward-looking, however,
and its well-structured projects and
clear vision have brought steady
expansion to the brewery and to its
portfolio of 127 pubs.

HOOK NORTON

Banbury, Oxfordshire, England OX15 5NY
www.hooky.co.uk

A particularly striking example of a
Victorian tower brewery, Hook
Norton is partly powered by steam,
via a series of belts, cogs, and shafts.
Drays pulled by shire horses deliver to
local pubs, further demonstrating how
the brewery likes to preserve
traditional practices. While doing this,
Hook Norton also produces some of
the country's most outstanding ales.

HOP BACK

Downton, Salisbury, Wiltshire,
England SP5 3HU
www.hopback.co.uk

Having soon outgrown its humble
1980s pub-cellar beginnings at the
Wyndham Arms in Salisbury, Hop
Back developed and expanded
through a series of premises for
brewing and drinking its beers, picking
up significant awards along the way.
At the core of the range is the multi-
award-winning Summer Lightning.

BEER

HOLDEN'S GOLDEN
BITTER 3.9% ABV
Fuggles hops and Maris Otter malt
combine in this medium-bodied,
straw-hued pale ale.

BLACK COUNTRY MILD
MILD 3.7% ABV
Bold chestnut red, with nutty biscuit
notes and wrappings of chocolate,
caramel, and earthy hops.

HOLT 1849
BEST BITTER 4.5% ABV
A 150-year anniversary ale, with a
vibrant and generous celebratory
hop flavor to match.

HOLT BITTER
BITTER 4% ABV
Spicy hops dominate the aroma
with tart fruitiness tempered by
biscuit malt and bittersweet fruit.

OLD HOOKY
STRONG BITTER 4.6% ABV
Beautifully poised, with a piquant,
fruity nature and malt character
rounding off a bitter finish.

HOOKY BITTER
BITTER 3.6% ABV
Subtly hoppy on the nose, then
malt and fruit appear, before a
returning hop finish.

SUMMER LIGHTNING
STRONG BITTER 5% ABV
Intensely bitter, with a grassy, fresh,
hoppy aroma and some malt
lingering on the palate.

CROP CIRCLE
BITTER 4.2% ABV
Cleverly blended aroma and bittering
hops combine with corn nuances
for a delicate fruity crispness.

HURNS

Unit 3, Century Park, Swansea
Enterprise Park, Wales SA6 8RP
www.hurns.co.uk

The Hurns beer distribution and pub
company moved into brewing in 2002
with the acquistion of the liquidated
Tomos Watkin Brewery, which had
built an enviable reputation in its
short life. Since then, the enterprise
has developed considerably, with no
little assistance from a dose of
wholehearted Welsh passion.

HYDES

46 Moss Lane West, Manchester,
England M15 5PH
www.hydesbrewery.com

Hydes is another of those remarkable
family-owned breweries that has
carved out a niche in its home region.
Hydes Original has persevered with
the same recipe and exacting
standards that were applied on day
one—back in 1863. The business
continues to face the future with
enthusiasm and in confident style.

ICENI

Mundford, Norfolk, England IP26 5HB
www.icenibrewery.co.uk

The Iceni tribe was ruled by Queen
Boudica (or Boadicea, if you prefer) in
around AD60. The tribe occupied most
of East Anglia (including Norfolk, of
course) and the brewery has harnessed
this heritage in the naming of its beers.

BREWING SECRET The company has its
own hop garden, which contributes
to a breathtaking range of cask and
bottled beers.

INNIS & GUNN

PO Box 17246, Edinburgh, Scotland
www.innisandgunn.com

Whisky distiller William Grant & Son
commissioned a special beer to season
oak casks for an ale cask-finished
whisky. It was then discovered that the
disgorged ale had taken on novel and
exciting flavors. The possibilities for a
new beer style were realized, and it is
now produced by Innis & Gunn, which
bought the concept from Grants to
develop the brand further.

TOMOS WATKIN CWRW HAF
BITTER 4.2% ABV
Refreshingly zesty, with citrus
flavors emerging from a clever
blend of three distinct hop varieties.

CWRW BRAF
BITTER 4.5% ABV
Amber-colored, with a gentle hop
aroma easing in a light bitterness
and temperate maltiness.

HYDES ORIGINAL
BITTER 3.8% ABV
A northwest classic: copper-
colored, full-bodied, with a
distinctive bittersweet flavor.

DARK MILD
MILD 3.5% ABV
A fruit and malt nose and complex
flavorings that meander through
berry fruits, malt, and chocolate.

ICENI BOADICEA CHARIOT ALE
BITTER 3.8% ABV
The original brew, it combines an
attractive hop nose with a cultured
and composed flavor profile.

CELTIC QUEEN
BITTER 4% ABV
An undemanding, hoppy nose and
a palate that reveals distinct bitter
notes and scatterings of malt.

INNIS & GUNN OAK AGED BEER
SPECIALITY STRONG BITTER 6.6% ABV
A butterscotch sweet aroma
crosses into the beer's flavor,
blending with vegetable and banana
notes, and a green apple sourness.

BEER TRAIL

COTSWOLDS

The village of Hook Norton in north Oxfordshire is the perfect base for any visitor exploring the Cotswolds or the city of Oxford. For the traveler, three of the village's pubs—the Sun, the Pear Tree, and the Gate Hangs High—all offer accommodation.

Pear Tree, Hook Norton

JOURNEY STATS

3 days

100 miles (160 km)

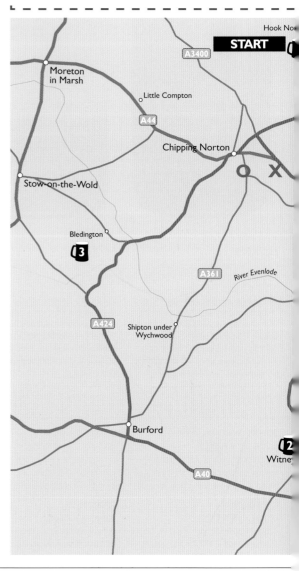

DAY 1: HOOK NORTON BREWERY

This is a near-perfect example of a Victorian tower brewery. It is still powered by a steam engine, and the making of Hook Norton's beers is a tactile, aural, and visual experience. Only the finest malted barley is used in the mash tun, and this needs to be manually removed when the wort is drained off the grist. The seemingly magical transformation of turning sweet wort into alcohol takes place in the brewery's hard-working open fermenters. A horse-drawn dray still delivers beer to local pubs. The Visitor Center is open from Monday to Saturday, though tours of the brewery must be booked beforehand via the website. The tour is followed by some sampling of Hook Norton beer. *Brewery Lane, Hook Norton (www.hooky.co.uk)*

DAY 2: WYCHWOOD BREWERY

The drive from Hook Norton to Witney takes in some glorious countryside, and at the end of the trip is the Wychwood Brewery. Tours of the brewery can be booked online. They last for two hours and go through the brewing process for Wychwood and Brakspear beers, from raw ingredients to the finished product. The tour takes in Brakspear's famous "Double Drop system" fermenting vessels. *Eagle Maltings, The Crofts, Witney (www.wychwood.co.uk)*

3 DAY 2: THE KING'S HEAD INN

Before returning to Hook Norton, pass by Cotswold Brewing (www.cotswoldbrewingcompany.com) at Foscot. Unusually for a British micro, brewer Richard Keene makes continental-style lagers. With a meandering stream at its side, the King's Head Inn, at nearby Bledington, is the perfect place to drink a glass of Cotswold Brewing's beer. *The King's Head Inn, The Green, Bledington (thekingsheadinn.net)*

| 0m | 10 miles |
| 0km | 23km |

4 DAY 3: OXFORD

The third day of the trail offers a chance to sample some of the fabulous pubs in the historical city of Oxford—a place where good beer, culture, and a convivial atmosphere sit cosily together.

TURF TAVERN

Hard to find but worth the search, the Turf Tavern is built on the only remaining part of the city wall. It sells a fabulous collection of British beers. *Bath Place, Holywell, Oxford; for directions go to the pub's website: www.theturftavern.co.uk*

KING'S ARMS

The King's Arms sits at the end of Broad Street, which is famous for its colleges and bookshops. The large pub is a warren of rooms and is much loved by locals and students. *40 Holywell Street, Oxford*

THE BEAR

Small and friendly, The Bear is on a narrow lane between Christ Church and Oriel colleges. It claims to be the oldest pub in Oxford, and is built on the site of a former bear-fighting pit. The walls are decorated by a collection of 5,000 ties. *6 Alfred Street, Oxford*

EAGLE & CHILD

Near Oxford's dreaming spires and the Ashmolean museum, Eagle & Child was a haunt of writers J.R.R. Tolkein and C.S. Lewis, who belonged to a literary group in the 1930s and 40s called the Inklings. *49 St. Giles, Oxford*

Traditional pubs, such as the Eagle in Oxford, offer temporary, "guest" beers, as well as serving a range of regular beers.

BREWERY

INVERALMOND

Perth, Perthshire, Scotland PH1 3UQ
www.inveralmond-brewery.co.uk

Several bottled waters available nationally are sourced from Perthshire's natural mineral springs, and it is little wonder that world-renowned whisky distilleries and this award-winning brewery put them to even better use. Plans are well advanced for increasing the production capacity at Inveralmond, with export markets a major focus.

ISLE OF ARRAN

Brodick, Isle of Arran, Scotland KA27 8DE
www.arranbrewery.com

Arran is often described as "Scotland in miniature," and its high-tech brewery, set among the stunning surroundings of castles, mountains, and an extraordinary shoreline, reflects tradition, substance, and native inventiveness. The plaudits it receives are matched by awards for design.

BREWING SECRET Gulf Stream-driven rainfall is a factor in the beer's character.

ISLE OF SKYE

Uig, Isle of Skye, Scotland IV51 9XP
www.skyebrewery.co.uk

The ferry terminal serving the Outer Hebrides also boasts an award-winning ale producer in the form of the Isle of Skye Brewery. There, a former teacher has been joined in beermaking duties by two ex-chefs—one of them Scotland's only female brewer.

BREWING SECRET These beers make the most of traditional Scottish produce, such as barley, oats, and honey.

JARROW

Primrose Hill, Jarrow, Tyne & Wear, England NE32 5UB
www.jarrowbrewery.co.uk

Set up in 2002, originally to supply the owners' two pubs, Jarrow met immediate success, and its soaring reputation meant its beers were soon more widely available. Jarrow's well-structured ales reflect Tyneside's industrial and social importance—Old Cornelius, for example, was named after the last surviving member of the Jarrow March protesters of the 1930s.

BEER

OSSIAN

BEST BITTER 4.1% ABV
Spicy and spritzy orange aromas blend with malt flavors and develop through further fruit notes.

INDEPENDENCE

BITTER 3.8% ABV
Full-bodied, earthy, and malty, with subtle hints of mixed fruit and punches of spice.

ARRAN BLONDE

STRONG BITTER 5% ABV
New-mown grass and floral aromas slip into citrus fruit and tangy, succulent malt flavors.

ARRAN DARK

SCOTTISH HEAVY 4.3% ABV
Rich ripe fruit aroma, with full malt bittersweet flavors typical of a traditional Scottish "heavy."

HEBRIDEAN GOLD

BEST BITTER 4.3% ABV
Softly fruity, using porridge oats for exceptional body smoothness and a full, creamy head.

RED CUILLIN

BITTER 4.2% ABV
Malt-laced, with nut and caramel fillings developing evermore malt all the way to a bittersweet finale.

RIVET CATCHER

BITTER 4% ABV
A subtle hoppiness and light malt veil persist throughout this consistently award-winning bitter.

JOBLING'S SWINGING GIBBET

BITTER 4.1% ABV
Superbly composed, with prominent hop aromas and fruit developing throughout the palate.

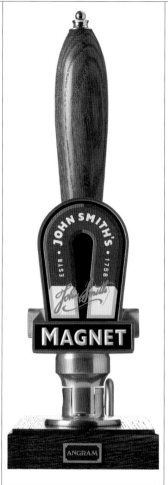

JENNINGS

Cockermouth, Cumbria,
England CA13 9NE
www.jenningsbrewery.co.uk

John Jennings had already been brewing
for 46 years when he built his own
brewery in 1874 in the shadow of
Cockermouth Castle. The brewery
stands at the confluence of the rivers
Cocker and Derwent, and has been
owned by Marstons since 2005.

BREWING SECRET Pure Lakeland water
is a key ingredient in Jennings ales.

JOHN SMITH

Tadcaster, North Yorkshire,
England LS24 9SA
www.johnsmiths.co.uk

John Smith (from the same family as
Samuel Smith) began brewing in 1847
to cater for the local mill trade. The
enterprise was taken over by the
Courage group in 1970, then
absorbed by Scottish & Newcastle.
John Smith's is the top-selling bitter in
the British Isles, selling more than a
million pints a day.

KELHAM ISLAND

Sheffield, South Yorkshire,
England S3 8SA
www.kelhambrewery.co.uk

Since Kelham Island opened in 1990,
Sheffield's four large breweries have
closed down, which makes Kelham's
success all the more remarkable. An
astonishing range of awards has been
collected along the way.

BREWING SECRET Pale Rider and Easy
Rider both make great use of highly
fragrant American hops.

LEES

Manchester, England M24 2AX
www.jwlees.co.uk

Established by the far-sighted John
Lees in 1878, when Manchester was
becoming the "workshop of the world,"
Lees expanded rapidly, matching the
growing local thirst. Sixth-generation
family members currently run the
brewery and pub estate, and they
remain faithful to the brewery's
maxim: "We think of ourselves as
old-fashioned and cutting-edge."

CUMBERLAND ALE
BITTER 4% ABV
Florally hoppy, its intense, full flavor
and firm, creamy body slide into a
dry aftertaste.

SNECK LIFTER
STRONG BITTER 5.1% ABV
Dark and fascinating, with complex
aromatics, and generous flavors of
fruit and roasted malt.

JOHN SMITH'S ORIGINAL
BITTER 3.8% ABV
A moderate-bodied and fruity-
flavored bitter, possessing a
short, hoppy finish.

JOHN SMITH'S MAGNET
BITTER 4% ABV
Balanced bittersweet flavors,
including caramel and liquorice, head
an easy-drinking, full-flavored beer.

PALE RIDER
STRONG BITTER 5.2% ABV
Strong but delicately fruity multi-
award winner, which profits from an
adventurous use of American hops.

EASY RIDER
BITTER 4.3% ABV
A subtle pale ale, its initial crisp
bitterness surrendering only to a
lingering fruity palate.

MOONRAKER
BARLEY WINE 7.5% ABV
Powerfully fruity on a rich roast
malt base, with a sweet tendency
and dryish finish.

JW LEES BITTER
BITTER 4% ABV
Classic amber-colored northern
bitter, with layers of malt in the
mouthfeel and a citrus finale.

BREWERY

LITTLE VALLEY

Hebden Bridge, West Yorkshire,
England HX7 5TT
www.littlevalleybrewery.co.uk

All beers made by master brewer
Wim van der Speck are certified as
100 percent organic. Awards have
followed Wim's career, in his native
Holland, then Germany, Scotland,
and now England.

BREWING SECRET Wim has a flair for
extracting spicy, fruit, chocolate, and
cereal flavors from malts and hops.

MARSTON'S

Burton upon Trent, Staffordshire,
England DE14 2BW
www.marstonsbeercompany.co.uk

The company operates three sites:
the Park Brewery in Wolverhampton,
which brews Banks's, Hanson's, and
Mansfield beers; Jennings Brewery at
Cockermouth in the Lake District,
and the Albion Brewery in Burton
upon Trent—"the home of British
beer." Throughout its long
existence—which stretches back to

1834—it has acquired several of
its competitors in the Midlands,
Cumbria, and Wales. Then, in 1999,
Marston's itself was taken over by
Wolverhampton & Dudley Breweries,
which changed its name to Marston's
PLC in 2007.

BREWING SECRET The brewery still uses
the fabled Burton Union fermenting
system for its classic Pedigree beer,
capitalizing on the renowned, hard,
and sulfur-rich local water.

MCMULLEN

Hertford, Hertfordshire,
England SG14 1RD
www.mcmullens.co.uk

Peter McMullen started his business in
1827. Several breweries and three
artesian wells later, the brewery today
is now more compact, but no less
efficient, dependable, and successful.
Emphasis on training, in the
brewhouse and throughout the 50-
strong pub estate, encourages the
team to work to exacting standards.

BEER

STOODLEY STOUT
STOUT 4.8% ABV
Rich and roasted flavors, with
chocolate malt, oat, and wheat
chasing orange and berry aromas.

CRAGG VALE BITTER
BITTER 4.2% ABV
Three complementary hop varieties
manipulate lemon aromas around a
full, rounded, crisp, fruity body.

PEDIGREE
BEST BITTER 4.4% ABV
A British institution—sweetly hop-
laden, with the vague sulfur aroma
that's characteristic of Burton ales.

BURTON BITTER
BITTER 3.8% ABV
Malty biscuit flavors counterbalance
a delicate hop nature; distinctive
sulfurous aroma.

OLD EMPIRE
INDIA PALE ALE 5.7% ABV
A stylish India Pale Ale, with hop
and fruit flavors and a dry extra-
hop finish.

DRAUGHT BASS
PREMIUM BITTER 4.4% ABV
Beautiful fruit aromas diffuse into
hoppy sweetness, with a touch of
malt and a lingering bitterness.

AK MILD
MILD 3.7% ABV
Its soft biscuit palate stems from a
carefully targeted blend of pale and
chocolate malts.

MCMULLEN COUNTRY BITTER
BEST BITTER 4.3% ABV
A distinct fruitiness combines with
nutty layers to create a complex
but refreshingly balanced palate.

MEANTIME

Greenwich, London, England SE7 8RX
www.meantimebrewing.com

Preferring to be known as the brewery that can't be pigeonholed could be self-regarding, but the approach of master brewer Alastair Hook is purposeful—to demonstrate the exciting flavor potential that beer has to offer.

BREWING SECRET Research into, and recreation of, beers from the past is an abiding passion here, as exemplified by Meantime's India Pale Ale.

MELBOURN BROTHERS

All Saints Street, Stamford, Lincolnshire, England PE9 2PA

Owned by Samuel Smith, Melbourn Brothers is a fruit beer specialist, selling principally to the US market. The 1825 stone-built brewery is steam-powered, and uses equipment that dates back to the Industrial Revolution of the early 19th century.

BREWING SECRET The spontaneously fermented beers that are produced here make use of wild, airborne yeasts.

MOORHOUSE'S

Burnley, Lancashire, England BB11 5EN
www.moorhouses.co.uk

Mineral water and low-alcohol "hop bitters" were William Moorhouse's forte. He started his business in 1865, but his successors failed to achieve a great deal in terms of brewing beer until fresh investment in infrastructure arrived in 1988. Further improvements and additions accelerated growth and helped create the admirable reputation that Moorhouse ales have today.

MORDUE

North Shields, Tyne & Wear, England NE29 7XJ
www.morduebrewery.com

When two enterprising, home-brewing brothers discovered the house they shared was formerly owned by 19th-century brewer Joseph Mordue, there was no doubting what to call their business. Several expansions, high customer demand, large investment, award upon award, and relocation have since brought the brewplant virtually back to Joseph Mordue's roots.

CHOCOLATE BEER
SPECIALITY STRONG BEER 6.5% ABV
Complex malt structure, with dark chocolate releasing vanilla notes to create a rich, memorable infusion.

INDIA PALE ALE
INDIA PALE ALE 7.5% ABV
Massively hoppy, with herbal, spice, and grass tiers grasping the strength of the original IPAs.

STRAWBERRY
FRUIT BEER 3.4% ABV
A clean, fresh taste, with ripe fruit flavors that quickly disappear into a short, slightly tart finish.

APRICOT
FRUIT BEER 3.4% ABV
Deliciously dry, tartly fresh, with a contrasting, well-balanced ripeness lingering in the mouthfeel.

PENDLE WITCHES BREW
STRONG BITTER 5.1% ABV
Distinctive and amber-colored, the beer has a full malty palate and a resonant fruity hop finale.

BLACK CAT
MILD 3.4% ABV
Full, dark, and complex, with distinctive chocolate malt and liquorice flavors, and a hoppy finish.

GEORDIE PRIDE
BITTER 4.2% ABV
Well poised, with hop and fruit aromas following through the palate, and a long, bitter finish.

WORKIE TICKET
BEST BITTER 4.5% ABV
A well-constructed bitter, with an intricate malt and hop blend, and a long, satisfying finish.

BEER STYLES

PORTER AND STOUT

Porter is the beer that came back from the dead. A revolutionary citizen of the turbulent 18th century, it was a dark, strong, restorative thirst-quencher, and a favorite of London's market porters, hence its name. Porter was the rock on which the British brewing industry was built—massive vats of it once matured in the cellars of brewers such as Whitbread. Yet porter sales declined in the 19th and 20th centuries, and it seemed dead and buried by the 1970s. Recently, it has been resurrected by American craft brewers, with British microbrewers following suit.

Unlike porter, stout has never been away. In the early 19th century, Irish brewer Arthur Guinness made porter but, by using roasted barley in the mash tun, he created a beer with a dry, roasted edge. Irish dry stout was born, and Guinness bestrode the world. Modern stouts retain a smoky and acrid dry edge, though some stray into porter territory with a more luscious touch—excellent examples include Titanic Stout, Porterhouse's Wrasslers, Murphy's, and Rogue's Shakespeare Stout. Other variations on a dark theme include milk stout (sweetish and low in alcohol), imperial stout (ideal as an after-dinner drink and, for historical reasons, often called Imperial Russian Stout), and oatmeal stout (smooth and silky). Imperial stout was originally brewed with lots of hops and to a high alcohol content to withstand lengthy journeys on which an even temperature would be impossible to maintain. Samuel Smith's makes a good example, though for intensity of flavor, it is hard to beat Rogue's Imperial Stout.

DARK MALTS Porter and stout use highly kilned, dark malts that contain more caramelized sugar than lighter malts, and carry notes of bitter chocolate and coffee.

MODERN STOUTS Stouts such as Oregon's Rogue Brewery expression feature malty and fruity flavors, and notes of mocha coffee, chocolate, and even condensed milk.

BALTIC PORTER Baltic porters tend to be very strong, with an almost medicinal quality, as exemplified by the Polish Okocim Porter.

BREWERY

MURPHY'S

Lady's Well, Leitrim Street, Cork,
County Cork, Ireland
www.murphys.com

The story has it that James J. Murphy's
1856 brewery was financed by his aunt,
Paris-based Marie-Louise Murphy, after
she posed nude for painter Francois
Boucher. Profound success followed,
but trading difficulties arose in the
1970s. They were resolved only in 1983
when Heineken bought and proceeded
to develop the Murphy's brand.

NETHERGATE

Pentlow, Essex, England CO10 7JJ
www.nethergate.co.uk

The popularity of ten impressive
permanent beers complemented by
seasonal and specialty ales have
necessitated the brewery's expansion,
then relocation, in 2005. Significant
awards have been gathered since
Nethergate's inception in 1986—at
the Great British Beer Festival and the
Chicago International Beer Festival.

NEWCASTLE
FEDERATION

Dunston, Tyne & Wear, England NE11 9JR
www.scottish-newcastle.com

The 33 million gallon brewery, two
miles from Newcastle city center,
has been home to Scottish &
Newcastle's flagship brand Newcastle
Brown Ale since 2005. The iconic
beer was first brewed in 1927, and
is now the UK's best-selling premium
bottled ale and is exported to more
than 40 countries worldwide.

NORTH YORKSHIRE

Guisborough, North Yorkshire,
England TS14 8HG
www.nybrewery.co.uk

The brewery is housed in a former
dairy at a moated country house
hotel on the fringes of the North
York Moors National Park. More than
20 organic beers are produced.

BREWING SECRET North Yorkshire uses
natural spring water; that, and the
brewery's own yeast lends a
distinctiveness to the beer.

BEER

MURPHY'S IRISH STOUT
STOUT 4% ABV
A beguiling aroma of roasted malt,
coffee, and chocolate blends into a
smooth, peaty sourness.

MURPHY'S IRISH RED
IRISH RED ALE 5.2% ABV
Nut, bread, and chocolate aromas
develop creamy malt flavors and a
degree of drying hoppiness.

OLD GROWLER
PORTER 5% ABV
A complex and distinctive porter,
with roast malt, liquorice, and fruit
layers; powerful, hoppy finish.

UMBEL ALE
BITTER 3.8% ABV
Freshly toasted coriander seeds are
added to the boil for an explosion
of spicy flavors.

NEWCASTLE BROWN ALE
BROWN ALE 4.7% ABV
Full-bodied and silky-textured with
a caramel and fruit individuality and
sweet aftertaste.

NEWCASTLE EXHIBITION ALE
BITTER 4.3% ABV
Full-bodied pale ale with a hoppy
aroma that develops sweetness on
the palate.

FLYING HERBERT
STRONG BITTER 4.7% ABV
An assured, full-flavored bitter,
with a grainy malt layer and fruit-
influenced dry finish.

FOOL'S GOLD
STRONG BITTER 4.6% ABV
Premium, hoppy, and pale-colored,
with bittersweet citrus notes
throughout its well defined flavor.

BREWERY

OAKHAM

Peterborough, Cambridgeshire, England PE2 7JB
www.oakhamales.com

Impressive growth from modest homebrew origins has led to the brewery now occupying its third site since 1993. The original owner sold the business on in 1995 but the early vision and ambitions prevail.

BREWING SECRET American hop varieties, with powerful floral characteristics, are a feature of the range.

O'HANLON'S

Whimple, Devon, England EX5 2NY
www.ohanlons.co.uk

A move from its origins under London railway arches to the West Country has undoubtedly paid off for the small specialist team. Craft brewing standards, its own water source, and an insistence on premium ingredients have reinforced the brewery's reputation. Export sales, encouraged by an impressive bottling plant, continue to develop.

OKELL'S

Douglas, Isle of Man, England IM2 1QG
www.okells.co.uk

Dr. William Okell's steam-powered brewery—which he designed himself in 1874—was regarded as one of the most sophisticated in the world at the time. Okell's new plant, which it moved to in 1994, is the modern equivalent. It is controlled by computers rather than steam, but the passion and commitment to quality beer production remains unaltered.

OLD LUXTERS

Henley-on-Thames, Oxfordshire, England RG9 6JW
www.chilternvalley.co.uk

Part of Chiltern Valley Winery, Old Luxters was set up in 1990 by David Ealand, who was eager to revive the tradition of farm-brewed ale. The latest production technology complements traditional practices.

BREWING SECRET This is the first microbrewery with a royal warrant of appointment to the Queen.

BEER

JEFFREY HUDSON BITTER / JHB
BITTER 3.8% ABV
Dominant citrus fruit hop aroma, which continues on the palate, blending into luscious malt flavors.

WHITE DWARF
WHEAT BEER 4.3% ABV
An English-style wheat beer, with flinty bitterness that mellows and reveals fruit nuances.

THOMAS HARDY'S ALE
BARLEY WINE 11.7% ABV
Powerfully hoppy, this beer can be stored for at least 25 years to mature and develop the flavors.

YELLOW HAMMER
BITTER 4.2% ABV
Pale yellow and fruit-led on the nose, continuing through to the somewhat bitter finish.

DOCTOR OKELL'S IPA
INDIA PALE ALE 4.4% ABV
Potential sweetness, offset by a high hopping regime for overall roundness, spiced by lemon notes.

OKELL'S BITTER
BITTER 3.7% ABV
Light colored and complexly flavored, with hints of honey and a long-lingering dry finish.

BARN ALE BITTER
STRONG BITTER 4% ABV
Initially aromatic from its blend of English hops, with a veneer of savory dried fruit.

BARN ALE SPECIAL
BEST BITTER 4.4% ABV
A full malt-and-fruit palate is tempered by a dry citrus finale.

ORKNEY

Stromness, Orkney,
Scotland KW16 3LT
www.orkneybrewery.co.uk

Commendable ecological awareness allows the brewery's waste water to be filtered through two neighboring lochs that support fish and waterfowl. It was first set up in 1988, and then thoroughly modernized in 1994. Expansions are planned for 2008 that will see the addition of a visitor center and shop, as well as increased output.

OSSETT

Ossett, West Yorkshire,
England WF5 8ND
www.ossettbrewery.co.uk

A lengthy career in some highly respected breweries prepared owner Bob Lawson perfectly for opening his own business in 1997. Significant expansion, driven by customer demand for its light-colored, florally aromatic, and flavorsome ales, has resulted in a new, purpose-built brewery and expanding pub chain.

PALMER'S

Bridport, Dorset,
England DT6 4JA
www.palmersbrewery.com

Palmer's is able to claim continuous production on its original site over a period of more than 200 years. From the outside it has altered little, but this is a contemporary brewing operation, offering a diverse range of ales.

BREWING SECRET Maris Otter malted barley and Golding hops combine to give these beers their fruitiness.

RCH

Weston-Super-Mare, Somerset,
England BS24 6RR
www.rchbrewery.com

Starting life in a hotel could never have been easy, but the decision was made to relocate when guests started complaining about all the water being used for brewing. Now situated in a former cider mill, continuous demand has prompted brewhouse expansion and upgrading to a 30-barrel (4,900-liter) plant.

DARK ISLAND
STRONG BITTER 4.6% ABV
Ruby-red and mysterious, with blackcurrant fruit on the nose and a full-roasted malt palate.

SKULLSPLITTER
BARLEY WINE 8.5% ABV
Forcefully malty nose; hints of apple, spicy hop, and some nut in the complex flavorings.

EXCELSIOR
STRONG BITTER 5.2% ABV
Fresh citrus floral aromas slip into toffee mellowness, a full flavor, and dry afterglow.

PALE GOLD
BITTER 3.8% ABV
Light and refreshing, with a floral and spicy aroma highlighting its American hop infusion.

TRADITIONAL BEST BITTER
BEST BITTER 4.2% ABV
Styled on an India Pale Ale; deliciously hoppy, with fruit and malt undercurrents.

TALLY HO!
STRONG BITTER 5.5% ABV
Distinctly nutty and dark, with full-bodied complexity emerging slowly, then on to a lingering afterglow.

PG STEAM BITTER
BITTER 3.9% ABV
Complex and multilayered, with leafy hop aromas and a core flavor of malt and fruit.

HEWISH IPA
INDIA PALE ALE 3.6% ABV
Lightly floral hopping, with a subtle sweetness plus some malt and fruit on the palate.

BREWERY

RINGWOOD

Ringwood, Hampshire,
England BH24 3AP
www.ringwoodbrewery.co.uk

A brewery with the best of all birth
certificates—it was launched in 1978
by Peter Austin, the acknowledged
"father of British microbrewing."
Enthusiastic local support ensured it
outgrew its plant and premises, but
it remains unarguably the tidiest, most
efficient of operations. Marston's
acquired it in 2007, hopefully to
develop its spirited potential further.

ROBINSON'S

Stockport, Cheshire,
England SK1 1JJ
www.frederic.robinson.co.uk

One of the British Isles' largest regional
breweries, Robinson's began as the
Union Inn in 1838. Sixth-generation
family members are still in charge of its
development, overseeing huge advances
in brewing and bottling techniques.

BREWING SECRET Tradition continues
here, and the brewery still uses its
surviving 1920s yeast strain.

ROOSTER'S

Knaresborough, North Yorkshire,
England HG5 8LJ
www.roosters.co.uk

The rules are simple: unconditional care
taken in the selection and preparation
of raw materials is repaid in flavor.
Beer is not an alcoholic commodity to
master brewer Sean Franklin, but a
serious sensory product, and inventive
infusions of lychees, roses, coffee,
grapefruit, and chocolate are teased
from hop varieties.

RUDGATE

Tockwith, York,
England YO26 7QF
www.rudgate-beers.co.uk

More than 60 brewers' barrels (9,800
liters) are produced weekly from a
former armory building on the
disused World War II Marston Moor
airfield. "Special" ales are brewed each
month, one on a Viking theme and
another in the Brewer's Choice range,
which encourages experimentation
with hop flavors and idiosyncrasies.

BEER

OLD THUMPER
STRONG BITTER 5.6% ABV
Peppered spice and apple aromas
develop rounded malt and caramel
flavors all the way to a fruity finish.

BEST BITTER
BEST BITTER 3.8% ABV
Tempting citrus aroma; slightly tart,
dry, and fruity flavors, with an
underlying malt sweetness.

OLD TOM STRONG ALE
BARLEY WINE 8.5% ABV
Full-bodied with an aroma and
flavor alliance of malt, chocolate,
fruit, and port wine.

UNICORN BEST BITTER
BEST BITTER 4.2% ABV
Golden, with some spicy hop and
malt on the nose, countered by a
bittersweet release.

ROOSTER'S YANKEE
BITTER 4.3% ABV
Aromatic, softly bitter, with aromas
of tropical fruit and Muscat grapes
lingering alongside tangy malt.

OUTLAW WILD MULE
BITTER 3.7% ABV
New Zealand hops create a
Sauvignon Blanc wine character in a
remarkable and imposing beer.

VIKING
BITTER 3.8% ABV
With a malt base, this is full and
warming; then hop and fruit
develop and linger in the finish.

BATTLEAXE
BITTER 4.2% ABV
A distinct hoppiness, with just-
perceptible sweetness; complex
fruit notes and significant aftertaste.

ST. AUSTELL

St. Austell, Cornwall,
England PL25 4BY
www.staustellbrewery.co.uk

The enterprising spirit that drove
Walter Hicks to mortgage his farm for
£1,500 in 1851 and set up a brewery
remains at the core of today's
business. Many of his descendants are
still involved in the company—in its
estate of 168 pubs and in the brewery,
which produces in excess of 40,000
barrels (6.5 million liters) annually.

ST. PETER'S

St. Peter South Elmham, Bungay,
Suffolk, England NR35 1NQ
www.stpetersbrewery.co.uk

A custom-built brewery, St. Peter's is
laid out around a farm courtyard. Raw
ingredients enter at one end; brewing
proceeds along one side of the
quadrangle, with fermentation, cask-
filling, and bottling in neighboring barns.

BREWING SECRET St. Peter's uses locally
grown, floor-malted barley and water
drawn from its own well.

SAMUEL SMITH

High Street, Tadcaster, North Yorkshire,
England LS24 9SB
www.tadcaster.uk.com

Tadcaster has three breweries, with
"Sam's" by far the smallest—although
it can claim to be Yorkshire's oldest.
A plentiful supply of water is drawn
through limestone from its own wells.

BREWING SECRET Fermentation takes
place in traditional slate "Yorkshire
squares," which lends distinctive
characteristics to flavor and body.

SHARP'S

Wadebridge, Cornwall,
England PL27 6NU
www.sharpsbrewery.co.uk

Facing the Atlantic from the Cornish
coast undoubtedly has an influence,
not only on how the beer is made,
but also on people's objectives and
horizons. Sharp's commendable
approach to sustainable energy and
water recycling is echoed by an
energetic attitude, which is inspiring
for the future of cask ale production.

TRIBUTE
BITTER 4.2% ABV
Specially grown Cornish Gold
barley delivers a rich biscuit aroma,
tempered by intense fruit flavors.

ST. AUSTEL IPA
INDIA PALE ALE 3.4% ABV
Full of flavor and packed with fresh
hoppiness; the rounded palate
arrives with veils of caramel.

GOLDEN ALE
BITTER 4.7% ABV
Robust, with a strong hop bouquet
and distinct, Czech lager-style malt
and fruit balance.

BEST BITTER
BEST BITTER 3.7% ABV
Distinctly fruity, with caramel notes
pushing its full-bodied complexity
to a dry, hoppy finish.

NUT BROWN ALE
BROWN ALE 5% ABV
A hazel-colored specialty, with a
flavor profile of beech nuts,
almonds, and walnuts.

OLD BREWERY BITTER
BEST BITTER 4% ABV
A typical Northern malty bitter,
with a dash of hop and some fruit
on the palate.

DOOM BAR
BITTER 4% ABV
Spicy resinous hop aromas and
sweet, delicate malts blend with
dried fruit and assertive bitterness.

ATLANTIC IPA
INDIA PALE ALE 4.8% ABV
Four hop varieties are added at
different stages to create cotton
candy aromas and delicate flavors.

BREWERY

SHEPHERD NEAME

Faversham, Kent,
England ME13 7AX
www.shepherdneame.co.uk

It didn't take 12th-century monks long to discover that Faversham's pure spring water could be combined with locally grown malting barley to produce particularly fine ale. When the town's mayor founded a brewery in 1698 over an artesian well, he launched the country's longest-surviving brewery, which, through various partnerships, was by 1864 called Shepherd Neame. The community-focused company is still run by the Neame family, whose heritage and traditional values go hand-in-hand with contemporary standards of service and technological advances.

BREWING SECRET The brewery still makes use of mash tuns made from Russian teak, which were installed in 1914.

SLATER'S

Stafford, Staffordshire, England ST16 3DR
www.slatersales.co.uk

Expertise, enthusiasm, and 10 years' experience provided this family-run business with the confidence and ambition to open new premises in 2004, since when production has increased threefold. Numerous national and local awards were briefly eclipsed by an invitation to "guest" at the Strangers' Bar in the House of Commons in the UK Parliament.

SPRINGHEAD

Sutton-on-Trent, Nottinghamshire, England NG23 6QS
www.springhead.co.uk

From being one of England's smallest microbreweries, Springhead has developed significantly through two massive expansions, highlighting how well the specialty ales sector is flourishing in the British Isles today. Now produced in a 50-barrel (8,300-liter) plant, Springhead beers are named with English Civil War themes in mind.

BEER

BISHOP'S FINGER
STRONG BITTER 5% ABV
Generously fruity, with banana and pear prominent, a biscuit-rich maltiness, and dried fruit flavors.

SPITFIRE
PREMIUM BITTER 4.5% ABV
A underlying deep maltiness is combined with a subtle hint of toffee and boldly fruity citrus hops.

WHITSTABLE BAY ORGANIC ALE
BITTER 4.5% ABV
Organic barley and New Zealand hops orchestrate this elegant ale's bittersweet and floral flavors.

MASTER BREW BITTER
BITTER 3.7% ABV
Distinctly hoppy, well-balanced, with a dusting of sweetness and a slight bitterness to the finish.

TOP TOTTY
BEST BITTER 4% ABV
A voluptuous aroma broadens into more complex hop notes, generous fruitiness, and rich malt infusions.

SLATER'S ORIGINAL
BITTER 4% ABV
A savory malt aroma and ensuing succulent palate is countered by bitter pepper-spiced hops.

PURITANS' PORTER
PORTER 4% ABV
Dark, with a heavier appearance than its roasted barley smoothness eventually confirms.

SPRINGHEAD BITTER
BITTER 4% ABV
A copper-colored, easy-drinking, hoppy ale, with some malt, slight fruitiness, and long, bitter finish.

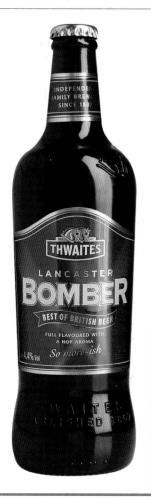

TETLEY

PO Box 142, Hunslet Road, Leeds,
West Yorkshire, England LS1 1QG
www.carlsberg.co.uk

The historic brewery has been fully
owned by Carlsberg since 1998, with
the Carlsberg-Tetley name dropped in
2004. As it has a reputation for some
fine ales, Tetley is a disappointingly
rare sight outside its native Yorkshire.

BREWING SECRET Tetley still uses
traditional square-shaped slate
fermenters for its cask English ales.

THEAKSTON

Masham, North Yorkshire,
England HG4 4YD
www.theakstons.co.uk

Ownership battles may have swept in
numerous changes during its 180-year
history but, fortunately today, tradition
survives and thrives. Now returned to
the Theakston family following Scottish
& Newcastle's management, the
company lives up to the name of its
most famous beer—Peculier, a 12th-
century word meaning "particular."

THORNBRIDGE

Bakewell, Derbyshire, England DE45 1NZ
www.thornbridgebrewery.co.uk

Resounding success has followed from
the brewery's philosophy of being
"never ordinary." While brewing
heritage is of prime importance,
innovation, enthusiasm, experience,
and a commitment to creating new
and exciting recipes have driven the
business since it was established in
2005 in the grounds of Thornbridge
Hall country manor house.

THWAITES

Blackburn, Lancashire, England BB1 5BU
www.thwaites.co.uk

Adaptation, modernization, and
progression have been watchwords
for more than two centuries. Dating
back to 1807, Thwaites remains
resolutely independent and family-
controlled—by descendants of its
founder, Daniel Thwaites. An estate of
more than 400 pubs reaches from the
Midlands to Cumbria.

TETLEY'S MILD
MILD 3.3% ABV
Light malt and caramel aromas, and
a well-balanced flavor structure,
developing an appealing bitterness.

TETLEY'S CASK BITTER
BITTER 3.7% ABV
A modest malt and hop aroma,
and a touch of preserved fruit
on the palate.

OLD PECULIER
STRONG BITTER 5.6% ABV
Rich and deep dark ruby in hue,
with a mellow fruit aroma and a
malty, full-bodied flavor.

BLACK BULL BITTER
BITTER 3.9% ABV
Bright amber colored, with a
crisp, dry palate weaving through
citrus fruit flavors.

JAIPUR
INDIA PALE ALE 5.9% ABV
Tantalizingly complex; emphasis on
citrus hoppiness; its powerful
length develops a bitter finish.

LORD MARPLES
BITTER 4% ABV
Easy-drinking bitter, with hints of
honey and caramel, and a long,
bitter afterglow.

LANCASTER BOMBER
BEST BITTER 4.4% ABV
Its inviting, malty aroma is crossed
with floral hop and some fruit in
the flavor.

THWAITES ORIGINAL
BITTER 3.6% ABV
A clean, dry-tasting, amber-glowing
bitter, with a citrus crispness and
firm malted base.

THE STORY OF ...

Thornbridge

Thornbridge Hall, Ashford in the Water, Derbyshire DE45 1NZ

For owner Jim Harrison, the idea of founding a brewery came shortly after he and his wife Emma had bought Thornbridge Hall, a stately home set in 100 acres of stunning parkland in the heart of the Peak District in Derbyshire. "The next step had to be to serve my own beer in my own bar, reviving the tradition once common of country house brewing."

But whereas many of Britain's new wave of craft brewers are content with brewing traditional English bitters, ordinary beer isn't part of the Thornbridge mindset. Unusually, an Italian head brewer, Stefano Cossi, was appointed and an international brewing team assembled, together drawing on diverse brewing experiences and a wide knowledge of ingredients—from herbs and fruits to intriguing varieties of hops. An example of this is the fruitily aromatic Nelson Sauvin hop from New Zealand, which is at the juicy heart of the Kipling South Pacific Pale Ale.

If the Thornbridge methods have been inventive and experimental, the results have been largely spectacular, and the beers are already garnering accolades, backed up by several awards.

▲ **THORNBRIDGE HALL** The grand manor house acts as an impressive beacon for the brewery, and also houses the brewery's bar for hosting special events.

▶ **WORKSHOP** The brewery itself is located in an old stonemason's and joiner's workshop, in the grounds of the hall.

◀ **CONDITIONING ROOM** The conditioning tanks—partly reclaimed vessels that came from Scottish & Newcastle— are where the beers settle and mature for between one and two weeks. Thornbridge is experimenting with far longer maturation periods, and a barley wine called Alliance has been conditioning for 12 months.

Some of the UK's most innovative beers are created at Thornbridge. The brewing team is small, and made up mostly of qualified food technologists. This brings a more scientific approach to the methods of beer production. Plans are already under way to expand the brewing plant, while the current three-room brewery will become a brewing laboratory for trialling new beers.

▲ **HERB GARDEN** The philosophy of Thornbridge is to brew small batches of original beers using the finest raw materials. Sometimes this means the inclusion of local plants, fruits, and herbs, such as elderflower, sage, and nettle, to add new notes to the chorus of flavors. The hall has a walled garden where herbs and other plants are being grown specifically for this purpose.

▲ **CASK CONDITIONING** One of the latest Thornbridge ventures is to condition beers in wooden casks previously used to hold whiskey. Saint Petersburg's Imperial Russian Stout was condition finished in whiskey barrels from three distinct whiskey regions, each lending its own characteristics to the beer. The Speyside Reserve has a dry, herbal edge, with an astringent finish; the Highland Reserve has a sweeter grassy palate; while the Islay Reserve has a bold peaty and marvelously smoky finish.

◀ **THE CRICKET INN** Thornbridge has the lease of a number of pubs locally, including The Cricket Inn in Totley, near Sheffield, which marries great food with a range of Thornbridge beers, including the award-winning Jaipur IPA, the even fruitier Kipling, the more bitter-edged Lord Marples, and Cricketers, a bitter brewed just for the pub.

BREWERY

TIMOTHY TAYLOR

Keighley, West Yorkshire,
England BD21 1AW
www.timothy-taylor.co.uk

The Taylor family guides the enterprise, as it has done since the brewery's inception in 1858.

BREWING SECRET Pure Pennine water from the brewery's own spring is a natural companion to the Golden Promise barley (also used extensively for malt whiskey); together, they form the legendary "Taylor's taste."

TITANIC

Burslem, Staffordshire, England ST6 1JL
www.titanicbrewery.co.uk

What began with brewing for demonstration purposes on log-fired Victorian equipment developed into the production of in excess of 17 million pints a year. Ecologically friendly business practices—recycling and conservation—are a priority. The name is taken from the world's most famous passenger ship, whose captain, John Edward Smith, was born nearby.

TRADITIONAL SCOTTISH ALES

Bandeath, Stirling, Scotland FK7 7NP
www.traditionalscottishales.com

Possibly the only brewery in the world to occupy a former torpedo factory, TSA developed out of Bridge of Allan Brewery, which already had an impressive portfolio of ales.

BREWING SECRET King James IV of Scotland purchased beer for his coronation in 1488 from the old Tullibardine brewery (now a whisky distillery).

TRAQUAIR

Innerleithen, Peeblesshire,
Scotland EH44 6PW
www.traquair.co.uk

The 18th-century brewing equipment in a house where Bonnie Prince Charlie once sought refuge remained untouched until their rediscovery in 1965. Since then, they have been put to use for brewing in authentic style.

BREWING SECRET Unusually in this day and age, Traquair's beers are fermented in oak over a seven-day period.

BEER

LANDLORD
PREMIUM BITTER 4.3% ABV
Complex hoppy aroma, well-balanced spice and citrus fruit flavors, tinged with biscuit malt.

BEST BITTER
BEST BITTER 4% ABV
A full measure of maltiness following citrus fruit, hoppy aromas define an honest Yorkshire bitter.

TITANIC STOUT
STOUT 4.5% ABV
Full roast, preserved fruit aromas; the malt-influenced palate accentuates more fruit and liquorice tiers.

BEST BITTER
BEST BITTER 3.5% ABV
Straw colored, with a waft of sulfur in the aroma and persistent hop flavorings.

BEN NEVIS ORGANIC
SCOTTISH HEAVY 4% ABV
A ruby-red, traditional Scottish 80 shilling ale, with succulent malt matched by light hop flavors.

1488 WHISKY ALE
SPECIALTY STRONG BITTER 7% ABV
Matured in malt whisky casks, it is peppery and slightly smoky, with a whisky-chased edge.

TRAQUAIR HOUSE ALE
BARLEY WINE 7.2% ABV
A dark and oaky winter brew, with ripe malt, fruit cake, and sweet sherry mystique.

JACOBITE ALE
BARLEY WINE 8% ABV
Herbal notes from the use of coriander warm the bittersweet chocolate and port wine flavors.

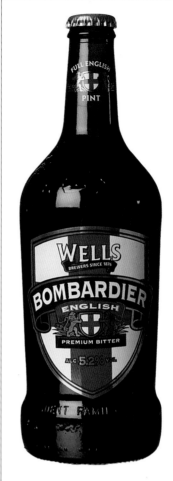

TRING

Tring, Hertfordshire, England HP23 6AF
www.tringbrewery.co.uk

Since the brewery was founded in 1992, Tring has earned increasing success through a commitment to quality. The beers' names are unusual—Side Pocket for a Toad is local parlance for something useless—and the pumpclip illustrations originate as watercolors.

BREWING SECRET Besides the core and seasonal ranges, Tring produces monthly "specials" to trial new recipes.

WADWORTH

Devises, Wiltshire, England SN10 1JW
www.wadworth.co.uk

Established by Henry Wadworth, the brewery began producing beer in 1875 and was expanded 10 years later into an impressive, red-brick Victorian tower brewery. The original open copper is still operational and wooden casks are used for local deliveries. A full-time cooper and a team of dray horses continue traditional customs.

WELLS & YOUNG'S

Bedford, Bedfordshire, England MK40 4LU
www.charleswells.co.uk
www.youngs.co.uk

A major force in British brewing was created in 2006 from the partnership of London brewer Young's and Bedford-based Charles Wells, two of the most prodigiously accomplished operators in the industry. Charles Wells founded his brewery in 1876, and, five generations later, it remains family owned. When the companies merged, Young's left its London-based Ram Brewery, where brewing had been recorded on the site since 1551. Wells & Young's cask and bottled ale portfolio is one of the broadest in the brewing sector, particularly after Courage brands—Best Bitter and Directors Bitter—were added in 2007 under an agreement with Scottish & Newcastle.

BREWING SECRET Heavy on Crystal malt, Well's Bombardier uses Challenger and Goldings hops for its fruity palate and spicy nose.

SIDE POCKET FOR A TOAD
BITTER 3.6% ABV
Distinct citrus notes appear through a floral aroma and crisp, dry, well-balanced palate.

JACK O'LEGS
BEST BITTER 4.2% ABV
Four malt varieties and two hop types support a full fruit flavor and undoubted bitterness.

WADWORTH 6X
BEST BITTER 4.3% ABV
A malt and fruit nose, with restrained hop characteristics developing an intensity on the palate.

JCB
STRONG BITTER 4.7% ABV
Aromatic wafts of tropical fruit; a rich malt mouth with some nutty sweetness on the palate.

WELLS BOMBARDIER
PREMIUM BITTER 4.3% ABV
Powerful citrus hop aromas meet malt and dried fruit in a richly complex medley.

EAGLE IPA
INDIA PALE ALE 3.6% ABV
Preposterously flavor-packed, with malt and ripe apple sweetness, belying its relatively low strength.

YOUNG'S BITTER
BITTER 3.7% ABV
Well-balanced, with citrus hop notes and enough malt for a flowery and bready finish.

YOUNG'S SPECIAL
BEST BITTER 4.5% ABV
Sweet hop aroma, but a robust malt and hop arrangement persists throughout layers of toffee.

BREWERY

WENTWORTH

Wentworth, South Yorkshire,
England S62 7TF
www.wentworth-brewery.co.uk

Water is drawn from the
independent brewery's own spring
and, indeed, part of the business
is bottling this water in natural
form. An extensive range of beer is
offered, covering all the major styles,
with strikingly labeled, monthly
"seasonal" ales a specialty. A 2006
refurbishment has allowed production
to increase dramatically.

WICKWAR

Wickwar, Gloucestershire,
England GL12 8NB
www.wickwarbrewing.co.uk

A million-pound refurbishment has
hoisted Wickwar from microbrewery
status to regional heights, increasing
its brewing capacity almost fourfold.
Beers are matured in below-ground
vaults at the former Arnold Perret &
Co. Brewery. The export market is an
increasing area of interest, with
encouraging European sales.

WILLIAMS

Alloa, Clackmannanshire,
Scotland FK10 1NT
www.heatherale.co.uk

Alloa was once second only to Burton
upon Trent as a brewing center, so it
is encouraging to observe innovative
beer styles still being developed there.
Historic recipes and traditional
folklore methods are skilfully applied.

BREWING SECRET In the Fraoch Ale,
flowering heather is used instead of
hops, reviving an ancient Celtic recipe.

WOODFORDE'S

Woodbastwick, Norwich, Norfolk,
England NR13 6SW
www.woodfordes.co.uk

Now on its third site, the brewery
continues to increase production
capacity and to broaden its ambitions.
A tremendous local following has
developed, and the country's top
awards have been accrued—even for
the beermats. Underpinning all this is
high-quality water, which comes
bubbling from an on-site borehole.

BEER

WPA (WOPPA)
PALE ALE 4% ABV
An India Pale Ale-style beer, with
teeming hoppiness and a bitterness
that leans toward astringency.

OATMEAL STOUT
STOUT 4.8% ABV
Touted as "deeply delicious," this
dark persuader revels in layers of
roast malt, toffee, and chocolate.

STATION PORTER
PORTER 6.1% ABV
Richly smooth, with roast coffee,
chocolate, and dried fruits combining
with complex spiced flavors.

IKB
BEST BITTER 4.7% ABV
Bold in its multi-malt flavors,
with rich cherry and plum fruit
breaking through.

FRAOCH HEATHER ALE
SPECIALTY BITTER 4.1% ABV
Abundantly floral and aromatic,
with a spicy mint piquancy, malty
character, and whiff of peat.

KELPIE SEAWEED ALE
SPECIALTY BITTER 4.4% ABV
Organic barley from coastal farms
and bladderwrack seaweed in the
mash produce beguiling flavors.

WHERRY BEST BITTER
BEST BITTER 3.8% ABV
Floral and citrus fruit aromas
unlock a malt-infused middle,
then a sustained finish.

NORFOLK NOG
BITTER 4.6% ABV
Deep red, with a roasted malt
background developing through
liquorice nuances and dried fruit.

WORTHINGTON'S WHITE SHIELD

Burton upon Trent, Staffordshire,
England DE14 1YQ
www.worthingtonswhiteshield.com

The brewery, which dates from 1920,
was reopened in 1995 as a museum
and in order to recreate discontinued
Bass ales, which it has done successfully
under head brewer Steve Wellington.

BREWING SECRET White Shield became
a cult beer for aficionados, as it is
bottled "live" and improves with age.

WYCHWOOD

Witney, Oxfordshire,
England OX28 4DP
www.wychwood.co.uk

Striking beers and striking imagery
quickly developed a huge fan base and
younger market for traditional ales
when Wychwood launched the
celebrated Hobgoblin in bottles in
1996. Until 1990 it had been the Eagle
Brewery, but now as Wychwood it
produces 50,000 barrels (eight million
liters) of craft ale annually.

WYLAM

Heddon-on-the-Wall, Northumberland,
England NE15 0EZ
www.wylambrew.co.uk

Production capacity was tripled in
2006 with a 20-barrel (3,200-liter)
investment in the then six-year-old
farm-based premises. An oil-fired
steam generator proves that 19th-
century technology can adapt to
state-of-the-art beer production.
Several industry awards have
reinforced its reputation.

YORK

York, North Yorkshire, England YO1 6JT
www.yorkbrew.co.uk

The phrase central to the company's
philosophy is "professionally managed
in a fun atmosphere"—and York
manages to be an extremely well-run
brewery and a tourist attraction at
the same time. Visitor-friendly
galleries overlook a much-expanded
brewhouse with its 20-barrel capacity
(3,200 liters), 10 conditioning tanks,
and five fermenters.

WHITE SHIELD
INDIA PALE ALE 5.6% ABV
Enthusiasts appreciate its hop
attack, its smokiness, treacle toffee
sweetness, dusting of paprika, and
serving of fried banana, stilton
cheese, and sliced apple.

HOBGOBLIN
STRONG BITTER 5% ABV
Hefty in roasted, chocolate, and
toffee malt flavors, with moderate
hoppy bitterness and fruitness.

FIDDLER'S ELBOW
BEST BITTER 4.5% ABV
Superb combination of citrus and
floral aromas, with tart fruit flavors
and a long, hoppy finish.

WYLAM ROCKET
STRONG BITTER 5% ABV
Copper-hued strong bitter with
memorable malt fruitiness and
pleasant hop bitterness that lingers.

WYLAM GOLD TANKARD
BITTER 4% ABV
Abundantly hoppy golden ale,
with layers of malt and hints of
citrus in the finish.

YORKSHIRE TERRIER
BITTER 4.2% ABV
An assertive bitterness is tempered
by fruit and hop aromas, audacious
flavors, and a hoppy finish.

CENTURION'S GHOST ALE
STRONG BITTER 5.4% ABV
Dark ruby, warming, and mellow,
with a roasted malt complexion
livened by autumn fruit flavors.

Worthington's White Shield, a cult beer for ale lovers, is a British bottle-conditioned pale ale.

Buggenhoot

Bosteels
De Landtsheer

Bosteels

De Kor

Van Steenberge

Proefbrouwerij

OOST-VLAANDEREN

Palm

Duvel Moortga

Brugge

Halve Maan
De Regenboog

De Dolle Brouwers

Urthel

De Struise

WEST-
VLAANDEREN

Westvleteren

Rodenbach

Vanhonsebrouck

Bavik

Alvinne

Bockor

Verhaeghe

De Ranke

Cazeau

Huyghe

Sint Canarus

Contreras

Glazen Toren

De Ryck

Cnudde

Van Den Bossche

Slaghmuylder

De Block

Affligem

Mort Subite

Girardin

Timmermans

De Cam

Cantillon

BRUSSELS

Lindemans

Drie Fonteinen

Ellezelloise

Boon

Hanssens Artisan

Lefebvre

BRABA
WALL

Watou

Van Eecke
Sint Bernardus

Légendes

Silly / Mynsbrughen

Brabant

Dubuisson/
Vapeur

Dupont

Brunehaut

HAINAUT

Blaugies

La Binchoise

Abbaye Des Rocs

Oudenaarde

Liefmans
Roman

Brootcoorens

Silenrieux

Chimay

St.Bernardus
Abt 12

Abbey Ale

St.Bernardus

Abt 12

Sint Bernardus

PROVISION BEER
'GOUDENBAND'

Liefmans

Oudenaarde
BELGIUM

BELGIUM

Abbey ales, witbiers, lambics, gueuze, kriek—Belgians have a staggering choice of beer styles for the size of the country, and many more regional variations are available to add subtlety to the selection process of a connoisseur. And Belgians certainly are connoisseurs when it comes to beer. They choose it much as the French choose wine: the right style and weight for the right occasion. Often it is chosen to accompany wonderful cuisine. Pullout boxes appear where a city has more than one brewery.

Westmalle

ANTWERPEN

Strubbe

Westmalle

Achelse Kluis

LIMBURG

Loterbol

VLAAMS BRABANT

Domus Huisbrouwerij

Kerkom

Hoegaarden

Grain D'orge

Val-dieu

LIÈGE

Bellevaux

Bocq

NAMUR

Caracole

Fantôme

Rochefort

Achouffe

LUXEMBOURG

Orval

Rulles

Orval

Sainte-Hélène

Bellevaux

BREWERY

ABBAYE DES ROCS

37, Chaussée Brunehault, B7387
Montignies-sur-Roc, Belgium
www.abbaye-des-rocs.com

Jean-Pierre Eloir, a former exciseman,
took up brewing in 1979. The business
has since expanded, with the beers
gaining a good reputation, particularly
abroad, and some are now being
developed with export in mind.

BREWING SECRET Core beers are true to
the spiced and well-bodied Walloon
style; keg beers are often unfiltered.

ACHELSE KLUIS

De Kluis 1, B3930 Hamont-Achel,
Belgium
www.achelsekluis.org

At a time when there were many
brewery closures, the Belgian beer
world had cause to celebrate in 1998.
That was when De Achelse Kluis—a
Trappist abbey on the Dutch
border—started up brewing again
after 84 unproductive years! It is run
as a pub-brewery, and draws in many
passing walkers and cyclists.

ACHOUFFE

32, Rue du Village,
B6666 Achouffe, Belgium
www.achouffe.be

One of the first new-wave micros,
Achouffe was set up in 1982 by two
Flemish and Walloon brothers-in-law.
In doing so, they started an unlikely
success story, finalized in the takeover
by Moortgat, the brewers of Duvel.
Prior to that, Achouffe had already
expanded into foreign markets in
Europe and elsewhere.

AFFLIGEM

Ringlaan 18, B1745 Opwijk, Belgium
www.affligembeer.be

Brouwerij De Smedt was a well-
established family brewer, especially
known for its Affligem abbey range,
when mondial brewer Heineken
stepped in 1999 to streamline the
brews—and change its name.

BREWING SECRET Affligem Blonde is the
staple, but specialists prefer the
Paters Vat Postel abbey range, formerly
made at defunct Campina Brewery.

BEER

BLANCHE DES HONNELLES
WITBIER 6% ABV
Not your usual wheat beer, this one
is made from malted barley, malted
wheat, and home-malted oats.

ABBAYE DES ROCS BRUNE
BELGIAN DARK STRONG ALE 9% ABV
Very spiced and sustaining, with a
nourishing touch. Well-liked in
Anglo-Saxon countries.

ACHEL BRUIN 8
TRAPPIST BEER 8% ABV
More than the draft beers on tap,
this is a classic Trappist brew; heavy,
estery, and filling.

ACHEL EXTRA BRUIN
DARK TRAPPIST 9.5% ABV
The flagship of brewmaster
Knops—who refuses to drink
anything else—rich and rewarding.

MC CHOUFFE BRUNE
SCOTCH ALE 8.5% ABV
Scotch ale is a tradition in Wallonia.
This is the Chouffe version, with
Belgian spicing and high strength.

LA CHOUFFE BLONDE
BELGIAN ALE 8% ABV
The bottle-conditioned staple beer:
sweet, bitterish, and spicy. A real
classic, and much praised.

POSTEL DOBBEL
ABBEY ALE 7% ABV
This estery brown "double"
abbey ale possesses chocolate
notes, and a dry finish.

AFFLIGEM PATERS' VAT
ABBEY ALE 6.8% ABV
Not always easy to find, but you
will be rewarded with a more
hoppy abbey ale than usual.

BELGIUM'S BEST-SELLING BEERS

For the enthusiast, Belgium is the country of unique and beguiling beers, but the vast majority of beer consumed there is bottom-fermented lager, locally known as "pils."

The brand of pils best-known abroad is Stella Artois, but in Belgium itself Jupiler is much more frequently seen. However, both hail from the same giant Anheuser-Busch InBev. The InBev part of the company was itself the result of the 2004 merger of of Belgium's (largely family-owned) Interbrew and South-American AmBev. Anheuser-Busch InBev owns different breweries all over the world, including several in Belgium, the main two being in Leuven and Jupille-sur-Meuse. Aside from the oceans of rather dull pils, they also offer an extensive range of other beer types, including the well-known Leffe range of abbey ales and the more-or-less "lambic-y" Belle-Vue beers (gueuze and different fruit concoctions). Thanks to their universal availability, they are often mistaken abroad—and indeed in Belgium itself—for being Belgiums' best. The Alken-Maes brewing group own the popular Grimbergen range.

JUPILER (PILS 5.2% ABV) *left*
STELLA ARTOIS (PILS 5.2% ABV)
LEFFE (ABBEY ALE 6.6% ABV) *center*
BELLEVUE EXTRA KRIEK (CHERRY-LAMBIC 4.3% ABV) *right*
BELLEVUE GUEUZE (FILTERED GUEUZE 5.2% ABV)
GRIMBERGEN BLOND (ABBEY ALE 6.7% ABV)
GRIMBERGEN DUBBEL (ABBEY ALE 6.5% ABV)

ALVINNE
Mellestraat 138, B8501 Heule, Belgium
www.alvinne.be

Davy Spiessens and Glenn Castelein started as homebrewers, going professional in the smallest way possible—in a shed in the garden. Word got around about the quality of their beer, however, and in 2007 they moved to the current location. Their range of beers is constantly evolving, while others they produce have been specially commissioned.

ANKER
Guido Gezellelaan 49, B2800 Mechelen, Belgium
www.hetanker.be

Now here's a brewery with a history. The owners claim it began in 1369, but it was in 1873 that the family Van Breedam took over and began its modern brewing age. In the 1990s, the end for the classic Gouden Carolus seemed near, but a family buy-out from the ill-fated RIVA empire succeeded, and now the brewery is productive and innovative once more.

BAVIK
Rijksweg 33, B8531 Bavikhove—Harelbeke, Belgium
www.bavik.be

With the fourth generation of the De Brabandere family, this brewery is run efficiently and encompasses a large number of tied pubs too.

BREWING SECRET Abbey ales and pilsners form an important role in the annual output (especially to supermarkets), but the most interesting brews are in the oud bruin tradition.

GASPAR
WINTER ALE 8% ABV
A real connoisseurs' beer, Gaspar is a hoppy treat—and pretty strong!

PODGE BELGIAN IMPERIAL STOUT
IMPERIAL STOUT 10.5% ABV
Pitch-black and incredibly strong, Podge is the brainchild of a British admirer of Belgian beers.

GOUDEN CAROLUS CLASSIC
STRONG DARK ALE 8.5% ABV
This malt bomb has a characteristic taste of raisins in portwine. An exemplary strong, dark Belgian ale.

GOUDEN CAROLUS CHRISTMAS
10.5% ABV
The raisins and molasses from the Carolus Classic are present, but with a greater alcohol kick.

PETRUS OUD BRUIN (DARK)
OUD BRUIN 5.5% ABV
Recently, the brewery invested in giant wooden barrels for fermenting this vinous, quite traditional ale.

PETRUS AGED PALE
OUD BRUIN 7.3% ABV
In the new barrels, you'll find this: the undiluted pale beer, ageing for years, gaining sourish, fruity notes.

BREWERY

BELLEVAUX

5, Bellevaux, B4960 Malmedy, Belgium
www.brasseriedebellevaux.be

Though the name doesn't give anything away, this Walloon brewery is actually run by a … Dutchman! In a true idyllic setting, this brand new brewery has very modern equipment. Wil Schuwer doesn't like to do things half-heartedly, and his beers are the result of extensive and careful experimentation.

LA BINCHOISE

38, Faubourg Saint Paul,
B7130 Binche, Belgium
www.brasserielabinchoise.com

Situated in the Hainaut province, this brewery was started in 1987 by André Graux. New management took over in 2001, and while they might have a more commercial agenda, La Binchoise is still worth a visit, both for the brewery tap and for the developing range of beers.

BLAUGIES

435, Rue de la Frontière,
B7370 Dour-Blaugies, Belgium
www.brasseriedeblaugies.com

Hard by the French border, Blaugies is another small family brewery in which the children have taken over from the parents—who, in this case, started up the business in 1988. The aim of De Blaugies is to produce beers in the style of the region, and the brewery often creates highly unusual brews.

BOCKOR

Kwabrugstraat 5, B8510 Bellegem, Belgium
www.bockor.be

This brewery is probably best known for its Jacobins (would-be lambics that use spontaneous fermentation). However, the brewery turns out a whole range of other beers, not least a traditional style oud bruin, created by former head brewer Omer Vander Ghinste. Bockor are currently revamping the range of beers.

BEER

BELLEVAUX BLACK
OLD ALE 6.3% ABV
Nearly every taster would agree that the Black is Bellevaux's most interesting beer. Though fruity in character, it is simultaneously very dry.

BIÈRE DES OURS
FLAVORED ALE 8.4% ABV
Bears know why: honey! Another traditional ingredient for Belgian specialty ales.

LA BINCHOISE SPÉCIALE BELGE
SPÉCIALE 5% ABV
This light, refreshing ale was once the staple Belgian beer, and known as a "Spéciale." Great revived style.

LA MONEUSE
SAISON 8% ABV
Down-to-earth, spicy Hainaut brew: yeasty, estery; strong for a *saison*, with the characteristic metallic tang.

BIÈRE DARBYSTE
FLAVORED ALE 5.4% ABV
Fig's juice? Alcoholic variant of Yesteryear, a non-alcoholic brew. Sweet only when fresh.

BELLEGEMS BRUIN
MIXED FERMENTATION BEER 5.5% ABV
Oud bruin relies both on wild and cultivated yeasts. The result: a beer in which flavors of berries, wood, and lactic sourness abound.

BOCQ

4, Rue de la Brasserie,
B5530 Purnode-Yvoir, Belgium
www.bocq.be

One of the few breweries in the
Namur province, Du Bocq is actually
one of the larger Belgian regionals,
not least because of the commission
brewing side of the business.
However, a few of Du Bocq's own
brews are well known nationally,
including the Gauloise range, the
Saison Regal, and their witbier.

BOON

Fonteinstraat 65,
B1520 Lembeek, Belgium
www.boon.be

In 1975, when lambic-based beers and
lambic brewers were dying out, Frank
Boon took over the De Vits range.
Deemed crazy, he still proves his
detractors wrong, by constantly
growing and improving his business.

BREWING SECRET Most Boon beers are
deemed "oude," meaning "in the old
style" of unadulterated lambics.

BOSTEELS

Kerkstraat 96,
B9255 Buggenhout, Belgium
www.bestbelgianspecialbeers.be

It is now the seventh generation of
the Bosteels family that owns and
runs this brewery. In recent times,
they have shown a flair for flowing
with fashion—not only in the beers,
but also with spectacular glassware.

BREWING SECRET Tripel Karmeliet, one
of the flagship beers, uses three grains
in the mash: barley, wheat, and oats.

BRUNEHAUT

17, Rue des Panneries,
B7653 Rogny-Brunehaut, Belgium
www.brunehaut.com

In another part of Brunehaut village
known as Guignies, Brasserie Allard &
Groetembril had operated until 1990.
That place closed, but, less than a year
later, a new page was turned when the
owners opened this brewery in Rogny.
They have a broad range of regional
beers, and are tentatively moving into
organic production with the "b" and
"Terroir" beers.

LA GAULOISE AMBRÉE

SPÉCIALE BELGE 5.5% ABV
Liquorice and citrus peel flavors,
along with the hops, clearly reveal
the beer's Walloon character.

CORSENDONCK AGNUS

ABBEY TRIPLE 7.5% ABV
Citrussy and hoppy nose; initial
grainy flavor, with a flowery
and citrus finish.

GEUZE MARIAGE PARFAIT

GUEUZE 8% ABV
"Perfect marriage," meaning the
lambics, of course, resulting in the
brewers' favorite dry gueuze.

BOON OUDE KRIEK

KRIEKEN 6.5% ABV
A fully unsweetened krieken (sour
cherry) lambic, which makes this
beer a delight for tongue and eyes.

TRIPEL KARMELIET

ABBEY TRIPLE 8% ABV
Smoked and spicy nose announces a
malt-dominated brew with a roasted
character—unusual for a pale beer.

DEUS BRUT DES FLANDRES

BELGIAN STRONG ALE 11.5% ABV
The Dom Perignon lookalike
bottle shows that this is aimed at
upmarket drinkers; dry and spritzy.

LA RAMÉE BLONDE

BLONDE ABBEY ALE 8% ABV
A strong beer that seems even
more powerful through its
liqueurlike finish.

NE KOPSTOOT

BLENDED BEER 7% ABV
This beer is mixed with genever
(the Dutch/Belgian version of gin),
creating a strong, fragrant brew.

BEER STYLES
WILD BEERS

The Belgian brewery of Cantillon seems from another time and a world away from the gleaming stainless-steel brewing behemoths that pump out millions of gallons of mass-market lager. Here, beer is brewed using spontaneous fermentation, a process that harks back to the very dawn of brewing. After the wort has been produced, it is left overnight in massive cooling trays high up in the eaves of the brewery. During this time, wild yeasts drift in through holes in the roof and trigger the fermentation process. Once this is under way, the fermenting beer is transferred to oak and chestnut barrels, lined up in a dark and musty room, to undergo a "long sleep." This ancient way of brewing has survived in the Payottenland region, close to Brussels in Belgium, and the beers produced here and in this way are known as lambics.

If the variety of beer styles is a family, then lambic and its other wild cousins must surely be the mad relations of the brood. Letting wild yeast, or *Brettanomyces* (Brett), infect the newly brewed wort is anathema to the majority of brewers; unpredictable and requiring great skill and experience to handle, it creates sour and challenging flavours. Yet the technique has not only continued and flourished in this corner of Belgium, it has also gone on to influence brewers around the world in recent years.

LAMBIC This is one of the most challenging beers in the world. When young it is sharp and acidic, somewhat reminiscent of a very dry English West Country cider. When aged, the effect is a more complex interplay of toasty, earthy, zesty, fruity flavors, and an assertive sourness. Some lambics have distinct grapefruit notes on the nose and palate.

GUEUZE Fresh lambics are blended with their more mellow elders, which have been ageing in wooden barrels for a year or more, to create Gueuze. This is the Champagne of the beer world—sprightly, elegant, sparkling.

AMERICAN WILD ALE Brewers in the US have also begun brewing with wild yeasts, usually in conjunction with wooden barrels, producing ales even more quenchingly sour than their Belgian forefathers. Glacier Brewhouse in Alaska and Russian River in California are two of the keenest exponents.

The Delirium bar in Brussels stocks somewhere in the region of 2,000 different beers, 400 of which are from Belgium.

BREWERY

CANTILLON

Gheudestraat 56, B1070 Brussel/
Anderlecht, Belgium
www.cantillon.be

As early as 1900, the Cantillon family had beer blending facilities here, in the old southern suburbs of Brussels. In 1970, Jean-Pierre Van Roy, who had married Claude Cantillon, took over the business, despite not being a brewer. Even though his background was not in beer, he turned into the staunchest defender of old-style brewing without compromises.

His son Jean, however, has shown in the last 10 years or so that the brewery is not averse to experimentation, and recent years have seen the use of fresh hops, and even American "C-hops"—both anathema to the lambic tradition

BREWING SECRET Cantillon's range of fruit beers uses whole fruit rather than being syrup-based.

CARACOLE

86, Côte Marie-Thérèse, B5500
Falmignoul, Belgium
www.brasserie-caracole.be

Started in around 1990, Caracole moved after a few years from Namur to the present location. The brewery offers beers in two varieties: a "normal," and a "bio" (organic) version. Caracole means "snail," and production isn't rushed—but the beers are enjoying growing international recognition.

CHIMAY

8, Route Charlemagne,
B6464 Baileux, Belgium
www.chimay.com

Though the bottling is done in Baileux, the brewery is still in the monastery at Forges-les-Chimay. Since 1861, monks have brewed here, but Chimay became the leading Trappist brewery through Père Theodore, who went to Leuven University to study brewing in a contemporary way. Chimay never stopped growing and is vital to the economy of the region.

BEER

CANTILLON GUEUZE
ORGANIC LAMBIC 5% ABV
Nose of citrus, horse blanket, wood, and hay; woody flavors, with green fruit and some sulfur; sour and tart in mouthfeel.

LOU PEPE FRAMBOISE
FRUIT BEER 5.5% ABV
A mix of lambic beer with a pure sugar solution. One of the most intense fruit beers on earth.

CANTILLON IRIS
SPÉCIALE BELGE 5% ABV
Lots of hops on the nose: cheesy aged ones, and fresh aromatic ones. Quite fruity, with a hoppy finish.

CANTILLON ST LAMVINUS
FRUIT BEER 5.5% ABV
Wet wood, sour fruit, sulfur, and horse blanket aromas. The fruit is very prominent, but it is difficult to distinguish the grapes that are used.

TROUBLETTE BIO
WITBIER 5% ABV
A fully organic Belgian white, with no excess coriander, but a fine citrussy and refreshing finish.

NOSTRADAMUS
BELGIAN DARK ALE 9.5% ABV
Caracole's strong dark ale is a mix of roasted, fruity, malty, and higher alcohol notes.

CHIMAY TRIPEL
ABBEY ALE 8% ABV
Sweet, grapey taste, with bittering hops and herbal qualities; not entirely unlike a dry white wine.

GRANDE RÉSERVE / BLEUE
BELGIAN STRONG ALE 9% ABV
Roasted malts, with some quite dominant bitterness, and dark, ripe fruit (plums, blue grapes), and pears.

CONTRERAS

Molenstraat 110, B9890 Gavere, Belgium
www.contreras.be

Contreras is an unlikely brewing
survivor. When Willy Contreras
retired, his daughter could not see
her future in brewing, but in 2001 her
husband, Frederik De Vrieze, took
the business in hand. He set out on
a straightforward modernizing path,
and the first beer to benefit from a
revamp was the breweries' top
offering, Mars.

DE BLOCK

Nieuwbaan 92,
B1785 Peizegem, Belgium
www.satanbeer.com

This is another family brewery that
was saved by the son-in-law (who, in
this case, had to prove himself capable
of holding his drink—and being able
to smoke!). The history of the
brewery is well documented in
the on-site museum. A very quiet
brewery, but interesting nevertheless.

DE DOLLE BROUWERS

Roeselarestraat 12B,
B8600 Esen, Belgium
www.dedollebrouwers.be

By buying and renewing the old
Costenoble Brewery in the far west
of Belgium in 1980, Kris Herteleer
and his two brothers started,
unknowingly, the country's
microbrewery revolution. Fame soon
reached international quarters—but
then the "mad brewers" never
searched for simplicity, a quiet life, or
easy money. "Quality does the trick"

is the motto of Kris—the only
remaining brewer of the original
three. Adding to the complexity are
the beer names, virtually all of which
use Dutch word play of some sort.

BREWING SECRET Kris also makes
specially oak-aged versions of some of
his beers, dubbed "Réserva". They
fetch vertiginous prices, are rare, and
rather difficult to hunt down.

MARS ESPECIAL

BELGIAN AMBER ALE 6.5% ABV
Mars is brewed with March water,
which according to the lore of the
brewery is "in bloom," and creates
a better beer. It used to be a dry,
metallic oud bruin, but today is
more of a classic Belgian amber
ale—moderate acidity on top of
crystal and amber malt sweetness.
Creamy, but not full-bodied.

KASTAAR

AMBER ALE 6% ABV
A somewhat darker "Spéciale
Belge," with lots of caramel and
some coriander for spicing—and a
flashy name for export: K-Star.

ARABIER

BELGIAN PALE STRONG ALE 8% ABV
A dry-hopped, citrussy beer that can
age beautifully to a potent brew.

STILLE NACHT

SEASONAL CHRISTMAS ALE 12% ABV
Overripe grapes, raisins, and other
dried fruits. Some hoppy bitterness
hiding behind lots of sweet malts;
acidic lining for a great balance.

OERBIER

BELGIAN DARK ALE 9% ABV
Fruitiness throughout, from nose to
finish. Very vinous character, grapey,
and clearly strong in alcohol.

OERAL

PALE BELGIAN ALE 6.5% ABV
An old ale that's been renamed;
creamy and hoppy.

ALL ABOUT ...
GLASSES

We are what we drink from. A book-lined study on a winter's night demands Cognac in a voluminous balloon; a gourmet feast requires an array of different glasses especially suited to Champagne, Burgundy, Bordeaux, and so on. But what about beer? The best glassware for the best long drink in the world should be the priority. It's about showing a beer in the best possible light, and revealing its aroma, condition, appearance, and flavor. Nations, towns, and individual breweries have developed a wide range of different and distinguished glassware—some simple and straightforward, such as those for a kölsch or a British pint; others more ostentatious and theatrical, like the quirky Kwak glass. In the USA, Samuel Adams' Boston Lager has a newly devised glass, specially shaped to maintain the beer's temperature, and to maximize its aroma and flavor—yet another development in the ongoing refinement and reinvention of the beer glass.

SNIFTER For some of the strongest beers, a small, brandy-balloon-like glass, known as a snifter, is the best choice. The shape holds aromas well, and its scale lends itself to rich, powerful beers, such as the Austrian Samichlaus.

FLUTE In Germany, pilsners and wheat beers are commonly served in tall, thin, wasp-waisted flutes.

BALLOON Duvel is served in a balloon-shaped receptacle resting on a flat-bottomed stem. This allows the drinker to appreciate the beer and its soft foamy head at the same time, while also savoring its fine aroma.

GOBLET Go to a Belgian bar and every beer gets a different glass. It has been known for drinkers to be refused their choice because no suitable glass is available. Trappist beers such as Orval and Westmalle should be served in goblets.

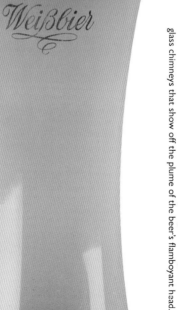

TUMBLER Whereas German wheat beer has an elegant, long-legged supermodel of a glass, Belgian-style wheat beers have adopted a more robust, chunky tumbler, popularized by the Hoegaarden Brewery.

TEST TUBE Kwak has its very own glass—a vessel that looks rather like a test tube. Because it has a rounded bottom, it has to be served held in a wooden bracket, like a test-tube holder, to keep it from toppling over.

CYLINDER Kölsch is served in small, light, cylindrical glasses—little glass chimneys that show off the plume of the beer's flamboyant head.

TULIP Ask for a pint in Britain and you are most likely to get it in either a nonic glass (straight-sided with a small bulge two-thirds of the way up) or a tulip-shaped glass, in which the contour is smoother. The last manufacturer of the traditional "pint pot" (a sturdy, dimple-sided glass tankard) went out of business in 2001.

BREWERY

DE KONINCK

Mechelse Steenweg 291,
B2018 Antwerpen, Belgium
www.dekoninck.be

De Koninck is an icon—as is its
main beer. It embodies the town of
Antwerp—whose inhabitants are a
proud lot, and will say so. The amber
"bolleke" (actually the glass) is still
the staple diet in many bars.

BREWING SECRET The draft version
is unpasteurized and should be
tried at its source.

DE LANDTSHEER

Mandekensstraat 179,
B9255 Buggenhout, Belgium
www.malheur.be

The brewery maintains the old family
name, but the beers are better known
under the brand name Malheur
("accident"). The company's steep
rise might have shocked some of
its competitors, but one of the men
driving this venture was for many
years a distributor for Westmalle,
and so was very well connected.

DE RANKE

1a, Rue du Petit Tourcoing, B7711
Dottignies/Dottenijs, Belgium
www.deranke.be

A fully integrated Belgian brewery:
the brewers are Flemish, the plant
was set up in Wallonia in 2005,
and a Brussels brewer was hired to
help them out! They have a distinct
keeness for lambics, for quality, and
for outspoken taste profiles—as
their beers amply testify.

DE REGENBOOG

Astridlaan 134,
B8310 Assebroek-Brugge, Belgium

Johan Brandt might currently be
operating in rather cramped
conditions, but then he needs space
for his wine and beermaking shop,
as well as for his beekeeping. He is
building up a new brewery in a
different location, however, which is
an indication of his ambition. His
beers are very characterful, and
sometimes entirely unique.

BEER

DE KONINCK

AMBER "SPECIALE BELGE" 5% ABV
Amber malts, residual sugars, and
hops give excellent balance to a
fine ale, with a slight but distinct
sulfury aroma and biscuit character.
The draft version is particularly
good—available in cask in the
UK as well.

MALHEUR BIÈRE BRUT RÉSERVE

BELGIAN STRONG ALE 11% ABV
Bottle fermented in the *méthode
Champenoise* manner. Alcoholic,
sweet brandy nose, then bitterish
and fruity flavors.

MALHEUR DARK BRUT

BELGIAN STRONG ALE 12% ABV
A dark version, but even more
complex, with vinous, chocolate,
fruity, and tannic notes.

XX BITTER

BITTER 6.2% ABV
Inspired by English bitters, but at
a very Belgian 6.2% ABV, this is a
wonderfully refreshing, hoppy brew.

KRIEK DE RANKE

FRUIT BEER 7% ABV
Mixed with lambic and cherries, this
sourish fruit ale is close to fruit
lambics—and yet quite different.

'T SMISJE SLEEDOORNBIER

FRUIT BEER 7% ABV
Made with sloe berries picked by
his family, the beer has a sharp,
fruity tang. Though normally
produced at 6% ABV, the "Extra"
version weighs in at 7%.

DE RYCK

Kerkstraat 24, B9550 Herzele
www.brouwerijderyck.be

Female brewmaster An De Ryck has
been the motor driving a lot of the
recent modernization at this family
brewery, the roots of which stretch
back to the 19th century. From keg
only production, the brewery now
handles all kinds of bottlings, often
with beer on lees.

BREWING SECRET A 40% ABV
Bierschnaps is produced here too.

DE STRUISE

Struise Brouwers, Noordhoek 13,
B8647 Lo-Reninge, Belgium
www.struise.noordhoek.com

Strictly speaking, the brewery here is
Deca—an old established regional
brewer—but De Struise Brouwers hire
their facilities to such an extent that
they claim 60 percent of the overall
output. Struise's Urbain Cotteau and
Carlo Grootaers aim for the wild,
complex, strong, flavor-packed beers
so loved by new brew countries, such
as the US, Denmark, and Sweden.

DOMUS HUISBROUWERIJ

Tiensestraat 8, B3000 Leuven, Belgium
www.domusleuven.be

In the same town as megabrewer
Stella Artois, Belgium's first brewpub
saw the light of day in 1985. But
then Leuven is Belgium's foremost
university town, and students do like
a drink. The brewing may occur
rather haphazardly, but the unfiltered
pilsner is a peach—thanks to Mark
Knops and Sam Croonen, huge
hopheads that they are!

DRIE FONTEINEN

Hoogstraat 2A, B1650 Beersel, Belgium
www.3fonteinen.be

Armand Debelder, a blender and later
brewer, rose to prominence in the
beer world through the Drie Fonteinen
("3 Fountains") pub and restaurant.
Debelder is the driving force behind
this micro-venture in brewing, though
other gueuze blenders and enthusiasts
of the beer style have helped him to
keep going through some difficult years.

AREND WINTER
SPÉCIALE BELGE 6.3% ABV
Formerly known as "Christmas
Pale-ale," this *Spéciale Belge* was
often regarded as a real treat for
the holiday season. A brown sugar
aroma is matched by a herbal smell.
Fairly sweet on the palate, with
caramel notes; the hop flavoring
varies from year to year.

PANNEPOT
DARK BELGIAN STRONG ALE 10% ABV
Fruity, vinous, and spiced; the
complexity of this beer amazed
everyone—an instant success.

AARDMONNIK—EARTHMONK
OUD BRUIN 8% ABV
Lighter than Pannepot, but it makes
up for this in taste: lactic, earthy,
vinous, and unfathomably complex.

CON DOMUS
PILSNER 5% ABV
An unfiltered, hazy pilsner, and
very good on draft. A malty
and grassy nose makes way for
a herbal, peppery, and grassy taste,
with plenty of bitterness. You can
figure out the word play on the
name yourself.

3 FONTEINEN OUDE GEUZE
GUEUZE 6% ABV
A top gueuze: horse blanket,
leather grease, and lemon juice
notes are all there, but so too is
tarragon—the Belgian Chablis?

3 FONTEINEN HOMMAGE
FRUIT LAMBIC 6.5% ABV
A mix of raspberries and sour
cherries, in homage to Gaston
Debelder, founder of the 3 Fonteinen.

BREWERY

DUBUISSON

28, Chaussée de Mons,
B7904 Pipaix-Leuze, Belgium
www.br-dubuisson.com

Leuze is a town with three breweries, two of them in the Pipaix village. Dubuisson is probably the most dynamic, and its location, next to a major road, has made their brewery tap a very successful venture. The brewery excels in high alcohol ales, so extreme caution is advised when drinking these beers.

DUPONT

Brasserie Dupont, 5 Rue Basse, B7904 Tourpes-Leuze, Belgium
www.brasserie-dupont.com

Western-Hainaut enjoys rich soil, and farmsteads here were huge—usually operating a brewery in the winter, making beer to be consumed on the land in summer (hence the style of beer known as *saison*). Brasserie Dupont became solely a brewery, but owner Olivier Dedeycker has re-engaged with the history of the land, by reintroducing farming and cheese-

making into this marvellous brewery—arguably one of Belgium's finest.

BREWING SECRET Most *saisons* of old carried a ferric tang because of the water, but Dupont always was the exception, as their well delivers very soft water. They are masters in restrained spicing.

DUVEL MOORTGAT

Breendonkdorp 58-66, B2870
Breendonk-Puurs
www.duvel.be

Started as a small family brewery, Moortgat continued producing top-fermented ale at a time when everywhere lager reigned. The Moortgat ale evolved into the iconoclastic Duvel, a beer that has become so popular that the brewery group renamed itself. Moortgat now owns breweries in Belgium and abroad.

BEER

BUSH PRESTIGE

BELGIAN STRONG ALE 13% ABV
This oak-aged version of the Ambrée is a true marvel in balance, despite its impressive strength.

BUSH AMBRÉE

BELGIAN STRONG ALE 12% ABV
In some markets known as "Scaldis," this is a treacherously drinkable alcohol-bomb.

AVEC LES BONS VŒUX

SEASONAL WINTER ALE 9.5% ABV
Once a complimentary winter ale, but so superb that it is now brewed year round. Barnyard and earthy aromas mingle with citrus zest. Grainy flavor: fresh white bread with nuts, spices, and walnut oil.

SAISON DUPONT

SAISON 6.5% ABV
Formerly brewed in winter with the hot summer months in mind – hence a dry, refreshingly light brew.

MOINETTE BLONDE II

BELGIAN STRONG ALE 8.5% ABV
Related to the *saison* in style, but stronger, and spiced—paradise seed especially takes up a major role.

DUVEL

BELGIAN STRONG ALE 8.5% ABV
Sometimes dubbed "red," to distinguish it from the filtered version, this ultra dry ale hides its potency as no other.

MAREDSOUS 8°

BROWN ABBEY ALE 8% ABV
Arguably the best from the Maredsous Abbey range. Estery, fruity notes, and tobacco leaf.

ECAUSSINNES

118, Rue Restaumont,
B7190 Ecaussinnes, Belgium
www.brasserieecaussinnes.be

The Van Poucke couple arrived on the brewing scene in 2000 with the Brasserie d'Ecaussinnes, a microbrewery and tavern. Its rise has been meteoric, and nobody would call it a micro today. The lion's share of the production is for export only, and the brewery even makes a beer exclusively for the Australian market.

FANTÔME

8, Rue Préal, B5454 Soy-Erezée, Belgium
www.fantome.be

Dany Prignon started this micro in a shed in the Ardennes, and while today he exports his beers to many countries, the shed is still the brewery's home—though it now contains far more equipment.

BREWING SECRET More works of art than products of brewing science, many of the beers are never brewed the same way twice.

GIRARDIN

Lindeberg 10-12,
1700 Sint-Ulriks-Kapelle, Belgium
www.brouwerijgirardin.com

As rural as you can get, Girardin is still very much a farm and brewery, and this authentic lambic brewer and gueuze blender has no time for curious visitors. If, however, you come simply to stock up on lambic—as the locals and other blenders do—the brewers will gladly help you to their citrussy, spontaneously fermented brews.

GRAIN D'ORGE

16, Centre, B4852 Hombourg, Belgium
www.brasserie-graindorge.be

Benoît Johnen started brewing professionally in 2002, in his hometown, close to the "three countries" border of Belgium, Germany, and the Netherlands. His small but versatile brewing plant enables him to vary the output, following demand. Most of the beer names are in reference to the idyllic region in which his brewery is located.

ULTRADÉLICE
BELGIAN STRONG DARK ALE 8% ABV
Ecaussinnes beers tend to be sweet, and so is this one. But this cinnamon-spiced beer has greater complexity than most.

BLACK GHOST
BELGIAN STRONG DARK ALE 8% ABV
One of the few regularly seen: malty, with fruity depths, but also flavors of cypress and pine.

FANTÔME
SAISON 8% ABV
The brewery's staple blonde beer: fruity, lactic, variable, and in the style of a *saison*.

FARO GIRARDIN
BLENDED LAMBIC 5% ABV
Caramel, meaty, and woody aromas; slight sour edge around the caramel. Filtered, as the yeast would wreak havoc with sugars from the syrup.

GIRARDIN FOND GUEUZE
GUEUZE 5% ABV
This delectable unfiltered gueuze has a marked grapefruit flavor.

BRICE
ABBEY BLONDE-STYLE ALE 7.5% ABV
With a little spice edge, this dry blonde hides its strength very well.

3 SCHTÉNG
BELGIAN DARK ALE 6% ABV
Rustic aromas come forth: pine, root, and other spicy nuances; chewy for its moderate strength.

Hoegaarden

Stoopkenstraat 46, 3320
Hoegaarden, Belgium

A village called Hoegaarden, near Tienen in Flanders, is the modern birthplace of Belgian white beer. Records of brewing in the village date back to 1445, when the local monks were enthusiastic brewers, but the tradition died out in the 1950s.

The beer's revival began in 1965, when milkman Pierre Celis decided to brew a beer in his hayloft that would be like the one he missed so much from his youth. With the help of a veteran brewer he founded the Cloister brewery—
De Kluis in Flemish.

His brew soon gained cult status, especially among younger drinkers. In the 1980s, with demand for the beer continuing to grow, Celis bought a local soft drink factory that he rebuilt into a brewery. A fire at the brewery in 1985 led to Interbrew (now InBev) lending Celis money to rebuild. Over time, the loan became full ownership, and the relationship between the parties grew ill-tempered. Interbrew wanted a consistent, mass-market beer, while Celis continued to tinker with his recipe in the pursuit of brewing excellence. Eventually Celis left the company and set up in the US. In Europe, the Hoegaarden brand went from strength to strength and, in the last few years, the beer has been rolled out worldwide, with sales in excess of 120 million liters per annum.

▲ **THE KEY INGREDIENTS** Celis used the traditional ingredients for a white beer: water, yeast, raw wheat, malted barley, hops, cilantro seeds, and dried Curaçao orange peel.

▲ **HOEGAARDEN'S COPPERS** The brewing vessels at Hoegaarden are now used to brew more than the single style of witbier that Celis set out to recreate. The Speciale is a stronger version of Hoegaarden, while the Grand Cru is brewed without wheat at all, and uses only barley; as a bottle-conditioned beer, it improves over a number of years. There is also a beer brewed to an old German recipe, and a beer called Forbidden Fruit— a full-bodied, sweet, and malty brew.

▼ **VISITOR CENTER** The brewery is open to visitors and there can be few better places to enjoy a glass of Hoegaarden than in its own taproom and restaurant.

▲ **STAYING PUT** Tradition plays a big part in the story of top-fermented beers, and InBev came in for stinging criticism worldwide when it announced plans to close the Hoegaarden plant in 2005 and move production to Jupille. This sparked protests locally and worldwide, with beer lovers demonstrating their anger at the plan. Finally, in September 2007, InBev had a change of heart and, as part of a €60 million investment in its Belgian breweries, the Hoegaarden site will stay open.

◀ **THE HOEGAARDEN BRAND** While Celis wanted to continually adjust his recipe for Hoegaarden, Interbrew (now Anheuser-Busch InBev) wanted a consistent beer that they could market internationally

BREWERY

HALVE MAAN

Walplein 26, B8000 Brugge, Belgium
www.halvemaan.be

At the dawn of the 1980s—just as the Maes family were reinventing their old, pilsner-brewing family brewery as a specialty beer brewery—the business ran into difficulty, and RIVA took over. But heir Xavier Vanneste had the brewing bug in his veins, and managed to raise the funds for a buy-out. Since 2005, he has been brewing here again, with new appellations.

HANSSENS ARTISANAAL

Vroenenbosstraat 15,
B1653 Dworp, Belgium
www.proximedia.com

Not a brewery, but a gueuze blender, and yet another family business saved by the son-in-law. Sidy Hanssens married the right man in the right place, and now blending has resumed in the small town of Dworp—once an important center of lambic brewing and gueuze blending. A strawberry lambic is also produced.

HOEGAARDEN

Stoopkensstraat 46,
B3320 Hoegaarden, Belgium
www.inbev.com

Although this is now a brand in the portfolio of brewing giant InBev, it is the lifeblood and spirit of Pierre Celis, Belgium's preeminent brewing revolutionary, that still haunts this brewery. Proof of this came in 2007, when InBev's moguls wanted to close the plant: fate, however, obliged them to reverse their decision.

HUYGHE

Geraardsbergse Steenweg 14b,
B9090 Melle
www.delirium.be

Huyghe is a large regional, turning out both top and bottom-fermented beers. In recent years, the brewery has diversified by undertaking many commissions, sometimes with very specific demands, such as for gluten-free beers, beers for fair trade sale, and beers with unusual ingredients (coconut, palm oil). Huyghe also brews a range of low-alcohol fruit beers.

BEER

BRUGSE ZOT
GOLDEN ALE 6% ABV
Fruity and yeasty esters dominate on the nose. Outspoken citrus flavors, make it fruity, even slightly sour, yet quite dry.

HANSSENS OUDE GUEUZE
GUEUZE 6% ABV
All the necessary notes are here: horse blanket, citrus, tannins, and lactic. Tart, rather than sour.

HANSSENS OUDE KRIEK
KRIEK 6% ABV
Another tart one, yet this ruby kriek (cherry beer) has a profound, sweetish background.

HOEGAARDEN WIT
WITBIER 4.9% ABV
From as early as the 18th century, the town of Hoegaarden was importing blue Curaçao oranges. The peel was mixed with coriander seeds, and, as the rich soil of the area yielded lots of wheat, a very distinct, fruity, and spicy style of beer evolved.

DELIRIUM TREMENS
BELGIAN STRONG ALE 8.5% ABV
Fruity-estery nose; fiery, alcoholic taste. Flavors of pie crust, orange zest, and apricots; quite sweet.

DELIRIUM NOËL
BELGIAN STRONG ALE 10% ABV
Perfumey beer, characterized by alcohol that intensifies the already sweet main taste. Quite spicy too (coriander, sweet woodruff, juniper).

KERKOM

Naamsesteenweg 469,
B3800 Kerkom bij Sint Truiden, Belgium
www.brouwerijkerkom.be

Jean Clerinckx used to work at the big Cristal Alken Brewery, but never forgot the ancestral one, which his father had closed. He restarted it, in the original location, in 1988. Eleven years later, Marc Limet took over and, since then, the brewery has been in constant evolution. Currently, the brewing apparatus is being renewed—but always with tradition in mind.

LEFEBVRE

54, Rue du Croly,
B1430 Quenast, Belgium
www.brasserielefebvre.be

The first member of the Lefebvre family to be involved in brewing was Jules in 1876. The brewery is now in the hands of the sixth generation, with Paul Lefebvre.

BREWING SECRET For a family brewery, this one is very outward looking, and now 80 percent of its beer production is exported.

LÉGENDES

Brasserie des Légendes, 19 Rue du Castel, B7801 Irchonwelz; and 75 Guinaumont, B7890 Ellezelles, Belgium
www.brasseriedeslegendes.be

When Philippe Gérard, brewer/owner of Ellezelloise, started to feel old age encroaching, he joined forces with microbrewery des Géants, run by Pierre Delcoigne and his wife, Vinciane. The companies merged at the end of 2006, though both sites have been kept active (hence the two addresses above). *Brasserie des Géants* is situated in a grand farmhouse, and its brewing paraphernalia combines state-of-the art equipment with a mash tun from 1890 and a copper from 1930. With the exception of the *saison*, the beers are classic strong Belgian ales. Ellezelloise has a more eclectic portfolio, with regional styles such as a *saison*, and more modern-looking beers, like the famous Hercule Stout.

BINK BLONDE

BELGIAN BLONDE ALE 5.5% ABV
Sweet and citrussy aromas, but seriously bitter in the taste, with both hop and citrus peel flavors.

KERKOMSE TRIPEL

ABBEY-STYLE TRIPLE 9% ABV
Everybody needs a triple today—Marc Limet's is a very hoppy, ultra-dry version, with a respectable ABV.

FLOREFFE DOUBLE

BROWN ABBEY ALE 6.3% ABV
An ale of a chocolatey kind, which develops madeira and port notes with a little ageing.

SAISON 1900

SAISON 5.2% ABV
One of the few that refers to the brewery's past; delicate farmyard and rose water aromas.

ELLEZELLOISE HERCULE STOUT

IMPERIAL STOUT 9% ABV
Proclaimed abroad as the first Belgian Imperial stout, this musty, inky brew is a fine, unspiced stout.

ELLEZELLOISE QUINTINE AMBRÉE

BELGIAN STRONG ALE 8.5% ABV
Under a huge head, this strong ale has an inviting medley of citrussy, spicy, and malt flavors.

DES GÉANTS SAISON VOISIN

SAISON 6% ABV
Referring to a former *saison* beer from neighboring Flobecq, it has some farmyard and iron touches.

ELLEZELLOISE SAISIS

WITBIER 6.2% ABV
A Hainaut interpretation of the spicy, citrussy Belgian wheat beer. Strong on wheat, stronger in its ABV.

BREWERY

LIEFMANS

Aalststraat 200,
B9700 Oudenaarde, Belgium
www.liefmans.be

Although Liefmans parent group went into receivership at the end 2007, it looks likely that Duvel Moortgat will take over, and so the Oudenaarde plant has a good chance of survival—if, as before, for lagering purposes only.

BREWING SECRET Liefmans beers are rare survivors from the once famous Oudenaards bruin style.

LINDEMANS

Lenniksebaan 1479, B1602 Vlezenbeek, Belgium
www.lindemans.be

When considering lambic breweries, we tend to think about small farm brewers. Lindemans may seem to fit this bill at first glance, yet it is also on the margins of the 10 largest breweries in Belgium. Its success is owed to the rather sweetish fruit concoctions it excels in, with nearly half of the produce destined for foreign markets.

LOTERBOL

Michel Theysstraat 58a,
B3290 Diest, Belgium
www.loterbol.be

Brewing on this site started in the 18th century, the name of the brewery then being Duysters. However, that brewery languished in the 1970s and beermaking only resumed here when the site became a brewpub in 1995. The owner, being a Trappist breweries agent, has infinite wisdom in all things beery.

MORT SUBITE

Lierput 1, B1730 Kobbegem, Belgium
www.alken-maes.be

In 1970, De Keersmaeker Brewery took over Brussels' famous Mort Subite bar (named after a dice game), where mainly gueuze and kriek were consumed. From then on, "Mort Subite" spontaneously fermenting beers became the force of the brewery. It has subsequently been taken over by Alken-Maes, Scottish & Newcastle, and now Heineken.

BEER

LIEFMANS GOUDENBAND
OUD BRUIN 8% ABV
A strong interpretation of the style, its underlying acidity lending the beer outstanding ageing possibilities.

LIEFMANS KRIEK
OUD BRUIN 6% ABV
The lighter version, refermented with sour cherries. The rare, un-sweetened draft version is stellar.

LINDEMANS GUEUZE CUVÉE RENÉ
GUEUZE 5% ABV
Initially produced on demand for export, now this caramel-and-sour-apple gueuze is fairly common.

LINDEMANS KRIEK CUVÉE RENÉ
KRIEK 5% ABV
Unfiltered kriek is rare and this bottled beer is a dry notch above the draft sweet version.

TUVERBOL
BEER STYLE 11% ABV
Mixed with Drie Fonteinen lambic, this beer excels. Sugar, caramel, liquorice, and honey balance the horse blanket aromas and tart lambic flavors.

MORT SUBITE OUDE GUEUZE
GUEUZE 7.2% ABV
A woody gueuze with notes from green apples and grapefruit. Lactic acid dominates other acids, making it fairly mellow, and with a marked wheat character.

ORVAL

2, Abbaye de Notre-Dame d'Orval,
B6823 Villers devant Orval, Belgium
www.orval.be

The single Orval Trappist ale is a
symbol of the whole abbey: the best
in early 20th-century Art Nouveau
styling, blending with the medieval
ruins that surround it. The bottle,
glassware, and everything else is
designed with an eye for beauty and
peace. The ruins can be visited, but
alas, not the newly revamped brewery.

PALM

Steenhuffeldorp 3,
B1840 Steenhuffel, Belgium
www.palm.be

Ranking among the largest
independently owned Belgian
brewers, Palm seems to hover
between fiery independence and base
commercialism. It operates breweries
throughout Belgium as well as abroad,
but the beers from the main plant,
although they do follow traditional
styles, are rather blandly executed.

PROEFBROUWERIJ

Doornzelstraat 20, B9080 Hijfte-
Lochristi, Belgium
www.proefbrouwerij.com

The brewery hirer's dream: a state-of-
the-art brewery, capable of caring for
myriad brews at the same time, with
a vast array of ingredients and yeasts
to choose from. No wonder it has
been brewing not only for Belgian
clients but also for many others from
abroad. De Proefbrouwerij is the
brainchild of Dirk Naudts, himself a
tutor of brewing sciences in Gent and

Leuven. A group of brewing students
known as The Musketeers decided to
have their own beer, Troubadour
Obscura, brewed here. Initially clients
come and have trial brews made
before deciding which composition
and which strains of yeast will work
best for them—after an intensive
tasting session, of course.

ORVAL

AMBER ALE 6.2% ABV
An ultra dry ale that owes a
large part of its character to
Brettanomyces yeasts, (not unlike
those that define lambic) and
to a high proportion of dry hops.

BRUGGE TRIPEL

ABBEY BLONDE ALE 8.2% ABV
A style that originated in Brugge's
center; the beer shows fierce
alcoholic and caramel notes.

DOBBEL PALM

SEASONAL ALE 5.5% ABV
The holiday offering—slightly
darker, slightly stronger than usual
Palm, and a flavor of gingerbread.

VICARIS GENERAAL

DARK ABBEY ALE 8.8% ABV
Brewed in the style of a dark abbey
ale, this one made an immediate
impression on beer festivalgoers.

VLAAMSE PRIMITIEF

BELGIAN WILD BEER 9% ABV
Fruity nose—not-quite ripe peach
or nectarines—and buttermilk
aroma. Taste is more bitter, even
burnt and rubbery.

TROUBADOUR OBSCURA

BELGIAN DARK STRONG ALE 8.5% ABV
Obscura takes the middle ground
between a stout and a Belgian
strong ale.

REINAERT GRAND CRU

BELGIAN PALE STRONG ALE 9.5% ABV
One of the few non-commissioned
beers. Sweet, but complex.

BEER TRAIL
BRUSSELS

"B" is for Belgium, Brussels, and Beer. Today, Belgium beers can be drunk worldwide, but the very best place to embrace Belgian beer culture is in Brussels itself, with its unique cafés, bars, and brasseries.

JOURNEY STATS

2 hours, plus drinking time

7 miles (10 km)

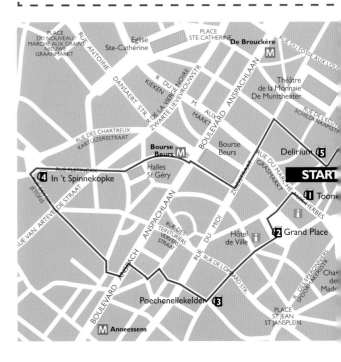

TOONE
The Beer Temple (*Rue Marché Aux Herbes 56*) is one of the world's best beer shops. It stocks most of Belgium's artisanal brewers. It is close to a narrow alleyway that forms the entrance to Toone, a puppet theater with a bar. The walls of this hidden gem are adorned with staring marionettes and the atmosphere is as good as the Kwak beer served here—in the correct glass of course.
6 Impasse Schuddevelde, off 21 Petit Ruedes Bouchers, Brussels

POECHENELLEKELDER
Opposite one of the world's most improbable tourist attractions, the Manneken Pis, is the Poechenellekelder. Loved by the people of Brussels, the bar has a list of 90 fine beers—a perfect introduction to the world of Belgian beers.
5 Rue du Chêne, Brussels

GRAND PLACE
Brussels' famous Grand Place is home to the Belgian Brewers Association and Brewery Museum—both occupy the opulent Brewers House. Several bars surround the square, but there are even better places to drink nearby. In September the square hosts an annual beer festival.

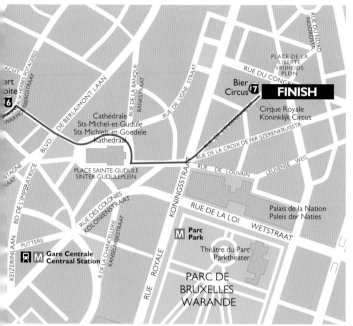

0 yards 200
0 metres 200

IN 'T SPINNEKOPKE

Away from Grand Place, but not too far, can be found In 't Spinnekopke. "The Little Spiders Head" is a small, intimate two-bar restaurant and café. It is as Bruxellois as you can get and has to be one of the best places in Brussels to eat and drink beer. Chef Jean Rodriguez prides himself on pairing food and beer superbly. Who needs wine when you can pair a draft lambic with a plate of mussels? *1 Place du Jardin aux Fleurs, Brussels*

DELIRIUM

Ilot Sacré is a clamor of medieval lanes and fish restaurants with outrageous menu boards, and energetic and sometimes insistent waiters trying to coerce people inside to dine. Down one such alley is Delirium. Don't wait at your table for service, go to the bar, which claims to stock more than 2,000 beers. *4a Impasse de la Fidélité, Brussels*

MORTE SUBITE

Along the road is Galeries Royales St Hubert. Built in 1846, it was the world's largest covered shopping mall when it opened. It leads the way to Morte Subite—a magnificent Art Nouveau bar, which is said to be the best surviving fin-de-siecle long bar in the world. Here is the place to try wildly fermented lambic or gueuze beers—which are best ordered with a plate of marvellous *tête pressée* (brawn) or *kip kap* (pig cheeks). *7 Rue Montagne aux Herbes Potageres, Brussels*

BIER CIRCUS

Up the hill from Central Station is Bier Circus. This friendly, bustling bar is the place to seek out beers from Belgium's growing band of artisanal brewers. It is the perfect place to experience the creative diversity of Belgian brewing. But take some friends with you—many of the beers are served only in 75cl bottles. But then, beer is always better drunk with a friend than alone. *89 Rue de l'Enseignement, Brussels*

Morte Subite in Brussels is celebrated for its Art Nouveau interior and superb range of Belgian beers.

ROCHEFORT

8, Abbaye de Notre Dame de St-Remy, B5580 Rochefort, Belgium
www.trappistes-rochefort.com

Though brewing has been carried out here since 1900, it is only since 1998 that Rochefort has used labels on their bottled beer. Small may well be beautiful, but that does not preclude the search for innovation, and recently the smallest of the Walloon Trappist breweries decided to employ a lay brewmaster, Gumer Santos, to work on their beer production. Since then,

an amazing new lagering room has begun taking shape next to the abbey church, and the few visitors allowed into the abbey are now proudly shown the brand new tasting room.

BREWING SECRET All beers share one basic recipe, but are separately brewed and so may vary a little. As with most Trappist breweries, production is voluntarily limited.

RODENBACH

Spanjestraat 133-141,
B8800 Roeselare, Belgium
www.rodenbach.be

The Rodenbach family started making beer in Roeselare in 1821. Now under the wing of Palm breweries, Rodenbach has turned resolutely modern, yet without doing away with its age-old traditions.

BREWING SECRET The "cathedral" of wooden fermenters is one of the most impressive sights in Belgian brewing.

ROMAN

Hauwaart 105, B9700 Mater-Oudenaarde, Belgium
www.roman.be

Located just outside Oudenaarde town, Roman's commercial products are primarily mainstream lagers and pilsners. Even their new Ename abbey ale range is a rather discreet interpretation of the style, and this also applies to the oud bruin-type beers, which are less bold than those of smaller producers.

ROCHEFORT 6 (RED)
ABBEY ALE 7.5% ABV
Six is a veiled reference to the beer's density (1060 OG)—and this lightest and rarest Rochefort enjoys a very fruity taste.

ROCHEFORT 8 (GREEN)
ABBEY ALE 9.2% ABV
On top of the fruit flavors are the bready, dark, and roasted malts—a nourishing Trappist ale.

ROCHEFORT 10 (BLUE)
ABBEY ALE 11.3% ABV
A superior Trappist ale, with toffee, chocolate, raisins, and port flavors, and incomparable complexity.

RODENBACH CLASSIC
OUD BRUIN 5% ABV
Bearing the signs of its mixed fermentation and wood ageing, it is vinous in character and refreshing.

RODENBACH GRAND CRU
OUD BRUIN 6.5% ABV
A sour beer that has been aged in barrels: very severe and dry; one for the connoisseur.

ENAME 974
ABBEY ALE 7% ABV
The Ename abbey ales range includes this red-brown beer, which is wheaty and spicy.

ROMAN OUDENAARDS
OUD BRUIN 5% ABV
This beer is more bready, nutty, and malty than really lactic in the usual Oudenaards bruin style.

RULLES

Artisanale de Rulles, 36, Rue Maurice Grevisse, B6724 Rulles, Belgium
www.larulles.be

Seldom does a brand new brewery (established only in 2000) meet with such immediate success. Grégory Verhelst's brews are mesmerizingly characterful, and the quality of the labels is equally amazing.

BREWING SECRET Grégory Verhelst enlisted the help of the Orval brewmaster to develop his beers.

SAINTE—HÉLÈNE

21, Rue de la Colinne, B6760 Ethe-Belmont, Belgium
www.sainte-helene.be

After a hectic start, this brewery really got going in 2005, when new brewing equipment was installed. The very southwest corner of Belgium seems to be particularly suited to brewing, as new breweries keep popping up there. Ste-Hélène is enthusiastic about promoting its beers, and is a regular at Belgium's many beer festivals.

LA SENNE

www.brasseriedelasenne.be

Currently there is no address for La Senne, and, for the time being, Yvan Debaets and Bernard Leboucq are brewing their beers at De Ranke. Bernard used to produce the beers in his own brewery, but when the lease ran out, he looked to find another home for the brewery. Hopefully that will happen shortly, as the beers are truly excellent.

SILENRIEUX

Rue de Noupré,
B5630 Silenrieux, Belgium
http://users.belgacom.net/gc195540/#

One of the earlier Walloon micros, Silenrieux started in 1991. Where possible, the ECOCERT (organic certificate) has been obtained. Several commissioned beers are also produced.

BREWING SECRET From the beginning, the emphasis has been on the use of alternative grains, such as spelt (an ancient form of wheat) and buckwheat.

LA RULLES TRIPLE
BELGIAN PALE STRONG ALE 8.4% ABV
No lack of body here; herbal and dry-bitterness on the palate, yet well fermented and strong.

LA RULLES ESTIVALE
SEASONAL ALE 5.2% ABV
A refreshing, citrussy, blossom-laden summer ale—one of the best of its kind.

LA SAINTE HÉLÈNE AMBRÉE
BELGIAN AMBER STRONG ALE 8.5% ABV
Close in character to the triple, but with more caramel and tobacco notes; well-balanced.

LA DJEAN TRIPLE
BELGIAN AMBER STRONG ALE 9% ABV
A beer with many flavors and impressions, from phenolic to fruity and dry to creamy.

TARAS BOULBA
SEASONAL BLONDE ALE 4.5% ABV
A blonde Summer ale that's very easily drinkable, grassy, and malty, with a dry-bitter finish.

STOUTERIK
STOUT 4.5% ABV
The Senne stout is complex like none other, with American hops, parsley, tobacco, mushroom, and peppery flavors.

SARA BRUNE BIOLOGIQUE
BUCKWHEAT BEER 6% ABV
Brewed with organically grown buckwheat, the beer is slightly sour, with some solvent notes.

NOËL DE SILENRIEUX
SEASONAL BEER 6% ABV
A winter offering, with smoked, red fruit, and nutty overtones. Contains buckwheat as well.

SILLY / MYNSBRUGHEN

2, Ville Basse, B7830 Silly, Belgium
www.silly-beer.com

Established in the 19th century, this family brewery walks a fine line between maintaining traditions and employing technical developments geared toward satisfying changing market niches. A *saison* is still produced—bottled and, better yet, on draft—and they have recently launched a beer flavored with rum and named after a regional rock band.

SINT BERNARDUS

Trappistenweg 23,
B8978 Watou, Belgium
www.sintbernardus.be

This brewery really took off at the end of World War II, when St. Bernard(us) received the license for making the St. Sixtus ales from Westvleteren Brewery. That agreement ended in 1992, and now Sint Bernard produces abbey ales and other styles of beer, some broadly in the vein of the St. Sixtus ales. They have diversified, however, partly

thanks to the influence of Pierre Celis, founder of Hoegaarden and grandfather of the Belgian brewing revival. The beers are particularly popular in Denmark, and several beers have been specially designed exlusively for the Danish market.

BREWING SECRET An original strain of yeast from the Trappist Westvleteren Brewery is still used at Sint Bernard.

SLAGHMUYLDER

Denderhoutembaan 2,
B9400 Ninove, Belgium
www.witkap.be

This regional determined its future when gradually, in around 1980, they obtained the rights to brew the Witkap Abbey ale range. It gave a dash to the company for several decades, and they carefully honed the recipes. With the Witkap fame now firmly established, the brewery has recently brought attention to their own range of lagers.

SAISON
SAISON 5.2% ABV
Fruity, madeiralike, thin-bodied. Even when young, this is more like an *oud bruin* than a real *saison*.

SCOTCH SILLY
SCOTCH ALE 8% ABV
Scotch ales are a Walloon tradition. This very malty dark beer is full-bodied and rich.

ST. BERNARDUS WITBIER
WITBIER 5.5% ABV
One of the best witbiers available, since Pierre Celis himself advised on this sweet and sourish recipe.

ST. BERNARDUS BOCK
BOCK 6.5% ABV
This dark beer is top-fermented, with honey, caramel, earthy, and roasted notes.

ST. BERNARDUS TRIPEL
ABBEY ALE 8% ABV
Special malts, coriander, and lots of sweetness reign in this blonde abbey ale.

ST. BERNARDUS ABT
ABBEY ALE 10.5% ABV
The flagship ale; imagine liquid Baba au Rum or the Sachertorte chocolate cake with added fruit, and you'll be close to the flavor.

WITKAP PATER TRIPEL
ABBEY ALE 7.5% ABV
A triple with a very vinous character, like a dry white wine; easily drinkable for its strength.

WITKAP PATER STIMULO
ABBEY ALE 6% ABV
Fruity and spicy, and made with local hops, this blonde ale is quite floral. An excellent session ale.

TIMMERMANS

Kerkstraat 11, B1701 Itterbeek, Belgium
www.anthonymartin.be/Public/

Once a traditional lambic brewery, Timmermans was among the first to habitually mix top-fermented beer into its blends. The brewery has also been eager to produce all kinds of syrup-lambic concoctions, designed to appeal more to the younger generation. Timmermans products, including Tradition, are easily found in Belgian supermarkets.

TRADITION GUEUZE

GUEUZE 5% ABV
Once known as "Caveau," this beer is a mix of tradition and commercialism, and so are its flavors: more pineapple than citrus, and herbal rather than the typical horse blanket notes.

URTHEL

Krommekeerstraat 21,
B8755 Ruiselede, Belgium
www.urthel.com

Though brewmaster Hilde Van Ostaden lives in Belgium, production of his beer has been moved from Van Steenberge to the Dutch Trappist brewery La Trappe. The beers are widely available in Belgium, and the distinctive gnomes on the bottle labels—from illustrations by Hilde's husband Bas—have contributed much to Urthel's popularity.

URTHEL SAMARANTH

BELGIAN BARLEY WINE 11.5% ABV
Barley wine in a Belgian style, with cake, fruit, and liqueur notes; a real after-dinner drink.

URTHEL PARLUS MAGNIFICUS

BELGIAN STRONG DARK ALE 7.5% ABV
Warming, with a slightly chocolatey and bready flavor that is reminiscent of a bock.

VAL-DIEU

225, Val-Dieu, B4480 Aubel, Belgium
www.val-dieu.com

Benoît Humblet set up this brewery in 1997 in the former agricultural section of the Cistercian monastery of Val-Dieu. Since then the brewery has produced a series of abbey ales that are executed with great respect for the local artisanal traditions of brewing. Here, the aim is for consistent quality rather than sudden and dramatic brilliance.

VAL-DIEU BLONDE

BELGIAN BLONDE ALE 6% ABV
A blonde beer with a leafy, grainy flavor and an overall impression of wheat.

VAL-DIEU GRAND CRU

BELGAIN STRONG ALE 10.5% ABV
A chewy, dark ale, with flavors of roasted malts and spice; bitterish notes ride above the sweeter malts.

VAN DEN BOSSCHE

St Lievensplein 16,
B9550 St-Lievens-Esse, Belgium
www.paterlieven.be

A long-standing family brewery in a brewery-rich part of Flanders. Long did it thrive on the local Buffalo ale, weaving colorful stories about its origins. Changes in the beer market have driven it to strengthen the Pater Lieven range—vaguely abbeylike in style—and, tentatively, to produce a beer expressly made for export.

PATER LIEVEN BLONDE

ABBEY ALE 6.5% ABV
Blossomy notes can be found in this abbey blonde, while hops promised on the nose are delivered on the palate.

BUFFALO BELGIAN STOUT

STOUT 9% ABV
Not the legendary Buffalo Spéciale, but a high alcohol, roasted stout, geared for foreign markets.

THE STORY OF ...

Orval

2, Abbaye de Notre-Dame d'Orval,
B6823 Villers devant Orval

In the world of beer there are many blessed brews, but the best must surely be those from the Trappist breweries. Today there are seven breweries that can use this appellation, meaning that their beers have been brewed within the enclosed community of a Trappist monastery. The magnificent seven abbeys where this brewing takes place are Ache, Chimay, Orval, Rochefort, Westmalle, and Westvleteren in Belgium, and Koningshoeven in the Netherlands. Beer mythology has it that monks have been brewing continuously since medieval times. It's a good story, but one that omits the Reformation, when many monasteries were abandoned for years and were used as a source of building stone.

In 1926, the de Harenne family, who had acquired the Orval ruins and surrounding lands in 1887, donated them to the Cistercian order so that monastic life could be re-established at Orval.

In 1931, the monks decided to take up the tradition of brewing once again. Their goal is not profit but a "*redevance*"—that is, to generate enough funds for the upkeep of the abbey, to support the local community, and for charitable projects.

▲ **THE MONASTERY** Orval Abbey's lovely grounds are open to the public; unfortunately, the brewery is not. However, its beers, including Petit Orval (the beer that the monks can drink), can be bought from the adjacent Ange Gardien pub.

▲ **MOVING WITH THE TIMES** As part of its commitment to technological advancement, Orval is in the process of replacing its mash tuns.

▲ **THE LONG VIEW** The abbeys share a common commitment to quality. As part of their philosophy, Trappist breweries not only use the finest ingredients but also invest in top-of-the-range brewing equipment. Orval director Francois de Harenne says: "The monks take a view of the long term, and want the very best equipment. The tradition of Trappist breweries is for the equipment to be sophisticated. We have a high level of quality and we must keep it."

▼ BREW KETTLES Orval maintains its equipment in splendid condition, as evidenced by the glowing state of these 1930s kettles. As in all Trappist breweries, the beer is top-fermented. Other characteristics of Trappist beers are that they all tend to be strong, bottle-conditioned, aromatic, and full of yeasty and fruity flavors.

▲ DRY-HOPPING Sacks of dry Styrian Goldings hops are added to the beer while it is undergoing secondary fermentation. These add balance to the beer and give it a rich, round, earthy, sweet aroma.

▲ THE ORVAL TROUT Local legend has it that a widow called Matilda lost a golden ring in a lake and promised that, if it were found, she would thank God by building an abbey. The ring was brought to the surface by a trout, as depicted on the Orval label and bottle-tops, and in images at the abbey.

▲ THE BEER While some Trappist beers are dark and heavy, Orval is light and dry, and perfectly partners the cheeses that are made in the abbey's dairy. Three Belgian malts and white cane sugar produce a beer with a distinctive pale orange hue.

VAN EECKE

Douvieweg 2, B8978 Watou, Belgium
www.brouwerijvaneecke.tk

The family that owns this brewery in rural Watou also owns another brewery, Leroy, in the vicinity. While Van Eecke specializes in abbey ales and posher brands, Leroy takes care of more mundane lagers and stouts.

BREWING SECRET The Kapittel range used to be in the oud bruin style, but in recent years, the brewery has given it a more classic abbey ale profile.

VANHONSEBROUCK

Kasteelbrouwerij Vanhonsebrouck, Oostrozebekestraat 43, B8770 Ingelmunster, Belgium
www.brouwerijvaneecke.tk

Defining a brewery as a "niche jumper" may hardly sound like praise, but Luc Van Honsebrouck describes his brewery this way himself, claiming that its strength lies in being flexible and more adaptable to market trends than the giants. Luc has a flair for PR, and his magnificent castle in the village acts as a signpost for the brewery.

VAN STEENBERGE

Lindenlaan 25, B9940 Ertvelde, Belgium
www.vansteenberge.com

A very expansive regional brewer, Van Steenberge specializes in making tweakings and blendings for anybody interested in having their very own beer made. Yet, at the core, it has a range of very decent beers, both abbey ales and oud bruins.

BREWING SECRET Unusually, the abbey ales were formulated with the help of a Latvian brewmaster.

VAPEUR

1 Rue du Maréchal, B7904 Pipaix-Leuze, Belgium
www.vapeur.com

Jean-Louis Dits and his late wife, both school teachers by profession, saved this brewery from demolition in 1985. Jean-Louis now owns one of the world's last steam operated breweries.

BREWING SECRET Voluntarily limiting the brewing to every last Saturday of the month, Jean-Louis also bows to his own, rather inflexible ecological logic.

HET KAPITTEL PRIOR
ABBEY ALE 9% ABV
Strong and dark, and now with a bitter-sweet character. Rich, fruitcake in fluid form.

HET KAPITTEL ABT
ABBEY ALE 10% ABV
A very strong blonde ale, with a dry, spicy character, and sweet alcoholic overtones.

ST LOUIS GUEUZE FOND TRADITION
GUEUZE 5% ABV
Can West Flemish beer be real gueuze? This citrussy, unfiltered fresh beer certainly comes close.

KASTEELBIER BLONDE
STRONG BELGIAN ALE 11% ABV
An unfiltered strong blonde beer, with sultanalike, alcoholic sweetness.

AUGUSTIJN
BELGIAN STRONG ALE 8% ABV
An amber ale, bottle-conditioned, dry, and fairly sweet; but with a citrus note too, like orange zest.

BIOS VLAAMSE BOURGOGNE
OUD BRUIN 5.5% ABV
An excellent oud bruin, with a spritzy acidity, a little like balsamic vinegar: velvety and refreshing.

SAISON DE PIPAIX
SAISON 6% ABV
Working from a long-kept recipe, Dits has cleaned it up to tart and citrussy flavors, with the metallic tang of old *saisons* all but gone.

VAPEUR EN FOLIE
SAISON 8% ABV
A lovely, spicy, malty, and alcoholic interpretation of *saison*—with unexpected ageing potential.

VERHAEGHE

Beukenhofstraat 96,
B8570 Vichte, Belgium
www.proximedia.com

The outlook for a small family brewer locked in the clasp of supplying oud bruin and pilsner for local pubs may not appear especially bright, but in the case of Verhaeghe, that summation would be wrong. The variety of oud bruins produced here is remarkable, and the "Duchesse de Bourgogne" in particular has attained cult beer status in new markets, especially the US.

WESTMALLE

Antwerpsesteenweg 496,
B2390 Malle, Belgium
www.trappistwestmalle.be

Monks started brewing here in 1836, selling beer at the gate 20 years later. Today, the abbey operates one of the world's most modern breweries, hidden behind the old brewhouse. Westmalle has come to define abbey ales through their "Dubbel" and "Tripel" styles. The "Extra" could be another world classic, if the monks were to commercialize it.

WESTVLETEREN

Donkerstraat 12,
B8640 Vleteren, Belgium
www.sintsixtus.be

Does this brewery need introduction? The Abbey of St. Sixtus of Westvleteren is the reclusive star of the beer world. It sells its beer by telephone reservation only—unwillingly even—as if to emphasize that the operation is run by monks who brew in order to be able to pray, instead of pray in order to sell. Westvleteren voluntarily limits production. As Joris, the brother responsible for the brewery, says: "We refuse to go into an endless spiral of producing more, then having to sell more, and bring more brothers into the process, or even having to hire outside staff."

BREWING SECRET This is the only remaining Trappist brewery that still employs solely in-house monks.

VICHTENAAR
OUD BRUIN 5.1% ABV
Probably the most basic of the oud bruins: tart, refreshing, and with complex aromas.

ECHT KRIEKENBIER
OUD BRUIN 6.8% ABV
Sour cherries were often put on oud bruins. The cherries give an explosion of fruity, tart flavors.

WESTMALLE DUBBEL
ABBEY ALE 7% ABV
Dark and vinous, with sugar sweetness coming through; surprisingly hoppy. A classic.

WESTMALLE TRIPEL
ABBEY ALE 9.5% ABV
The dry Champenoise triple that made all triples blonde. Sweetish and fruity, with a hoppy finish.

WESTVLETEREN BLONDE
ABBEY ALE 5.8% ABV
A blonde ale that starts with a big grain flavor, followed by very serious hops; best bitterlike.

WESTVLETEREN EXTRA 8°
ABBEY ALE 8% ABV
Dark and strong: roasted, faint bitterish notes, with pears, plums, hazelnuts, and coffee.

WESTVLETEREN ABT 12°
ABBEY ALE 10.2% ABV
A truly massive dark Trappist ale: chewy like no other beer, and with a perfect balance between the sweet and bitter notes.

MORE BEERS OF

BELGIUM

Characterful beers are made by a number of other microbreweries in Belgium, but distribution may be limited to a few small outlets at certain times of the year. These Belgian beers may be hard to track down, but they are worth the effort. Some have won awards.

BREWERY

BRABANT
59, Rue Banterlez
B1470 Baisy-Thy, Belgium
www.labrasseriedubrabant.tk

Frédéric Magerat had been trying his hand at brewing for a long time before he finally turned professional in 2003. In a part of Wallonia that is rather poorly supplied with breweries, Brabant Brewery tries to reawaken local brewing traditions, and some of the names of its beers are taken from former local breweries.

BROOTCOORENS
197, Rue de Maubeuge, B6560
Erquelinnes, Belgium
www.brasserie-brootcoorens-erquelinnes.be

Alain Brootcoorens started his microbrewery in the very last month of the 20th century. His staple beers, Angélus and La Sambresse, can be found at the brewery tap, but are also gradually finding wider distribution.

BREWING SECRET The brewery can also make individually commissioned beers.

CAZEAU
67 Rue de Cazeau,
B7520 Templeuve, Belgium
www.brasseriedecazeau.be

Laurent Agache and Quentin Mariage resurrected Cazeau in 2004. It had operated since the mid-18th century, but in 1969, when Laurent' father Jean was in charge, brewing stopped.

BREWING SECRET The new saison is an indication that these brewers are eager to create styles of beer with more complex, less obvious flavors.

CNUDDE
Fabrieksstraat 8,
B9700 Eine, Belgium

When Louis Cnudde died in 1995, nobody would have wagered a penny on his brewery's future. But his three sons kept the brewery alive, even when brewing only sporadically. Though the beer is available elsewhere, admirers of this brew often like to drink it in the Casino under the brewery tower.

BEER

ARCHIDUC-DUVIEUSART
SAISON 6.5% ABV
A modern-day saison, with all the characteristic farmyard, spicy, and herbal aromas. One of the beers in which the name refers to a former brewery.

ANGÉLUS BLONDE
BELGIAN BLONDE ALE 7% ABV
A flowery and seriously spicy beer, yet one that's also delicate and refreshing.

SAISON CAZEAU
SAISON 4.8% ABV
This is a truly light and refreshing saison. Elderflowers counterbalance the spicy touch.

TOURNAY DORÉE
BELGIAN STRONG ALE 7.2% ABV
The nose offers honey and overripe bananas; the taste is bittersweet, with a sourish, citrus peel note.

LOUIS V OUD BRUIN
OUD BRUIN 4.7% ABV
One of the very last beers of this sort, brewed in and around Oudenaarde town. Slight sourish flavor, lactic, and metallic, while balancing flavors of liquorice and sweet malts. Keg only.

BREWERY

DE CAM
Dorpstraat 67A, B1755 Gooik, Belgium
www.decam.be

Karel Goddeau is brewmaster at Slaghmuylder Brewery, but in his free time he blends gueuze, selling it under the De Cam brand name. The lambic for the gueuze comes from different lambic brewers. Once blended, the beer is lagered in barrels that have a history of their own: they hail from the famous Czech Plzeňský Prazdroj Brewery, home of Pilsner Urquell.

GLAZEN TOREN
Glazen Torenweg 11,
B9420 Erpe-Mere, Belgium
www.glazentoren.be

When three friends got together to make their hobby professional, what transpired was a very modern microbrewery in which originality was the watchword.

BREWING SECRET Glazen Toren brews are very individualistic interpretations of well-known styles, such as saison, Abbey Triple, or Belgian witbier.

SINT CANARUS
Polderweg 2,
B9800 Deinze-Gottem, Belgium
http://users.telenet.be/SintCanarus/home_EN.htm

Piet Meirhaeghe started brewing here in 2002, right in the shadow of the church in the delightful, rural town of Gottem. However, demand for Piet's beer is such that part of the output is now outsourced and hails from the Proefbrouwerij. The Sint Canarus Brewery is open to visitors on weekends.

STRUBBE
Markt 1, B8480 Itegem, Belgium
www.brouwerij-strubbe.be

Marc Strubbe inherited the family brewery, and made it a point to incorporate advanced laboratory techniques into the traditional brewing methods. Brewing commissioned beers and foreign beers under license helps things tick over.

BREWING SECRET The barrels and fermentation tanks allow Marc to work with variable blending.

BEER

DE CAM OUDE GEUZE
GUEUZE 6.5% ABV
Tart, with yogurt, wood, grapefruit, and horse blanket notes—a classic gueuze from the newest blender.

DE CAM OUDE KRIEK
FRUIT LAMBIC 5% ABV
Overwhelming fruit flavors, as well as notes from the cherry stones; a headless and spritzy fruit lambic.

ONDINEKE OILSJTERSEN TRIPEL
ABBEY BLONDE ALE 8.5% ABV
The name is only pronounceable by Aalst town-inhabitants. Fruity, very balanced, and dangerously drinkable.

JAN DE LICHTE
WITBIER 7.5% ABV
A sweet-sour balance, with the unmistakable spice of coriander.

POTTELOEREKE
BELGIAN STRONG DARK ALE 8% ABV
Semi-sweet, richly bodied, with notes of gingerbread, caramel, and pear drops.

ICHTEGEMS GRAND CRU
OUD BRUIN 6.5% ABV
The newest in the range, and an interesting, stronger variation of an Oudenaarde bruin, resulting in a velvety, yet woody dark ale.

BEER STYLES
FRUIT BEER

The addition of fruit to beer is not a recent invention. Over many centuries, raspberries, blackberries, peaches, apricots, damsons, lemons, bananas, and even coconuts have been used to create unusual and distinctive flavors. In the county of Kent, in England, surplus cherries were traditionally used to produce the local favorite cherry ale. Sadly, the last few decades have seen most of the cherry orchards disappear, and the beer along with them. In Belgium, however, fruit beer retains a strong presence. In the Brussels region, lambic brewers have been adding cherries to their beer for hundreds of years. While some fruits may be added in the form of a purée, syrup, or flavoring, the use of whole cherries does more than affect the flavor of the beer—wild yeast on the fruit's skin helps to spark off a secondary fermentation.

LAMBIC Authentic Belgian lambic fruit beer is both fermented and flavored with whole cherries, and known as kriek, or raspberries (frambozen or framboise). Eminent examples of this style of beer include Cantillon's Kriek Lambic and Oud Beersel Oude Kriek.

FLEMISH Another classic Belgian fruit beer is Flemish brown ale, which is also flavored with cherries or raspberries. The stylishly tissue-wrapped Liefmans' Kriek and Frambozen are good examples.

AMERICAN Craft brewers in the USA are now raiding the fruit bowl for their beers. New Glarus's Raspberry Tart remains faithful to the Belgian framboise style, while using berries from Oregon. Other notable American fruit beers are Samuel Adams' Cherry Wheat and New Belgium's seasonal Frambozen.

BRITISH Although less in evidence now than in the past, British fruit beers do exist. Melbourn Brothers specialize in such brews, with cherry, strawberry, and apricot beers, and Old Luxters produces a tasty Damson Ale using Cumbrian fruits.

Liefmans, in the Flemish city of Oudenaarde, Belgium, brews a local style of ale called oud bruin.

Plzeň

Gambrinus

Pilsner Urquell

Prague

Staropramen

U Medvídků

U Fleků

České Budějovice

Budweiser Budvar

Budweiser Burgerbrau

Zlatopramen

Svijany

Klášter

Dětenice

Žatec

Louny

Nymburk

Krušovice

Chodovar

Kutná H

Kozel

Ferdinand

Lobkowicz

Herold

Poutník

Platan

Regent

Eggenberg

Budweiser burgerbrau

CZECH REPUBLIC

The Czech Republic is one of the great brewing nations. It was here that the first golden beer, pilsner, was pioneered in the town of Plzen in the mid-19th century, and it is here also that some of the world's most prized hops are grown at Žatec. The Czech brewing industry is justly proud of its heritage, and is mostly concerned with preserving traditions of brewing excellence that have been developed and nurtured over generations. Pullout boxes appear where a city has more than one brewery.

Novopacké Pivo

Náchod/Primátor

Primator

Holba

Pernštejn

Rychtář

Polička

Radegast

Ostravar

Rebel

hard

Ježek

Černá Hora

Zubr

Radegast

Starobrno

Rebel

Janáček

Zubr

BREWERY

BERNARD

5 Května č.1, 396 01 Humpolec,
Czech Republic
www.bernard.cz

While reviving 16th-century Humpolec brewery in 1991, Stanislav Bernard and two partners took the daring decision to produce traditional unpasteurized beers using microfiltration. Since then, awards and an expanding export market have followed.

BREWING SECRET Bernard has its own floor maltings and uses spring water.

BUDWEISER BUDVAR

Karoliny Světle 4, 370 21
České Budějovice, Czech Republic
www.original-budweiser.cz

The town of České Budějovice (Budweis) has been a home of brewing since 1265. Today, the Budějovický (Budweiser) Budvar product name has Protected Geographical Indicator status within the EU (like Cognac and Parma ham), but in the US, where Anheuser-Busch's Budweiser is trade-marked, it is called Czechvar.

BUDWEISER BURGERBRAU

Lidická 51, 370 54,
České Budějovice, Czech Republic
www.budweiser-burgerbrau.cz

Much of the beer from České Budějovice's oldest extant brewery—operating since 1795—is marketed under the Samson label. The brewery underwent a major modernization program in the 1990s to greatly increase its output.

ČERNÁ HORA

Černá Hora 3/5, 679 21 Černá Hora,
Czech Republic
www. pivovarch.cz

The nearby Black Hill (Černá Hora)—one of the Czech Republic's finest skiing areas—gives this brewery its name. The town's first written brewing record is dated to 1530, but brewing here is believed to predate that considerably. The brewery's traditional techniques and high quality ensure frequent competition successes.

BEER

CELEBRATION / SVÁTEČNÍ LEŽÁK
PREMIUM LAGER 5% ABV
Delicate herblike hop and yeast aromas overlay a peppery bitterness for a grassy finish.

AMBER / JANTAROVÝ LEŽÁK
AMBER BEER 4.4% ABV
Brewed using caramalt for a nutty bitterness, offset by toffee aromas and a honeyed palate.

BUDWEISER BUDVAR / CZECHVAR
PREMIUM LAGER 5% ABV
Spritzy, with an attractive head, floral and grapefruit fruitiness on the nose, and a dry, biscuit malt palate.

CZECH DARK LAGER
DARK BEER 4.7% ABV
Its distinct malty flavor develops a cinnamon spiciness before rolling into biscuit undertones.

SAMSON BUDWEISER BIER
PREMIUM LAGER 4.7% ABV
Some butterscotch and citrus aromas and a honeyed, sweet malty palate, finishing peppery hop dry.

BB BUDWEISER BIER ORIGINAL
PILSNER 5% ABV
Vanilla and herb hop aromas, a bittersweet, malt-veiled mouthfeel, with final traces of tobacco.

MORAVSKÉ SKLEPNÍ NEFILTROVANÉ
PREMIUM LAGER 4% ABV
Unfiltered, with a light body and lingering biscuit malt finish.

GRANÁT
DARK BEER 4.8% ABV
A reddish-brown, award-winning lager, with a distinct caramel palate complementing a plummy aroma.

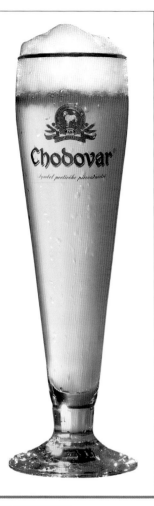

CHODOVAR

Pivovarská 107, 348 13 Chodová Planá,
Czech Republic
www.chodovar.cz

Albi, a dog said to have discovered the bountiful spring that provided water for brewing here in the Middle Ages, was symbolically reinstated by the brewery in 2000, and he now stands proudly on the company emblem.

BREWING SECRET The brewery has an on-site beer spa, complete with a dark beer bath and herbal remedies.

DĚTENICE

Pivovar Dětenice, 507 24 Dětenice,
Czech Republic
www.krcmadetenice.cz

The castle-based brewery—once owned by the Prague chapter of the Knights of Malta—closed in 1955 after several years of nationalization, and reopened only in 2000.

BREWING SECRET Beers are brewed in direct-fired vessels and are filtered through straw, fermented in wooden vats, then lagered in oak barrels.

EGGENBERG

Latrán 27, 38115, Český Krumlov,
Czech Republic
www.eggenberg.cz

Nowhere but in Bohemia could two towns merge over brewing disputes. Years of arguing about wheat beer privileges were resolved simply by uniting neighbors Latrán and Krumlov, and establishing a single brewery. Over time, the brewery passed from the Eggenberg family to the Schwarzenbergs and down the centuries to its present owners, Dionex.

GAMBRINUS

U Prazdroje 7, 304 97 Plzeň,
Czech Republic
www.gambrinus.cz

There are several versions of the origins of the name Gambrinus, but all trace their origins back to beer in some way, be it brewing, cellars, or hops.

BREWING SECRET The brewery shares its malthouse, filtration facilities, and filling lines with Pilsner Urquell. The brewhouses, however, are separate.

PRESIDENT
BLENDED PILSNER 5% ABV
Southern Bohemian malt lager and refined pilsner blend for a full body and bitter finish.

ZLATÁ JEDENÁCTKA
PREMIUM LAGER 4.5% ABV
Brilliantly golden, with unmistakable hop aromas and velvety malt fullness to a soft bitter finish.

SVETLÉ DETENICKÉ PIVO 12°
PREMIUM LAGER 4% ABV
Aromatically floral, finely structured body; sweet malt and honey influences, and hoppy afterglow.

TMAVÉ DETENICKE PIVO 13°
DARK BEER 4% ABV
A typically full-bodied dark lager; malty, some spice, and faintly bitter toward the finish.

EGGENBERG SVĚTLÝ LEŽÁK
PREMIUM LAGER 5% ABV
Powerfully floral with sweet butterscotch notes; zesty, firm, and delightfully balanced to a bitter finish.

EGGENBERG TMAVÝ LEŽÁK
DARK BEER 4.2% ABV
Deep and dark, with a hop pungency, then a malty caramel and toffee bittersweet palate.

GAMBRINUS PREMIUM
PREMIUM PILSNER 5% ABV
A fresh, grassy, and lemon aroma, with hints of butter throughout a full malt flavor.

GAMBRINUS SVĚTLÝ
PILSNER 4.1% ABV
A malt and vanilla palate follows a honeyed, grassy nose to a spicy, bitter finale.

BREWERY

HEROLD
262 72 Březnice, Czech Republic
www.heroldbeer.com

The town's Baroque castle is fully restored, and its attached brewery continues to produce pilsner-style beers in a traditional, hand-crafted manner to a "small is beautiful" philosophy. The range includes wheat beers and Bohemian Black Lager.

BREWING SECRET Open fermenters, home-drawn water, and resident maltings accentuate its heritage.

HOLBA
Pivovarská 261, 788 33 Hanušovice, Czech Republic
www.holba.cz

Among the largest and best equipped breweries in the country, Holba—based in the Jeseníky Mountains—is intensely proud of its regional heritage and independence as a traditional beer producer. It describes its portfolio as "genuine beer from the mountains" and reinvests much of its profits in quality control.

JANÁČEK
Neradice 369, 688 16 Uherský Brod, Czech Republic
www.pivovar-janacek.cz

Weary of leasing the Kaunic family brewery, František Janáček built his own in 1894, and it was soon regarded as the best in southeast Europe. His son Jaromír turned it into one of the most modern, then his nephew guided it through a period of considerable reconstruction. Today it combines modernity with tradition.

JEŽEK
Vrchlického 2, 586 01 Jihlava, Czech Republic
www.pivovar-jihlava.cz

From its earliest days, Ježek beer was exported to Austria—the Viennese monarchy showed particular interest. Wholesale reconstruction in the mid-1990s saw environmentally friendly production methods put in place and improvements made to the quality, taste, and stability of the beer. Ježek also has an on-site restaurant.

BEER

BOHEMIAN BLACK LAGER
DARK LAGER 4.1% ABV
A schwarzbier-type lager; bitter chocolate flavors, plus a little malty sweetness, and a long, dry, slightly smoky finish.

PREMIUM BOHEMIAN LAGER
PREMIUM LAGER 5.1% ABV
Full-bodied, yet softly textured, with a classic creamy malt veil and late hop dryness.

HOLBA CLASSIC 10°
PREMIUM LAGER 4% ABV
A thirst-quencher with a mild, slightly bitter flavor, some malt, and an earthy hop aroma.

HOLBA ŠERÁK
PILSNER 4.5% ABV
Bitterly hoppy, with a surprising malt richness. The brewery's advice is to drink "at least one a day".

JANÁČEK EXTRA
PREMIUM LAGER 5% ABV
Full and robust, with a malt-filled aroma and affable, leafy hop-influenced bitterness.

KVASNIČÁK 10°
PILSNER 4% ABV
An unfiltered "yeast beer", lightly hopped, with refreshing carbonation and a spicy breadlike palate.

JIHLAVSKÝ GRAND
EXTRA PREMIUM LAGER 8.1% ABV
An extraordinary honey-gold beer, with malt and bread aromas and a rich malt palate.

JEŽEK 10° DARK
DARK BEER 4.1% ABV
Typical dark lager (marketed as "women's beer") with caramel and coffee layers and a firmly sweet finish.

KOZEL

Ringhofferova 1, 251 69 Velké Popovice, Czech Republic
www.beer-kozel.cz

The famous goat emblem was created by a traveling French artist in return for hospitality. The town's new brewery opened in 1874 and, by 1912, German innkeepers would boast they kept Kozel's beer. Since 2002 it has been part of Plzeňský Prazdroj—owned by SABMiller—with massive investment driving development.

KRUŠOVICE

270 53 Krušovice 1, Czech Republic
www.pivo-krusovice.cz

When the original owner, Jiří Birka, offered the brewery for sale in 1581 to Emperor Rudolf II, the inventory read: "The brewery kettle is made of stone, so it may be cooked upon immediately." Those documents still exist, but Birka would hardly recognize the highly-mechanized, industrial brewery today—currently the nation's fifth-largest producer.

KUTNÁ HORA

U Lorce 11, 284 15 Kutná Hora, Czech Republic
www.drinksunion.cz

The heritage-rich town of Kutná Hora bought its brewery in 1589 and ran it for 360 years until nationalization brought it under government control. It returned briefly to town ownership in 1992 and is now operated by the Drinks Union group. The brewery's beers are sold at many local restaurants and bars.

LOBKOWICZ

Vysoký Chlumec 29, 262 52 Vysoký Chlumec, Czech Republic
www.lobkowicz.cz

The noble Lobkowicz family has owned the brewery since 1466 and is proud that it is a relatively small operation. Some of the beer is exported as Premium Czech Lager.

BREWING SECRET The brewery promotes ecologically sensitive production methods and uses water from an artesian well.

VELKOPOPOVICKÝ KOZEL PREMIUM
PREMIUM LAGER 5% ABV
Florally hoppy, with a biscuit malt palate and engaging bitterness.

VELKOPOPOVICKÝ KOZEL DARK
DARK BEER 3.8% ABV
Aromatic hops dominate, and dark malts give spicy caramel flavors.

KRUŠOVICE IMPERIAL
PREMIUM LAGER 5.5% ABV
A dry straw aroma heightens a bitter palate, with a floral hop and malt finish.

KRUŠOVICE DARK BEER
DARK BEER 3.8% ABV
Roast malt and caramel generosity meet earthy and nutty nuances before a citrus hop finale.

DAČICKÝ SVĚTLÝ LEŽÁK
PILSNER 4.1% ABV
A classic and popular Bohemian beer, lavishly malted with a compatible medium bitterness.

LOREC SPECIAL LAGER
PREMIUM LAGER 6.1% ABV
Pleasantly and distinctly hop-bittered, with a sweetness emerging from its generous malt layers.

LOBKOWICZ KNÍŽE 12°
PILSNER 5% ABV
A traditional pilsner, with a malt-layered, bittersweet palate following an earthy, honeyed hop nose.

LOBKOWICZ BARON 12°
DARK BEER 4.7% ABV
A dark lager, with flavor notes of chewy caramel and chocolate emerging from sweet malt.

Prague's Old Town Square is thronged with visitors throughout the year, enjoying its many pavement bar-cafés.

BREWERY

NÁCHOD / PRIMÁTOR

Dobrošouska 130, 547 40 Náchod,
Czech Republic
www.primator.cz

One of the most technically advanced breweries in the country, Náchod draws its water from the Ardšpach-Teplice protected landscape region. The brewery's origins lie in 1872, with enlargement following in 1925 and 1930. More recent improvements include a new brewhouse, and better storage and filling facilities.

NOVOPACKÉ PIVO

Pivovarska 400, 509 01 Nová Paka,
Czech Republic
www.novopackepivo.cz

The advantages of brewing and malting houses sharing the same site was recognized in Nová Paka almost 500 years ago, and its significance persists today through passionately traditional practices. Emphasis on tourism at the Art Nouveau-style complex keeps its profile high at home, while 40 percent of production is exported.

NYMBURK

Pražská 581, 288 25 Nymburk,
Czech Republic
www.postriziny.cz

In the mid-19th century, a monopoly was broken up in Nymburk when beers from other towns could be offered for sale on one condition—that they must be tasty! The present brewery's first beer flowed in 1898. The acclaimed writer Bohumil Hrabel was raised in the town and now features on most of the bottle labels.

OSTRAVAR

Hornopolní 57, 728 25 Ostrava 1,
Czech Republic
www.ostravar.cz

The Czech Republic's third-largest city lies closer to Katowice in Poland and Vienna in Austria than to Prague, and so prides itself on being "different" to other Czech breweries. Ostravar beers reflect this strategic position, and are carefully considered with local tradition in mind. It has, however, been internationally owned (now by InBev) since 2000.

BEER

PRIMÁTOR PREMIUM
PREMIUM LAGER 5% ABV
Soft vegetable hop aroma, a distinct bitterness on the palate, lapping in full malt richness.

PRIMÁTOR 24° DOUBLE
DARK LAGER 10% ABV
A spirited kick detectable from its sweet malt aroma, then spice and dried fruit lusciousness.

KUMBURÁK
PREMIUM LAGER 5% ABV
A rich malt palate follows some citrus fruit aromas through to a memorable hop aftertaste.

PODKRKONOŠSKY SPECIÁL
DARK BEER 6.3% ABV
An intriguing dark color and deep flavors that unearth chocolate and coffee notes.

POSTŘIŽINSKÉ ZLATOVAR
PREMIUM LAGER 4.7% ABV
Hrabel is indeed depicted on the label of this fully malty and mildly bitter charmer.

TMAVÝ LEŽÁK
DARK BEER 4.5% ABV
Dark amber in color, with a rich coffee and caramel palate and chocolate-coated finish.

OSTRAVAR PREMIUM
PREMIUM LAGER 5.1% ABV
A rich head promoting malt and hop aromas straddle a full-bodied strong bitter bite.

OSTRAVAR KELT
STOUT 4.8% ABV
Irish-style stout; pronounced hop and roasted barley aromas which continue throughout the palate.

PERNŠTEJN

Palackého 250, 530 33 Pardubice,
Czech Republic
www.pernstejn.cz

In the late 19th century, the brewery's porter was renowned throughout Europe for its flavor and strength, winning international medals almost at will. This rare example is still produced today, alongside fruit drinks and non-alcoholic beverages (similarly with several of the country's breweries) in an impressive portfolio.

PILSNER URQUELL

U Prazdroje 7, 304 97 Plzeň,
Czech Republic
www.pilsner-urquell.cz

The Czechs have blessed us with the microwave oven, soft contact lenses, and beer that changed the world. It was, however, a Bavarian who was the key player in the Pilsner Urquell story. As a young brewer, Josef Groll presented the nation with its first pilsner on 4 October 1842. This sensational clear golden beer spread across Europe like wildfire from its "original source."

RADEGAST

739 51 Nošovice, Czech Republic
www.radegast.cz

Radegast, roughly meaning "dear guest," was the Slavic god of fertility and crops, and consequently became proclaimed god of hospitality too. Despite its nominal connections with the dawn of time, the brewery actually began operating only in 1970. It continues to be one of the country's most technologically advanced and best equipped beer producers.

REBEL

Dobrovského 2027,
Havlíčkův Brod, Czech Republic
www.hbrebel.cz

In 1995, ownership returned to the descendants of the original 1843 brewery owners with a renewed reconstruction impetus. Havlíčkův Brod's brewing tradition has survived centuries of disruption—destruction by Hussites, a town-razing fire, two wars, and political upheaval. The Rebel name honors Czech nationalist and dissident Karel Havlíček Borovský.

PERNŠTEJN SVĚTLÝ LEŽÁK

PREMIUM LAGER 5.2% ABV
Invitingly deep gold in color, with high malt levels counterbalancing a final hop bitterness perfectly.

PARDUBICKÝ PORTER

PORTER 8% ABV
Spice and coffee notes get intimate with sweet malt—an accomplished, bottom-fermented stunner.

PILSNER URQUELL

CLASSIC PILSNER 4.4% ABV
The ideal one-and-a-half inch (35 mm) tight head leaves a lacing down the glass with every sip of spiced leaf and preserved fruit flavors, developing a sweet malt piquancy and long, enveloping finish.

RADEGAST ORIGINAL

PILSNER 4% ABV
A light malt and spiced hop nose, malt-sweet flavors and a crisp, grainy bitterness.

RADEGAST PREMIUM

PREMIUM LAGER 5% ABV
A characteristic herbal hoppy aroma and medium-sweet malt intensity dwell on cereal notes.

REBEL TRADIČNÍ

PILSNER 3.9% ABV
Light bodied, developing citrus fruit flavors to counterbalance its malt and fragrant hop finale.

REBEL ORIGINAL PREMIUM

PREMIUM LAGER 4.8% ABV
Fragrantly aromatic and fully malty in the classic Czech style, then a dry hop finish.

THE STORY OF …

Pilsner Urquell

U Prazdroje 7,
304 97 Plzeň, Czech Republic

Pilsener, pilsner, or pils are the names often given to the most famous lager style in the world. And the birthplace of the world's first bright golden beer is the city of Plzeň, in Bohemia, in the Czech Republic. Czech beers were brown in color and probably cloudy until 1842, when Josef Groll from Bavaria was contracted by the town of Plzeň to brew a beer for the new citizens' brewery (the Plzeňský Prazdroj) which could rival a new style of copper-colored beers emerging from Vienna. He created a fresh, clear, gold beer, topped with a wispy, snow-white head. The lightness of the beer was made possible by advances in malting, in which direct heat from hot coals was replaced by a more controllable heat in the form of warm air, which enabled paler shades of malt to be produced.

It was given the name Pilsner Urquell (meaning from Plzeň, the original source) and the style has been mimicked, but rarely bettered, all over the world. A true pilsner, at 4.4% ABV, has a moderate amount of alcohol; typically most beers from continental Europe have an alcoholic strength of 5% ABV. The unfermented sugar in the beer contributes to its assertive richness. Today the Pilsner Urquell Brewery produces one in five of the Czech Republic's beers and is its biggest exporter.

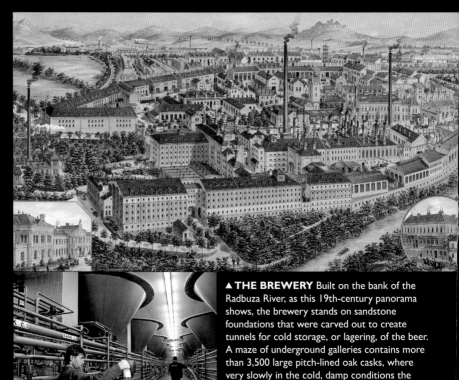

▲ **THE BREWERY** Built on the bank of the Radbuza River, as this 19th-century panorama shows, the brewery stands on sandstone foundations that were carved out to create tunnels for cold storage, or lagering, of the beer. A maze of underground galleries contains more than 3,500 large pitch-lined oak casks, where very slowly in the cold, damp conditions the beer is matured from a precocious brew into one with a majestic fullness.

▲ **STEEL FERMENTERS** The beer was originally fermented in open vessels made of Bohemian oak. Today, steel fermenters are used, and Pilsner Urquell's master brewer Václav Berkais is convinced that his predecessor Josef Groll would have used steel rather than wood had it been available.

▲ **COLD FERMENTATION** Because it is cold fermented, the beer maintains more of its flavors from the spicy Žatec hops and sweet Bohemian or Moravian barley malt. The hops impart an especially fresh, herbal aroma, and contribute to a certain and classy finish.

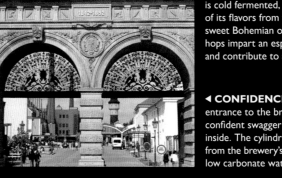

◄ **CONFIDENCE AND PRIDE** The grandiose entrance to the brewery exudes a pride and confident swagger in the work that takes place inside. The cylindrical water tower holds supplies from the brewery's own springs. This low sulfite, low carbonate water is ideal for making pilsner.

▼ THE BREWING HALL Large, graceful, copper-colored vessels dominate the brewing hall. Pilsner Urquell uses a triple decoction mash in its brewing. Portions of the mash are drawn off at three different times, and each portion, or decoction, is heated, boiled briefly, then returned to the main mash. The process helps break down the complex carbohydrate in the malt into simpler fermentable sugars.

◄ THE MUSEUM AND VISITOR CENTER The brewery is much more than a workplace. It also welcomes people to its visitor center, and offers a sensory exhibition of raw materials and an insight into how beer was brewed over 100 years ago in the on-site museum.

▲ STONE CELLARS The highlight for any visitor has to be a walk into one of the dimly lit, ice-cool sandstone cellars, where filtered and non-pasteurized Pilsner Urquell can be sampled straight from the barrel.

BREWERY

REGENT
Trocnovské náměstí 124, 379 01 Třeboň, Czech Republic
www.pivovar-regent.cz

The brewery's name was inspired by an accountant who became a knight, then regent and uncrowned king of the entire Bohemia kingdom. Today's brewery was created in the mid-19th century, and delivery trains exporting Regent beer soon traversed Europe. Owners have included the ubiquitous Schwarzenbergs and, from 2000, brothers Ferdinand and Václav Stasek.

STAROBRNO
Hlinky 160/12, 661 47 Brno, Czech Republic
www.starobrno.cz

Brewing around Brno began in monasteries and convents, notably those of the Augustinian Brothers and Cistercian Sisters. The highest production and technical standards—features of its Mandell and Huzak family ownership since 1872—have earned Starobrno a coveted "Czech Made" quality certificate. It is now owned by Dutch firm Heineken.

STAROPRAMEN
Nádražni 84, 150 54 Prague 5, Czech Republic
www.staropramen.com

Far-sighted developers situated the Smíchov Brewery in Prague's future industrial area, where demand for beer was assured. From the start, Staropramen—Prague's biggest brewer—was perceived as a Czech beer for Czech people, which gave it an advantage among nationalist-leaning consumers. Today it is owned by global giant InBev.

SVIJANY
Svijany 25, 463 46 Příšovice, Czech Republic
www.pivovarsvijany.cz

Beer was crucial to the region's economy long before this brewery's foundation in 1564, and family dynasties have marked Svijany's long history. That stopped in the mid-20th century with nationalization, but further changes of ownership followed the brewery's privatization in 1998, and under current ownership, Svijany is seeing a revival in fortunes.

BEER

BOHEMIA REGENT PREZIDENT
PREMIUM LAGER 6% ABV
Flamboyant hop aromas prepare the palate for a well-rounded malt sweetness of flavor.

STAROBRNO PREMIUM LAGER
PREMIUM LAGER 4% ABV
A nose of hay, melon, and malt, then heightening traces of caramel on the palate.

STAROPRAMEN DARK BEER
DARK BEER 4.5% ABV
Its light body loops around malty caramel, liquorice, and aniseed notes to a floral finale.

SVIJANSKÝ RYTÍŘ 12°
PILSNER 5% ABV
Pilsner-style with a yeast-rich, sweet malt aroma and high levels of fruit vitality.

BOHEMIA REGENT PALE LAGER
PILSNER 4.8% ABV
The floral aroma leaves traces of cinnamon then a toffee palate with hints of honey.

STAROBRNO REZÁK
DARK BEER 4% ABV
A deep amber Vienna-style lager unveiling slight bitter hop and joyous caramel mouthfuls.

STAROPRAMEN PREMIUM LAGER
PREMIUM LAGER 5% ABV
A rich floral bite unveils a full-bodied satisfier with a *riz* ("just right") finish.

SVIJANSKÝ KNÍŽE 13°
PILSNER 5.6% ABV
Fragrantly hoppy "special light" lager with a full sweet malt body and bitter finale.

U MEDVÍDKŮ

Na Perštýně 7, 100 01 Prague 1,
Czech Republic
www.umedvidku.cz

The restaurant and brewhouse date back to 1466, though the brewery has been reinstalled in recent years—along with extensions and additions to the *pension*, which retains its original Gothic rafters and Renaissance painted ceilings. This is one of the biggest beer halls in Prague, and it hosted the city's first cabaret.

ŽATEC

Žižkovo náměstí 81, 438 01 Žatec,
Czech Republic
www.zateckypivovar.cz

There is no escaping it in Czech beer production—every brewery uses the town's succulent hops, and, as far back as 1585, Žatec beer was praised for "its essence, strengths, and virtues."

BREWING SECRET Significant recent investment has upgraded its yeast plant, restored open fermenters, and introduced state-of-the-art kegging.

ZLATOPRAMEN

Drážďanská 80, 400 07 Ústí nad Labem,
Czech Republic
www.zlatopramen.cz

Modernization may have accelerated in recent years, but this brewery's history is as long as the existence of brewing privileges. The use of Austrian Emperor Franz Joseph II's eagle for its emblem was granted in the early 20th century, while the Zlatopramen trademark was adopted in 1967. It is now owned by Drinks Union.

ZUBR

Komenského 35, 751 52 Přerov,
Czech Republic
www.zubr.cz

The Zubr (buffalo) label is a well-regarded one, with more than 20 national and international brewing awards to its name. It also has a "mark of quality" certificate for best food product. It is one of the country's largest volume producers, with 12 percent of its output going for export throughout Europe.

OLDGOTT BARIQUE LEŽÁK
PILSNER 5.2% ABV
Earthy and melon-fruity aromas, yeasty characteristics developing into a roasted malt, caramel infusion.

X-BEER
SPECIALITY BEER 12.6% ABV (VARIABLE)
Matured for 28 weeks in oak vessels for an elaborate, sweet flavor and indulgent complexity.

ŽATEC BLUE LABEL
PREMIUM LAGER 4.6% ABV
Hints of grassy hop and sweet malt, then banana with biscuit malt on the palate.

ŽATEC EXPORT
PILSNER 4.6% ABV
Bready aroma with herbal notes, some sweet malt, delicate spicy hop, and appropriate apple sourness.

ZLATOPRAMEN 11°
PILSNER 4.7% ABV
A faint, earthy hop aroma unfolds into a full biscuit flavor with a potent bitterness.

ZLATOPRAMEN 11° DARK
DARK BEER 4.6% ABV
Aromatically floral, its sweet palate, composed from inventive blends of barley malts, edges toward toffee.

ZUBR CLASSIC 10° LIGHT
PILSNER 4.1% ABV
A good-quality hop aroma and sweetly malty, driving its medium body to a flinty bitterness.

ZUBR PREMIUM 12°
PREMIUM LAGER 5.1% ABV
Golden, with a glass-embracing froth throughout its rounded mouthfeel and a medium bitterness.

MORE BEERS OF
THE CZECH REPUBLIC

The Czech Republic has a long and proud brewing heritage. Unlike the new wave of brewing that has swept through the US and parts of Europe in recent years, most of these Czech breweries have been around very much longer, largely supplying a local market.

BREWERY

FERDINAND
Táborská 306, 256 01 Benešov,
Czech Republic
www.pivovarferdinand.cz

Brewing is entrenched in Benešov, as is evident by street names such as Na Chmelnici ("At The Hop Garden"). The core of today's brewery dates from 1897, while extensive 1970s reconstruction stimulated steady growth. The trademark Ferdinand, adopted in 1992, triggered a series of national awards for the range.

KLÁŠTER
294 15 Klášter Hradiště nad Jizerou,
Czech Republic
www.pivovarklaster.cz

Unpasteurized beers are fermented and aged here in caves hewn out of solid rock deep beneath the handsome brewery in 1570. Traditional brewery methods and maturation processes have elevated Klášter's award-winning beers to connoisseur status.

BREWING SECRET Medieval recipes are used for some of the beers.

LOUNY
Husova 64, 440 01 Louny, Czech Republic
www.pivovarlouny.cz

Encircled by impressive ramparts, the royal town in which Louny resides was once known for its vineyards and hop gardens. The brewery was founded in 1892 by a Schwarzenberg prince. It is now owned by the Drinks Union group.

BREWING SECRET The brewery was the first in Austro-Hungary to use artificial cooling. It has its own maltings.

PLATAN
Pivovarská 1, 398 12 Protivín,
Czech Republic
www.pivo-platan.cz

The avenue leading to the brewery is explanation enough that Platan means "plane tree." Brewing has taken place here since 1598, and the Schwarzenberg family—who have owned it since 1711—built a new plant in 1876.

BREWING SECRET Its Schwarzenberske Knížecí 21° (10.5% ABV) is one of the nation's strongest beers.

BEER

LEŽÁK SVĚTLÝ FERDINAND
PREMIUM LAGER 5% ABV
Medium-bodied, vigorous, and fragrantly hoppy, with a finely balanced malt and bitter integrity.

LEŽÁK TMAVÝ FERDINAND
DARK BEER 4.5% ABV
Dark amber in color, with a sweet and slightly spiced flavor and lengthy sweet finish.

LEŽÁK 11° SVĚTLÉ PIVO
PREMIUM LAGER 4.6% ABV
A fine, grainy, generous malt texture performs effectively with a faint hoppiness and bittersweet finale.

LEŽÁK 11° TMAVÉ PIVO
DARK BEER 4.3% ABV
Deep amber is reflected in its head, with a caramel sweetness and delicate hop bitterness.

LOUNY SVĚTLÉ VÝČEPNÍ
PREMIUM LAGER 4.3% ABV
An impressive head and a medium, vibrant maltiness, with dried fruit nuances and bittersweet finale.

LOUNY TMAVÉ VÝČEPNÍ
DARK BEER 4.15% ABV
Hoppily bitter aromas introduce a fine caramel malt center with hints of spice and liquorice.

PLATAN JUBILEJNÍ
PREMIUM LAGER 5% ABV
Distinct hop aromas with fruit, grainy malt, toasted nut, and vanilla flavors, then honey sweetness.

PLATAN JEDENÁCT
PILSNER 4.9% ABV
A lightness of aroma steadies a cornlike delicate palate that finishes sharp and clean.

BREWERY

POLIČKA
Pivovarská 151, 572 14 Polička,
Czech Republic
www.pivovar-policka.cz

The small walled town of Polička began brewing in the 16th century and has never stopped. Some of the equipment still in use at the brewery today dates back to a 1865 rebuild.

BREWING SECRET Beer is bottled unpasteurized, as is some cask production—well worth seeking out in its wide-ranging sales territory.

POUTNÍK
Pivovarská 856, 393 17 Pelhřimov,
Czech Republic
www.pivovarpoutnik.cz

Centuries of brewing in Pelhřimov have earned this brewery a reputation for quality through progress, but it wasn't until 2003 that the new owners—the DUP Coop, adopted Poutník (Pilgrim) as the brewery's brand name. New methods, strategies, and recipe alterations were also introduced to concentrate output on unpasteurized beers in distinctive styles.

RYCHTÁŘ
Resslova 260, 539 01 Hlinsko v Čechách,
Czech Republic
www.rychtar.cz

Beginning life in 1913 as the "Social Brewery", Rychtar has undergone impressive modernization at the hands of its current Czech investment group owners.

BREWING SECRET A new fermenting cellar and microfiltration plant have improved levels of production quality, particularly for unpasteurized beers.

U FLEKŮ
Křemencová 11, 110 01 Prague 1,
Czech Republic
www.ufleku.cz

A brewpub of wide renown, its restoration has remained true to its 1499 origins. The atmosphere is heightened by stained glass, stylish furniture, a picturesque courtyard, and Gothic vaulted beer halls.

BREWING SECRET Traditional oak fermenters and stacked cooling vats are among the unusual brewery features.

BEER

HRADEBNÍ SVĚTLÉ VÝČEPNÍ
PILSNER 3.9% ABV
A bready aroma, thin body, but surprising level of caramel malt.

OTAKAR SVĚTLÝ LEŽÁK
PREMIUM LAGER 4.2% ABV
Microbiologically filtered to retain natural flavors of floral-to-fruity hop and bittersweet malt.

POUTNÍK PRÉMIUM 12°
PREMIUM LAGER 4.8% ABV
Unmistakably malty, but well balanced with earthy notes, then a bittersweet aftertaste.

POUTNÍK SPECIÁL 14°
PREMIUM LAGER 5% ABV
Fully rounded with plumlike aromas complementing a superbly malty body and bitter finish.

KLASIK 10°
PILSNER 4% ABV
Often described as the brewery's "daily drinker", it is typically pale but malty and bittersweet.

PREMIUM 12°
PREMIUM LAGER 5% ABV
Distinctly malty, with a light, natural carbonation and a developing, sharply-defined hop finish.

FLEKOVSKY TMAVÝ LEŽÁK
DARK BEER 5.5% ABV
A classic dark lager—and one of the world's greats—unfiltered and complex, with roasted coffee and cream aromas meeting a bitter palate via spiced hop, then liquorice and coffee influences.

Folk musicians frequently entertain drinkers in the traditional bar-restaurants of Prague's Old Town.

BEER TRAIL

PRAGUE

The city of Prague is one of the world's greatest beer destinations. And where better to start a beer trail than in the Old Town Square (Staroměstské náměstí), location of the famous 15th-century Astronomical Clock—one of the world's oldest clocks still in working order. Many bars edge the square, each spilling out on to the cobbles with seating and canopies.

A short walk away is the dramatic Powder Tower, built in 1475 on the site of one of Prague's 13 city gates. Nearby is the impressive 14th-century Charles Bridge. Walk over it and see Na Kampe, where Hollywood actor Tom Cruise, as Special Agent Ethan Hunt, blew up a car in the film *Mission Impossible 3*. Less frenetic than the Old Town side of the bridge, Na Kampe is home to several new bars that have recently opened in the area.

JOURNEY STATS
1 hour, plus drinking time
3 miles (5 km)

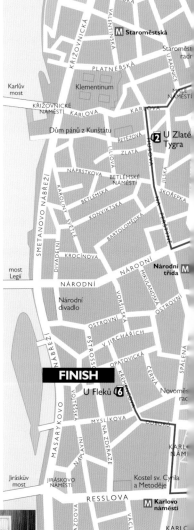

OLD TOWN SQUARE
Here it is possible to sit outside and savor a beer, while watching the thousands of visitors who now flock to the Czech capital. Displays of folk dancing and music can often be enjoyed here too.

2 U ZLATÉHO TYGRA
One of the Old Town's most atmospheric and oldest bars, U Zlatého Tygra is crowded with small tables, which always seem to be full with locals deep in energetic conversations—so be prepared to stand. It's a favorite of the writer and former Czech President Václav Havel, and President Clinton has also drunk here. The unfiltered Pilsner Urquell is said to be the best in Prague. *Husova 17, Prague*

3 U PINKASŮ
In 1843 U Pinkasů was the first bar in Prague to serve Pilsner Urquell, and it is still available today. The bar was saved from extinction in 2000, when it was extensively refurbished. A more recent refurbishment has opened up more of the building. *Jungmannovo nám, 16/15, Prague*

START

Old Town Square

4 NOVOMĚSTSKÝ PIVOVAR

An Art Deco-style entrance leads visitors down an alleyway of shops to this wood-paneled brewery, pub, and restaurant. Unfiltered light and dark beers are available. The food is unashamedly Czech, with specialties such as a goulash, tripe soup, and roast knuckle of pork. *Vodickova 20, Prague*

5 PIVODUM

The Pivodum restaurant and bar is dominated by gleaming coppers. Traditional Czech beers are served, as well as other interesting brews, including a sour cherry beer, a coffee beer, and Samp—a beer champagne. Groups can order eight beers for the price of seven, and they are served in a large giraffelike container. A sample tray of eight beers is available too. *Ječná/Lípová 15, Prague*

6 U FLEKŮ

Crowded it may be, a haunt of many tourists it certainly is, but U Fleků should not be missed. Brewing began here in 1499, and it is said to be the world's oldest brewpub. It comprises many large rooms, including one for a booming oompah band. It has a small museum and daily brewery tours. The superb house beer is Flekovsky tmavy lezáck, which comes in dark and light versions. *Kremencova 11, Prague*

BEERS TO TRAVEL FOR

REST OF THE WORLD

EUROPE • THE AMERICAS • ASIA • AUSTRALASIA • AFRICA

Fat Cat, Canada

■ CANADA

Desnoes and Geddes, Jamaica

■ MEXICO

■ CUBA

JAMAICA

■ ANTIGUA

TRINIDAD
& TOBAGO

REST OF THE WORLD

PERU ■

■ BRAZIL

■ ARGENTINA

Beba, Italy

Hue, Vietnam

Quilmes, Argentina

Stiegl, Austria

REST OF THE WORLD

The world of beer is expanding. Markets are growing in territories less associated with brewing, but of more interest are the nations where craft brewing is burgeoning. Italy is one of the most interesting of these: not only are its brewers producing flavor-rich, experimental beers, but they are also showing how to market beer in elegantly designed bottles. This is true, to some extent, in Denmark and Scandinavia too, while over in East Asia, Japan is developing great variants of European beers, with their own, quirky take on classic design.

Herslev Bryghus, Denmark

SWEDEN

FINLAND

NORWAY

ESTONIA

LATVIA

DENMARK

LITHUANIA

NETHERLANDS

POLAND

Ochakovo, Russia

RUSSIA

LUXEMBOURG

SLOVAKIA

UKRAINE

AUSTRIA

FRANCE

HUNGARY

SWIZERLAND

ROMANIA

SLOVENIA

MONGOLIA

CROATIA

SERBIA

SPAIN

ITALY

Fujizakura Heights, Japan

PORTUGAL

GREECE

MALTA

CYPRUS

SOUTH
KOREA

JAPAN

CHINA

INDIA

LAOS

THAILAND

VIETNAM

SRI LANKA

SINGAPORE

INDONESIA

Thaibev, Thailand

AUSTRALIA

Mac's, New Zealand

SOUTH AFRICA

Little Creatures, Australia

NEW ZEALAND

BREWERY

32 VIA DEI BIRRAI
Via Cal Lusent 41, 31040 Onigo di Pederobba (TV), Italy
www.32viadeibirrai.com

Born into a brewing family, Belgian-Italian Fabiano Toffoli founded his microbrewery in 2006 after working as a brewer and a brewing consultant.

BREWING SECRET Toffoli brews with pure water from several sources to lend distinct characteristics to different beers; the hops are from Poperinge.

ALMOND 22
Via Dietro le Mura 36/38, 65010 Spoltore (PE), Italy
www.birraalmond.com

This microbrewery was founded in 2003, in the seaside town of Pescara, by Swedish-Italian Jurij Ferri. He brews highly praised ales inspired by British and Belgian styles, as well as some original, experimental beers that use local ingredients.

LE BALADIN
Piazza V Luglio 15, 12060 Piozzo (CN), Italy
www.birreria.com

Charismatic, pioneering Teo Musso is internationally known as one of the most creative brewers in the world. He has turned beer into a type of wine and created beer truffles—not even he knows what he will do next.

BREWING SECRET Musso plays music to his yeasts during the fermentation process, believing that they respond.

BARLEY
Via C. Colombo, 09040 Maracalagonis (CA), Sardinia, Italy
www.barley.it

Skilful home brewer Nicola Perra established this microbrewery in 2006 in southern Sardinia, challenging the mass-market lagers so popular in the region (consumption here is the highest in Italy).

BREWING SECRET Local ingredients such as Sardinian wine wort and organic honey are used in the ales.

BEER

OPPALE
BELGIAN BLOND ALE 5.5% ABV
Refreshing, easy-to-drink, cloudy ale with a very pleasant dry, bitter finish of chives.

AUDACE
BELGIAN GOLDEN STRONG ALE 8.4% ABV
Strong golden ale, rich in ester flavors. Warming, spicy, and dry, with a long, bitter, citrussy finish.

TORBATA
BARLEY WINE 8.7% ABV
Peated ale with a smoky flavor similar to a Scotch whisky. Easy to drink despite its strength.

FARROTTA
SPELT WHEAT ALE 5.7% ABV
Cloudy golden ale brewed using barley and locally grown spelt; easy-drinking and thirst-quenching.

XYAUYÙ
BARLEY WINE 12% ABV
Radical oxidization gives "solera" sherry-like favors. A flat, warming, velvety nightcap. A masterpiece.

NORA
SPICED ALE 6.8% ABV
Inspired by ancient Egypt, using kamut grains, ginger, and myrrh. A balsamic bitterness comes from Ethiopian resins.

TOCCADIBÒ
GOLDEN STRONG ALE 8.4% ABV
A warming ale; spicy, hoppy and dry, with intriguing bitter-almond notes of amaretto.

BB 10
BARLEY WINE 10% ABV
A unique brew made with sapa, the boiled wort of local Cannonau grapes. A highly distinctive nightcap.

BEBA

Viale Italia 11,
10069 Villar Perosa (TO), Italy
www.birrabeba.it

Pioneering brothers Alessandro and Enrico Borio brew a wide range of regular and seasonal lagers at their microbrewery founded in 1996 near Turin. The adjoining tap-room serves all the house beers on draft along with excellent food. The local specialty is *gofri*, a crisp unleavened bread stuffed with cheeses, cured meats, or preserves.

MOTOR OIL
STRONG DARK LAGER 8% ABV
Ebony-colored, with strong notes of liquorice and roasted coffee, beans and a long, bitter finish. As viscous as its namesake.

TALCO
RYE LAGER 4.2% ABV
Seasonal "rye weizen-lager" is a thirst-quenching treat on a hot summer afternoon.

BIRRA DEL BORGO

Via del Colle Rosso,
02021 Borgorose (RI), Italy
www.birradelborgo.it

Birra del Borgo was founded in 2005 by former homebrewer Leonardo Di Vincenzo. Having learned his trade at a brewpub in Rome, he established his own in a small village around 60 miles (100 km) from the capital. Here, he brews fine ales, often inspired by British styles, and also experiments with unusual ingredients such as tobacco, tea leaves, and gentian roots.

KETO REPORTER
TOBACCO PORTER 5.5% ABV
Kentucky Toscano tobacco leaves are infused in this smoky, peppery porter. Surprisingly easy to drink.

RE ALE EXTRA
IPA 6.4% ABV
Generously hopped with Amarillo and Warrior; well balanced, with sweet caramel and fruity notes.

BIRRIFICIO ITALIANO

Via Castello 51, 22070 Lurago Marinon (CO), Italy
www.birrificio.it

Agostino Arioli founded his renowned brewpub in 1994 with his brother Stefano and other friends. His pils and bock soon became cult favorites. He brews a large range of seasonal beers such as a sparkling blackcurrant lager and a cask-conditioned ale spiced with cinnamon and ginger. The restaurant serves great regional food and has live music.

SCIRES
CHERRY ALE 7% ABV
Whole black Vignola cherries, lactic bacteria, wild yeast, and wood chips create this fantastic sour beer.

FLEURETTE
FLAVORED LIGHT ALE 3.7% ABV
Made with barley, wheat, and rye, and flavored with rose and violet petals, elderberry juice, black pepper, and citrus honey.

BREWERY

BRÙTON

Via Lodovica 5135, 55100 San Cassiano
di Moriano (LU), Italy
www.bruton.it

Named, they say, after the beer made
by the Minoans of ancient Crete, this
stylish Tuscan brewpub offers good
regional food and interesting ales,
bearing a logo of the minotaur,
created by young former home
brewer Alessio Gatti.

CITABIUNDA

Via Moniprandi1/a Fraz. Bricco di Neive,
12052 Neive (CN), Italy
www.birrificiocitabiunda.it

Brewpub Citabiunda ("blonde girl" in
the local dialect) is set in a charming
former village schoolhouse in high
Piedmont. It offers original, intriguing
beers and home-cooked food.

BREWING SECRET Marco Marengo, who
was taught the art of brewing by Teo
Musso of Le Baladin, uses Champagne
yeasts to create his distinctive brews.

CITTAVECCHIA

Z.A. Stazione di Prosecco 29/E, 34010
Sgonico (TS), Italy
www.cittavecchia.com

Cittavecchia was founded in 1999 in
this wine-producing village between
Trieste and the Slovenian border.
Former home brewer Michele Barro
was compelled by his passion for good
beer to leave his job as designer and
take up brewing full time. Now his
lagers and ales are sold in the region's
best restaurants and bars.

DUCATO

Via Strepponi 50/A, 43010 Roncole Verdi
di Busseto (PR), Italy
www.birrificiodelducato.it

Young brewer Giovanni Campari set
up his microbrewery in 2007 near
Giuseppe Verdi's birthplace, not far
from Parma. He proved his skills from
the outset, brewing four beers full of
character. Further new lines are
confirming Ducato as one of the most
promising Italian craft breweries.

BEER

MOMUS
STRONG AMBER ALE 7.5% ABV
Inspired by Belgian abbey ales with
a touch of local *millefiori* (thousand-
flower) honey. An easy-drinking ale
despite its strength.

LILITH
AMERICAN PALE ALE 5.5% ABV
Well balanced, rich in caramel notes,
with grapefruit flavors from a
generous amount of Cascade hops.

BIANCANEIVE
BELGIAN WITBIER 4.8% ABV
Strongly spiced wheat beer, easy
to drink, refreshing, and thirst-
quenching, with flowery notes
from the Champagne yeasts.

SENSUALE
BELGIAN ABBEY AMBER ALE 7% ABV
Well-balanced strong ale, rich in
vinous and citrus fruit notes; sweet
right through to the aftertaste.

FORMIDABLE
STRONG DARK ALE 8% ABV
Strong, fruity, Belgian-style ale with
liquorice notes. George Simenon's
sleuth Maigret drank his beer from
a *formidable* two-pint (liter) tankard.

SAN NICOLÒ
SPICED ALE 6% ABV
Amber ale, generously spiced with
cardamom, brewed once a year for
Saint Nicholas's Day.

NEW MORNING
SAISON 5.6% ABV
Amazing *saison*, flavored with
camomile flowers. Easy-drinking
and thirst-quenching, with lovely
earthy notes.

AFO
AMERICAN PALE ALE 5.2% ABV
AFO means "Ale For the Obsessed"
and is dedicated to hop lovers. Nice
citrus fruit aromas, caramel notes.

GRADO PLATO

Viale Fasano 36/bis,
10023 Chieri (TO), Italy
www.gradoplato.it

This brewpub near Turin was founded in 2003 by former home brewer Sergio Ormea. His son Gabriele helps him run the pub, which is well known for its food—notably snails cooked in over 20 different ways!

BREWING SECRET Regional produce, such as chestnuts and barley, feature strongly in these inventive, eclectic ales.

LAMBRATE

Via Adelchi 5, 20131 Milano, Italy
www.birrificiolambrate.com

The first (and still the best) brewpub in Milan, founded in 1996 by brothers Davide and Giampaolo Sangiorgi and their friend Fabio Brocca after a visit to 't IJ Brewery in Amsterdam. They have recently expanded production, adding some new interesting ales. The menu features some creative beer-influenced dishes, such as pork cooked in beer mash.

L'OLMAIA

Strada Foce e Fornace 22,
Podere Olmaia,
53042 Chianciano Terme (SI), Italy
www.birrificioolmaia.com

A tiny, pretty microbrewery founded in 2005 near Siena, in the green and leafy Val d'Orcia. Young, enthusiastic brewer Moreno Ercolani creates intriguing, natural ales with passion, often using local produce, such as honey from the elms that grow profusely here (*olmaia* means elm).

MALTUS FABER

Via Fegino 3,
16131 Genova-Rivarolo, Italy
www.maltusfaber.com

This brand new microbrewery is located on the industrial archeological site of a former brewery in Genoa. It was founded by two friends, Fausto Marenco, a former home brewer, and Massimo Versaci, a well-known collector of "breweriana." Inspired by a love of Belgium, they brew clean, interesting, and promising ales.

CHOCARRUBICA

COFFEE-CHOCOLATE STOUT 7% ABV
An original brew, featuring cocoa and carob beans from Sicily. Soft and velvety on the palate.

STRADA SAN FELICE

CHESTNUT STRONG LAGER 8% ABV
Dark, strong lager made with local nuts, giving a gentle smoked aroma and a marked taste of chestnuts, with a slightly bitter finish.

GHISA

SMOKED ALE 5% ABV
Ebony in color with a "cappuccino" foam; lighty smoked, easy to drink, and balanced, with plum notes and a long, hoppy finish.

MONTESTELLA

BLONDE ALE 4.9% ABV
Their flagship ale; pale, with fresh aromas of hay and hops with a long, dry finish cleansing the palate.

PVK

BELGIAN WITBIER 6% ABV
Easy-drinking blonde ale brewed with durum wheat, barley, oats, red pepper, coriander, and orange rind.

CHRISTMAS DUCK

BELGIAN STRONG DARK ALE 8.5% ABV
Remarkable seasonal winter warmer using local elm-tree honey that gives bittersweet and fruity notes.

AMBRATA

BELGIAN AMBER ALE 6.5% ABV
Rich in caramel and nutty notes, well balanced, with a long, dry, and bitter finish.

BRUNE

BELGIAN STRONG DARK ALE 8% ABV
Complex dark ale with strong coffee, chocolate, and liquorice. Dry enough to be easily drinkable despite its strength.

BREWERY

MONTEGIOCO

Frazione Fabbrica 1,
15050 Montegioco (AL), Italy
www.birrificiomontegioco.com

Riccardo Franzosi, who left a secure job in the family construction firm to assemble his own beers, is one of the most eclectic brewers in Italy. He brews a wide range of regular and seasonal ales, using local products —cherries, peaches, and blueberries.

BREWING SECRET The coriander he uses comes from his neighbor's garden.

PANIL (TORRECHIARA)

Strada Pilastro 35/a,
43010 Torrechiara (PR), Italy
www.panilbeer.com

Renzo Losi, a biology graduate, got his brewing break in 2000, when his winemaker father gave him permission to make beer at the family's vineyard estate, south of Parma.

BREWING SECRET The links with the family winemaking tradition are retained in the use of oak barrels and *spumante* yeasts.

PICCOLO BIRRIFICIO

Via iv Novembre 20,
18035 Apricale (IM), Italy
www.piccolobirrificio.com

This microbrewery, founded in 2005, is housed in a former olive-oil mill in the lovely medieval village of Apricale, near the French border. Brewer Lorenzo Bottoni produces a range of fine ales under the brand name of Nüa ("naked"), including some amazing brews using unusual local fruits and plants.

SCARAMPOLA

Loc. Monastero 9,
17017 Millesimo (SV), Italy

Founded in 2004 in the cellars of an old mansion, this brewpub has now moved to a charming nearby abbey. Brewer Maurizio Ghidetti likes to use local ingredients such as chestnuts and chinotto fruits. Beers are available on draft in the tap room Osteria del Vino Cattivo in nearby Cairo Montenotte.

BEER

DOLII RAPTOR

STRONG ALE 8.5% ABV
Matured in Barbera wine barrels for over six months, then re-fermented with white wine yeasts.

QUARTA RUNA

SOUR PEACH ALE 7% ABV
Volpedo peaches are heated in an oven before fermentation for extra "peachiness." The sourness comes from wild yeasts on the peach skins.

PANIL BARRIQUÉE SOUR

FLEMISH SOUR RED 8% ABV
The flagship ale, barrel-aged for three months. Sour, vinous, and uncompromising.

DIVINA

WILD BEER 5.5% ABV
Spontaneously fermented by being left, uncovered, on the back of a truck in a field overnight. Sweet-sour, yeasty, and citrussy.

SESONETTE

BELGIAN SAISON 6.5% ABV
Matured in Chardonnay barrels with spices and local chinotto peel (from a small, bitter citrus fruit).

CHIOSTRO

SPICED ALE 5% ABV
Spiced with *Artemisia absinthium* (wormwood), then fermented with Trappist yeasts, giving complex and unique aromas and flavors.

IPA

FRUIT BEER 7.6% ABV
In this case IPA doesn't mean India Pale Ale but Italian Pompelmo (grapefruit) Ale. Grapefruit peel and Cascade hops are used.

NIVURA

CHESTNUT ALE 7.5% ABV
A new style, very popular in Italy. Smoked notes from chestnuts dried in traditional stoves called *tecci*.

MORE BEERS OF

ITALY

Italy has a growing band of small-batch, craft producers who are experimenting with many ingredients and methods.

BI-DU

Via Confine 26,
22070 Rodero (CO), Italy
www.bi-du.it

This brewpub was founded in 2002 in the tiny village of Rodero, close to the Swiss border. It takes its name from a Sumerian beer used to pay workers. Beppe Vento is one of the best, and most awarded, brewers in Italy.

BREWING SECRET Vento brews beers only in styles that he personally loves.

KÖLSCH
KÖLSCH 5% ABV
A cloudy, fresh digestif with a lovely touch of bitterness; typical of the brewer's philosophy.

ARTIGIANALE
BITTER ALE 6.2% ABV
A celebrated strong bitter ale, with a good balance between malts and hops, and a long, bitter finish.

MOSTO DOLCE

Via Fra' Bartolomeo 211,
59100 Prato, Italy
www.mostodolce.it

This microbrewery was founded in 2003 by Francesca Torri and Elio Dall'Era. Francesca is the brewer, creating her successful range of lagers and ales with passion. There are two beautiful tap rooms in which to sample her brews, one in Prato (Via dell'Arco 6) and the other in Florence (Via Nazionale 114 R).

BOCK
BOCK 6.3% ABV
An award-winner, brewed with five different malts and generously hopped for a good balance.

MARTELLINA
CHESTNUT HONEY ALE 7.3% ABV
Uncompromising, strong, but very drinkable amber ale with a great punch coming from the flavor of local chestnut honey.

TROLL

Strada valle Grande 15/A,
12019 Vernante (CN), Italy
www.birratroll.it

Beer enthusiast Alberto Canavese transformed his bar, set in a charming alpine village, into a brewpub in 2002. Brewer Daniele Meinero is well known for the unusual herbs and spices he adds to his ales.

BREWING SECRET Meinero was trained by radical brewer Teo Musso of Le Balandin in Piozzo.

PALANFRINA
CHESTNUT ALE 9% ABV
Intense flavor from local chestnuts, used in several different ways, such as dried, smoked, and in the form of chestnut honey.

SHANGRILA
SPICED ALE 8.5% ABV
A deep amber ale enlived with a Himalayan blend of spices, giving exotic aromas and flavors.

ZAHRE

Via Razzo 50,
33020 Sauris di Sopra (UD), Italy
www.zahrebeer.com

Sauris, a mountain village in the Friuli region close to the Austrian and Slovenian borders, was known as Zahre in ancient times. Sandro Petris who founded his microbrewery in 1999, is able to use the purest, freshest mountain spring water for his highly appreciated lagers.

AFFUMICATA
SMOKED LAGER 6% ABV
A deep red, well rounded lager full of smoked barley malt aroma. Perfect with the acclaimed local crudo ham.

CANAPA
FLAVORED LAGER 5% ABV
A surprisingly elegant, delicate, easy-drinking lager flavored with local Carmagnola hemp flowers.

VECCHIO BIRRAIO

Via Caselle 87, 3510 Marsango di Campo S. Martino (PD), Italy
www.vecchiobirraio.it

Beer enthusiast pioneer Stefano Sausa founded his family brewery in 1995 not far from Padua with the goal to brew tasty, natural, and genuine craft beers without any adjunct. Good food alongside fine lagers and ales seem to be the secret of this successful brewpub.

SAUSA PILS
PILSNER 5% ABV
Flagship of the brewery, awarded pils from Bohemian inspiration, with dry and long hoppy finish.

BLACK HORSE
FOREIGN EXTRA STOUT 6.5% ABV
Full-bodied strong stout with pleasant notes of coffee, chocolate, and dried fruit.

VILLA POLA

Via Batt. S. Pomini 3,
41050 Barcon di Vedelago (TV), Italy
www.villapola.com

This brewpub, founded in 2002 not far from Treviso, is in the spectacular setting of an 18th-century villa. Skilful brewer, Paolo de Martin, is a great lover of German beers, and brews his ales accordingly.

BREWING SECRET De Martin was the first Italian brewer to produce a chestnut beer.

POLA PILS
PILSNER 4.7% ABV
Lovely, well-balanced, quenching, clean pils in the German style, with a long, dry, and hoppy finish.

SOCI'S SCHWARZ
GERMAN SCHWARZBIER 4% ABV
Based on an recipe from the Soci dea Bira home-brew society. Well hopped, with coffee, dried fruits, plums, chocolate, and liquorice.

BREWERY

BEER

BREWERY

BEER

ALL ABOUT ...
FLAVORINGS

The *Reinheitsgebot* dictates that German brewers use only malt, hops, yeast, and water for their beers. But cross the border into Belgium and the shelves of a native brewhouse will groan under the weight of jars of spices and herbs. Crushed coriander seeds and dried orange peel add spicy and rich citrus notes to a witbier such as Hoegaarden, while ginger, aniseed, cumin, and star anise also find their way into various brews. Eclectic brewer Dany Prignon at Fantôme plays around with oregano—no doubt that beer is great with pizza. There are even Belgian beers brewed with tea, honey, and mustard.

Herbal flavorings have a long history in brewing: before hops, brewers in the British Isles experimented with sweet gale, wild rosemary, ground ivy, and bog myrtle. In northern Europe, the mixture of herbs used for flavoring beer was called "gruit." And, as European countries colonized the world, all sorts of spices were brought back, and it was only natural that some, such as ginger, ended up in the brewing kettle.

Contemporary use of flavorings is on the increase, and is no longer confined to Belgian mavericks like Prignon. For example, Scottish brewmaster Bruce Williams has brought back to life heather ale— an ancient style of beer that was brewed by the Picts, while Italian brewers are experimenting with chestnuts, myrrh, and tobacco.

HEATHER
Scottish heather flowers are used in the boil alongside a minimum of hops to create the Williams Brothers' Fraoch. The ale has an almost peaty, floral nose and dry, astringent finish.

GINGER, MYRRH, AND HONEY
Brewers in Italy are getting somewhat spicy with the fruits of their labors. Le Baladin's Nora contains ginger root and myrrh, while heather honey goes into the brewery's Erika. Honey is also a traditional ingredient of some Belgian beers, such as Binchoise's Bière des Ours.

CHESTNUTS AND TOBACCO
Birra del Borgo's Keto Reporter uses Kentucky Toscano tobacco leaves to help give this porter a peppery character, while Strada San Felice from Grado has chestnuts in the brew.

COFFEE AND CHOCOLATE
The ever-inventive Meantime Brewery of London has produced beers with Fairtrade coffee beans in the mix. In the US, Rogue Ales Chocolate Stout is a chocoholic's delight. Both coffee and chocolate harmonize beautifully with similar notes in the malts of these dark beers.

GOOSEBERRIES, PINE, AND SEAWEED
Williams Brothers of Scotland brews beers made with gooseberries and bog myrtle; Scots pine and spruce shoots; and bladderwrack seaweed.

NOUGAT France's Bourganel Brewery produces artisan beers using regional ingredients, such as chestnuts and bilberries, and nougat from Montélimar, which lends an almond flavor to the beer.

BREWERY

ANNOEULLIN
5 Grand Place,
59112 Annoeullin, France
brasserie.annoeullin@wanadoo.fr

Established in 1905, this tiny brewery is run by the Lepers family, brewers for five generations. Their most well-known beer features a reproduction of Jean-François Millet's masterpiece *L'Angelus* (1857) on its label. It is a jewel of the northern French style of long-matured beers known as *bière de garde* (beer for keeping).

AU BARON
2 rue du Piémont,
59570 Gussignies, France
Aubaron@wanadoo.fr

Set on a riverbank in a charming valley, this microbrewery and restaurant has been owned by the Bailleux family since the 1970s. It's a delightful place, where you can take a tour of the brewery, dine on grilled meat or fish, and sample beers such as the Cuvée des Jonquilles—a brew as golden as the daffodils after which it is named.

BOURGANEL
7 avenue Claude Expilly,
07600 Vals les Bains, France
www.bieres-bourganel.com

In 1997 Christian Bourganel, a drinks distributor in the Ardèche, decided to develop a range of blonde artisan beers flavored with regional produce.

BREWING SECRET Unusual ingredients include chestnuts *(marrons)*, bilberries *(myrtilles)*, nougat from Montélimar and Verveine du Velay liqueur, which is flavored with verbena.

CASTELAIN
13 rue Pasteur,
62410 Bénifontaine, France
www.chti.com

Founded in 1926, this family brewery was passed into the hands of Yves and Annick Castelain from their parents in 1978. Under the name of Ch'ti (local patois for a northerner), they have developed a range of strong, mellow lager beers with a long, cold secondary fermentation period.

BEER

L'ANGÉLUS
WHEAT BEER 7% ABV
Rich, smooth, and wonderfully aromatic, with hints of coriander and a syrup sweetness.

CUVÉE DES JONQUILLES
ALE 5% ABV
Strong but thirst-quenching, this ale is packed with delicious flavors of citrus and exotic fruits.

BOURGANEL AU NOUGAT
FLAVORED LAGER 5% ABV
An amazing nougat bouquet and, in the mouth, the flavor of grilled almonds.

BOURGANEL AUX MARRONS
FLAVORED LAGER 5% ABV
An amber beer; elegant, very fruity and refreshing, with a hint of vanilla as well as chestnut.

MALTESSE
PREMIUM LAGER 7.7% ABV
Blonde, rich, and strong, with a taste of barley, and an appealing hint of bitterness in the finish.

CH'TI BLONDE
LAGER 6.4% ABV
Full-bodied, with just enough bitterness to be very refreshing. Mellow and tasty.

LA CHOULETTE

18 rue des Écoles,
59111 Hordain, France
www.lachoulette.com

Founded in 1885, this farmhouse brewery is a rare survivor from the thousands of breweries that existed in the region in the late 19th century. Alain Dhaussy, the current brewer, has succeeded in creating artisan beers of real quality, faithful to the traditions of northern France, but with a real sense of innovation too.

COREFF

2 place de la Gare,
29270 Carhaix, France
www.coreff.com

This Breton brewery's foundation, in Morlaix in 1985, pioneered the revival of artisan breweries in France. Now in Carhaix, in central Brittany, it produces British-style real ales (stout and porter are in the range), but wheat and blonde beers are also made here.

BREWING SECRET All of Coreff's beers are unpasteurized and unfiltered.

DUYCK

113 route Nationale, 59144 Jenlain, France
www.duyck.com

Originally a farmhouse brewery, Duyck was established in 1922, producing beers in the northern *bière de garde* style—brewed and bottled in the winter for laying down and drinking in the summer. In the 1950s, the family began bottling their beers in recycled champagne bottles. Raymond Duyck, the present manager, is the fourth generation of this family of brewers.

FISCHER

7 route de Bischwiller,
67300 Schiltigheim, France
www.heineken-entreprise.fr

Founded in 1822, this industrial brewery has for many years been an icon of Alsace beer, with its logo of a little fisherman drinking from a huge glass. Fischer was acquired by Heineken in 1996, and lost its autonomous status ten years later. Malt whiskey, which is avidly consumed in France, is a key flavoring in Fischer's Adelscott beer.

CHOULETTE FRAMBOISE
FRUIT BEER 6% ABV
Refreshing, with a slight sourness. The note of ripe raspberries is present, but not too intrusive.

PORTE DU HAINAUT AMBRÉE
AMBER ALE 7% ABV
Medium-bodied fruity beer, with flavors of cooked apples, pears, and caramel; slight bitterness.

COREFF AMBRÉE
AMBER ALE 5% ABV
Deep, appealing ale with notes of brown sugar, toasted malt and caramel, and a good bitterness in the finish. A classic since 1985.

JENLAIN AMBRÉE
AMBER ALE 7.5% ABV
Full bodied, with a hint of bitterness, the mellowness of roasted malt and aromas of stewed prunes and caramel. A perfect accompaniment to food, but also an ingredient in rustic local dishes such as *Carbonnade Flamande* (beef cooked in beer).

ADELSCOTT
LAGER 5.8% ABV
Reddish-brown in color, combining caramel notes with the aroma of peat smoke, and with a sweet finish. Refreshing, however.

BREWERY

GAYANT
63 Faubourg de Paris,
59500 Douai, France
www.brasseurs-gayant.com

Established in 1919, this independent, family-owned brewery has always embraced and pioneered new styles of brewing, from ales made using the top-fermentation technique, to Celta, the first non-alcoholic beer.

BREWING SECRET Brasseurs de Gayant brews the strongest beer in France, called Bière du Démon (12% ABV).

KRONENBOURG
67 route d'Oberhausbergen,
67037 Strasbourg, France
www.brasseries-kronenbourg.com

A tiny Strasbourg brewpub, opened in 1664, grew to become France's largest brewery in the 20th century, a feat achieved by selling refreshing lager beer at low prices all over the world. Nowadays its sales have declined somewhat, and it is owned by the Danish Carlsberg group.

LANCELOT
La Mine d'Or,
56460 Le Roc Saint-André, France
www.brasserie-lancelot.com

Established in 1990, and now housed in the buildings of a 19th-century gold mine, Lancelot creates beers that are—in their names and imagery on the labels at least—linked to Breton and Celtic traditions, and Arthurian legends. Lancelot's production methods, however, are very much in the mold of Belgian beermaking.

BRASSEURS DE LORRAINE
3 rue du Bois le Prêtre,
54700 Pont à Mousson, France
www.brasseurs-lorraine.com

In 2003, three dynamic young partners opened a new brewery in the heart of the Lorraine region, in northeast France. Their aim was to revive a regional tradition of beermaking that had almost entirely died out there. The brewery now produces six main brands, all of them in distinct styles.

BEER

GOUDALE
ALE 7.2% ABV
Golden, dense, and full of malty aromas, with a slight bitterness imbued by the Flemish hops.

AMADEUS
WHEAT BEER 4.5% ABV
Cloudy and pale yellow, this is a light and refreshing beer, with aromas of citrus fruit and coriander.

1664
SPECIAL LAGER 5.5% ABV
A smooth, golden, and refreshing lager: slightly bitter on the palate and with hints of malt.

BLANC
WHEAT BEER 5% ABV
Fresh and fruity notes and a touch of coriander make for a crisp and refreshing beer.

MORGANE
ALE 5.5% ABV
This organic beer is pleasantly refreshing and light in style.

CERVOISE
ALE 6% ABV
The color is amber, the flavor fruity and malty beer, with hints of honey and spices.

ABBAYE DES PRÉMONTRÉS
ABBEY BEER 6% ABV
Amber, malty in taste, but with a delicate bitterness. Stewed fruits and caramel in the finish.

DUCHESSE DE LORRAINE
RED BEER 5.5% ABV
Malty, spicy, and with a hint of dried fruits, this beer is made using an 18th-century recipe.

METEOR

6 rue du Général Lebocq,
67270 Hochfelden, France
www.brasserie-meteor.fr

Brewing on the same site since 1640, Meteor is now the longest-established independent family brewery in France. Alsace traditions are in evidence, but Meteor also develops new beer styles.

BREWING SECRET Meteor was the first French brewery to be granted the rights to use the term "Pils," by the Czech authorities in 1927.

MICHARD

6 place Denis Dussoubs,
87000 Limoges, France

Jean Michard was a pioneer in the revival of artisan brewing in France, opening his first brewpub in 1987 in Limoges. Using Bavarian styles, he and his daughter Julie develop fine beers in traditional ways, by hand, and with no use of electronics. Rare and hard to acquire, these beers are sold only at the brewpub.

PIETRA

Route de la Marana,
20600 Furiani, France
www.brasseriepietra.com

The first Corsican brewery in history opened in 1996. Brewers Armelle and Dominique Sialelli use raw materials native to the island, such as *maquis* herbs and chestnut flour, which forms an ingredient rather than just a flavoring in their Pietra beer. *Biera Corsa* has been a great success, both in Corsica and overseas.

ROUGET DE LISLE

Rue des Vernes,
39140 Bletterans, France
www.larougetdelisle.com

Opened in 2002, and named after the locally born composer of *The Marseillaise*, this brewery develops up to 15 new beers each year, some of them using local ingredients instead of hops for their bitter notes.

BREWING SECRET Among the ingredients used to replace hops are wormwood, dandelion, blackcurrant, and gentian.

METEOR PILS
PILS LAGER 5% ABV
A classic blonde Pilsener beer. Unpasteurized, it is smooth, very malty, and has a good bitterness. Very refreshing.

MICHARD AMBRÉE
BAVARIAN 5.5% ABV
Brillant copper color; very smooth on the palate, with a light sourness and bitterness in the finish.

COLOMBA
WHEAT BEER 5% ABV
Very fresh and sharp, with unusual aromas of arbutus, myrtle, and juniper. A refreshing summer beer.

PIETRA
AMBER LAGER 6% ABV
Elegant flavors of toasted malts, nuttiness, and a slight bitterness.

FOURCHE DU DIABLE
LAGER 5.4% ABV
Amber in color; aromas of spring flowers and an unusual bitter note contributed by gentian roots.

ABISINTHE
LAGER 6% ABV
Golden and very refreshing, with aromas of mint, balm, and the special bitterness of wormwood.

BREWERY

SAINT GERMAIN

26 route d'Arras,
62160 Aix-Noulette, France
www.page24.fr

Two young but experienced brewers opened this brewery in 2003, with top-fermentation beers in the *bière de garde* style. One takes its name from Saint Hildegard, a German abbess of the 11th century, who is often (though incorrectly) credited with the introduction of hops into the beermaking process.

ST-SYLVESTRE

121 rue de la Chapelle,
59114 St-Sylvestre-Cappel, France
www.brasserie-st-sylvestre.com

There has been a brewery in this small Flemish village since 1789. The Ricour family has brewed traditional beers, using barley malts and hops, for many generations.

BREWING SECRET Three different strains of yeast are used to develop strong and rich aromas in the beers.

THEILLIER

11 rue de la Grande Chaussée,
59570 Bavay, France

In this small town near Valenciennes, the Theilliers have been brewing since 1832. Very little has changed since then, in fact—from the equipment used to the art of brewing one of the most splendid French beers.

BEWING SECRETS A very long cooking time, in old copper kettles, is one of the secrets of Michel Theillier, the current brewer.

THIRIEZ

22 rue de Wormhout,
59470 Esquelbecq, France
http://brasseriethiriez.ifrance.com

From working as a manager in a food distribution company, Daniel Thiriez changed his life to become an artisan brewer. He established his brewery on an old farm in Flanders in 1996, and uses traditional brewing methods.

BREWING SECRET Thiriez's unfiltered beers have a second fermentation in the bottle, on their lees.

BEER

RESERVE HILDEGARDE AMBRÉE
ALE 6.9% ABV
Golden, with a rich nose of cereals, spices, and honey. Very smooth with a good bitterness and a long finish.

PAGE 24 RHUBARBE
ALE 5.9% ABV
Gold in color, with floral aromas. Very refreshing, with a special acidity contributed by rhubarb.

TROIS MONTS
ALE 8.5% ABV
Brilliant gold, with a rich and malty nose. Very fruity, it has good bitterness and a long finish.

GAVROCHE
AMBER ALE 8.5% ABV
Deep amber, with aromas of toasted malts and stewed red fruits; a little bitterness and a long finish.

BAVAISIENNE
AMBER ALE 6.5% ABV
A hue of amber, and with cereal aromas on the nose, this is a complex, deep, and malty beer, with notes of brown sugar and caramel, and a rich bitterness. Wonderful.

ÉTOILE DU NORD
BLONDE ALE 5.5% ABV
The moment the bottle is opened, an extraordinary smell of fresh hops comes to the nose. The beer's refreshing bitterness is in perfect harmony with its fine malt aromas.

1516 BREWING COMPANY

Schwarzenbergstrasse 2,
A-1010 Vienna, Austria

Essentially, this is an American-style brewpub in downtown Vienna. Not all the beers are brewed in accordance with the German Purity Law passed in 1516—the date that lends this establishment its name—but then the brewpub was only founded in 1998.

BREWING SECRET 1516 specializes in extremely hoppy brews, most of which are extremely strong.

EGGENBERG

Eggenberg 1, A-4655 Vorchdorf, Austria
www.schloss-eggenberg.at

Schloss Eggenberg is a small castle in Upper Austria that has been brewing for more than 500 years. A broad range of lagers (including a non-alcoholic one) are produced for the local market, and some fine bock beers are brewed for export; these include an urbock and even a blonde version of the traditionally dark Samichlaus beer.

FORSTNER

Dorfstrasse 52, A-8401 Kalsdorf bei Graz, Austria
www.hofbraeu.at

One of the more adventurous new brewers, Gerhard Forstner has recently made inroads into brewing Belgian and American-style ales. His brewery is in an old farmhouse building that has also served as a school. Some of his beers are endorsed by the Slow Food movement and are sold at Slow Food festivals.

FREISTÄDTER

Promenade 7, A-4240 Freistadt, Austria
www.freistaedter-bier.at

The town of Freistadt lies close to Austria's border with the Czech Republic, and its brewery is owned by the townspeople. Since 1777 every owner of a building inside the old city walls automatically owns a certain number of shares of the brewery; those shares can be sold only along with the building itself.

YANKEE STICKE

STICKE 7.3% ABV
Sticke is a bock-strength *altbier*—and this one comes with great bitterness, derived from whole hops.

HOP DEVIL

IPA 6.5% ABV
Orange of hue, with an intense grapefruit aroma and a full body. Distinct flavor of Cascade hops.

SAMICHLAUS

DOPPELBOCK 14% ABV
Intense malt aroma, with noticeable alcohol. Sweet and fruity (dried cherries, figs, and plums); very little hop character present.

HOPFENKÖNIG

PILSNER 5.1% ABV
Very pale, with a firm head and hay-like spicy hop aromas. Light body followed by some dry bitterness.

STYRIAN ALE

BITTER ALE 5.6% ABV
Very dark burgundy; roasty and fruity (grapefruit?) aromas; slightly tart and very refreshing, with a medium bitterness.

TRIPLE 22

BELGIAN STYLE TRIPLE 9.5% ABV
Copper, with firm head and aroma of pawpaw and mango. Sweet and full-bodied; spicy and bitter finish.

RAUCHBIER

SMOKED LAGER 5.3% ABV
Pale amber, with a smoky nose; dry and aromatic, with a nice balance of smoked malt and hops.

RATSHERRN TRUNK

EXPORT 5.1% ABV
A firm head and a full body. Low hop bitterness, with a hint of grass in the aftertaste.

BREWERY

GÖSSER

Brauhausgasse 1,
A-8707 Leoben-Göss, Austria
www.goesser.at

Part of the Heineken group, Gösser is one of the most popular and most valuable brands in Austria, and its best-selling beer is a *märzen*.

BREWING SECRET Head brewer Andreas Werner uses locally grown Fuggles hops, known as Styrian Goldings, for the Reininghaus Jahrgangspils.

GUSSWERK

5020 Salzburg,
Söllheimer Strasse 16, Austria
www.brauhaus-gusswerk.at

Established in 2007 in a former bell foundry, Brauhaus Gusswerk is a very small operation. There is a stylish brewery tap, but the bottled beers can be found in organic shops nationwide.

BREWING SECRET Brewer Reinhold Barta adheres strictly to the standards of organic beer production issued by the international Demeter organization.

HIRT

Hirt 9, A-9322 Micheldorf, Austria
www.hirterbier.at

This old brewery, founded in 1270 in the southern province of Carinthia, offers a broad variety of beer styles. The fame it has won, however, is focused on the pilsner beers—these are widely available nationwide and through export. Hirter's *weizen* and *märzen* beers, on the other hand, are much harder to find.

KALTENHAUSEN

Salzburgerstrasse 67,
A-5400 Hallein-Kaltenhausen, Austria
www.edelweissbier.at

Though its history stretches back to 1475, Kaltenhausen is best known for its wheat beer, which came into production only in the 1980s. The brewery's Edelweiss is now the best-selling wheat beer in the country.

BREWING SECRET Fissures in a nearby mountain cause a stream of cold air that's used to cool the fermenters.

BEER

GÖSSER MÄRZEN
AUSTRIAN MÄRZEN LAGER 5.2% ABV
Malty nose, with notes of hay and hops; sweet, malty, well-balanced flavor, with a robust bitterness.

REININGHAUS JAHRGANGSPILS
PILSNER 4.9% ABV
Herbal and haylike aromas; dry and hoppy, with some fruity (ripe red apples?) aromas in the aftertaste.

KATHARSIS
OLD ALE 6.6% ABV
Very low head and carbonation. Fruity nose (dried apricots) and a rich, full body; tart finish.

EDELGUSS
BLONDE ALE 5.1% ABV
Golden and slightly hazy. Some grainy aromas and a hint of sponge cake. Herbal notes in the aftertaste.

PRIVAT PILS
BOHEMIAN-STYLE PILSNER 5.2% ABV
Pale golden, with a faint floral hop aroma and an overall mild bitterness that is embedded in an almost sweetish, malty body.

BIO HANF
FLAVORED LAGER 4.8% ABV
Locally grown hemp gives this pale lager a nutty aroma.

EDELWEISS HOFBRÄU
BAVARIAN-STYLE HEFEWEIZEN 4.5% ABV
Spicy, clovelike aromas, with a little hint of banana. Very spritzy and refreshing, with a rather slight body.

GAMSBOCK
WEIZENBOCK 7.1% ABV
Intense banana aromas, and dangerously refreshing for such a strong beer. Extremely dry finish.

MOHRENBRÄU

Dr Waibel Strasse 2,
A-6850 Dornbirn, Austria
www.mohrenbrauerei.at

Austria's westernmost brewery has won fame for brewing strong beers. The brewery building is also home to a small museum, which showcases the brewing traditions of the province of Vorarlberg.

BREWING SECRET The soft palate of the Mohrenbräu's Kellerbier is due to a small amount of wheat in the mash bill.

SCHWECHATER

Mautner Markhof-Strasse 11, A-2320
Schwechat, Austria
www.schwechater.at

A large brewery that claims to have brewed the first lager beer in 1840, though, to be precise, it was the Vienna lager that was invented here by Anton Dreher. Production of that beer was discontinued in the early 20th century. Nowadays the brewery is part of Heineken and produces golden lagers.

SIEBENSTERNBRÄU

Siebensterngasse 19,
A-1070 Vienna, Austria
www.7stern.at

Siebensternbräu was the first brewpub in Austria to brew specialty beers—IPA, chili, and fruit flavored. Owner Sigi Flitter also helped reintroduce many of Austria's indigenous but forgotten beer styles.

BREWING SECRET The range varies with each season, but expect a wheat beer in summer and a smoked in winter.

STIEGL

Kendlerstrasse 1,
A-5017 Salzburg, Austria
www.stiegl.at

Austria's largest independent brewery produces Austria's single most successful beer, Goldbräu. The brewery itself dates back to 1492 and, over time, has built up a splendid collection of beer-related exhibits for the "Brauwelt"—the largest museum on the continent entirely devoted to brewing.

KELLERBIER
LAGER 5.7% ABV
Very fruity and yeasty on the nose; soft on the palate and with hardly any bitterness.

BOCKBIER
BOCK 7% ABV
Intense haylike hop aromas. Full-bodied and well-balanced, with not too much sweetness or bitterness.

SCHWECHATER ZWICKL
UNFILTERED PILSNER 5.5% ABV
Herbal hop aromas and a hint of lemon zest. A lot of wheat in the mash bill. Dry and hoppy finish.

SCHWECHATER BIER
PALE LAGER 5% ABV
Golden color, malty aromas. Full bodied with hops being noticeable from the start to the finish.

RAUCHBOCK
SMOKED BOCK 7.9% ABV
Intense smoky nose; full, almost sweet, body, with hints of chocolate and liquorice, and a smoky finish.

PRAGER DUNKLES
DARK LAGER 4.5% ABV
While most dark beers in Austria are terribly sweet, this one is dry. Intense toasty notes, very little hop aroma. Roasty finish.

GOLDBRÄU
AUSTRIAN MÄRZEN-TYPE
LAGER 4.9% ABV
Relatively low bitterness and a hint of malty sweetness in the aroma and on the palate.

PARACELSUS ZWICKL
ORGANIC LAGER 5% ABV
Unfiltered, so hazy orange in hue; aromas of malt and yeast; medium body and very low bitterness.

ALL ABOUT ...

BEER AND FOOD

Even though beer is great on its own, it is also a perfect companion at the dining table. In the past, wine has garnered all the culinary kudos, while beer has been dismissed as of little consequence when it comes to fine dining. Yet beer is a natural friend of food, as an increasing number of chefs, brewers, and drinkers are discovering.

European beer nations such as Belgium, Germany, Austria, and Hungary have been in on this great secret for centuries, and their bars and restaurants have never had qualms about cooking with beer or serving it alongside their dishes. In Belgium, *cuisine à la bière* includes the likes of rabbit cooked in cherry beer, and Flemish beef stew. Visit the Czech Republic and a glass of Budvar or Bernard is an essential accompaniment to Bohemian staples such as potato pancake stuffed with spicy pork. The same goes for Bavaria, where pork dishes share table space with a dark and delicious dunkel or doppelbock.

This approach is now spreading throughout the rest of the world, as chefs and brewers catch on to the pleasures of matching beer with food. For example, American brewpubs take great delight in pairing up adventurous beer styles with creative modern cuisine, as well as splashing their brews about in the kitchen. In both dining room and kitchen, beer is at last beginning to vie for space with wine, and has earned the right to be regarded with equal respect.

BEER AND OYSTERS
In the British Isles, an affinity between stout and oysters has long been appreciated, and brown ale traditionally plays a part in steak-and-kidney pudding.

ACIDITY Sour beers such as lambics and Flemish reds can hold their own in partnership with pickled dishes; perhaps surprisingly, they also work superbly with a big-flavored, ripe, pungent cheese.

MALT FLAVORS

MALT FLAVORS The sweet flavors of malt harmonize with the natural sweetness of a meat such as pork, making this a winning combination. Roast malts deliver smoky, roasted notes, so beers made with them are ideal partners for grilled meats and barbecues.

HOP FLAVORS

HOP FLAVORS Beers that have a spicy, peppery finish chime exquisitely with aromatic Asian dishes, while the citrus and orange-marmalade notes in a hoppy beer elevate the great cheeses of the world to another plateau. Hop bitterness also cuts through fat and cleanses the palate for the next mouthful.

"DIFFICULT" FLAVORS

Beer wins the day when it comes to those foods that experts consider difficult to pair with a suitable wine: chocolate and asparagus are notable examples. A sticky chocolate dessert and a Belgian kriek are divine together, while a Bavarian-style weissbier, with its trademark custard-and-cream aroma and palate, is perfect with steamed asparagus. A smoky rauchbier sits well with a Bavarian dish like sausages and asparagus.

TASTING BOARDS

TASTING BOARDS In Sydney, Australia, the stylish Redoak Boutique Beer Café serves tasting boards that offer small plates of inventive culinary delights, each one accompanied by a different, complementing beer.

BREWERY

STIFTSBRAUEREI SCHLÄGL

Schlägl 1, A-4160 Schlägl, Austria
www.stift-schlaegl.at

The small village of Schlägl, close to the Czech and Bavarian borders, is home to the only Austrian brewery wholly owned by a monastery—in this case the Premonstratensian order. In recent years the product range has grown considerably and now includes several ales.

UTTENDORFER

Uttendorf 25, A-5261 Uttendorf, Austria
www.uttendorf-bier.com

Small and family-run, Uttendorfer is based in a 100-year-old tavern building on the road between Salzburg and Braunau. The tavern itself is worth a visit because it offers local food, including game—the brewer is a passionate hunter—in a rustic setting.

BREWING SECRET The brewery has built a good reputation for brewing distinctively hopped beers.

VILLACHER

Brauhausgasse 6, A - 9500 Villach, Austria
www.villacher-bier.at

Austria's southernmost brewery was founded in 1858. It began as a strictly regional brewery, but has become a national one in the last 25 years and has even developed an export market in Italy. The beers are branded as Villacher, though the brewery's official name is Vereinigte Kärntner Brauereien. It now owns Schleppe (a specialty brewer) and Piestinger near Vienna.

DIE WEISSE

A-5020 Salzburg, Rupertgasse 10, Austria
www.dieweisse.at

Founded in 1901, Die Weisse could be considered Austria's oldest brewpub. Until the early 1990s, its modest output was sold exclusively in the two-room pub, but, since then, it has become fashionable, and its beers are now served in bars and restaurants across the country. The range has broadened too, and now includes seasonal bocks and a *märzen*.

BEER

STIFTER BIER
RED ALE 5.7% ABV
Malty sweetness with a refreshing fruit (peach and melon) undertone. Just a faint hint of hops.

DOPPELBOCK
DOPPELBOCK 8.3% ABV
A big, malty nose. Fruity (pears and apples) and sweet from the start, but very well balanced finish.

EINHUNDERT
GERMAN PILSNER 5% ABV
Reputedly the hoppiest pilsner in the world, this beer has 100 IBUs and an extremely dry aftertaste.

DUNKLER BOCK
BOCK 7% ABV
Bottom-fermented Bock, with roasty aromas, full body, and little sweetness. Finish: dry; quite bitter.

VILLACHER EDITION 07
VIENNA LAGER 4.9% ABV
Sweet aroma, with hints of fruit (red apple). Refreshing yet full bodied and almost sweet, but then balanced with some hops.

VILLACHER GLOCKNER PILS
PILSNER 4.9% ABV
Pale golden; intense carbonation. Grassy hop aroma. Crisp and dry on palate, with hoppy aftertaste.

DIE WEISSE
BAVARIAN HEFEWEIZEN 5.2% ABV
Gold and cloudy, with a large pillowy head, intense spicy aromas, and a surprisingly dry, bitter finish.

WEITRA BRÄU

Sparkassaplatz 160,
A-3970 Weitra, Austria
www.bierwerkstatt.at

Weitra claims to hold Austria's oldest brewing privilege, issued in 1321. In medieval times, most of the buildings around the town square exercised their right to brew, now there is only one brewpub and this brewery left.

BREWING SECRET This organic specialty brewery, bought by Zwettler in 2002, still brews using open fermenters.

ZILLERTAL BIER

Umfahrungsstrasse 3,
A-6280 Zell am Ziller, Austria
www.zillertal-bier.at

This brewery in the small Zillertal-valley in Tyrol has been around for more than 500 years. Each May it celebrates the Gauderfest, a festival that dates back to 1428, with a beerfest that lasts for four days.

BREWING SECRET A special bock beer is brewed for the festival, and is available only on that weekend.

ZIPFER

A-4871 Zipf, Austria
www.zipfer.at

A mass production brewery now owned by Heineken, Zipfer creates beers that tend to be extremely pale and show a distinct hop aroma due to the use of whole hops. The flagship beer is the crisp Urtyp, introduced in 1967, which should not be confused with the Pils. Head brewer Günther Seeleitner finds time to occasionally brew one-off beers.

ZWETTLER

Syrnauer Strasse 22 – 25,
A-3910 Zwettl, Austria
www.zwettler.at

A large, family-owned brewery, Zwettler grew to its present size over the last 40 years when owner Karl Schwarz decided first to mass-produce relatively cheap lager and then subsequently to establish more prestigious brands of specialty beers.

BREWING SECRET Zwettler introduced the first unfiltered Zwickl in the late 1970s.

HADMAR
ORGANIC VIENNA LAGER 5.2% ABV
Sweet and malty on the nose and palate; hints of roastyness, bitterness; variable from batch to batch.

WEITRA HELL
LAGER 5% ABV
Straw colored, with estery aroma and very little carbonation. Soft on the palate, with a mild hoppyness.

GAUDER BOCK
MAIBOCK 7.4% ABV
Aromas of vanilla and alpine herbs. Unusually intense bitterness helps balance the malt to give a dry finish.

ZILLERTAL WEISSBIER
HEFEWEIZEN 5% ABV
Aromas of citrus and banana. Refreshing and prickly, light and aromatic (cloves), rather than sweet.

PILS
PILSNER 5.2% ABV
Pale, with stable white head. Intense floral hop aromas (Tettnanger); extremely dry and hoppy.

STEFANIBOCK
BOCK 7.1% ABV
Citric and haylike aromas dominate. Malty, but hardly sweet on the palate; lighter and more easy-drinking than other bock beers.

ORIGINAL
PILSNER 5.1% ABV
Malty and quite full-bodied; balanced with a mild bitterness from locally grown Perle and Select hops.

ZWETTLER ZWICKL
UNFILTERED LAGER 5.5% ABV
Yeast and lemon in the nose. Refreshing, smooth, and balanced, with a moderate hop bitterness.

CALANDA

Kasernenstr. 36, CH-7007 Chur, Switzerland
www.calanda.com

Heineken has turned Calanda into the largest brewery in eastern Switzerland. Aside from brewing ubiquitous international brands for the swiss market, Calanda still produces five traditional, local beers, as well as Ittinger, originally created by Actienbrauerei Frauenfeld, but which was sold off in 1994.

EICHHOF

Obergrundstrasse 110, CH-6005 Luzern, Switzerland
www.eichhof.ch

Founded in 1834, Eichhof has been listed on the Zurich stock exchange since 1927. Their general assembly sees more than 1,000 beer-loving investors showing support for the largest independent Swiss brewery.

BREWING SECRET This brewery uses water from the Pilatus, a landmark mountain in the central Swiss alps.

FALKEN

Brauereistrasse 1, CH-8201 Schaffhausen, Switzerland
www.falken.ch

The Falken Brewery is located in Schaffhausen, where the Rhine River forms the border with Germany. Founded in 1799, it is one of the larger independent breweries in Switzerland. Although slightly hoppier than many other Swiss beers the "falcon" beers give a very smooth overall impression that resembles traditional Czech lagers.

LOCHER

Industriestrasse 12, CH-9050 Appenzell, Switzerland
www.appenzellerbier.ch

Appenzell is Switzerland's smallest province (kanton), but the beer produced by the local brewery has won it a lot of fame.

BREWING SECRET In the 1990s, the Locher family found out that beers brewed on the full moon ferment more easily; they have, therefore, created a line of "Vollmond-brews."

CALANDA
LAGER 5% ABV
Sweetish-estery nose; an almost fruity and refreshing first impression that gives way to a mild bitterness.

ITTINGER KLOSTERBRÄU
AMBER LAGER 5.8% ABV
Malty, slightly roasted aroma. The flavor is sweet with grains, caramel, and bitter hops. Short, dry finish.

BÜGEL BRÄU
LAGER 4.9% ABV
Pale golden, with a somewhat yeasty nose. Full-bodied, with hints of vanilla, and very mildly hopped.

BARBARA
LAGER 5.9% ABV
Slightly sweetish, toffeelike nose and very balanced on the palate. Fruity (red apple) notes in the finish.

FIRST COOL
LAGER 4.5% ABV
Very little aroma. Sweet and soft on the palate due to a generous portion of corn on the mash bill.

FALKEN PRINZ
LAGER 5.5% ABV
Butterscotch and herbal aromas; full body, with lots of carbonation, sweet and spicy (perhaps ginger) notes, and butterscotch in the finish.

VOLLMOND
ORGANIC LAGER 5.2% ABV
An aroma of hops and lemon zest; medium body—chewy; hoppy, but not excessively bitter.

HOLZFASS-BIER
LAGER 5.2% ABV
Aromas of sweetcorn, very little carbonation, and a distinctive note from the oak in which it is matured.

BIERVISION MONSTEIN

Monstein, CH-7278 Davos, Switzerland
www.biervision-monstein.ch

Andreas Aegerter and Christian Ochs started this village brewery high up in the mountains near Davos in 2001, along with 756 small investors (each of them a devoted customer). They all shared the vision that there is a market for unusual beers, as well as beer-related products, such as cheese crusted with malt and spirits distilled from beer.

RUGENBRÄU

Wagnerenstrasse 40, CH-3800 Matten, Switzerland
www.rugenbraeu.ch

This family-run brewery is located in the tourist resort of Interlaken, close to the Eiger and Jungfrau mountains—landmarks of Berner Oberland. Owner-president Bruno Hofweber promotes beer and gourmet cuisine in cooperation with the chefs of the larger hotels in the vicinity, most notably the Victoria-Jungfrau.

SONNENBRÄU

Alte Landstrasse 36, CH-9445 Rebstein, Switzerland
www.sonnenbraeu.ch

This is the only surviving brewery of 34 that once existed in the Rhine valley on Switzerland's eastern border. It has been quick to introduce new beers to the market – including Switzerland's first "Light" beer in 1978.

BREWING SECRET It focuses on local produce, and uses corn from the region in the brewing process.

BRAUHAUS STERNEN

Hohenzornstrasse 2, CH-8500 Frauenfeld, Switzerland
www.brauhaussternen.ch

This is an intriguing brewpub, set up on the site of the Aktienbrauerei Frauenfeld, where Martin Wartmann created Ittinger (now brewed at Calanda). The present brewery was built in 2003 with financial help from many prominent European brewers eager to see Martin brew interesting beers, some in limited editions ("Nur für Freunde"—"for friends only").

MUNGGA
KÖLSCH 3.5% ABV
Brewed from organic Swiss ingredients, Mungga ("groundhog") has aromas of violets, a dry taste, and an elegant bitterness.

ROYAL 11
SPICED BEER 6.5% ABV
Reddish, with pleasant cherry aromas (from the local liqueur Röteli); fruity and only faintly bitter.

ALPENPERLE
LAGER 4.8% ABV
Pale golden, with a sweetish nose and a light body. Some sweetness but very little hops in the aftertaste.

ZWICKEL BIER
UNFILTERED LAGER 4.8% ABV
Straw colored and slightly hazy; a faint aroma of lemon zest; dry and balanced, with a herbal bitterness in the finish.

RHEINTALER MAISBIER
LAGER 5% ABV
Grassy hops hide the maize aromas. Very smooth mouthfeel and late, not very intense, hop bitterness.

FIRST SWISS ALE
BROWN ALE 5.4% ABV
Aroma of caramel, bread, toasted malt and fruit. Medium body and medium bitterness in the finish.

WARTMANN'S NUR FÜR FREUNDE NO1
BELGIAN DUBBEL 9.6% ABV
Chocolaty, slightly sweet aroma. Full-bodied and fruity (ripe plums); very mild bitterness in the finish.

HONEY BROWN ALE
BROWN ALE 6% ABV
Sweet and fruity. Quite refreshing for its strength. Very low bitterness and a hint of honey in the finish.

BREWERY

BEIERHAASCHT
Avenue de Luxembourg 240,
4940 Bascharge, Luxembourg
www.beierhaascht.lu

Tradition and the 21st century combine in this hotel and brewpub, where gleaming kettles are central to the design of the bright, airy bar. The menu features traditional regional specialties, as well as dishes made with beer.

BREWING SECRET The beers adhere to German brewing purity rules (the *Reinheitsgebot*).

CORNELYSHAFF
Maison 37,9753 Heinerscheid,
Luxembourg
www.cornelyshaff.lu

Situated in a nature park, Cornelyshaff comprises a popular bar, restaurant, and hotel, as well as a brewery that is open to visitors. It is modern, gleaming, and energy efficient—the cooperative that owns it prides itself on minimizing its environmental impact. The bar and restaurant showcase the beers and much farm produce from the area.

DIEKIRCH
1 Rue de la Brasserie,
9214 Diekirch, Luxembourg
www.mouseldiekirch.lu

The roots of La Brasserie Diekirch stretch back to 1871; by 1900 it had become the most productive brewery in Luxembourg. It joined Interbrew in 2002, becoming part of InBev in 2004.

BREWING SECRET An unfiltered (*gezwieckelte*) version of the standard beer is available in the adjoining brewery tap, Mousel's Cantine.

SIMON
Rue Joseph Simon 14,
9550 Wiltz, Luxembourg
www.brasseriesimon.lu

Situated in the very hilly and heavily forested Ardennes countryside, the brewery has operated within sight of the church in the lower town of Wiltz since 1824, and used to provide beer to the Grand Duke in its early years.

BREWING SECRET Open fermenters and copper kettles, visible through the brewery windows, are still used here.

BEER

BIÈRE MEESCHTERBÉIER
LAGER 5% ABV
Light, pale orange, thirst-quenching beer produced during, and for, the summer months.

BIÈRE AU FROMENT CLAIRE
WITBIER 6% ABV
Pale and slightly cloudy. Strong, with a crispness of taste that is sharp and refreshing.

OURDALLER WAÏSSEN TARWEBIER
WITBIER 4.6% ABV
An unfiltered, cloudy wheat beer; assertive in character, it is full of spice.

KORNELYSBÉIER
RYE BEER 4.2% ABV
A spicy aroma gives way to a strongly flavored deep, earthy taste brought on by the use of rye grain.

DIEKIRCH GRAND CRU AMBRÉE
VIENNA LAGER 5.1% ABV
Sweetness and fruit on the palate give way to a malty character. A soft amber in color.

DIEKIRCH EXCLUSIVE
LAGER 5.1% ABV
Pale to the eye and somewhat thin on the palate, it is an uncomplicated, easy-drinking beer.

SIMON DINKEL
SPELT WITBIER 4.5% ABV
Brewed from 70% barley, 30% unmalted spelt—an ancient form of wheat grown in the area—the beer is pale and has a soft, fruity aroma.

OKULT NO 1
WITBIER 5.4% ABV
Cloudy to the eye, it is tart and refreshing, with a zesty aftertaste.

Stiegl is Austria's largest independent brewer, and its Goldbräu lager is one of the country's biggest-selling beers.

BREWERY

3 HORNE

Marktstraat 40, 5171 GP Kaatsheuvel,
Netherlands
www.de3horne.nl

Founded in his garage by homebrewer
Sjef Groothuis in 1991, De 3 Horne
was transferred to the larger premises
of a former shoe factory in 1993. The
building also houses a tasting room and
a shop. Most of the beers are Belgian-
inspired, and some are produced for
third parties, such as Kandinsky Bier,
which is made for a Tilburg beer café.

ALFA

Thull 15-19, 6365 AC Schinnen,
Netherlands
www.alfa-beer.nl

One of the few independent, family-
run breweries left in the Netherlands,
Alpha has been controlled by the
Meens family since its foundation in
1870. The beers are brewed from
spring water, each bottle numbered to
keep tabs on the amount used.

BREWING SECRET One of the few Dutch
brewers to adhere to the *Reinheitsgebot*.

BRAND

Brouwerijstraat 2-10,
6321 AG Wijlre, Netherlands
www.brand.nl

Despite being incorporated into the
Heineken empire in 1989, Brand has
managed to maintain its reputation
and identity. Dating back to 1340, it
is easily the oldest Dutch brewery.

BREWING SECRET It brews a highly varied
range of bottom-fermented beers:
pilsners, a dubbelbock, an amber bock,
Imperator, and the pale Meibock.

BROUWERIJ 'T IJ

Funenkade 7, 1018 AL Amsterdam,
Netherlands
www.brouwerijhetij.nl

Amsterdam's favorite micro is now
the city's oldest brewery, even though
it was founded only in 1985. Strong
Belgian-style ales form the backbone
of the output, though there's also a
pils and a witbier. Set in an old
windmill, the taproom is thronged on
warm summer afternoons, its outdoor
seating taken up by drinkers enjoying
the lowest beer prices in Amsterdam.

BEER

TRIPPELAER
ABBEY-STYLE TRIPLE 8.5% ABV
A biscuity, bready aroma is followed
by lots of sweet malt and a touch
of bitter orange.

DOBBELAER
ABBEY-STYLE DOUBLE 6.5% ABV
Malty, sweetish beer, with a nutty
finish. Clean, flavorful, and as good
as most Belgian dubbels.

ALFA EDEL PILS
PILS 5% ABV
Tobacco and citrus hop aromas
overlay a buttery maltiness. One of
the most distinctive Dutch pils.

ALFA SUPER DORTMUNDER
DORTMUNDER EXPORT 7.5% ABV
A bitter Export, that combines
grassy hops, honey, and vanilla with
the trademark Alfa butteriness.

BRAND IMPERATOR
AMBER LAGER 6.5% ABV
Dried fruit, toffee, and spicy hops
fight for supremacy in this
beautifully balanced amber beer.

BRAND URP
PILS 5% ABV
Aromatically hoppy; lemon, pepper,
and pine notes predominate. First
brewed in 1952 and still one of
Holland's best pils beers.

TURBOCK
DOPPELBOCK 9% ABV
Packed with dark fruits and
molasses sweetness, the trademark
Ij spiciness adds a dimension not
found in German bocks.

COLUMBUS
STRONG ALE 9% ABV
A balance of biscuity malt, coriander,
lemon, and resinous, minty hops.
Assertive, but not overpowering.

THE BEST-KNOWN DUTCH BEERS

The vast majority of beer drunk in Holland is pils put out by one of four large brewing groups: Heineken, Bavaria, Grolsch, and Anheuser-Busch InBev.

Between them, these brewing companies control about 95 percent of the Dutch beer market —Heineken leading the way with 50 percent, and its three competitors following with around 15 percent each. Heineken's main offerings are their ubiquitous Pils, Amstel Pils, the better-quality Amstel 1870 (another pils) and witbier Wieckse Witte. During the autumn bock season, sweet Heineken Tarwebock and the surprisingly-good Amstel Bock are available. Bavaria, now the largest wholly Dutch-owned brewer, concentrates on the cheaper end of the market. In addition to their branded Bavaria Pils, they also produce several own-label beers for supermarket chains. Anheuser-Busch InBev closed their largest Dutch brewery, Oranjeboom, in Breda, in 2002. Dommelsch, their largest remaining plant, is much smaller, and large quantities of Jupiler Pils are imported from Belgium. Dommelsch Pils, strong lager Dommelsch Dominator, and autumn seasonal Dommelsch Bokbier Primeur are the main Dutch-brewed brands.

HEINEKEN PILS (PILS 5% ABV) *left*
HEINEKEN TARWEBOCK
  (BOCK 6.5% ABV)
AMSTEL PILS (PILS 5% ABV) *center*
AMSTEL 1870 (PILS 5% ABV)
AMSTEL BOCK (BOCK 7% ABV)
BAVARIA PILS (PILS 5% ABV) *right*

BUDELS

Nieuwstraat 9,
6020 AA Budel, Netherlands
www.budels.nl

Budels is among the few established, predominantly bottom-fermenting Dutch breweries. Started in 1870, the business is currently run by the fourth generation of the founding Aerts family.

BREWING SECRET In recent years Budels has diversified into top-fermenting beers, such as kölsch, altbier, and an abbey-style dubbel.

GROLSCH

Brouwerslaan 1, Boekelo, 7548 XA
Enschede, Netherlands
www.grolsch.nl

Now owned by SABMiller, Grolsch used to operate two breweries, one in Groenlo (from which the name derives) and one in Enschede. In 2004 a new hypermodern plant was opened in Boeklo, just outside Enschede, and the two older breweries were closed. The bulk of Grolsch's sales are pils, though it has tried, with varied success, to diversify its product range.

GRUNN

Boumaboulevard 55,
9723 ZS Groningen, Netherlands
www.grunn-speciaalbier.nl

The brewery was established by Jaap van der Weide and Egbert Timmerman in 2000, with their beers being brewed under contract. The eventual aim is to build a brewery and pub close to the FC Groningen football stadium; for now, though, the beers are being brewed in Belgium and Germany.

BUDELS LAGER
PILS 5% ABV
A gentle, piney hop aroma is followed by fruity, sweetish taste; perhaps closer to a helles than a pils.

BUDELS CAPUCIJN
ABBEY-STYLE DOUBLE 6.5% ABV
Sweet toasted malt aromas are complemented by bitterness, dates, and the merest hint of smoke.

GROLSCH PREMIUM WEIZEN
HEFEWEIZEN 5.5% ABV
Hazy golden, with the orange, cloves, and basil aromas typical of a German-style wheat beer.

GROLSCH PREMIUM PILSNER
PILS 5% ABV
Good aroma of noble hops and a pleasant spiciness in the finish; a little too much sweetness perhaps.

GRUNN DREIDUBBEL
TRIPEL ALE 5% ABV
A sweet, honeyish tripel in which biscuity, even sugary, malt is complemented by a tart fruitiness reminiscent of pears.

GRUNN HOAGELWIT
WITBIER 5% ABV
An unspiced wheat beer with subtle hopping and delicate elderflower, lemon, butter, and pepper aromas.

BREWERY

GULPENER

Rijksweg 16, 6271 AE Gulpen, Netherlands
www.gulpener.nl

Like the majority of the country's older brewers, Gulpener is located in the south of the country. A wide range of both top- and bottom-fermented beers are produced.

BREWING SECRET Gulpener's Mestreechs Aajt is a blend of sour beer that has been aged for at least a year in wood and freshly brewed beer.

HERTOG JAN

Kruisweg 44, 5944 EN Arcen, Netherlands
www.hertogjan.nl

A management buyout in 1981 saved this old brewery from closure when it was part of the Oranjeboom group. A clause in the agreement prohibited brewing bottom-fermented beer, however, and so a range of Belgian-style ales was developed. Oranjeboom bought back the brewery to get hold of its specialty brands, before selling it on to Interbrew (now InBev) in 1995.

JOPEN

Minckelersweg 2a,
2031 EM Haarlem, Netherlands
www.jopen.nl

Jopen was founded in 1995 with the intention of recreating old beer styles specifically from the Haarlem locale—once an important brewing center. This is Holland's only brewery to concentrate on local recipes, and no other in the world produces beer in these styles. A brewpub to showcase the beers is due to open soon.

KLEIN DUIMPJE

Parallelweg 2, 2182 CP Hillegom, Netherlands
www.kleinduimpje.nl

This is the brewery of a prize-winning amateur brewer, Erik Bouman, whose porter was chosen as the best of more than 400 entries at the Dutch Homebrewing Championship of 1997. Bouman's competition success prompted him to start brewing professionally. His extensive range of top-fermenting ales includes his celebrated porter.

BEER

GULPENER KORENWOLF
WITBIER 5% ABV
A Belgian-style white beer packed with orange, ginger, wheat and coriander flavors. It's brewed from barley, wheat, spelt and rye.

GULPENER GLADIATOR
STRONG LAGER 10% ABV
A big bruiser of a beer. Apple, grapes, and caramel flavors are wrapped in a blanket of sweetness.

HERTOG JAN GRAND PRESTIGE
STRONG DARK ALE 10% ABV
A big, fruity strong ale, overflowing with caramel, liquorice, toffee, and apple flavors topped off with hops.

HERTOG JAN PRIMATOR
PILS 5% ABV
Though quite sweet for a pils, there are plenty of grassy hop aromas to provide a spicy backbone.

JOPEN KOYT
GRUIT BEER 8.5% ABV
A recreation of a pre-hop beer brewed from three grains and herbs. Fruity, spicy, and delicious.

JOPEN HOPPENBIER
AMBER ALE 6.5% ABV
Based on a recipe from 1501 using barley, wheat, and oats; hints of coriander, ginger, and cloves complement spicy hops.

HILLEGOMS TARWE BIER
WITBIER 5.5% ABV
Flavored with coriander and orange peel, this wheat beer is spicy, citric, and just ever so slightly sweet.

PORTER
PORTER 5.5% ABV
Espressolike roast malt combines with a chocolate sweetness, backed up with liquorice and toast.

LINDEBOOM

Engelmanstraat 52-54, 6068 BD Neer, Netherlands
www.lindeboom.nl

Established by farmer Willem Geenen in 1870, Lindeboom is the country's smallest surviving lager brewery. Still owned by members of the Geenen family, it's a modest producer of mostly pils. It does also produce altbier, and further diversification into top-fermentation came with the development of the Governeur family of ales in the late 1990s.

VENLOOSCH
ALTBIER 5% ABV
The sugary fruit aroma is deceptive as the taste is dry and hoppy. A reasonable try at the altbier style.

LINDEBOOM OUD BRUIN
OUD BRUIN 3.5% ABV
A fruity and very sweet low-alcohol dark lager, in a style that is unique to the Netherlands.

DE MOLEN

Overtocht 43, 2411 BS Bodegraven, Netherlands
www.brouwerijdemolen.nl

Since starting Molen in 2004, brewer Menno Olivier has quickly gained an enviable reputation. This is one of only a handful of Dutch micros to export; its cask-conditioned beer, Engel, is designed especially for the UK market.

BREWING SECRET Aficionados regard Tsarina Esra, an Imperial porter, as one of Europe's very finest beers.

BOREFTS BLOND
BLONDE ALE 6.5% ABV
Unlike many blondes, hops dominate here. Orange, pine, resin, and grass flavors fill the mouth.

BOREFTS STOUT
STOUT 7% ABV
Packed with all the roasty malt flavors you expect from a stout. Complex, characterful, harmonious.

MOMMERIETE

Holthonerweg 9, 7779 DE Holthone, Netherlands
www.mommeriete.nl

Homebrewers Gert and Karina Kelder were delighted when they discovered that a local restaurant had a spare, unused room. It was the perfect location to finally brew professionally after 15 years as amateurs, and they set to work in 2004. Mommeriete beers are available on tap in De Ganzenhoeve restaurant and in bottles through specialist Dutch beer shops.

SCHEERSE TRIPEL
TRIPLE 9.5% ABV
Biscuit and yeast aroma, honey on the tongue, and a spicy hop finish with notes of tobacco and pepper.

VROUWE VAN GRAMSBERGH
STRONG DARK ALE 10% ABV
Black toffee, bread, plum aromas, and a honey sweetness slip into a resiny, roasty, bitter finish.

DE PRAEL

Helicopterstraat 13 - 15, 1059 CE Amsterdam, Netherlands
www.deprael.nl

Set up with the help of government grants, Amsterdam's smallest brewery has a workforce made up of recovering psychiatric patients. The first choice of name—De Parel ("The Pearl")—had to be changed when Budels complained that it infringed on the copyright of their Parel beer. The solution was simply to shuffle the letters of the name around.

HEINTJE
WITBIER 5.4% ABV
Unspiced, but with prominent citrus aromas, a touch of fruit, and an unexpectedly hoppy finish.

MARY
BARLEY WINE 9.6% ABV
Neither malt nor hops dominate this fruity strong ale, laced with pepper, toffee, and caramel.

BREWERY

DE SCHANS

De Schans 17, 1421 BA Uithoorn, Netherlands
www.schansbier.nl

Guus Rooijen started up De Schans when he began brewing professionally in 1998. Though objections from the Catholic church opposite prevented Guus from opening a sampling room, there is a shop on site.

BREWING SECRET More adventurous than most Dutch micros, De Schans also produces a *saison* and a *schwarzbier*.

SCHELDEBROUWERIJ

Rangeerstraat 1, 4431 NL 's-Gravenpolder, Netherlands
www.scheldebrouwerij.nl

One of the oldest and largest Dutch micros, Scheldebrouwerij has been through many changes since opening in 1994. The current owners, brothers Frans and Jan Ooms, are eager to expand the business further; with that in mind, they have moved the beer production over the border into neighboring Belgium.

ST CHRISTOFFEL

Metaalweg 10, 6045 JB Roermond, Netherlands
www.christoffelbier.nl

Operating since 1986, St Christoffel is one of the oldest Dutch micros, founded (but no longer run) by Leo Brand, a member of the Brand brewing dynasty. It produces the very best lagers brewed in the Netherlands.

BREWING SECRET The Robertus beer is a rare example of a Münchner dark lager that's true to the Bavarian style.

LA TRAPPE

Eindhovenseweg 3, Berkel-Enschot, Netherlands
www.latrappe.nl

There are just seven genuine Trappist breweries in the world; Koningshoeven (better known as La Trappe) is the only one outside Belgium. The monastery had problems recruiting new monks, and that was one of the factors that prompted the sale of the brewery to Bavaria. Brewing still takes place within the monastery grounds under the supervision of the monks.

BEER

VAN VOLLENHOVEN'S STOUT
STOUT 7% ABV
A complex yet light-bodied stout, combining espresso roastiness with dark fruit and chocolate flavors.

SCHANSBIER 6
ABBEY-STYLE DOUBLE 5.8% ABV
Thick and chocolatey but not sickly sweet. Black toffee, chicory, and coffee complete the complexity.

SCHOENLAPPERTJE
FRUIT BEER 6.5% ABV
Locally-grown blackcurrants give this ale an unusual bright red hue and a sweet, fruity taste, with just a touch of balancing acidity.

STRANDGAPER
AMBER ALE 6.2% ABV
The aroma of biscuit, orange, and elderflower is interlaced with grass and pepper notes from the hops.

CHRISTOFFEL BLONDE
PILS 6% ABV
Spicy hop flavors burst from the glass—basil, mint, ginger, grapefruit, and cloves are all there.

CHRISTOFFEL ROBERTUS
MÜNCHNER 6% ABV
The nutty flavor of Munich malt runs right through this beer, flanked by biscuit, toast, and toffee.

LA TRAPPE WITTE TRAPPIST
WITBIER 5.5% ABV
Unspiced, but a subtle use of aromatic hops more than compensates, providing delicious citrus and pepper flavors.

LA TRAPPE TRIPEL
STRONG ALE 8% ABV
Sweetness and fruit give way to coriander, orange, and hop bitterness in this supremely balanced beer.

The Dutch city of Amsterdam is said to have a bar for every 500 citizens — 1,200 in total.

BREWERY

BØGEDAL BRYGHUS

Høllundvej 9, DK-7100 Vejle, Denmark
www.boegedal.com

This farmhouse is the world's only commercial brewery producing the old Danish style of "Goodbeer," a strong, rich beer dating back to before the industrial age. The same recipe is always followed, and yet no two beers are alike, hence they are numbered rather than named.

BREWING SECRET Bøgedal is Scandinavia's only all-gravity brewery.

BREW PUB

Vestergade 29, DK-1456 Copenhagen, Denmark
www.brewpub.dk

This successful microbrewery with restaurant is located in the heart of Copenhagen, in a beautiful 17th-century building. It brews 11 varieties of beer. The pub offers a five-beer sampler menu and the chefs draw inspiration from the beer on tap to create their dishes. Advice on pairing beer with food is also provided.

BRØCKHOUSE

Høgevej 6, DK-3400 Hillerød, Denmark
www.broeckhouse.dk

A fast-growing and popular micro-brewery to the north of Copenhagen, established in 2002. It was the goal of owner Allan Poulsen, a former IT engineer, to create something different from ordinary Danish pilsner.

BREWING SECRET Poulsen uses quality ingredients and British, German, and Belgian brewing traditions to create exciting and memorable brews.

CARLSBERG

Vesterfælledvej 100,
DK-1799 Copenhagen V, Denmark
www.carlsberg.com

Denmark's leading brewing company was founded in 1847 by the visionary brewer J.C. Jacobsen. Carlsberg is a pioneer of steam-brewing, refrigeration techniques, and the propagation of a single yeast strain. The company has a wide portfolio of beers and sells to more than 150 countries. It has recently moved all of its production, with the exception of specialty beers

BEER

BREW NO. 127
DARK ALE 6.3% ABV
Smells of prunes and citrus. Fills the palate and lingers on with a faint smoky aftertaste.

BREW NO. 121
PALE ALE 5.9% ABV
Light amber in color with compact carbonation. Aromatic sweetness reaveals notes of honey, citrus, and fine wine.

COLE PORTER
PORTER 5.2% ABV
Deep black in color, with a rich, creamy head. Seven malts give a well-balanced depth of flavor.

AMARILLO
RED ALE 5.5% ABV
Fresh aroma and flavors of plum and citrus. Balanced bitterness from caramel and red ale malt.

BRØCKHOUSE IPA
INDIAN PALE ALE 6% ABV
Top-fermented ale brewed with three varieties of hops to achieve a sweet, balanced complexity.

BRØCKHOUSE ESRUM KLOSTER
ABBEY ALE 7.5% ABV
Developed with the monks of Esrum Abbey. Strong nose; sweet, spicy flavor with hints of aniseed, lavender, rosemary, and juniper.

CARLSBERG ELEPHANT
STRONG PILSNER 7.2% ABV
High alcohol lager with high hop and malt content, resulting in a rich and bitter character.

CARLSBERG PILSNER
PILSNER 4.6% ABV
Another bottom-fermented lager with flavors of hops, grains, pine needles, sorrel, and Danish apples.

and the Jacobsen brand, from its original brewery in Copenhagen to Fredericia, located 125 miles (200 km) from its former home. In its place, a new city district is being developed, which will conserve the historic brewery buildings, and be the site of the Carlsberg Visitors Center.

GOURMETBRYGGERIET

Bytoften 10-12,
DK-4000 Roskilde, Denmark
www.gourmetbryggeriet.dk

One of the largest microbreweries in Denmark, "The Gourmet Brewery" creates specialty beers that are designed to be paired with food. The brewery's partner is a trained chef who works together with a local restaurant to create recipes that are attached to 66cl bottles for sharing. The company recently acquired the Ølfabrikken Brewery.

HERSLEV BRYGHUS

Kattingevej 8 , Herslev,
DK-4000 Roskilde, Denmark
www.herslevbryghus.dk

This small microbrewery, established in 2004 by Tore Jørgensen, is part of a family farmhouse located in Herslev, a small village outside Roskilde. The beer here is unfiltered, unpasteurized, and naturally carbonated.

BREWING SECRET Four kinds of grain are the foundation of the brewing process, creating beers with unique character.

JACOBSEN BREWHOUSE

Gamle Carlsberg Vej 11,
DK-2500 Valby, Denmark
www.jacobsenbeer.com

Named after Carlsberg's founder, Jacobsen was established in 2005 to produce high-quality specialty beers with a Scandinavian touch. This brewhouse will remain in the original 1847 Carlsberg brewery complex.

BREWING SECRET Jacobsen also brews an exclusive Vintage series, matured in oak barrels.

CARLSBERG SEMPER ARDENS
BELGIAN ABBEY ALE 7.3%
Unfiltered; brewed with Münchener and chocolate malt, and featuring burnt undertones and a hint of blackcurrant on the palate.

TUBORG PILSNER
ABV PILSNER 4.6% ABV
Denmark's favorite beer. Bottom-fermented lager, lightly roasted, with aroma of flowers and grain.

ØLFABRIKKEN PORTER
PORTER 7.5% ABV
Black as the night, with a thick head of foam. Intense body with coffee, chocolate, and liquorice notes.

GOURMETBRYGGERIET BOCK
DOPPELBOCK 7.2% ABV
Deep reddish in color, with a heavy aroma of malt and caramel backing up the strong body.

HVEDE
WHEAT BEER 5.8% ABV
Southern-German inspired, with Bamberg wheat and buck malt. Sweet with fruity nuances, balanced with bitterness.

PALE ALE
PALE ALE 5.9% ABV
Combines English barley and oats, and Amarillo hops. Golden color, fresh and fruity aroma and flavor.

JACOBSEN SAAZ BLONDE
PALE ALE 7.1% ABV
Extract of angelica adds a juniper-like flavor that complements the fruity taste of the yeast.

JACOBSEN EXTRA PILSNER
PILSNER 5.5% ABV
A premium lager using Nordic ingredients such as Danish organic pilsner malt and Swedish sea buckthorn juice.

ALL ABOUT ...
BOTTLE SHAPES

Brewing folklore has it that we have a little-known 16th-century Tudor clergyman to thank for the advent of bottled beer. It is said that Alexander Newell, dean of St Paul's Cathedral in London, liked to fish, taking with him some home-brewed beer in an old medicine bottle. At the end of one trip, he left the bottle behind. On his return to the river bank, some time later, he found the bottle and opened it. There was a satisfying pop and hiss, and he realized that the beer had remained in good condition. Although glass bottles were probably used for storing beer before Newell's time, this piscatorial (and quite possibly apocryphal) anecdote has survived to mark the beginnings of bottled beer.

Due to the high cost of its labor-intensive production, bottled beer remained a luxury for the next couple of centuries. Matters changed for the better in the British Isles in 1845, when the abolition of a Glass Tax helped to boost the availability of glass bottles. To make sure that the beer didn't escape, they were stoppered with corks, then screw tops, and finally the crown corks (more commonly known as just bottle-tops), that are still in use today.

PAPER-WRAPPED Bottles wrapped in paper, such as those of Belgium's Corsendonk Agnus from Bocq Brewery, and Italy's Birrificio Montegioco beers, add a touch of mystique to the beer's presentation.

ELEGANT Recent years have seen some brewers reconfigure the aesthetics of beer bottles by looking to the world of wine and Champagne for inspiration. Italian craft brewers, such as Le Baladin and 32 Via dei Birrai, are at the cutting edge with stylish and graceful bottles that owe more to wine than beer.

COMMON SHAPES Most bottle profiles favor either a slender design with a long, tapering neck or a fatter form with a short neck and rounded, slumped shoulders, like that of Sierra Nevada ale from the US.

OVAL-SHAPED England's St Peter's Brewery uses bottles that hark back to an oval-shaped design of the late 18th century.

ARTISAN Some artisanal brewers are keen on corks, especially for their stronger beers. After all, these are beers that have been hand-crafted and are the beer equivalent of wine—why not make them special? The use of co¬ks has been prevalent in northern France and Belgium for a long time, but new wave brewers such as the Danish Bøgedal Brewery are also embracing the technique.

BØGEDAL
Bryghus

BØGEDAL № 127

Type: Mørk, Northern Brewer, Appelsin
Alkohol: 6,5 %
Brygget: 2/4 2008
Tappet: 15/4 2008

STUBBY Several Belgian brewers use a distinctive stubby bottle. Strong and heavy, it can withstand the high pressure created by secondary fermentation in the bottle, a crucial element of beers like Duvel and Steenberg's Gulden Draak.

Gulden Draak

SWING TOPS On the European mainland, many bottles are sealed with swing tops rather than with crowns. They are famously used for Grolsch in the Netherlands and by German breweries such as Berg. They are also popular with home-brewers.

32

OPPALE

Berg Brauerei
ULRICH ZIMMERMANN

BREWERY

MIDTFYN BRYGHUS

Marsk Billesvej 24,
DK-5672 Broby, Denmark
www.midtfyns-bryghus.dk

This microbrewery is on the island of Fyn off the eastern Danish mainland. Founded in 2005, it was bought by American entrepreneur Eddie Szweda in 2007. It has since found success with its quality, hand-crafted brews.

BREWING SECRET It first gained much appreciative attention for the now-discontinued Braveheart beer.

MIKKELLER

Slien 2, 2.tv,
DK-1766 Copenhagen, Denmark
www.mikkeller.dk

An innovative brewery producing an eclectic range of beer. Mikkeller adopts an American rule-breaking approach to brewing and has achieved significant international recognition with several of its brews.

BREWING SECRET The brewery recently introduced Black, the strongest beer ever made by a Danish brewer.

NØRREBRO BRYGHUS

Ryesgade 3,
DK-2200 Copenhagen N, Denmark
www.noerrebrobryghus.dk

Opened in 2003, this brewpub serves up to 10 hand-crafted beers. Founder-brewmaster Anders Kissmeyer aims to serve the best and most varied beer in Denmark. The beers he brews are also an integral part of the whole dining experience in the restaurant. The Nørrebro bottle won a Danish design award in 2004.

RAASTED BRYGHUS

Hobrovej 358,
DK-8900 Randers, Denmark
www.raastedbryghus.dk

This small, award-winning micro in the little town of Raasted is housed in an old dairy dating from 1888. The youngest brewmaster in Denmark, Martin Jensen founded it in 2005 when he was just 24 years old.

BREWING SECRET Jensen designed the brewing system himself and had it built to his specifications.

BEER

IMPERIAL STOUT

IMPERIAL STOUT 9.5% ABV
Dark, almost black, stout with a nice cream-colored head, good body, and some sweetness.

DOUBLE INDIA PALE ALE

DOUBLE PALE ALE 9.2% ABV
American-inspired dark amber-colored ale with a complex profile of hops. Intense and powerful taste.

BEER GEEK BREAKFAST

OATMEAL STOUT 7.5% ABV
An award-winning stout with a rich nose, smooth and balanced taste, and coffee and chocolate notes.

BLACK

IMPERIAL STOUT 17.5% ABV
Exceptional body of sugars, roasted coffee beans, and black chocolate; a complex and lingering aftertaste.

BOMBAY PALE ALE

INDIA PALE ALE 6.5% ABV
English Marris Otter malt gives a deeply intense malt character. Fruity aromas, high bitterness, and some sweetness.

LITTLE KORKNY ALE

BARLEY WINE 12.25% ABV
Made with Pale Ale and Crystal malt. A strong, sweet beer with hints of plums and caramel.

RAASTED TRIPPEL

ABBEY TRIPLE 8% ABV
Flavored with generous amounts of light cane sugar, with a delicate smell and taste of citrus.

RAASTED CASCADE IPA

INDIA PALE ALE 5.5% ABV
Fruity and full-bodied; a mix of American Cascade, and Centennial hops gives a spicy, citrussy touch.

REFSVINDINGE BREWERY

Nyborgvej 80,
DK-5853 Ørbæk, Denmark
www.bryggerietrefsvindinge.dk

Since 1885, four generations have run this farmhouse brewery. It was among the first to brew ales in Denmark and is credited with developing Danish white beer (*hvidtøl*) and the old-style smoked "ship's beer" (*skibsøl*), as well as two varieties of beer for children (not entirely alcohol free!).

ROYAL UNIBREW

Faxe Allé 1, DK-4640 Faxe, Denmark
www.royalunibrew.com

Formerly The Danish Brewery Group, Royal Unibrew is Denmark's second largest brewery and Scandinavia's largest exporter. The company owns two regional breweries, Faxe and Albani, Danish brands such as Ceres, Thor, and Maribo, and a number of international breweries. The Royal brand is its most popular in Denmark.

THISTED BRYGHUS

Bryggerivej 10,
DK-7700 Thisted, Denmark
www.thisted-bryghus.dk

Thisted Brewery is in the town of the same name on the second largest island in Denmark. Owned by the town's current and former residents, it has made traditional lagers since 1899 and is famous for its all-malt organic brews.

BREWING SECRET Thisted's malt mill was first used at the Carlsberg brewery as early as 1902.

AASS BRYGGERI

Postboks 1530,
N-3007 Drammen, Norway
www.aass.no

Norway's oldest brewery dates back to 1834. Named after Poul Lauritz Aass (pronounced "ouse"), it is a family-owned business run by four generations since 1860.

BREWING SECRET Aass brews according to the strict 1516 Bavarian Law of Purity, drawing its water from the nearby lake of Glitre.

ALE NO. 16
BROWN ALE 5.7% ABV
Well rounded, typical dark ale using original English yeast to produce a sweet, fresh taste.

MORS STOUT
PORTER 5.7% ABV
Dark, smooth porter brewed using malt that has been roasted with cocoa beans.

ROYAL EXPORT
PREMIUM LAGER 5.6% ABV
The best-selling beer in the range has mild, aromatic, and balanced taste. It uses a special yeast to give a smooth, vinous character.

CERES JULEHVIDTØL
WHITE BEER 1.9% ABV
A classic low-alcohol Christmas brew with dark malts and sugar giving a sweet, full-bodied taste.

LIMFJORDSPORTER
BALTIC PORTER 7.9% ABV
Almost black in color; rich and complex. Bottom-fermented and brewed with smoked malt and liquorice for rich flavor and aroma.

PORSE GULD
PALE LAGER 5.8 % ABV
A classic Thisted brew. Fruity and sweet golden lager flavored with locally gathered bog myrtle.

AASS BOCK
DUNKLER BOCK 6.5% ABV
Smooth and creamy; brewed using Munich malt and Hallertau hops. Lagered for at least three months.

AASS JULEØL
DUNKLER BOCK 6.2% ABV
The most sought-after Christmas beer in Scandinavia. Thick and malty with a smooth, rich flavor.

BREWERY

BERENTSENS BRYGGHUS

Jernbaneveien 28,
N-4370 Egersund, Norway
www.berentsens.com

This regional brewery uses fresh and natural raw materials to produce high-quality ales as well as cider, spirits, and soft drinks. Managing director Harald Berentsen is the fourth generation to run the company, which was founded by his great grandfather, Captain Wilhelm Berentsen in 1895.

HAANDBRYGGERIET

Thornegaten 39,
N-3015 Drammen, Norway
www.haandbryggeriet.net

This small brewery is known for its hand-made brews and for keeping Norwegian brewing traditions alive. Housed in a 200-year-old wooden building, it is run by volunteers, and experimentation is encouraged.

BREWING SECRET As well as using old oak wine barrels, they are now ageing beer in former Akevitt spirit casks.

HANSA BORG BRYGGERIER

Kokstaddalen 3, Kokstad,
N-5863 Bergen, Norway
www.hansa.no

Norway's second-largest brewing company also runs as a brewpub (Kalfaret Brygghus) in Bergen. Founded in 1891, Hansa merged with Borg Breweries in 1997. Its original name reflects Bergen's history as a member of the Hanseatic League, a historic Baltic regional trading alliance.

LERVIG AKTIEBRYGGERI

Vierveien 1, Hillevåg,
N-4016 Stavanger, Norway
www.lervig.no

Established by an enthusiastic group of brewers in 2003, the brewery began as a protest against the closure of the region's local brewery, Tou. Today, it is an established independent and industrial craft brewery, which supplies local beer-lovers, as well as bars and restaurants, with quality brews and non-alcoholic beverages.

BEER

BERENTSENS RAV AMBER ALE
AMBER ALE 5.5% ABV
This over-yeasted ale features a generous amount of American Cascade hops, giving a clear bitterness and complex character.

ROGALANDSPILS
LAGER 4.7% ABV
Made with Czech hops and Scottish malt. Rich and deeply flavorful with well-balanced bitterness.

DARK FORCE
WHEAT STOUT 9% ABV
Uses wheat and dark roasted malts and house wheat yeast. High hop aroma and ample bitterness.

NORWEGIAN WOOD
TRADITIONAL ALE 6.5% ABV
Made from naturally smoked Munich, Crystal, and chocolate malts; spiced with locally gathered juniper twigs and berries.

HANSA PILSNER
PILSNER 4.5% ABV
The brewery's most popular beer, this is a crisp, light lager with a citrussy finish.

HANSA BAYER
DARK LAGER 4.5% ABV
Semi-dark Munich-style beer. Dark malts give it a toffeelike finish.

FIINE LERVIG PREMIUM
PILSNER 4.7% ABV
Dark and elegant, with deep and aromatic malt character and a complex freshness of hops.

HERLIGE LERVIG PILSNER
PILSNER 4.7% ABV
The brewery's flagship beer is an easy-to-drink, light, and refreshing pilsner. Pale golden with a lacy head and floral hop aromas.

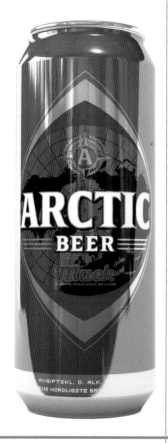

MACK'S BREWERY

Storgata 4, N-9291 Tromsø, Norway
www.mack.no

This brewery and soft drinks company was founded by Ludwig Markus Mack in 1877. It is best known for its highly popular pilsner, originally introduced in 1891. The brewery produces beer to honor special occasions and has a Party and a Seasonal series. Despite claims, it is not the world's northern-most brewery, since a microbrewery was set up in Honnigsvag in 2000.

NØGNE Ø

Gamle Rykene Kraftstasjon,
Lunde N-4885 Grimstad, Norway
www.nogne-o.com

Kjetil Jikiun launched Nøgne Ø ("naked island") in 2003 after learning home-brewing in the US. Now his brewery is Norway's largest supplier of bottle-conditioned ale.

BREWING SECRET Nøgne mixes British Marris Otter malt with American C-hops, including Cascade, Centenneal, Chinook, and Columbus.

RINGNES

Thorvald Meyersgate 2,
N-0555 Oslo, Norway
www.ringnes.no

Norway's largest brewery was founded by brothers Amund and Ellef Ringnes in 1876. Through a long succession of mergers, this historic brewery is now owned by the Carlsberg Group. As well as Carlsberg and Ringnes, its brands include Tuborg Lysholmer, Dahls, and Frydenlund.

CARLSBERG SWEDEN AB

Bryggerivägen 10
SE-161 86 Stockholm, Sweden
www.carlsberg.se

Sweden's largest brewing company, and fifth-largest worldwide, brews beer in Stockholm, Goteborg, and Falkenberg. It was established in 2001 through a merger of the Falcon and Pripps breweries. Its main beer brands in Sweden include Pripps, Falcon, Eriksberg, Carlsberg, and Tuborg.

ARCTIC BEER
PALE LAGER 4.5% ABV
A pale golden beer, with a hint of hops on the nose and a dry finish.

MACK HAAKON
LAGER 4.75% ABV
A commemorative beer launched to celebrate the 1994 Winter Olympics in Lillehammer. Rich-tasting and amber in color.

SAISON
SAISON 6.5% ABV
East Kent Goldings and Crystal hops and Belgian ale yeast produce a light and refreshing brew, available all year but ideal in summer.

IMPERIAL STOUT
IMPERIAL STOUT 9% ABV
A dark, rich ale with a generous sweetness and bitterness coming from the roasted malts.

DAHLS PILS
PILSNER 4.5% ABV
Golden, smooth, aromatic lager with a rich taste, malty, and fruity flavor, and lingering bitterness.

RINGNES PILS
PILSNER 4.5% ABV
Fresh and pure, with a slightly dry character, light sweetness, low fruitiness, and a well-balanced hop bitterness.

CARNEGIE STARK-PORTER
PORTER 5.5% ABV
The oldest active brand, dating from 1836. Fruity flavor with elements of caramelized sugar, coffee, and chocolate.

FALCON EXPORT
LAGER 5.2% ABV
Brewed since 1896; it has a rich and malty taste with a well-balanced bitterness.

BREWERY

ÅBRO BRYGGERI

SE-598 86 Vimmerby, Sweden
www.abro.se

Sweden's oldest family-run brewery is located in the southern Småland region. Lieutenant Per W. Luthander founded Åbro in 1856. Axel Herman Johansson purchased the brewery in 1898, and it is still owned and operated by his descendents today.

BREWING SECRET The brewery is located beside the source of fresh spring water that it uses in its brewing.

DUGGES ALE & PORTERBRYGGERI

Möbelgatan 3, SE-43133 Mölndal, Sweden
www.dugges.se

The brewery was founded in 2005 by Mikael Dugge Engström. His series of beers include Gothenburg, marrying old Swedish traditions with British and American inspiration, and Express Yourself, a collection of specialty brews with names like Holy Cow (an IPA) and Fuggedaboudit! (a brown ale).

GOTLANDS BRYGGERI

St Hansgatan 47,
SE-621 56 Wisby, Sweden
www.gotlandsbryggeri.se

Gotland is the largest island in the Baltic sea. This experimental microbrewery, owned by Spendrups, is in the old Hanseatic town of Visby, housed in a brewery and church dating from the 1700s. It is known for its specialty and seasonal beers.

BREWING SECRET The range includes an authentic Maclay's Scotch Ale.

JÄMTLANDS BRYGGERI

Box 224, SE-831 23 Östersund, Sweden
www.jamtlandsbryggeri.se

This innovative small microbrewery was established in 1996 in the capital of the Jämtland region of central Sweden. It brews a wide variety of beer, including a strong English ale, Baltic Porter, and Vienna lager. It consistently wins awards at the Stockholm Beer Festival.

BREWING SECRETS It draws from British, German, and Alsace beer styles.

BEER

SMÅLAND
PILSNER 5.2% ABV
Brewed with Czech yeast. Full-bodied, moderately bitter taste, with elements of hops and apricot.

ÅBRO ORIGINAL
PREMIUM LAGER 5.2% ABV
A full-bodied, light lager; rounded bitterness and sweetness, and an aromatic hoppy character.

DUGGES AVENYN ALE
AMERICAN PALE ALE 5% ABV
Aromas of hops, flowers, and citrus fruits; flavors of grapes, pine, and a hint of caramel.

HIGH FIVE!
INDIAN PALE ALE 7.5% ABV
Dark amber. Intense hop aroma; notes of strawberry jam, pine, and chocolate, and a dry bitterness.

WISBY KLOSTERÖL
ALE 5% ABV
Scottish yeast plus Pilsner, Munich, and wheat malts give an orangey fruitiness and a honeyed flavor.

WISBY WEISSE
WEISSBIER 5.2% ABV
A Bavarian-style wheat beer containing 60 percent wheat and caramel malt. Unfiltered and unpasteurized.

PRESIDENT
PORTER 4.8% ABV
This bottom-fermented beer has a medium bitterness and the soft aroma of Czech Saaz hops.

OATMEAL PORTER
PORTER 4.7% ABV
An unfiltered and top-fermented porter with a ruby-black color. Espresso in a glass!

NYNÄSHAMNS ÄNGBRYGGERI

Box 186, Lövlundsvägen 4,
SE-149 22 Nynäshamn, Sweden
www.nyab.se

Nynäshamns Ängbryggeri, meaning
"steam brewery," produces mainly
ales, stouts, and porters using
British and American methods.
Founded in 1997 by four enthusiasts,
all of its beers are named after places
in the archipelago and the harbor
town of Nynäshamn.

NILS OSCAR

Fruängsgatan 2, SE-611 31 Nyköping,
Sweden
www.nilsoscar.se

This microbrewery and distillery was
established in 1996 and makes well-
balanced beers that go well with food.
It has won many awards, including
four medals in the World Beer Cup.

BREWING SECRET Nils Oscar has its own
maltings, and a farm where barley and
other cereals for malting are grown.

SPENDRUPS BRYGGERI

SE-143 03 Vårby, Sweden
www.spendrups.se

The largest Swedish-owned brewing
company was founded in 1897.
It owns three breweries in
Grängesberg, Vårby, and Gotlands.
Its CEO and brewmaster, Johan
Spendrup, is the fourth generation
of his family to run the brewery.

BREWING SECRET This is the only brewer
in Sweden to produce beer according
to the 1516 Bavarian Purity Law.

FINLANDIA

Suokulmantie 237, Matku,
Forsaa FI-31110, Finland
www.finlandiasahti.fi

Finlandia is a specialist brewer of *sahti*,
a traditional Finnish home-brew made
with rye and other grains, flavored
with juniper twigs and berries. Beer
enthusiasts can sample Finlandia Sahti
in Helsinki at St. Urho's Pub and the
Restaurant Savotta. The best time to
do so is during Helsinki's Sahti Week,
which takes place in May each year.

BEDARÖ BITTER
PREMIUM BITTER 4.5% ABV
A well-balanced, hoppy ale with
a fruity taste and a bitter, dry finish.

FATLAGRAD SMÖRPUNDET
PORTER 5% ABV
A full-bodied porter with chocolate
notes and a mild bitterness.

IMPERIAL STOUT
IMPERIAL STOUT 7% ABV
Well balanced and rich from ageing.
Chocolate aromas with caramel
giving way to a bittersweet finish.

INDIA ALE
INDIA PALE ALE 5.3% ABV
Heavily hopped with Amarillo,
giving an aroma of tropical fruits;
the fruitiness is balanced by the
crystal malt sweetness.

SPENDRUPS OLD GOLD
PILSNER 5% ABV
German-style pilsner made with
Czech Saazer hops. Citrus notes, a
dry, bitter finish and long aftertaste.

MARIESTADS EXPORT
PALE LAGER 5.3% ABV
A Dortmunder-style beer with
German hops. Aromas of toasted
malt and spicy hop flavors.

SAHTI STRONG
SAHTI 10% ABV
Sweet and somewhat oily on the
palate; the juniper nose gives way
to a bubblegum aftertaste.

TAVALLINEN
SAHTI 8% ABV
A deep chestnut color, with a heavy
juniper nose and a hint of
blackcurrant.

BREWERY

HARTWALL

Atomitie 2a, FI-00371 Helsinki, Finland
www.hartwall.fi/en

Hartwall, part of the Heineken Group, has breweries in Lahti and Tornio. Brands include Hartwall Jaffa, Hartwall Novelle, Upcider, Lapin Kulta, and Karjala beers. Victor Harwall founded it in 1836 as the first mineral water supplier in Scandinavia. Brewing began in 1966 with Karjala beer—its Karelian name and logo defied the Soviet Union, then occupying much of the region.

HUVILA

Puistokatu 4, FI-57100, Savonlinna, Finland
www.panimoravintolahuvila.fi

This craft brewery, making British-style ales, *sideri* (cider), and *sahti*, is located in Savonlinna, a popular tourist area in the Lake Saimaa area. The complex offers good food at the brewery-restaurant Huvila, bed and breakfast, live music, brewery tours, and a brewing school.

BREWING SECRET All of Huvila's products are unfiltered.

LAITILAN

Sirppukuja 4, FI-23800 Laitila, Finland
www.laitilan.com/english

This is one of the fastest-growing breweries in Finland. Founded in 1995, it brews a range of full malt beers under the Kukko (rooster) name, Oiva Scandinavian cider, and old-fashioned lemonades.

BREWING SECRET The brewery uses wind power for all its energy needs, and was the first in the world to develop a gluten-free full malt beer.

NOKIAN PANIMO

Nuijamiestentie 17, 37120 Nokia, Finland
www.nokianpanimo.fi

Nokian Panimo was founded in 1991 and specializes in unfiltered lagers sold under the Året Runt, Kommodori, and Jouluolut brands. It also brews filtered lagers including Keisari Pils and Keisari Strong. It produces approximately 4,400,000 pints (2.5 million liters) of beverages per year, including beer, mineral water, and juice-based soft drinks.

BEER

LAPIN KULTA PREMIUM
LAGER 4.5% ABV
Crisp and smooth; now brewed to a new recipe using only natural ingredients, and with more malts and hops in the mix.

KARJALA IVB
STRONG LAGER 8% ABV
Golden, strong lager with a generous head; smooth malts and hops give a robust character.

HUVILA PORTER
PORTER 5.5% ABV
English roasted malts give a strong coffeelike, roasted aroma with a hint of chocolate.

HUVILA ESB
STRONG BITTER 5.2% ABV
Robustly hopped with a fruity and floral aroma, complex flavors, and a long and bitter aftertaste.

KUKKO PILS
PILSNER 4.5% ABV
A German-style pilsner with the strong bite of aromatic hops. Won best beer in Finland three times.

KUKKO PORTER
PORTER 6.5% ABV
A Baltic porter that has a powerful, full malt roasted body and the perfect base.

ÅRET RUNT IV
STRONG LAGER 5.7% ABV
Deep brown, unfiltered lager. Fruity, slightly sweet, and mildly roasted, with a strong hops flavor.

KEISARI STRONG IV
STRONG LAGER 5.7% ABV
A Munich-style dark lager. Amber-colored, high in aroma with a delicate sweetness; moderate hops.

OLVI

Olvitie I-IV, FI-74100 Iisalmi, Finland
www.olvi.fi

Finland's third largest brewer, Olvi is also the only Finnish-owned brewery with national operations. A publicly traded company, founded in 1878, Olvi has subsidiaries in Estonia (A. Le Coq), Lithuania (Ragutis), and Latvia (Cesu Alus). It is a regular sponsor of Oluset, Finland's largest and oldest annual summer beer festival.

PLEVNA BREWERY

Itäinenkatu 8, FI-33210 Tampere, Finlayson Finland
www.plevna.fi

This brewpub and restaurant was established in 1994 and is situated in the historic Finlayson cotton mills of Tampere, Finland's third largest city. The brewery produces a variety of beer, including dark and pale lager, stout, and wheat beer. Following tradition, all beers conform to the *Reinheitsgebot* purity laws.

SINEBRYCHOFF

Oy Sinebrychoff Ab, Sinebrychoffinaukio I PL 87, FL-04201 Kerava, Finland
www.koff.fi

Sinebrychoff is part of the Carlsberg Group, and its abbreviated name and main brand range, Koff, is one of the most popular in Finland. It is the oldest Nordic brewery, founded by Russian Nikolai Sinebrychoff in 1819.

BREWING SECRET Karhupanimo, their new microbrewery, is producing a range of hand-crafted lagers.

TEERENPELI

Hämeenkatu 19, Lahti, Finland
www.teerenpeli.com

Teerenpeli operates breweries, bars, and restaurants in Helsinki, Lahti, and Tampere. Its first brewery was founded in 1995. A new brewery and whiskey distillery opened in 2002, set within the Restaurant Taivaanranta in Lahti. Teerenpeli's beers have won medals at the Helsinki Beer Festival.

OLVI TUPLAPUKKI
PALE DOPPELBOCK 8.5% ABV
Finland's best-selling strong beer, rich in malt and hops. A spicier version is produced for Christmas.

OLVI III
LAGER 4.5% ABV
Olvi's most popular beer, a Pilsner-type full-bodied lager with sweet and malty flavor.

RAUCHBIER JAMES
SMOKED BEER 5.2% ABV
Dark copper in color; a slightly roasted, tarry flavor, and full-bodied with a bite of bitter in the aftertaste.

IMPERIAL STOUT SIPERIA
IMPERIAL STOUT 8% ABV
A strong, rich stout with a typical tar-like flavor combined with a roasted fruitiness.

SINEBRYCHOFF PORTER
IMPERIAL STOUT 7.2% ABV
Robust and brimming with coffee flavors, this beer has a long, warming finish.

KARHU III
LAGER 4.6% ABV
Described by the brewer as "untamed." Full-bodied, with stronger flavors of hops and malt than are usual for a lager.

LAISKAJAAKKO
DARK LAGER 4.5% ABV
Full-bodied, malty dark lager, brewed with Crystal 50 and Black malt, and Hallertau hops.

ONNENPEKKA
PALE LAGER 4.7% ABV
Golden and refreshing. Made with Pilsner barley malt from the Lahti region, and pure water from the Salpausselkä area.

BEER STYLES

WHEAT BEER

Little more than a generation ago, Bavarian *weissbier*, or *weizen*, was in sharp decline. Once the privilege of kings and princes, this historic brew had come to be regarded as an old person's drink in comparison to the youthful gloss of lager. In the early 1980s, all this changed. Hip drinkers rediscovered it, and word spread from Bavaria to intrigue and inspire beer-lovers and brewers all over the world. At about the same time, Belgium's spicy *witbiers* (white beers) also appeared on the beer-drinkers' radar, beginning with Hoegaarden, the creation of former milkman Pierre Celis.

The international appeal of these beers has been picked up on by brewers from the US, Britain, and many other nations. Some are now producing wheat beers in the Bavarian *weissbier* tradition; others favor spicy and zesty brews in the style of Belgian *witbiers*.

MALT Wheat beers are a mixture of pale and wheat malt, with the latter making up a sizeable percentage of the grist. This gives the beer a tart and refreshing flavor. Subtle hopping adds a lemony, spritzy fruitiness.

YEAST Bavarian *weissbiers* from breweries such as Schneider and Maisels feature banana, clove, and vanilla notes from the yeast, and may be cloudy (*hefeweizen*) with suspended yeast, or clear (*kristall*). Darker wheat beers are called *dunkel*, and stronger ones *weizenbock*.

SPICES Belgium *witbiers* tend to be spicy, almost peppery, due to the use of spices such as coriander seeds and rare African grains of paradise, as well as bitter Curaçao orange peel. Some examples, such as St Bernardus Wit, have a luscious silkiness.

BREWERY

AMBER

Bielkówko, ul. Gregorkiewicza 1,
83-050 Kolbud, Poland
www.browar-amber.pl

Owned by the Przybylo family, this medium-sized brewery is one of the most modern in Poland. Situated close to Gdansk in Pomerania, an area with a rich brewing tradition, the brewery is a supporter of the Slow Food movement, and organizes the Kozlaki Bielkowskie food and drink festival every September.

BROWARMIA

Ul. Królewska 1,
Warszawa, 00-065, Poland
www.browarmia.pl

Opened in 2005, this fine brewpub has a vibrant atmosphere—busy, convivial, and loud on music nights. Polish food with a modern twist is a specialty to match the beers on tap. Six beers are currently brewed in the smart cellar brewery, with six more planned for the future.

KOSZALIN

Koszalin ul. Spoldzielcza 8, Koszalin, Poland
www.royalunibrew.com

This brewery has been keeping the beer-drinkers of northwest Poland happy since it was established in 1874. In 2002 it was one of the first in the country to be privatized, and in 2005 was bought by the Danish company Royal Unibrew. Koszalin is one of the region's biggest employers, and its brews are available nationally.

OKOCIM

Ul Browarna 14, 32-8-Bresko, Poland
www.okocim.com.pl

Built in 1845, the Okocim brewery is one of the finest buildings in Bresko. Much of the original site is well preserved, and it is one of the few remaining breweries left from this period. Now owned by Carlsberg, there has been considerable investment in recent years.

BREWING SECRET Closed conical fermenters are a modern addition.

BEER

ZYWE
PILSNER 6.2% ABV
Pale in color, it has lemon flavors and uses hops and barley from the Lubin region.

KOZLAK
DUNKEL BOCK 6.5% ABV
A ruby-red beer, it is rich in malt and yeasty flavors, with a warming aftertaste.

PSZENCICZNE
PALE ALE 4.8% ABV
Not quite a Burton ale, it is strongly hopped in the kettle before being dry-hopped in the lagering tank.

RASPBERRY WHEAT BEER
WHEAT BEER 5% ABV
The house wheat beer is in the Bavarian style, with the addition of fresh raspberries. The fruit adds a refreshing, zesty tartness.

BROK SAMBAR
PILSNER 6.2% ABV
Golden in color, with a thin white head. Sweetcorn and candy flavors predominate, with little hop aroma.

BROK STRONG
LAGER 7.2% ABV
A complex, sweet beer with crisp orange overtones. Its recipe dates back more than 120 years.

ZAGLOBA
LAGER 4.8% ABV
Pale in color and light in body, it has a yeasty, biscuity zest with a hint of spicy hops.

OKOCIM PORTER
PORTER 9% ABV
A porter in the Baltic tradition, with a soothing, almost medicinal taste and hints of cinnamon.

BREWERY

KOMPANIA PIWOWARSKA SA

ul. Szwajcarska 11, 61-285 Poznan, Poland
www.kp.pl/eng

This company has won many brewing awards and has a reputation for quality. Owned by SABMiller, it is expanding quickly. It has recently bought the Browar Belgia Brewery in Kielce and is aggressively marketing its brands in home and world markets. All its beers are bottom-fermented brews.

RELAKSPOL

ul. Borkowska 30.32,
30-438 Kraków, Poland
www.relakspol.com.pl

It is unusual in Poland for a small brewery to sell beer both in bottles and on draft, but Relakspol, which opened in 1992, does just that. Krakow is the former capital of Poland and still its cultural heart. There is a small but growing beer culture in the city, and an increasing number of bars sell locally brewed beers.

WARKA

Gosniewska 655-660 Warka, Poland
www.warka.com.pl

The town of Warka is celebrated as the birthplace of Kazimierz Pulaski (1745–1779), a Polish nobleman who became a hero of the American Revolution. Brewing has taken place here since the Middle Ages, and, in 1478, Warka brewers were granted the exclusive rights to supply beer to the Warsaw royal court. Today, the Warka brewery is owned by Heineken.

ZYWIEC

ul. Browarna 88, 34-300 Zywiec, Poland
www.zywiec.com.pl

Established in 1852 by the Hapsburg family, this brewery fell into state ownership after World War II, and was acquired by Heineken in the mid-1990s. It is home to a lively brewing museum that takes visitors right through the brewing process.

BREWING SECRET The Zywiec Porter uses a recipe from 1881.

BEER

DEBOWE MOCNE
DARK LAGER 7% ABV
A strong, German-style *dopplebock*, its rich taste is the result of being matured in oak barrels.

TYSKIE GRONIE
LAGER 5.6% ABV
Crisp, clean-tasting beer with a clear yellow hue. Poland's favorite beer, it is sold worldwide.

PILS
PILSNER 5.7% ABV
An easy-drinking golden beer that is, nevertheless, worth seeking out. It has a soft and pleasant aroma, and a lingering dryness on the palate.

WARKA ORIGINAL
LAGER 5.7% ABV
A deep, rich golden color, topped with a bold white head. An easy-drinking, if strong, beer.

WARKA STRONG
LAGER 7% ABV
Copper-colored, it is light in malt and with a hint of hops. A complex, dry bitterness, but a sweet finish.

ZYWIEC
LAGER 5.6% ABV
Crisp, gold, and easy-drinking, with flowery, hoppy aromas, it is now exported worldwide.

PORTER
BALTIC PORTER 9.5% ABV
A dark, strong beer, brewed with Munich and other special malts for sweetness and color. Aromatic hops provide a rich aroma.

SLOVENSKO

Novozámocka 2,
947 12 Hurbanovo, Slovakia
www.heineken.sk

Once Heineken had three breweries in Slovakia, but only the Hurbanovo plant is now left. Heineken leads the Slovak beer market with a share of 45 percent (nearest rival SABMiller has 38 percent). Heineken has close relations with the region's farmers as it operates the largest malt-producing plant in the area.

TOPVAR

Krusovska cesta 2092,
Topolcany, Slovakia
www.topvar.sk

The brewery operates at two sites in Slovakia: Topolcany and Velký Šariš. In 2000, the brewery launched a beer called Brigita, named after the Slovak finance minister Brigita Schmögnerovà. A popular beer, it remained on sale for some time after her resignation in 2002. The company is now owned by SABMiller.

BORSODI SÖRGYÁR

Rákóczi út 81, Bocs, Hungary
www.inbev.com

One of the largest breweries in Hungary, Borsodi Sörgyár was privatized in 1991 after the fall of Communism and bought by drinks giant InBev in 1993. Typically, one of the characteristics of state ownership is a lack of investment in quality control, and that's something that has been rectified in recent years.

BLONDER SÖRGYAR

Futca 9 Vonyarcvashegy, Hungary
www.blonder.hu

One of a handful of microbreweries to have emerged in recent years in Hungary, Blonder Sörgyar is situated close to Lake Balaton, the largest lake in central Europe. As well as beer brewed on the premises, this roadside inn offers accommodation and has a restaurant. The food is very Hungarian—wholesome, and a fine accompaniment to the beer.

ZLATY BAZANT /
GOLDEN PHEASANT
Lager 4.2% ABV
Clear and golden, with a hint of straw, this is an easy-drinking beer without any complexities. Beers of this type were like "liquid bread" to factory workers. It is also available in a non-alcoholic version.

TOPVAR SVETLÉ
Lager 5.2% ABV
A sunburst of yellow tones, with a thin white head. This beer has an attractive nose, with plenty of citrus fruit flavors.

BORSODI SÖR
Lager 4.6% ABV
A golden-colored light beer, with a wispy head, it is sweet and easy to drink. A working man's beer.

BORSODI BIVALY
Lager 6.5% ABV
A bold, golden yellow, this is a strong, grainy beer with an overt sweetness on the palate.

VILÁGOS
Lager 5.6% ABV
Yellow in color, this is a strong, grainy beer with an overt sweetness. Somewhat rough at the edges, but it works very well with Hungarian cuisine.

BREWERY

DREHER

Magladi ut 17, Budapest, Hungary
www.dreher.hu

For many years this brewery was run by Anton Dreher, one of the great beer innovators. In the mid-19th century, he developed the technology to ferment beer at low temperatures and created a new kind of malty amber beer, called Vienna lager. For his achievements, Dreher was dubbed "The King of Beer." The company is now owned by SABMiller.

HEINEKEN HUNGÁRIA

Sörgyárak Nyrt 9400 Sopron,
Vándor Sándor st, Hungary
www.heinekenhungaria.hu

Sopron might be at the heart of Hungary's wine region, but it has also had a brewery for over 100 years. Founded by Gyula Lenck in 1895, Heineken Hungária (as it is now known) is one of the largest brewers in the country. It also has a production plant at Martfű.

ILZER SÖRGYÁR

Ilzer Sörgyár Rt., 2200, Monor, Hungary
www.ilzer.hu

Located 22 miles (35 km) south of Budapest, this brewery was founded in the early 1990s. Its range of brews now includes Alt Bayersicher Dunkel, a dark wheat beer; Diet, a beer that is low in sugar; and a kosher beer called Shalom.

BREWING SECRET Ilzer developed and brewed the first Hungarian wheat beer.

PÉCSI SÖRFŐZDE

Alkotmány utca 94, Pécs, H-7624,
Hungary
www.pecsisor.hu

This brewery was founded in 1848 by Hirschfeld Lipó. It is now Hungary's fourth-largest brewery and the largest not owned by a multinational (although most of the equity is owned by the Austrian company Ottakringer). Pécs is known for its warm climate and Mediterranean atmosphere. It will be European City of Culture in 2010.

BEER

DREHER CLASSIC
PILSNER 5.5% ABV
With a crisp, fresh aroma, this is a bitter, golden-yellow beer with an aroma of hops and a hint of malt.

DREHER BAK
DUNKLER BOCK 7.3% ABV
A rich, full-bodied dark beer, notes of caramel and malt, reminiscent of bittersweet chocolate.

SOPRONI ÁSZOK
LAGER 4.5% ABV
Light to taste, this beer is crisp on the palate. Not a complex beer, but very refreshing.

STEFFL
PILSNER 5.3% ABV
A clear, clean, sparkling golden pilsner. A nice level of hops and a sweet aroma.

ILZER HEFEWEISSBIER
WHEAT BEER 5% ABV
Cloudy yellow, with a wispy white head. Hints of banana and spice give way to a citrussy finish.

ILZER ROGGEN ROZS SÖR
RYE BEER 4.8% ABV
Hazy to the eye, this is a complex rye beer of some originality. The rye imparts rich spice notes.

SZALON SÖR
PILSNER 4.6% ABV
Brewed for over 100 years, this is the company's flagship beer. Golden-yellow with a thick, long-lasting head and barley aromas.

SZALON BÚZASÖR
WHEAT BEER 5.2% ABV
Unfiltered, hence its hazy appearance; fruit notes mingle with a yeasty scent.

BERE ROMANIA

Str. Manastur Nr. 2-6, Cluj Napoca,
Romania
www.sabmiller.com

Now a subsidiary of SABMiller, this
brewery first opened in 1878. Its main
brand, Ursus, is advertised under the
slogan "The King of Romanian Beers."
Each September the town of Cluj
Napoca, in the heart of Transylvania,
hosts a beer festival.

BREWING SECRET These beers are
fermented using Bavarian yeast.

HEINEKEN ROMANIA

Miercurea Ciuc, Romania 4100
www.heinekenromania.ro

The former Brau-Union Romania, the
country's biggest brewer was taken
over by Heineken in 2003. It now
controls about 26 percent of the
domestic market. Many Romanians buy
beer in plastic bottles and Heineken is
investing in the technology to package
beer in this way—a worthwhile move
given that the per capita consumption
is 157 pints (89 liters) per annum.

APATINSKA PIVARA

Trg Oslobodenja 5, Apatin,
Serbia 25260
www.inbev.com

The biggest brewer in Serbia
and the largest in the Balkans,
this InBev-owned company now
has 46 percent of the local market.
The town of Apatini, which is on
the Danube, is in a fertile barley-
growing area called Vojvodina.
Records show that brewing has
taken place in the town since 1756.

BIP-BEOGRADSKA

Bulevar Vojvode Putnika 5, PO Box 21
SCG-11000 Beograd, Serbia
www.bip.co.yu

Following privatization in 2007, a
consortium comprising Swedish
brewer United Nordic Beverages, and
Lithuania's Alita, plans to invest in the
development of the brewery to boost
its capacity. Currently, BIP has four
breweries—two in Belgrade, one in
the town of Cacak in central Serbia,
and another in Leskovac, in the south.

URSUS PREMIUM PILS

PILSNER 5.2% ABV
Lively carbonation, a malty aroma,
hints of fresh hops and bread, and
lemony notes in the finish.

TIMISOREANA

LAGER 5% ABV
A light yellow, easy-drinking beer
that doesn't challenge the senses.
Made to a recipe from 1718.

BUCEGI

LAGER 4.6% ABV
Blonde lager beer, with a soft hint
of citrus, unassuming on the palate.

CIUC PREMIUM

LAGER 4.8 % ABV
Golden lager with a decent head.
Dry, without much hop character,
but with a sweet aftertaste.

JELEN PIVO

LAGER 5% ABV
Light yellow in color, with a white,
wispy head. It has hints of grass and
grain and aromas of hops and malt.
Jelen means "deer."

APATINSKO PIVO

LAGER 5% ABV
A fresh-tasting beer with floral
notes and a citrus aroma.

BG

LAGER 5% ABV
The sparkling golden beer has a
pleasant bitterness and a soft aroma
with a hint of sweetcorn and bread.
One to enjoy at the Belgrade Beer
Festival, which takes place in August.

Ožujsko Pivo, the medium-strength lager produced by Zagrebacka, is one of Croatia's most popular beers.

PRODUCT OF CROATIA

Ožujsko

Pivo

Specijal - Svijetlo

ZAGREBAČKA PIVOVARA - ZAGREB

PIVNICA
TOMISLAV

KARLOVAČKA

Dubovac 22, Karlovač, Croatia 47000
www.karlovacko.hr

Karlovačka is Croatia's second-largest brewery, with about 22 percent of the domestic beer market. Founded in 1854, it is in the very heart of Croatia, on the delta of four rivers—the Korana, Kupa, Mrenica, and Dobra. Heineken bought the brewery in 2003. The town of Karlovač organizes a beer festival at the end of August in its city square.

ZAGREBACKA

Ilica 224, Zagreb, Croatia
www.inbev.com

Zagrebacka Pivovara, Croatia's largest brewer, was established in 1893 and is now owned by InBev. After years of falling beer consumption, the market is now growing again, with domestic lager brands being the most popular segment of the market.

BREWING SECRET Double-malted dark chocolate barley gives the dark lager its prized aromas, flavors, and color.

UNION

Pivovarniška ulica 2, 1000 Ljubljana, Slovenia
www.pivo-union.si

This brewery was founded in 1864 by the Kozler family, but state-of-the-art technology makes it is one of the most modern in Slovenia. A fascinating museum takes visitors through the brewing process. However, you have to be there on the first Tuesday morning of the month to enjoy it.

RIDNA MARKA

71 Mikgorod str.Radomyshl, Ukraine
www.etalon-beer.com.ua/en

Beermaking in Radomyshl dates from 1886, when this brewery was founded by the Czech Albrechtam brothers. They found that the soft water here was ideal for brewing. The modern brewery has adapted Bavarian technology to Ukrainian ingredients.

BREWING SECRET The brewhouse has been specifically designed to produce unfiltered, genuine wheat beers.

BREWERY

KARLOVAČKO
LAGER 5.4% ABV
Golden-yellow beer, with yeasty and toasted malt aromas and a refreshing bitterness; the favorite beer of visitors to Croatia.

OŽUJSKO PIVO
LAGER 5.2% ABV
A golden lager, with a deep, white head. A sweetcorn and malt nose gives way to a fruity finish.

TOMISLAV PIVO
DARK LAGER 7% ABV
Croatia's strongest beer, this deep ruby-red lager has aromas of roasted malt and coffee, and a dry finish.

UNION LAGER
LAGER 5% ABV
A Slovenian favorite. A sweet, golden beer, it has corn overtones.

ČRNI BARON / BLACK BARON
STOUT 5.2% ABV
A dark dessert beer, rich with caramel notes and aromas; its finish is warming but could be longer.

ETALON WEISSBIER
WHEAT BEER 5% ABV
Spicy with a rich, creamy malt note and a long, quenching flavor and finish. Hints of bananas and vanilla.

BEER

BREWERY

OBOLON

3 Bogatyrska Str. Kiev, Ukraine
www.obolon.com

Obolon was built in 1980 by the Soviets, who wanted a world-class brewery. Czech brewers acted as consultants. In 1992, the company was first in Ukraine to be privatized. Ukraine is the largest beer market in the CIS, the former Soviet Union. Obolon has a 26 percent share of the market, and is also the country's biggest beer exporter.

BALTIKA

6 Proezd, Parnas 4, St. Petersburg, Russia
www.eng.baltika.ru

The Russian beer market has been going through a period of rapid change as it continues to adjust to a capitalist economy. Baltika's rise has been swift, and it is now the country's largest beer producer. It brews the top two brands—Baltika and Arsenalnoye. The company accounts for more than seven out of ten beer sales, and exports to 46 countries.

BOCHKAREV

Telmana Street, 24,
St. Petersburg, Russia

Bochkarev started as a soft-drinks manufacturer in 1988 and began brewing in 1999. Owned by Heineken since 2002, it is now the sixth-largest single-site brewery in Europe. St. Petersburg is Russia's beer capital and has a fast-evolving beer culture. Bochkarev has 17 percent of the St. Petersburg market, and a seven percent market share in Moscow.

OCHAKOVO

44, Riabinivaya, Moscow, Russia
www.ochakovo.ru

Ochakovo is the last independent Russian brewery, and is trying to remain so. Its original brewhouse has been transformed into a museum, which takes visitors, step-by-step, through the brewing process and features many exhibits from the 19th century.

BREWING SECRET In 2005, Ochakovo launched an unpasteurized, unfiltered "live" beer, aimed at the health market.

BEER

OBOLON PREMIUM

LAGER 5.2% ABV
Light gold in color, with a sweet malt taste. The use of rice in the grist gives the beer a softness.

WEIZEN

WHEAT BEER 5% ABV
Unfiltered, top-fermented wheat beer, with a pleasant fruity and spicy flavor.

BALTIKA NO. 3 CLASSIC

LAGER 4.8% ABV
A malty nose gives way to a bitter finish. Widely available across Russia.

BALTIKA NO 6 PORTER

PORTER 7% ABV
A well-balanced beer. Dark roasted malts, chocolate and molasses flavors fill the glass, overlayed by a good hop finish.

BOCHKOVOE

LAGER 4.3% ABV
Its name means "barreled." Thin, clear, yellow, light in body, the nose is light and malty with corn flavors.

KREPKOE OSOBOE

LAGER 8% ABV
Full of malt flavors, this strong beer has a warming finish, but could do with more balance.

OCHAKOVO CLASSIC

LAGER 5% ABV
Corn-yellow in color, with intense malt overtones and a hoppy finish.

OCHAKOVO RUBY

VIENNA LAGER 3.9% ABV
Pale ruby in color, with aromas of winter fruits and floral notes, it has strong hints of caramel on the palate.

SUN INBEV

Vorontsovsky Park, 6 Moscow, Russia
www.suninterbrew.ru

Founded in 1999, the company is an amalgamation of two important players in the Russian and Ukrainian beer markets—Interbrew and SUN Brewing. SUN InBev now owns ten breweries in Russia, and is the second largest brewing company in the country. Brazilian beer is proving popular in Russia now that Brahma, also owned by InBev, is being brewed in Klin.

ŠVYTURYS-UTENOS

Kuliu Vartu g. 7, Klaipeda, Lithuania
www.svyturys.lt/en

Brewing began here in 1784, making this the oldest brewery in Lithuania. The company has a reputation for the quality of its beers and has won several international brewing awards. It is open to the public for tours twice a week for groups of five to 25 (via the tourist office at www.klaipedainfo.lt).

BREWING SECRET All the employees give their feedback on each new brew.

GUBERNIJA

Dvaro str. 179, LT-76176 Siauliai,
Lithuania
www.gubernija.lt/en

Lithuania has a long and proud brewing tradition, and records show that beer was being made in Siauliai in the 14th century. The first record of the Gubernija Brewery on its current site dates from 1786. Over the years the brewery has been rebuilt many times, most recently in 2000 when the modern plant was installed.

KALNAPILIS

Taikos Avenue 1,
LT-5319 Panevezys, Lithuania
www.kalnapilis.lt/en

Over 100 years old, the brewery was founded by German Albert Foight, who named it Bergschlösschen ("little castle on the hill"); later the name was changed to the Lithuanian Kalnapilis. Now owned by Danish Royal Unibrew, the company prides itself on its innovation—it was the first brewer in Lithuania to use twist caps on bottles and the first to market beer in cans.

TOLSTIAK DOBROYE
LAGER 5% ABV
A pale beer with a rich, sweet taste and a pleasant, hoppy bitterness.

KLINSKOYE SVETLOE
LAGER 4.5% ABV
Straw-colored, the mild flavor is achieved by the use of corn or rice in brewing. It has a soft hop aroma.

ŠVYTURYS EKSTRA
DORTMUND LAGER 5.2% ABV
Clear and golden, it has a firm white head, an intense aroma of hops, and a slight bitterness.

ŠVYTURIO
LAGER 5% ABV
Translucent gold in color, it has a good balance of rich malt and bitter hops. In Lithuania it's known simply as "red," due to its label color.

GUBERNIJOS EKSTRA
LAGER 5.5% ABV
Medium-gold in color. Strong, rich, and warming with caramel and sweetcorn overtones. A dry finish with citrus and hop flavors lingering on the palate.

ORIGINAL
LAGER 5% ABV
A pale golden-yellow with a good foamy head, it has a sweetcorn aroma with a hint of Saaz hops.

RED
LAGER 4.8% ABV
Russet hues and malty, sweet overtones, but the aftertaste quickly fades away.

BREWERY

ALDARIS
Tvaika iela 44, Rīga, Latvia
www.aldaris.lv/eng

This brewery, which was founded in 1865, became part of Baltic Beverages Holding (a joint venture between Carlsberg and Scottish & Newcastle) in 1992. It is the leading and most advanced brewery in Latvia, producing more than 12 different light and dark lagers, based on traditional recipes.

CĒSU ALUS
Aldaru laukums 1, Cēsis, Latvia - 4101
www.cesualus.lv

Cēsu Alus was founded in 1879 and is the oldest brewery in Latvia. In 1999 it was purchased by the Estonian brewer A. Le Coq. It is now one of the largest brewers in Latvia. It has a new, state-of-the-art brewhouse and further huge investment is being planned. The town is renowned for its beer festival, knights' tournaments, and open-air theater performances.

A. LE COQ
Tähtvere 56/62, 50050 Tartu, Estonia
www.alecoq.ee/en

This brewery was founded in 1826, and purchased in 1913 by A. Le Coq, a London-based company. At the time, it was looking for a brewery in the Russian Empire where it could produce its Imperial Stout rather than export it from England. Production was halted in the 1960s but revived in 1999. A small museum is housed in the former maltings.

SAKU
75 501 Saku, Estonia
www.saku.ee/english.php

First documented in October 1820, the brewery was built by Count Karl Friedrich Rehbinder, on his Saku estate. It is now the largest in Estonia and makes Originaal, the country's favorite beer.

BREWING SECRET Saku is working on a range of brightly colored, flavored beers called DLight; some will use pomegranate and lemon.

BEER

GAIŠAIS
LAGER 4.5% ABV
A light beer with a fresh, hoppy aroma and a softly bitter taste. Not too challenging, it is a refreshing drink.

ORIĢINĀLAIS
PILSNER 5% ABV
Amber-colored, with a light aroma of caramel and a pleasantly bitter taste of hops.

CĒSU BALSAM PORTER
PORTER 6% ABV
Sweet chocolate taste with hints of aromatic vanilla. In Latvia, balsam is commonly used to flavor drinks.

CĒSU PREMIUM
LAGER 5.2% ABV
A pale golden color, it has hints of sweet grass and hops on the nose.

LE COQ PORTER
PORTER 6.5% ABV
A strong, dark beer—a worthy successor to the famous Imperial Extra Double Stout.

DOUBLE BOCK
BOCK 8% ABV
A strong and warming light bock, it has a surprisingly mellow finish for a beer of this strength.

ORIGINAAL
LAGER 4.6% ABV
A mild-flavored beer, the color of pale straw, with pleasant hints of sweetcorn in the aroma.

HELE
LAGER 5.2% ABV
A strong hoppy flavor and hints of grass and hops on the nose. Thin in color, it lacks the body to be a star.

The cool crispness of pilsner-type lager is well-suited to the Spanish climate, and this is the most popular style of beer, however wine tends to dominate cultural tastes in Spain, as elsewhere in southern Europe.

BREWERY

ALHAMBRA

Avenida de Murcia 1,
18012 Granada, Spain
www.cervezasalhambra.com

The Alhambra group was founded in 1925 and is named after Granada's famed Moorish palace. Spain's purest water comes from the nearby Sierra Nevada mountain range, and is used in the making of Alhambra beers.

BREWING SECRET The brewery uses traditional techniques that include fermentation lasting up to 39 days.

HEINEKEN ESPAÑA

Carretera Córdoba,
23005 Jaén, Spain
www.heineken.es

Heineken España (formerly El Alcázar), in its current form, was created in 1999 when acquisitive Heineken bought the five breweries of the Cruzcampo group to add to the two El Águila breweries it already owned. It was then forced by the competition authorities to sell two breweries in Madrid and Valencia to Damm.

DAMM

Roselló 515, 08025 Barcelona,
Spain
www.damm.es

Auguste Kuentzmann Damm brought Alsace-style lager brewing to Barcelona in the 19th century. The original brewery operated until 1992, when the production plant was moved to the town of El Prat de Llobregat in order to increase beer production capacity and modernize processes.

SOCIEDAD CENTRAL DE CERVEJAS

Estrada da Alfarrobeira—2625 – 244
Vialonga, Portugal
www.centralcervejas.pt

This brewery has been influenced by the techniques of Germany and Denmark. It produces a wide range of dark and light beers using a spectrum of colored malts. From a crisp Pilsen to its fruity Bohemian, these are beers of some distinction.

BEER

ALHAMBRA PREMIUM
LAGER 4.6% ABV
A soft gold in color, its nose is lemony and fresh with a hint of malt. A well-balanced, quaffable beer.

MEZQUITA
WHEAT BEER 7.2% ABV
A full-bodied, assertive red wheat beer with caramel notes and hints of pepper in the aroma.

CRUZCAMPO
LAGER 5% ABV
Pale gold in color, light-tasting, with a fine balance of malt and hops and a floral, aromatic aroma. One of Spain's most popular beers.

BOCK-DAMM
STOUT 5.4% ABV
A Munich-style stout, rich with toasty flavors and a warming sweetness on the finish.

ESTRELLA DAMM
PILSNER 5.4% ABV
A light, refreshing beer with a creamy head and a rather dry and bitter taste.

SAGRES PRETA (DARK)
LAGER 4.3% ABV
A Munich-style dark lager with a mahogany hue, a creamy head, and a nutty aroma. It tastes slightly chocolatey, with hints of toffee and caramel, but balanced with plenty of bitterness from hops.

CEREURO—CERVEJEIRA EUROPEIA

Estrada da Portela n°8,
2795 – 643 Carnaxide, Portugal
www.sumolis.pt

Part of soft drinks manufacturer Grupo Sumol, this brewery was set up after the revolution of 1974, when the brewing industry was nationalized. It went into private ownership in the 1990s. The company also brews Magna, an interesting German-style dark beer, and markets Grolsch in Portugal.

SIMONDS FARSONS CISK

The Brewery, Notabile Road, Mriehel, BKR 01, Malta
www.farsons.com

Wherever the British army went, beer was soon to follow, and this brewery was built in lavish Art Deco style at the end of World War II in 1946. The site is being redeveloped, with the old brewing vessels at the heart of a visitor center.

BREWING SECRET It brews the potent XS (9% ABV) for the export market.

KEO

Franklin Roosevelt Ave, Limassol, 3602 Cyprus
www.keogroup.com

Limassol is the main port and fastest-growing city on the island of Cyprus. It is also home to the Keo Brewery, and no trip to Limassol is complete without visiting the plant, which lies just beyond the Old Port. During the week, there is a daily tour around the brewery—finishing, of course, in the tasting room.

MYTHOS

570 22 Sindos Thessaloniki, Greece
www.mythosbrewery.gr

One of Greece's largest breweries, Mythos is owned by Britain's Scottish & Newcastle. The biggest selling beer is Mythos itself. It is the leading Greek lager brand, and its sales are increasing at an average of 10 percent each year. Mythos also brews the Greek lager Golden and German beers Henninger and Kaiser.

TAGUS
LAGER 5.4% ABV
A clear golden color, this beer is rich and malty with caramel overtones. Its estery nose hints of its alcoholic strength and its warming finish.

FARSONS LACTO
MILK STOUT 3.8% ABV
Soft on the tongue, this black beer is a classic milk stout, with lactose added after fermentation.

HOPLEAF EXTRA
ALE 5% ABV
English malt, along with Challenger and Target hops, produce a complex beer with a refreshing bitter finish.

KEO
LAGER 4.5% ABV
A pale lager with a thick head and a sweet malt taste, it is easy on the palate and very drinkable.

FIVE BEER
LAGER 5% ABV
Deep amber in color, it is rich in malt and low in bitterness. Sweet in the finish.

MYTHOS
LAGER 5% ABV
An easy-drinking beer, with a bright blonde color and a thick white head. Light caramel aftertaste.

MYTHOS RED
VIENNA LAGER 5.5% ABV
A rich red color; low in bitterness, its flavor is dominated by sweet notes.

Portugal's Sociedad Central de Cervejas produces the Sagres brand, which comprises a range of beers based largely on German lager styles.

AMSTERDAM BREWING

21 Bathurst Street, Toronto,
Ontario, M5V 2NG, Canada
www.amsterdambeer.com

Purity, passion, and revelry are the watchwords for Toronto's first brewpub. Founded in 1986 on John Street in the entertainment area, it was an immediate success. Business was brisk, and it soon moved to another site before finding its current home in 2005. A large retail shop is part of the site, and tours are

organized twice a day throughout most of the year. The brewery stands opposite the historic Fort York, a National Historic site and the 1793 birthplace of modern Toronto. In 2003, when the Kawartha Lakes Brewing Company closed, its brands were sold to Amsterdam Brewing, who continue to brew a range of Kawartha Lakes' (KLB) beers, including a raspberry wheat beer and the KLB Nut Brown Ale.

BIG ROCK

5555-76th Avenue SE, Calgary,
Alberta T2C 4L8, Canada
www.bigrockbeer.com

Alberta's warm days and cool nights produce the finest two-row malting barley in the world. The most popular variety, Harrington, is the only malt used in Big Rock beers. There are regular brewery tours for visitors.

BREWING SECRET The brewery shuns the use of adjuncts and other processing aids in its beermaking.

CHURCH KEY BREWING

1678 County Rd 38, Campbellford,
Ontario, K0L 1L0, Canada
www.churchkeybrewing.com

Located in a former Methodist church where it was founded in 2000, Church Key Brewing is the brainchild of John Graham. John has put environmental principles into action here: solar hot water, bio-diesel, radiant floor heating, and heat recovery units are all employed to lower the carbon output of this award-winning brewery.

KLB NUT BROWN ALE
BROWN ALE 5% ABV
The unmistakable tang of East Kent Golding hops. Sweet to taste, it has hints of honey and chocolate.

AMSTERDAM WHEAT BEER
WHEAT BEER 4% ABV
Light in color, with malt sweetness and a hint of fresh bread. Often served chilled with a slice of lemon.

AMSTERDAM NATURAL BLONDE
LAGER 5% ABV
Crisp and clean with hints of citrus. Canadian malt combines with aromatic Czech and German hops.

AMSTERDAM SPRING BOCK
LAGER 6% ABV
Mahogany-hued with a rich, mouth-warming body; the three malts provide wonderful fruit flavors.

GRASSHÖPPER
WHEAT BEER 5% ABV
Crisp, refreshing, and only lightly hopped. Locals drink it with a slice of lemon, which adds assertiveness.

MCNALLY EXTRA ALE
STRONG IRISH ALE 7% ABV
A strong full-bodied Irish ale. It has a flowery aroma and a rich, fruity maltiness.

HOLY SMOKE SCOTCH ALE
SCOTCH ALE 6.25% ABV
A dark and malty ale, the use of whisky malt giving it an intense smoky aroma and peaty taste.

NORTHUMBERLAND ALE
ALE 5% ABV
Also known as Church Key, this is a crisp and light brew, with a dry, citrus finish.

CANADA'S BEST-KNOWN BEERS

In Canada today, the major brewers are either foreign-owned or have been forced to merge with international drinks corporations.

The most recent of these mergers affected Molson, which joined with US rival Coors in 2005. Anheuser-Busch InBev owns Labatt Breweries, and Japan's Sapporo owns Sleeman Breweries, which is currently Canada's third largest beer producer.
The market in Canada for domestic beer is dominated by two brands, Labatt Blue and Molson Canadian, both of which are marketed using strong Canadian imagery of mountains, the great outdoors, and ice hockey. The big two have a long history in Canada. John Molson founded a brewery in Montreal in 1786 and John Kinder Labatt started in London, Ontario, in 1847. Both Molson and Labatt have a wide range of niche brands. Canada has many fine craft brewers and brewpubs, many operated using environmentally responsible brewing methods. The Cheval Blanc exemplifies this spirit. It is one of Canada's best-known brewpubs and was the first to open in Montreal. A good time neighborhood tavern, it has been wowing locals and beer lovers from around the globe since 1986.

LABATT BLUE (PILSNER 5% ABV) *left*
MOLSON CANADIAN
  (LAGER 5% ABV) *center*
SLEEMAN CREAM ALE
  (ALE 5% ABV) *right*

CREEMORE SPRINGS

139 Mill Street, Creemore, Ontario, L0M 1G0, Canada
www.creemoresprings.com

Ownership by Molsons since 2005 has done little to lessen the independence of this 100-year-old brewery. The town of Creemore nestles between the curiously named Mad and Noisy rivers. Every August the brewery is a sponsor of a town-center party called the Copper Kettle Festival. Regular brewery tours are run.

PREMIUM LAGER
LAGER 5% ABV
Soft malt and fruit flavors give way to nutty overtones and a dry hoppy finish.

URBOCK
BOCK 6% ABV
Dark brown, with a sweet, nutty texture; fruit aromas can be found as the beer warms in the glass.

FAT CAT BREWERY

940 Old Victoria Road, Nanaimo, British Colombia V9R 6Z8, Canada
www.fatcatbrewery.com

Class and quality exude from this microbrewery, which was founded in 2000. Fat Cat Brewery is part of a new wave of thinking that says that beer is fun and fashionable, and should be made by hands-on brewers who have an affinity with the environment. The beers are distinctive, idiosyncratic, and very well made.

POMPOUS POMPADOUR
PORTER 4% ABV
A ruby black porter; very dark and luxurious, with lots of chocolate and cream overtones.

FAT CAT INDIA PALE ALE
INDIA PALE ALE 6% ABV
A very well balanced beer; amber in color and with a lot of hops.

GRANVILLE ISLAND BREWING

1441 Cartwright Street, Vancouver, BC V6H 3R7, Canada
www.gib.ca

When the brewery opened in 1984, the owners of Granville Island had an inkling that the British Columbian public was ready for a natural, pilsner-style beer. Sales of the first release, Island Lager, confirmed their thoughts.

BREWING SECRET All Granville Island's beers are unpasteurized.

ENGLISH BAY PALE ALE
PALE ALE 5% ABV
Copper hued and in the tradition of classic English ales. Smooth and mild, with a caramel malt aroma.

CYPRESS HONEY LAGER
LAGER 4.7% ABV
Honey from Fraser Valley gives a crispness and hint of sweetness in the finish. Lightly hopped.

BREWERY

MCAUSLAN

5080 St-Ambroise, Montréal,
Québec, H4C 2G1, Canada
www.mcauslan.com

McAuslan Brewing began in January
of 1989 when its founder Peter
McAuslan decided to turn his home-
brewing hobby into a business. It
quickly established itself as one of the
area's best microbreweries and was
one of the first in Canada to bottle its
products. It produces a challenging
range of seasonal beers.

MAGNOTTA BREWERY

271 Chrislea Road, Vaughan,
Ontario, L4L 8N6, Canada
www.magnotta.com

Magnotta focuses on brewing lagers
using traditional craft-brewing
methods. The whole process can
be seen by taking a brewery tour.

BREWING SECRET Beers are made
without adjuncts, such as corn or rice,
preservatives, pasteurization, or the
"high-gravity process" that requires
dilution and blending.

MOOSEHEAD

89 Main Street West, Saint John,
New Brunswick, E2M 3H2, Canada
www.moosehead.ca

Canada's oldest independent brewery
can trace its roots back to 1867,
when Susannah Oland first started
brewing in her Dartmouth, Nova
Scotia backyard. Today, the company
is still owned and operated by the
Oland family. Moosehead has stakes in
McAuslan and wholly owns the
Niagara Falls Brewing Company.

NIAGARA FALLS

6863 Lundys Lane, Niagara Falls,
Ontario, L2G 1V7, Canada

Well, what do you do once you've
seen the falls? Have a beer of course.
The brewery was founded in 1989,
and, through its early brews, it quickly
acquired a reputation for being
adventurous. Niagara Falls is now
wholly owned by Moosehead.

BREWING SECRET It is credited with
being the first North American
brewery to produce a true *eisbock*.

BEER

ST-AMBROISE APRICOT ALE
FRUITY WHEAT BEER 5% ABV
Apricot essence and malted wheat
combine to create an original
tasting beer with a clean, fruit nose.

ST-AMBROISE OATMEAL STOUT
STOUT 5% ABV
Brewed from dark malts and roasted
barley, this stout carries strong
espresso and chocolate notes.

TRUE NORTH INDIA PALE ALE
INDIA PALE ALE 6.5% ABV
Spicy, grassy, and fruity hop flavors
are combined with an assertive
bitterness. Very fruity.

TRUE NORTH WUNDER WEISSE
WHEAT BEER 5% ABV
Yellow color with a slight, natural
wheat beer haze. Subtle aromas of
yeast and delicate ripe banana.

MOOSEHEAD LAGER
LAGER 5% ABV
Pale, staw-colored, clean-tasting
session beer; best drunk cold.

CLANCY AMBER ALE
ALE 5% ABV
Top-fermented, Clancy's is a reddish
beer, with a distinct malt aroma and
overlays of caramel.

NIAGARA HONEY BROWN
AMERICAN BROWN ALE 5% ABV
An inherent sweetness, with hints
of honey and caramel. Light to
drink, it has a short dry finish.

NIAGARA EISBOCK
EISBOCK 8% ABV
A robust throat-warming beer;
each year's vintage has its own
unique characteristics. It's a classic!

PUMP HOUSE BREWERY

5 Orange Lane, Moncton, New
Brunswick, E1G 1S9, Canada
www.pumphousebrewery.ca

Today, the Pump House Brewery is
a group of brewing and bar catering
businesses. It was opened as a
brewpub in downtown Moncton
in 1999 by owners Shaun Fraser,
a local fire department chief, and
his wife Lilia. The couple have won
many awards for their beers and
for their business skills, and the

brewpub's popularity grew so quickly
that expansion was soon necessary.
In July 2002, a brewing and bottling
plant was built outside the city
center, and production began in the
same year. A restaurant called the
Barn Yard BBQ was also established
on the same site.

BREWING SECRET In the fall, the brewery
hosts an "Oktoberfest" and creates a
special lager in its honor.

SLEEMAN

551 Clair Road West, Guelph,
Ontario, N1L 1E9, Canada
www.sleeman.com

The Sleeman family started brewing in
Canada in 1834, the year John Sleeman,
an ambitious young brewer from
England, arrived in Ontario. In 1851
he started the first Guelph-based
Sleeman Brewery, making small, 100-
barrel batches with local well water,
prized for its purity and hardness. The
company is now owned by Sapporo.

STEAMWORKS

375 Water Street, Gastown,
Vancouver, V6B 5C6, Canada
www.steamworks.com

A popular pub and brewery located
in the historic Gastown area of
Vancouver, Steamworks offers
fabulous views of the harbor.

BREWING SECRET Steamworks produces
a wide range of seasonal brews using
a pot pourri of ingredients, including
fresh cherries, pumpkin, cinnamon,
nutmeg, ginger, and cloves.

PUMP HOUSE BLUEBERRY ALE
FRUIT BEER 5% ABV
Blond, with a blueberry aroma.
Sweet flavors of blueberry and malt,
with a hint of pepper.

FIRE CHIEF'S RED ALE
RED ALE 5.5% ABV
Reddish brown, with toffee and nut
flavors, followed by light chocolate
notes and a bitter aftertaste.

PUMP HOUSE SCOTCH ALE
ALE 4.8% ABV
Deep amber, with a smoky aroma.
Flavors of caramel are followed by
chocolate, then a slight bitter
aftertaste of roasted malt.

HONEY BROWN LAGER
LAGER 5% ABV
A refreshingly smooth, full-bodied
lager, with a subtle touch of honey
which creates a slightly sweet finish.

SLEEMAN CREAM ALE
ALE 5% ABV
Designed to combine the refreshing
quality of German lager with the
distinctive taste of English Ale.

HEROICA OATMEAL STOUT
STOUT 8% ABV
Rolled oats and black roasted barley
give this beer a warm, roasted nose
and distinct dryness.

SIGNATURE PALE ALE
ALE 5% ABV
British Crystal malt gives the beer a
rich color, caramel maltiness, and
adds a whiff of toffee to the nose.

UNIBROUE

80 Des Carrieres, Chambly,
Quebec, J3L 2H6, Canada
www.unibroue.com

In the spring of 1992, André Dion
launched his first unfiltered, bottled
sur lees beer. The yeast remains
living in the bottle, changing the
characteristics of the beer as it ages.
The beers are very popular, and the
company was bought by Sleeman in
2004. As with Sleeman, it is now
owned by Japanese brewer Sapporo.

VANCOUVER ISLAND

2330 Government St, Victoria, British
Colombia, V8T 5G5, Canada
www.vanislandbrewery.com

The inspiration for this company's
formation in 1984 was the absence of
locally made beers on Vancouver
Island. The brewery believes that
brewing should be a perfect blend of
art and science, with no short cuts.

BREWING SECRET Though the hops and
yeast are imported, only the finest
Canadian barley is used.

WELLINGTON BREWERY

950 Woodlawn Road West, Guelph,
Ontario, N1K 1B8, Canada
www.wellingtonbrewery.ca

The brewery is dedicated to Arthur
Wellesley, the 1st Duke of Wellington,
the British commander who defeated
Napoleon's French army at Waterloo
in 1815. The building is known for its
distinctive conical rooftop, which
replicates that of an oast house—a
structure traditionally used for drying
hops in the English county of Kent.

YUKON BREWING

102A Copper Rd, Whitehorse,
Yukon Y1A 2Z6, Canada
www.yukonbeer.com

Clean water makes clean beer. Yukon
beers start with North America's
cleanest water. Named by some the
Wilderness City, Whitehorse nestles
on the banks of the famous Yukon
River, surrounded by mountains and
clear mountain lakes. Yukon makes
eight beers, including one flavored
with coffee beans.

MAUDITE
RED ALE 8% ABV
Deep amber-red, with a rocky foam
head and an appealing aroma of wild
spices and floral hop notes.

BLANCHE DE CHAMBLY
WHITE BEER 5% ABV
Pale golden in color, with an
effervescent foam and a subtle
bouquet of spice and citrus notes.

HERMANNATOR
EISBOCK 9.5% ABV
Brewed and then frozen, it is a
symphony of complex chestnut
colors and spicy flavors.

HERMANN'S DARK
BAVARIAN LAGER 5.5% ABV
A toasty malt nose with similar
flavors on the palate; takes on a
somewhat nutty character.

ARKELL BEST BITTER
BEST BITTER 4% ABV
An amber-hued and refreshing
beer—light-bodied for a bitter.
More malty on the palate than
the nose, with caramel notes.

WELLINGTON IMPERIAL STOUT
STOUT 8% ABV
A rich, exceptionally complex beer,
with an almost coffeelike flavor.

LEAD DOG ALE
ALE 7% ABV
Intricate malt flavors predominate.
Reminiscent of a porter, it has a
slightly darkened, creamy head.

DISCOVERY ALE
PALE ALE 5% ABV
Brewed using honey made from
Fireweed, the official flower of the
Yukon. It finishes dry on the tongue.

MORE BEERS OF
CANADA

Canada has a small, stable core of brewpubs and craft breweries, many of which have a loyal following in the vicinity of their home towns. Some of these brewers do produce bottled beers that travel further afield, but many do not, and sell only draft beer locally.

BREWERY

BRICK BREWING

181 King Street South, Waterloo, Ontario, N2J 1P7, Canada
www.brickbrewery.com

Founder Jim Brickman traveled to no fewer than 29 countries and visited 68 breweries for research before achieving his ambition of setting up his own brewery in 1984. At the time, it was the first brewery to open in Eastern Canada for 37 years. The brewery's home town, Waterloo, hosts a Bavarian beer festival every October.

CHEVAL BLANC

809 Rue Ontaria Est, Montreal, Quebec, H2L 1P1, Canada
www.lechevalblanc.ca

Montreal's first brewpub—a good time neighborhood tavern that has been wowing locals and beer lovers from all over the world since 1986. Its small kitchen produces some fine Hungarian hot dogs too. Long regarded as one of the coolest bars in the city, it keeps its decor simple and hosts exhibitions and music evenings.

DIEU DU CIEL

29 West Laurier Avenue, Montreal, Quebec, H2T 2N2, Canada
www.dieuduciel.com

A small brewpub that opened in 1998, Dieu du Ciel is owned by Jean-François Gravel, who turned his passion for making beer into a business. Gravel is constantly pushing at the boundaries of brewing and loves to create new beers. He believes that beer is a wonderful adventure, which brings together both art and science.

FERME BRASSERIE SCHOUNE

2075 Ste-Catherine, St-Polycarpe, Quebec, J0P 1X0, Canada
www.schoune.com

All the beers draw on the Schoune family's Belgian links. All use pure barley malt, and the white uses a proportion of local wheat.

BREWING SECRET The beers are unfiltered, so the yeast remains in the bottle to help produce deep, rich fruit flavors to compliment the spiciness.

BEER

WATERLOO DARK
LAGER 5% ABV
Roasted malts give this beer a dark ebony color and an espresso nose. It is surprisingly light to taste.

BRICK BOCK
BOCK 7% ABV
Seasonal brew, the ingredients change annually, dark and malty with liquorice overtones.

AMBER
RED ALE 5% ABV
A classic caramelized red ale, with a clean, refreshing bitterness. A well-balanced, drinkable beer.

INDIA RED
INDIA PALE ALE 6% ABV
A reddish American style IPA. Dry hopped with Centennial hops, it has masses of bitterness.

CHAMAN
IMPERIAL PALE ALE 8% ABV
Strong amber hues and dominating hop flavors; very complex and bitter, but always well balanced.

ROUTES DES ÉPICES
RYE BEER 5% ABV
A rye beer to which pepper has been added during brewing to give a wonderful peppery flavor.

LA REB'ALE
STRONG ALE 7.5% ABV
The rock 'n' roll of the range: copper red, deeply malty, and a powerful caramel mouthfeel.

LA BLANCHE DU QUÉBEC
WHITE BEER 4.1% ABV
With a spicy character, it refreshes the palate with a citrus caress; an ideal partner with goat cheese.

BREWERY

GRANITE

1662 Barrington Street, Halifax, NS B3J 2A2, Canada
www.granitebrewery.ca

The Granite Brewery uses wholly natural ingredients in its brewing. They include Canadian two-row barley malt from western Canada, caramel malt, which provides flavor and color, and English black malt for a deeper color.

BREWING SECRET Crushed Canadian wheat flour is employed to enable good head retention on the beers.

RUSSELL

202-13018 80 Avenue, Surrey, British Columbia, V3W 3B2, Canada
www.russellbeer.com

When Russell Brewery was founded in 1995 its owners had a single goal in mind: to brew the best pure natural beer, with no pasteurization and no short cuts taken. Currently the beers are available on draft in the Vancouver area, though there are plans to put the brewery's output into bottles and cans in the near future.

SPINNAKERS

308 Catherine Street, Victoria, British Colombia, V9A 3S8, Canada
www.spinnakers.com

A must-visit brewpub, and, as it has accommodation, the perfect base to explore other creative craft brewers in the area. Its beers are eclectic, drawing on styles from all over the world. There is also a malt vinegar brewery on the premises, which uses traditional oak barrel ageing methods for its naturally brewed malt vinegars.

STORM BREWING

St John's, Newfoundland, A1B 3N7, Canada
www.stormbrewing.ca

The brewery was named Storm to reflect the harsh marine environment of Newfoundland. The brewery recently took part in a zero emissions experiment that saw oyster and shiitake mushrooms and earthworm cultivation on the brewers' spent grains. The beers are unpasteurized and contain no preservatives or additives.

BEER

PECULIAR
ALE 5.6% ABV
A dark red ale with a slightly sweet but dry palate.

GIN LANE ALE
BARLEY WINE 9% ABV
Dry hopped, with an assertive, almost winey character; the bitterness derives from Kent Golding and Fuggles hops.

RUSSELL PALE ALE
PALE ALE 5.5 % ABV
Amber in color, the malts come from Scotland, the hops Yakima. It has soft citrus overtones.

RUSSELL CREAM ALE
ENGLISH ALE 5% ABV
Made with English malts, it is dark, golden, and smooth, with Canadian barley married to American hops.

SPINNAKERS IMPERIAL STOUT
IMPERIAL STOUT 7.75% ABV
A strong stout, brewed with all English floor-malted grains; a rich and aromatic brew.

SPINNAKERS HONEY PALE ALE
BLOND ALE 4.7% ABV
Using English Pale malt and local honey, this is a smooth, light-bodied, slightly sweet, and very refreshing.

NEWFOUNDLAND RED ALE
RED ALE 5.5% ABV
A smooth ale with a deep reddish hue. A sugar sweetness is overlaid with butterscotch.

COFFEE PORTER
PORTER 5% ABV
A seasonal beer, brewed using imported black malt and dark roasted Arabica coffee beans.

OPENING HOURS
MON - SAT
6·30 am - 9·00 pm

The Carib brand, launched in 1950 on the island of Trinidad, soon enjoyed international success.

BUCANERO SA

Circunvalación Sur Km 3.5,
Holguin, Cuba
www.cervezacristal.com

A surprisingly modern and
sophisticated brewery, which is
increasingly gearing production
toward the burgeoning tourist trade
and exports. You can see the Cristal
logo everywhere in Cuba, especially
on the popular Cristal Bici-taxis, the
drivers of which are always ready to
take you to the nearest bar.

CARIB

Eastern Main Road,
Champs Fleurs, Trinidad
www.caribbeer.com

The sole brewery on Trinidad since
1957, Carib has formed business links
with InBev, Carlsberg, and Diageo—
the owner of Guinness. The company
also has breweries in Grenada,
St. Kitts and Nevis. The British brought
commercial brewing to Trinidad just
after World War I; the local taste
favors sweet lagers and strong stouts.

DESNOES AND GEDDES

214 Spanish Town, Kingston, Jamaica
www.jamaicadrinks.com

Now owned by global drinks giant
Diageo, Desnoes and Geddes was
established by two friends, Eugene
Desnoes and Thomas Geddes, who
set up a soft drink plant in 1918 and
began brewing in 1927 with Red Stripe.

BREWING SECRET Red Stripe was
originally produced as an English ale.
It didn't become popular until it was
offered as a chilled lager instead.

PHOENIX BEVERAGES GROUP

The Phoenix House, Pont-Fer, Mauritius
www.phoenixbeveragesgroup.com

This drinks group was created when
Phoenix Beverages (formerly Mauritius
Breweries) and Phoenix Camp
Minerals merged in 2003. Mauritius
Breweries had started brewing under
license in 1961, launching Phoenix
Beer, the first Mauritian beer, in 1963.
The brewery also brews Guinness
and Warsteiner under license.

BREWERY

CRISTAL
LAGER 4.9% ABV
Lightly-hopped, and full of cane
sugar sweetness. A drink best
suited to a hot day.

CARIB LAGER
LAGER 5.2% ABV
Pale, but full-bodied with a rich
head formation. Slightly aromatic,
balanced between sweet and bitter.

CARIB STAG
LAGER 5.9% ABV
European style lager. It is has a pale
golden straw color with a rich head
formation. Very sweet.

DRAGON STOUT
SWEET STOUT 7.5% ABV
Having been primed with sugar on
bottling, the flavor is malty, with
a distinct note of molasses.

RED STRIPE
LAGER 4.7% ABV
Yellow in color, it has a grainy
aroma, a crisp, clean taste, and is
best drunk very cold.

PHOENIX BEER
LAGER 5% ABV
A beer for a hot day on a beautiful
beach. Its malty nose gives way to
an overt sweetness.

BLUE MARLIN
LAGER 6% ABV
Lots of popcorn and bubble gum on
the nose; a clear, pale gold body.

BEER

MOCTEZUMA

Monterrey/Veracruz-Llave, Mexico
www.femsa.com

Mexico's most innovative brewer, Moctezuma also has operations in Brazil and is an important exporter of beer to the US. It has a powerful brand portfolio that includes Tecate, Dos Equis, Sol, Indio, Bohemia, and Carta Blanc, many of which are sold in style bars worldwide. Its beers tend to be smooth, with a spritzy finish.

GRUPO MODELO

Lago Alberto 156 Colonia Anáhuac, Mexico DF, 11320, Mexico
www.gmodelo.com

Founded in 1925, Grupo Modelo is the leader in Mexico, with more than 60 percent of the local beer market and seven brewing plants throughout the country. Currently, it brews and distributes 12 brands, including Corona Extra, the best-selling Mexican beer worldwide, Modelo Especial, Victoria, Pacifico, and Negra Modelo.

CERVESUR

Arequipa, Peru

Based in southern Peru in the Andes, the company, which is of German origin, has been brewing since 1898 and is now part of SABMiller. It is currently being merged with SABMiller's other Peruvian company Backus & Johnson. Its main brand, Cusqueña, is Peru's best-selling lager.

BREWING SECRET The water for brewing comes from a source high in the Andes.

ANTARES

17 Esquina 71, La Plata - P de Bs As, 7600, Argentina
www.cervezaantares.com.ar

Antares is the brightest star in the Scorpius constellation, and the brewpub that shares its name sparkles too. Stylish and smart, it offers a lively alternative to beers from international brewers. Brews include a kölsch, a Scotch ale, a honey beer, a cream stout, a barley wine, and an imperial stout, with some variations in style.

DOS EQUIS
VIENNA LAGER 4.8% ABV
Rich and dark red, with chocolate orange flavors; its warming sweetness gives way to a long finish.

SOL
LAGER 4.5% ABV
A crisp, light-bodied lager with a corn syrup aroma.

CORONA EXTRA
LAGER 4.6% ABV
Light straw in color, it's a refresher on a hot day. Best drunk with lime for taste.

LEON NEGRA
VIENNA LAGER 6% ABV
Caramel in color, with malt hints and has a toasty caramel edge. A satisfying sweetnesss when chilled.

CUSQUEÑA
LAGER 5% ABV
Pronounced "Cus-Ken-Ya," the beer is crisp and refreshing, with a lingering lemon aroma.

ANTARES STOUT IMPERIAL
IMPERIAL STOUT 8.5% ABV
Intense liquorice and toasted flavors give way to roasted coffee and caramelized orange intensities.

ANTARES KÖLSCH
KÖLSCH 5% ABV
A well hopped and highly drinkable ale style. Good fruity overtones make it an ideal partner to food.

MORE BEERS OF
SOUTH AMERICA

Argentina and Brazil have a smattering of excellent craft brewers, mixing styles from Europe and the Americas. Here are a few more.

BREWERY

BULLER BREWING COMPANY

RM Ortiz 1827, Buenos Aires, Argentina
www.bullerpub.com

Buenos Aires can have few better pub gardens, and this one has the added bonus that at least six beers are brewed on site. Inspiration is drawn from the old and new worlds.

BREWING SECRET Argentinean honey, German malts, and American hops vie for attention in a fine array of beers.

EISENBAHN

Cervejaria Sudbrack Ltda, Rua Bahia, 5181—Salto Weissbach, 89032-001 Blumenau SC, Brazil
www.eisenbahn.com.br

Owners Jarbas and Juliano Mendes established this brewery in 2002, and brew without the use of adjuncts or preservatives. They create a wide range of beers, from German-style weizenbier to special Belgian-style ales. Eisenbahn beers are exported to the United States and France.

BEER

HONEY BEER
FLAVORED BEER 8.5% ABV
Along with the malts used, the Argentinean honey gives the beer an assertive character.

OKTOBERFEST
GERMAN ALE 5.5% ABV
Vienna and Munich malts impart a strong flavor profile; with little hop bitterness, the malt dominates.

EISENBAHN KÖLSCH
KÖLSCH 4.8% ABV
Four malts, including wheat, combine in this malty, golden beer; slight fruity aroma and low bitterness.

EISENBAHN NATURAL
PILSNER 4.8% ABV
Brazil's first organic beer. Light and golden, and low in bitterness. The nose is malty biscuit.

BARBA ROJA

Ruta 25 N° 2567, Escobar, 1625 Buenos Aires, Argentina
www.cerveceriabarbaroja.com.ar

Part of a leisure park complex in Escobar, Barba Roja is a pirate-themed brewpub. The heritage of the range of beers is unashamedly German, but with a local twist.

BREWING SECRET The area is renowned for its flowers and fruit—all of which feature in some of the brewery's seasonal beers.

QUILMES

Tte. Gral. Juan D. Peron 667 103, Buenos Aires, Argentina
www.quilmes.com.ar

The dominant beer in Argentina, Quilmes is now part of the InBev embrace. Like many breweries in South America, it was begun by a German, the brewery and malt plant being founded in the 1880s by Otto Bemberg. "Quilmes" derives from an indigenous name for the place where the brewery is located.

SUL BRASILEIRA

BR 392, Km 05, Santa Maria—RS, 97000, Brazil

Local folklore says that Sul Brasileira's Xingu beer is the daughter of a beer brewed in ancient times by pioneering Amazonian brewsters. The name Xinghu (pronounced "shin-goo") is a tributary of the Amazon River, which is home to the few surviving cultures and species of native Amazonian life.

TERESÓPOLIS

BR-040 - Km 116, Serra do Capim, Teresópolis, RJ, Brazil
www.lokalbier.com.br

At an altitude of over 2,800 ft (900 m), Teresópolis is surrounded by mountains and verdant rainforest. According to the brewery, its Lokal beer derives from a German word meaning "beer of our land." The name exemplifies the company's proud links with the surrounding environment and the brewery's local community.

BREWERY

BARBA ROJA NEGRA
DARK LAGER 4.5% ABV
A European-style Münchner, the beer's darkness offset by a white head. Fresh tasting and smooth.

BARBA ROJA WINNER
DOPPELBOCK 4.8% ABV
Hints of chocolate and liquorice in this double bock. Sweet, with a warming finish.

QUILMES CRISTAL
LAGER 4.9% ABV
Thin and pale, with no aromatic distractions. Surprisingly drinkable, though, with refreshing sweetness.

QUILMES STOUT
STOUT 4.8% ABV
Three malts clamor for attention—but the expected coffee flavors are overwhelmed by sweetness.

XINGU BLACK BEER
SCHWARZBIER 4.7% ABV
Dark in color, but light and sweet to taste. Still in the glass, its head soon disappears.

LOKAL
PILSNER 4.7% ABV
Pale, yellow, and full of corn flavors. Mildly hopped and refreshing, it has little aftertaste.

TERESÓPOLIS BLACK PRINCESS
DARK LAGER 4.8% ABV
Lacks the malty overtones expected from a beer of this color. Refreshing when chilled through.

BEER

Asahi Super Dry, still a very popular lager in Japan and abroad, was first launched in the 1980s.

JAPAN'S BEST-KNOWN BEERS

On the international market, several Japanese beer names stand out, most notably Asahi, Kirin, Orion, and Sapporo.

Asahi, a major Japanese brewer, came strongly forward in the market with the release of enduringly popular Asahi Super Dry back in the 1980s. Asahi beers are noted for their subdued hop aroma profiles and clean, crisp taste; they are brewed in many locations, nationally and internationally. Asahi Stout is a rare exception to the signature Asahi flavor profile. Kirin once maintained as much as two-thirds of the Japanese beer market thanks to its classic Kirin Lager. That changed, however, with Asahi's introduction of Super Dry. Orion is based on the island of Okinawa and has more than 50 percent of the market there, as well as a sizeable export market. Sapporo has dropped to fourth place among the major breweries in sales terms, but many fans love its soft mouthfeel and pleasant drinkability. Founded on the northern island of Hokkaido in the 1870s, it soon became a popular national, then international brand. It is, however, the brewery's Edel Pils that stands out in terms of quality and flavor.

ASAHI (STOUT 8% ABV) *left*
KIRIN (LAGER 5.5% ABV) *center*
SAPPORO (PILSNER 5% ABV) *right*

BAIRD BREWING

9-4 Senbonminato-cho, Numazu City, Shizuoka 410-0845, Japan
www.bairdbeer.com

Founded by Ohio native Bryan Baird and his wife Sayuri in January 2001, Baird has come to be considered Japan's best brewery. After the six regular beers were established—later augmented by an American-style wheat ale—Baird then focused on many seasonal beers. The Bairds have recently opened a taproom in Tokyo.

BAYERN MEISTER BIER

1254-1 Kawaharabata,
Inouede-aza, Fujinomiya City,
Shizuoka 418-0103, Japan
www.bmbier.com

Brewmaster Stefan Rager originally came to Japan to brew at several start-up microbreweries which opened after the 1995 liberalization. Later, with his Japanese wife, he founded a boutique-style brewery on the southern face of Mount Fuji, dedicated to German beer styles. The German Embassy in Tokyo is one of his most loyal customers.

ECHIGO

3970 Fukui, Nishiura-ku, Niigata City,
Niigata 953-0076, Japan
www.echigo-beer.jp

The brewers of the venerable Tsurukame saké of Niigata opened Japan's first microbrewery in February of 1995 to great fanfare. Operations have expanded from the original brewpub to a large-scale brewery with canning line today. While the canned products are well regarded, the more expensive small-production bottled products are even more highly prized.

RISING SUN PALE ALE
Pale Ale 5% ABV

A brilliant American-style Pale Ale made with British Maris Otter malt and with a unique US hop signature.

ANGRY BOY BROWN ALE
BROWN ALE 6.2% ABV
Exciting and complex, this strong brown ale has a complex flavor profile and a richly satisfying finish.

PRINZ PILS
PILSNER 5.5% ABV
Pale yellow, soft mouthfeel with low carbonation. The subtle flavors are in excellent balance.

AMADEUS DOPPELBOCK
DOPPELBOCK 8% ABV
Very deep reddish brown, with coffee, toffee, and caramel aromas. Rich tangy malt and high alcohol suggest rum-soaked fruitcake.

ECHIGO PILSENER
PILSNER 5% ABV
This reasonably priced craft beer has a rich malty flavor, moderate bitterness, and a clean, quick finish.

ECHIGO STOUT
STOUT 7% ABV
Higher gravity and more care in the brewing of this beer results in a brilliant interplay of rich, roasty flavors.

BREWERY

FUJIZAKURA HEIGHTS

3633-1 Funatsu, Fujikawaguchiko-machi,
Minami Tsuru-gun,
Yamanashi 401-0301, Japan
www.fuji-net.co.jp/beer/

Situated on the north side of Mount
Fuji, this small brewery specializes in
traditional German beers. While the
Pils seems to be the most popular in
their restaurant, the Weizen is easily
superior, and the smoky Rauch is the
brewery's leading award winner.

HAKUSEKIKAN

5251-1 Hirukawa Tahara,
Nagatsugawa, Gifu 509-8301, Japan
www.hakusekikan-beer.jp

One of Japan's most distinctive
breweries, Hakusekikan pushes the
envelope of possible beer styles. Head
brewer Satoshi Niwa is brilliant and
imaginative, experimenting with wild
beers using airborne yeast, while also
making use of long fermentation times,
barrel ageing, and other methods to
produce truly distinctive beers.

HARVEST MOON

Ikspiari 4F, 1-4 Maihama,
Urayasu City, Chiba 279-8529, Japan
www.ikspiari.co.jp/harvestmoon/

Set in a festive shopping complex
adjacent to Tokyo Disneyland, Harvest
Moon owes its strength to the fast
developing talents of head brewer
Mayumi Sonoda. Flavors are
understated but thrillingly complex,
with great balance and drinkability.

BREWING SECRET Yuzu Ale is often used
in traditional Japanese cuisine.

HIDEJI

747-56 Mukabaki,
Nobeoka 882-0090, Japan
www.hideji-beer.jp

Interest in this sleepy little micro was
enlivened after the election of maverick
prefectural governor Higashikokubaru,
whose corruption-fighting efforts have
won him immense public support.
A cartoon likeness of the governor
adorns Hideji's Stout. Hideji beer has
improved recently, along with the
fortunes of Miyazaki prefecture.

BEER

DOPPEL BOCK
DOPPELBOCK 8% ABV
Brewed only in spring, with a label
adorned with stylized cherry
blossoms, this rich and restorative
lager boasts a long malty finish.

RAUCH
RAUCHBIER 5.5% ABV
A rare rauchbier brewed regularly
in Japan, the smoky flavors last long
into the finish.

SUPER VINTAGE
STRONG ALE 14.3% ABV
Astonishingly fruity and complex
beer, yet boasts a surprisingly dry
finish. Permanently on tap at Beer
Club Popeye in Tokyo.

SMOKED PALE ALE
PALE ALE 5% ABV
A session pale ale given just a hint
of smoked malt, with the smoky
flavor appearing only in the finish.

YUZU ALE
ALE 4.5% ABV
An aromatic citrus fruit with a subtle
bitterness. The lovely aroma offsets
nicely the rich malty backbone.

SCHWARZ
SCHWARZBIER 4.5% ABV
Very dark, with red highlights;
chocolatelike flavor, with minimal
bitterness and fine carbonation for
a smooth mouthfeel.

HIDEJI STOUT
STOUT 4.1% ABV
Dry, with a fair measure of tartness,
the beer develops a roastiness and
soft texture as it warms.

SMOKING MOLE ALE
AMBER ALE 4.2% ABV
Bright amber gold, with a tangy rich
malt flavor, accented by plummy
fruit notes. Hops are subdued in a
more British interpretation.

HITACHINO NEST

1257 Konosu, Naka City,
Ibaraki 311-0133, Japan
www.kodawari.cc

The parent company is an old regional saké brewery that also produces shochu spirits and even wine. Beer was added to the range in 1996, followed by exports to the US. In fact, half of production is now exported, primarily to the US market. The best beers are Belgian in style.

ISEKADOYA

6-428 Jingu, Ise City, Mie 516-0017, Japan
www.biyagura.jp

Said to date back to the 16th century as an enterprise producing miso (fermented soya bean paste) and soy sauce, Isekadoya branched out into brewing in the 19th century for a brief time, supplying foreign ships with ale provisions. They resurrected their beer business in 1997, keeping to the same 19th-century label designs.

IWATEKURA

5-42 Tamuramachi, Ichinoseki City,
Iwate 021-0885, Japan
www.sekinoichi.co.jp

Located in a rather remote area of Northern Japan, Iwatekura has been distinguishing itself in recent years with a range of creative beers. They include a flavored ale with a striking caramel taste.

BREWING SECRET Local oyster beds renowned for their quality are harvested for the oyster stout.

KINSHACHI

1-7-34 Sakae, Naka-ku, Nagoya City,
Aichi 460-0008, Japan

Old line sake brewer Morita Shuzo produced beer briefly some 100 years ago for sale primarily to US whaling ships. One of the most internationally famous members of the family was Akio Morita, one of the founders of electronics giant Sony. In 1996, the company reopened a disused soft-drink bottling plant as a small brewery, under the old Kinshachi brand name.

WHITE ALE

WITBIER 5.5% ABV
Modeled on a Belgian wit, but with a pronounced orange flavor due to the use of real juice.

EXTRA HIGH

BELGIAN DARK ALE 8.3% ABV
Similar to a Belgian dark ale, XH (as it is known) is rich and malty, with a characteristic Belgian yeast flavor.

ISEKADOYA PALE ALE

PALE ALE 5% ABV
Initially produced in a more English style, recent versions have featured more assertive hopping, common to US pale ales. Still, it retains rather subdued characteristics.

CARAMEL ALE

FLAVORED ALE 5% ABV
The curiously accurate chewy caramel flavor is unmistakable in this ale aimed at female drinkers.

OYSTER STOUT

STOUT 7% ABV
The brewery revives this classic English style with a rich yet dry interpretation, minimal hopping, and only a faint hint of oyster flavor.

RED MISO LAGER

FLAVORED BEER 6% ABV
Miso is a specialty of the Nagoya region where Kinshachi is located. Only a small amount is used, giving the beer a faintly meaty flavor.

BLACK MISO LAGER

DARK LAGER 6% ABV
This newer version is made with very dark "hatcho" miso, and has an even richer, almost nutty taste.

BREWERY

MINOH AJI

3-19-11 Makiochi, Minoh City,
Osaka 562-0004, Japan
www.minoh-beer.jp

Established by liquor store owner
Masaji Oshita, and run by his
daughters Kaori and Mayuko, Minoh
AJI brewery mostly makes beers
based on American craft beer styles.

BREWING SECRET Among the more
distinctive beers are two that contain
hemp and one that uses Cabernet
Sauvignon grape juice.

NASU KOHGEN

3986 Oaza Takakukoh, Nasu-cho,
Nasu-gun, Tochigi 325-0001, Japan

Set in a picturesque forest just off the
primary highway leading north from
Tokyo, this brewery is known for its
superior quality, with prices to match,
and an emphasis on traditional English
styles. The brewery is in the vicinity
of the Japanese royal family summer
villa, and a beer named after Princess
Ai upon her birth has become one of
Nasu Kohgen's best sellers.

SANKT GALLEN

124 Kaneda, Atsugi City,
Kanagawa 243-0807, Japan
www.sanktgallenbrewery.com

This enterprise snuck under the
radar before the liberalization of
microbreweries with their less-than-
1 percent-alcohol brews back in the
early 1990s. Now, however, Sankt
Gallen seem to be specializing in high-
gravity "sweets beers," though their
golden, amber, and pale ales remain
popular too.

SHIGA KOGEN

1163 Hirao, Yamanouchi-machi, Shimo
Takai-gun Nagano 381-0401, Japan
www.tamamura-honten.co.jp

In September 2004, saké brewer
Tamamura Honten broke a little of
their 200-year tradition and began
brewing beer. Within three years
Shiga Kogen had become one of the
most respected Japanese craft beer
brands. Clear product identity and
superior label designs have
contributed to the beer's popularity.

BEER

MINOH AJI STOUT

STOUT 5.5% ABV
Brewed in the Irish style, with lots
of roast flavor and creamy texture,
this stout has a subdued bitterness.

DOUBLE IPA

STRONG IPA 9% ABV
Bold and exciting, this strong beer
is only produced as a seasonal so
far, but its popularity may lead to
it becoming available year-round.

NINE-TAILED FOX BARLEY WINE

BARLEY WINE 11% ABV
Remarkably subdued flavor profile
for a beer with such high alcohol.
In 2007 the brewery released a 10-
year vertical set, containing years
1998 to 2007 in 330 ml bottles,
which sold out quickly. These same
years are still available separately in
large 500 ml ceramic crocks.

IMPERIAL CHOCOLATE STOUT

IMPERIAL STOUT 8.5% ABV
The most popular of the "sweets
beers," this limited edition bottling
is released in time for St. Valentine's
Day and quickly sells out. Lots of
rich chocolate and caramel flavors
are tempered by a touch of acidity
and very low hopping.

HOUSE DPA / DRAFT PALE ALE

PALE ALE 8% ABV
American in style, with a brilliant
orange-gold hue, complex floral
hop aroma, and lingering sweetness.

MIYAMA BLONDE

SAISONLIKE BEER 7% ABV
Made using the Miyama Nishiki
strain of saké rice, along with
European hops and barley. Rich and
interesting, but with a brisk finish.

MORE BEERS OF
JAPAN

Suntory is famous for its whiskey, but its beer is also worth trying among these other Japanese brewers.

HELIOS

405 Kyoda, Nago City,
Okinawa 905-0024, Japan
www.helios-syuzo.co.jp

Originally a distiller of rum from Okinawa's abundant fields of sugar cane, Helios branched out into craft beer in 1996. Their flagship product is a rich weizenbier, which goes well in Okinawa's sub-tropical climate, while their Goya Dry is their most "local" and distinctive brew.

OTARU

3-263-19 Zenibako, Otaru City,
Hokkaido 047-0261, Japan
www.otarubeer.com

Japanese owners, a German brewer, and an American manager combine to make Otaru Beer an international endeavor. The bottom line here is quality. No beer is shipped beyond a 70-mile (100-km) radius of Otaru. The brewery's high production values are a match for those of most German brewers.

GOYA DRY
FLAVORED BEER 5% ABV
Bitter melon, the "national vegetable" of Okinawa, is used alongside hops to bitter this curiously refreshing beer. Naturally, it is ideal with pork-predominant Okinawan cuisine.

OTARU PILS
PILS 4.9% ABV
A stellar interpretation of the world's most popular beer style. Otaru's version is perfectly balanced.

WEISS
WEISSBIER 5.4% ABV
A clean, tart rendition of this German style wheat beer, with a fruity aroma and floral notes.

SHONAN

7-10-7 Kagawa, Chigasaki City,
Kanagawa 253-0082, Japan
www.kumazawa.jp

A saké brewing enterprise since 1872, Kumazawa Shuzo began brewing beer in 1996, naming the brand after the Shonan coastal region where the brewery is located. Quality has always been high, and Shonan has garnered many international awards over the past decade.

YOHO

1119-1 Otai, Saku City,
Nagano 385-0009, Japan
www.yonasato.com

Yona Yona Ale is perhaps the most popular craft beer in Japan, available in brightly colored cans and on draft all over Japan. While the recipe predates head brewer Toshi Ishii (who previously worked at Stone Brewing in San Diego), he is responsible for their second big success, Tokyo Black, a tasty porter with remarkable flavor and smooth balance.

OZENO YUKIDOKE

7-3 Nishi Honmachi, Tatebayashi City,
Gunma 374-0065, Japan
www.ryujin.jp

Quality and product stability was a bit uneven in the first few years of this brewery, which was founded in 1997. However, from around 2004 onward, Ozeno Yukidoke's beer began to improve dramatically and it now produces several tasty brews. The parent company is an old established saké brewer.

SUNTORY

3-1 Yazaki-cho, Fuchu City,
Tokyo 183-0025, Japan
www.suntory.co.jp/factory/musashino/

A long-standing whiskey enterprise with recent awards to their credit, Suntory is a relative newcomer to the world of beer. Established in the early 1960s to take advantage of their large distribution network, the brewery has only recently developed a repuation for quality lager.

LIEBE
SCHWARZBIER 5% ABV
Surprisingly dry and drinkable for such a dark, richly flavored beer, Liebe is an award-winning lager of superior depth and complexity.

WEIZEN BOCK
STRONG WEIZENBIER 7% ABV
Superb body, aroma, and balance for a high-alcohol beer, though it could be considered a bit staid by some.

YONA YONA ALE
PALE ALE 5.5% ABV
Square in the American Pale Ale category. Brisk and citrussy, with Cascade hops giving a sharp finish

TOKYO BLACK
PORTER 5% ABV
This tasty roasty beer can best be described as a session porter, with a unique twist. Brewer Ishii recently brewed a batch in England.

BROWN WEIZEN
HEFEWEIZEN 5% ABV
Unusual cloudy brown appearance, with a subtle lactic note. Richness suddenly comes in at mid-palate, leaving a long and satisfying finish.

INDIA PALE ALE
IPA 6% ABV
Patterned on the West coast style of IPA, it is boldly bitter with a quick hoppy finish.

THE PREMIUM MALT'S
LAGER 5.5% ABV
Having taken three Monde Selection awards in a row, this superior 100 percent malt lager is one of the best in Japan.

GUANGZHOU ZHUJIANG

Guangzhou PR, China
www.zhujiangbeer.com

Zhu Jiang is brewed in Guangzhou, in the South of China. Guangzhou is the third largest city in Mainland China with a population of 12 million. InBev has had a 24 percent stake in the brewery since 2002. Beers from the brewery are widely exported around the world.

SUN LIK

22 Wang Lee Street,
New Territories, Hong Kong, China
www.sunlikbeer.com

Sun Lik is Cantonese for San Miguel, one of the most famous beer brands worldwide. San Miguel Brewery Hong Kong is a non-wholly owned subsidiary of San Miguel Corporation. The brewery holds the franchise to produce and sell San Miguel's beer brands in Hong Kong, Macao, and Hainan province in mainland China.

TSINGTAO

Hong Kong Road, Central,
Qinqdao, China 266071
www.tsingtaobeer.com

The Tsingtao Brewery was founded in 1903 by German settlers in Qingdao. Today it is part owned by American giants Anheuser Busch, which is currently undertaking a massive investment in new breweries on the China mainland. The company runs over 40 breweries and malt plants in 18 provinces across China.

YANJING

9 Shuanghe Road, Shunyi District,
Beijing, China
www.yanjing.com.cn

The last remaining large independent brewer in China, Yanjing often rouses the attention of the global brewers. Over the past 25 years Yanjing has developed into one of the largest beer producing enterprises in China. It operates 20 other breweries on the China mainland, and its output is predicted to reach 1.1 billion gallons (5 million kiloliters) by 2010.

ZHU JIANG BEER
LAGER 5.3% ABV
The beer has a pale yellow strawlike appearance, with a subtle malt flavor highlighted by a delicate hop balance that finishes crisp and clean. Czech hops, German yeast, Chinese rice, and Canadian barley malt are used.

SUN LIK
LAGER 5% ABV
Rice is used in the beer's grist, which gives the beer a crisp if somewhat sugary finish. The beer is pale yellow in color and has a sweetcorn nose.

TSINGTAO
LAGER 4.8% ABV
Crisp, slightly malty flavor and nutty sweet taste. The color is a bright yellow; aroma grainy, with a hint of sweetness. A high level of carbonation makes it very fizzy.

YANJING BEER
LAGER 5% ABV
A sweet, golden syrup nose, it has overlays of biscuits and corn and pours a sun burst yellow into a glass. The brewing water is said to be from unpolluted mineral water deep under the Yanshan mountain.

BREWERY

HITE

640, Yeongdeungpo-Dong,
Yeongdeungpo, Seoul, South Korea
www.hite.com

Founded in 1933 as Chosun
Breweries, Hite is Korea's leading
brewer, with 60 percent of local sales.
Carlsberg is a substantial investor in
the brewery. The present production
at Hite amounts to approximately
150 million gallons (seven million
hectoliters) per annum. The company
also makes a rice-based wine.

ORIENTAL BREWERY

Hanwon Bldg, 1449-12 Seocho-dong,
Seocho-gu, 137-070 Seoul, South Korea
www.ob.co.kr

Founded by the Doosan Group in
1952, this brewery produces several
of Korea's most popular beverages,
including the OB, Cass, and Cafri
lagers; the company also produces
Budweiser under license. InBev
became involved in 2003 and took all
of its equity in 2006. It is the number
two brewer in Korea, with 40 percent
of the market.

KHAN BRÄU

Central Post Box 808,
Ulaanbaatar, Mongolia
www.khanbrau.net

The microbrewery was opened in
1996 as a joint Mongolian and
German venture. The company's pub,
the Khan Lonkh, offers draft pilsner in
a western-style environment. The
company says it is brewing beer to
comply with the German purity rules.

BREWING SECRET Khan Bräu takes its
water from the crystal pure Tull River.

BOON RAND

999 Samsen Road, Bangkok,
Thailand 10300
www.boonrawd.co.th

Boon Rawd was founded in 1933 by
Phraya Bhirom Bhakdi, who had toured
Germany and Denmark to learn about
brewing. The brewery is still owned
by the Bhirom-Bhakdi family. The
company operates three breweries
in Thailand.

BEER

HITE

LAGER 4.5% ABV
Golden in color, Hite is a light,
easy drinking beer—with an aroma
of bubblegum.

PRIME MAX

LAGER 4.5% ABV
Pale orange in color; with a
sweetcorn aroma, it has hints of
biscuit and citrus fruits.

OB BLUE

LAGER 4.4% ABV
Originally brewed in 1948. When
InBev purchased the company, the
recipe was altered to include rice.

CASS

LAGER 4.5% ABV
Pale and golden, Cass was once
Korea's biggest selling beer; it now
ranks number three.

BAADOG

VIENNA LAGER 4.8% ABV
Reddish brown in color, it has
sweet overtones with hints of
caramel and burnt sugar.

KHAN BRAU

PILSNER 4.8% ABV
A crisp beer that uses German malt
and hops. The Bavarian hops
provide a spicy flavor.

SINGHA

LAGER 6% ABV
A full-bodied barley malt beer with
a strong hop character. Clean to
taste, it complements spicy food.

SINGHA LIGHT

LAGER 3.5% ABV
Lacks the complexity and vitality of
its stronger stablemate. It is pale
yellow of hue and thin to taste.

THAIBEV

Vibhavadee Rangsit Road, Chomphon, Chatuchak, Bangkok, Thailand

Thailand's other major beer producer is in fierce competition with Boon Rand. Its Chang brand is the best-selling beer within the country and is widely exported. The company also makes the famous Mekhong rice whiskey.

LAO BREWERY

Km 12 Thadeua Road, Vientiane, Laos
www.beer-lao.com

The Lao Brewery began production in 1973 and was originally known as Brasseries et Glaci è res du Laos. Two years later, in 1975, it became state owned. In 2002, Carlsberg and TCC, a Thai company, each agreed to acquire a 25 percent stake in Lao Brewery; the remaining shares are still held by the Laos government.

HUE

243 Nguyen Sinh Cung
Hue City, Vietnam

The Hue Brewery is based in Hue City, the old capital of Vietnam, on the banks of the famous Perfume River in central Vietnam. Carlsberg—which entered Vietnam in 1993 with the acquisition of a 60 percent stake in South East Asia Brewery, based in the north of the country—now has a 50 percent share in the Hue Brewery.

ASIA PACIFIC BREWERIES

459 Jalan Ahmad Ibrahim, Singapore 639934
www.tigerbeer.com

Widely available across Asia, AP's beers are now brewed in seven different countries. Tiger Beer—its most famous—was first produced in the 1930s, when the "Time for a Tiger" slogan was first used. Anthony Burgess named the first novel in his The Long Day Wanes trilogy Time for a Tiger.

CHANG
LAGER 5% ABV
The export version is golden and light, aimed at an international palate. The domestic version is stronger (6.4% ABV), slightly darker, and brewed with rice as well as malt and hops.

BEERLAO
LAGER 5% ABV
Described as Asia's best beer, Beerlao has a pleasant sweetness. Light bitterness, with hints of honey.

BEERLAO DARK
LAGER 6.5% ABV
Reddish brown it is full of sweet toffee and toast flavors. A short but warming finish.

HUE
LAGER 5% ABV
A yellow corn color with a thin white head, and the body seems somewhat thin too. It is an easy-drinking beer, without surprises and a nose with hints of toast. Not much complexity, but a refresher nonetheless.

TIGER
LAGER 5% ABV
A golden colored refreshing lager. It is normally served so chilled that its taste and aromas are masked.

ABC EXTRA STOUT
STOUT 8% ABV
A strong but easy-drinking beer. The nose is robust, with roasted coffee and chocolate flavors.

BREWERY

MULTI BINTANG

Surabaya, Central Java, Indonesia
www.multibintang.co.id

Indonesia's largest brewery produces
and markets a range of drinks, including
Bir Bintang, Heineken, Guinness Stout,
and the low alcohol Green Sands. It was
founded in 1929, with Heineken taking
a share of the company in the 1930s.
Though taken over by the Indonesian
government in 1957, Heineken
became involved again in 1967, and
today it is largely owned by them.

MOUNT SHIVALIK

Mohangram, P.O. Bhankarpur,
Distt Mohali, Punjab, India
www.mountshivalik.com

The brewery was formally
incorporated in 1972. It was the first
in India to introduce the concept of
super strong beer in the country
under the name of Thunderbolt Super
Strong beer, which at 9 percent ABV
is a bit of a heavyweight. It also brews
the US brand Stroh.

UNITED BREWERIES

Bangladore, India
www.theubgroup.com

It is said the company's logo—
a Pegasus—once carried a cask of
beer between its wings as gift to the
gods. Its Kingfisher brand is the flying
leader in India's soaring beer market,
and what once was a company that
supplied beer to the troops of the
British Empire has now acquired a
worldwide reputation.

LION BREWERY

254 Colombo Road, Biyagama,
Sri Lanka
www.lionbeer.com

The company's best-known beer
is the bottle conditioned Lion Stout.
The beer is brewed from British,
Czech, and Danish malts, with Styrian
hops and an English yeast strain. All
the ingredients are transported along
precarious roads to the brewery,
located 3,500 ft (1,000 m) above sea
level in the midst of tea plantations.

BEER

BINTANG BIR PILSENER
LAGER 4.8% ABV
A fresh malty aroma gives way to
a dry hoppy bitter finish—the beer
clearly draws on its Dutch ancestry.

BINTANG GOLD
LAGER 4.8% ABV
A slightly darker variation of the
pilsener, brewed to commemorate
the republic's golden anniversary.

THUNDERBOLT 5.0
LAGER 5% ABV
Thinnish texture, with a hint of
hops. It is dry to the finish with
a touch of sweetness.

PUNJAB 6000 EXTRA STRONG
BEER 8.75% ABV
Strong in alcohol, the finish is a
little harsh but warming. Maltish
flavor, with no overlay of hops.

KINGFISHER
LAGER 5% ABV
Brewed under license in many
countries. It has a crisp taste with
a sweetish overtone.

LONDON PILSNER
LAGER 5% ABV
Thin yellow color, some hop aroma,
and a sweetish after taste, it smells
of grass.

LION STOUT
STOUT 8% ABV
A world-class beer, with pruney,
mocha aromas and flavors. It has
a tarlike oiliness of body and a
peppery, bitter-chocolate finish.
The alcohol gives it a long
warming finish.

CASTLE / SAB

65 Park Lane, Sandown,
Sandtona, South Africa
www.sablimited.co.za

SAB—South African Breweries—was
founded in 1895 and began producing
its Castle Lager brand in the mining
town of Johannesburg. The company
soon became the biggest brewer in
southern Africa. In 2002, SAB bought
Miller Brewing in the US, and as
SABMiller it has become one of the
biggest global drinks companies.

MITCHELL'S

Arend Street, Knysna Industria,
Knysna, South Africa
www.mitchellsknysnabrewery.com

Founded in 1983 by Lex Mitchell,
this microbrewery handcrafts a
characterful range of unfiltered
draft beers that are predominantly
British in style, combined with a
German influence. Some Mitchell's
ales are bottled and widely available
in the Cape region, but the beers
are not exported.

PAULANER

Clock Tower Precinct, Victoria & Alfred
Waterfront, Cape Town, South Africa
www.paulaner.co.za

The South African Paulaner is an
offshoot of the big Paulaner Bräuhaus
in Germany. Brewmaster Wolfgang
Ködel brews the Bavarian-style beers
on the premises and sells them on
draft in the glass-fronted brewpub and
beer garden located on Cape Town's
busy waterfront. German food
complements the beers.

SHONGWENI / ROBSON'S

B1 Shongweni Valley, Shongweni, near
Durban, KwaZulu-Natal, South Africa
www.shongwenibrewery.com

Shongweni mainly produces bottle-
conditioned beers, using the infusion
mash technique and fermentation in
open-top vessels. All its beers are
unfiltered and unpasteurized.
The family-owned brewery stands
out in a local market dominated by
mass-produced lagers. It exports to
the UK and elsewhere.

CASTLE LAGER

Lager 5% ABV
Award-winning lager made from
African Gold Barley and Southern
Star hops. It is brewed in nine
countries and sold in 40.

CASTLE MILK STOUT

Milk Stout 6% ABV
Dark, highly-hopped, strong stout
with a complex taste of roasted
black malts, coffee, and caramel.

OLD 90 / NINETY SHILLING ALE

Scottish-style Amber Ale 5% ABV
Aromatic with Pale, Crystal, and
Black malts, bark cinnamon, and
caramel. The name refers to an old
Scottish tax on a barrel of ale.

RAVEN STOUT

Milk Stout 5% ABV
Pale and Black malts with lactose
and some caramel. Full-bodied and
smooth, with a distinct hop aroma.

PAULANER LAGER

Lager 4.9% ABV
Unfiltered and unpasteurized,
golden in color, smooth, and
well balanced.

MÜNCHNER DUNKEL

Dunkel 5% ABV
An old-fashioned Munich-style
dark beer: dark golden, full-bodied,
malty, and smooth.

ROBSON'S DURBAN PALE ALE

India Pale Ale 5.7% ABV
Brewed with Pale malt, and
Cascade and Challenger hops.
Crisp, fruity, and well-balanced.

ROBSON'S EAST COAST ALE

Golden Ale 4% ABV
A smooth and refreshing golden
ale, made with a single malt variety
along with Brewers Gold and
Challenger hops.

BARONS
1 Moncur Street, Woollahra,
New South Wales 2025, Australia
www.baronsbrewing.com

"Beer barons" by name and nature, this relative newcomer has its brands produced under contract and is one of the country's fastest-growing craft beer players; they are also eyeing export markets in the US and Russia.

BREWING SECRET Barons makes use of indigenous "bush tucker" ingredients, such as wattle seed and lemon myrtle.

J BOAG & SON
39 William Street, Launceston,
Tasmania 7250, Australia
www.boags.com.au

From a once-moribund regional brewery, Boag's has ridden a wave of popularity since the launch of James Boag's Premium Lager in 1994. Lagers comprise the bulk of production, but Boag's has rolled out some fine limited-edition ales in recent years. The brewery was acquired by the Lion Nathan group in late 2007.

BOOTLEG
Corner Johnson & Pusey Roads,
Wilyabrup, Western Australia 6280
www.bootlegbrewery.com.au

"An oasis of beer in a desert of wine" is the mangled metaphor Bootleg use to state that they were the first craft brewery in the Margaret River wine region. Since opening in 1994, four other micros have joined them. Bootleg is housed in a sprawling homestead, with tasting room, restaurant (lunches only), and beer garden.

BRIDGE ROAD BREWERS
2 Bridge Road, Beechworth,
Victoria 3747, Australia
www.bridgeroadbrewers.com.au

Winemaker-turned-brewer Ben Kraus operates from his home town in regional Victoria—where renegade bushranger Ned Kelly was sentenced to death. Kraus has a wide range of beers on tap at his brewery door bar.

BREWING SECRET Ben is one of the few Australian brewers to produce styles such as *saison* and *bière de garde*.

LEMON MYRTLE WITBIER
BELGIAN WITBIER 5% ABV
Moderate carbonation, lime-scented mid-palate with spicy hints, followed by a clean, crisp finish.

BLACK WATTLE ORIGINAL ALE
SPICED AMBER ALE 5.8% ABV
Creamy mouthfeel, malt-driven, with hints of roasted nuts, chocolate, and milky coffee.

WIZARD SMITH'S ALE
BITTER ALE 5% ABV
A solid malt backbone, with toffee and spicy hop notes, is rounded out by a significant bitterness.

RAGING BULL
STRONG DARK ALE 7.1% ABV
Dark mahogany, complex coffee, treacle, and bitter chocolate notes; bristling late bitterness.

TOM'S AMBER ALE
ENGLISH BROWN ALE 4% ABV
Deep garnet-brown; roasty and bitter initially, with treacle notes; dry finish.

BEECHWORTH AUSTRALIAN ALE
AUSTRALIAN PALE ALE 4.4% ABV
Quaffable, easy-drinking cloudy ale, which balances fruity notes with moderate hop bitterness.

CHEVALIER SAISON
SAISON 6% ABV
Lively carbonation, complex palate, with hints of sherbet, wine, fennel, and yeast; a tingling, dry-ish finish.

THE BEST-KNOWN BEERS IN AUSTRALIA

Australia's biggest-seller is Victoria Bitter (produced by the Foster's group), which accounts for roughly one in every five beers consumed.

No one can really explain the phenomenal rise of "VB" over the past two decades, although it did coincide with changes in brewery ownership and an erosion of traditional loyalty to individual state brands. Somewhat ironically, Foster's Lager is one of the largest-selling brands globally and yet accounts for only around one percent of the domestic beer market. Carlton Draught (another Foster's group brand) remains strong in its Victorian home market, as do Toohey's in New South Wales and Castlemaine XXXX in Queensland. But the latter has been eclipsed recently by XXXX Gold, a "mid-strength" (lower alcohol) version; such mid-strength beers enjoy widespread popularity in the sun-belt states of Queensland and Western Australia, but have yet to make their mark elsewhere. Increasingly Aussie drinkers are turning to local premium and imported lagers, and to craft beers. The fastest-growing brand in the past couple of years has been Carlton Pure Blonde—a lower-carbohydrate beer that has already attracted a host of copycat brands.

VB (LAGER 4.9% ABV) *left*
CARLTON DRAUGHT
 (LAGER 4.6% ABV) *center*
TOOHEYS (LAGER 5% ABV)
XXXX GOLD (LAGER 3.5% ABV)
 right
CARLTON PURE BLONDE
 (LAGER 4.6% ABV)

BRIGHT

Great Alpine Road, Bright,
Victoria 3741, Australia
www.brightbrewery.com.au

A relative newcomer, Bright is situated in the regional Victorian town of the same name. The brewery door bar (open Fri–Sun) has a decidedly alpine feel, and is indeed close to ski runs. Flavor and balance have been at the forefront of each new style.

BREWING SECRET Bright's seasonal beers are available only at the brewery door.

CASCADE

131 Cascade Road, South Hobart,
Tasmania 7004
www.cascadebrewery.com.au

Australia's oldest operating brewery, complete with on-site maltings, is also the most striking, with the castellated sandstone building nestled in the foothills of the sometimes snow-capped Mount Wellington. Now part of the Foster's empire, Cascade attracts tens of thousands of beer lovers annually to its visitor center.

COOPERS

461 South Road, Regency Park, Adelaide,
South Australia 5010
www.coopersbrewery.com.au

While most Australian breweries were progressively "lagerized" during the 20th century, this family-run Adelaide brewing dynasty kept knocking out cloudy, bottle-conditioned ales and stouts. Since opening a new expanded brewery in 2001, surging demand for their beers has driven them to become the country's third-largest beermaker.

HELLFIRE AMBER ALE
BRITISH PALE ALE 5% ABV
Amber-gold; toffee and spice notes, dash of roasted malt; balanced, with satisfying bitterness.

CASCADE STOUT
MEDIUM STOUT 5.8% ABV
Coffee notes up front, with milk chocolate on the palate, followed by a moderately bitter finish.

CASCADE BLONDE
SUMMER ALE 4.8% ABV
Clean and crisp, with a hint of citrus hop flavor.

COOPERS SPARKLING ALE
AUSTRALIAN PALE ALE 5.8% ABV
Cloudy; fruity aromatics with a hint of peaches; rounded, dry, yeasty finish.

COOPERS EXTRA STOUT
DRY STOUT 6.4% ABV
Espresso and bitter chocolate notes, with banana hints too; robustly bitter finish.

BREWERY

FERAL

152 Haddrill Road, Baskerville,
Western Australia, 6056
www.feralbrewing.com.au

The Swan Valley wine region outside
Perth also boasts a handful of
microbreweries, including Feral. The
company's logo features a feral pig—
many of which roam the Aussie bush
and are keenly sought after by
hunters. Unusually, the flagship
brew is a Belgian witbier which,
fortunately, is free of any feral yeasts.

HOLGATE BREWHOUSE

79 High Street, Woodend,
Victoria 3442, Australia
www.holgatebrewhouse.com

Brewpubs serving hand-pumped real
ale are rare in Australia, and Holgate
is well worth seeking out. Paul and
Natasha Holgate took over the lease
of the stately Keatings Hotel in 2002,
relocating their microbrewery there
four years later (it had previously been
in a large shed beside their home).
They produce English-inspired ales.

KNAPPSTEIN

2 Pioneer Avenue, Clare,
South Australia, 5453
www.lion-nathan.com.au

Microbreweries in wine regions are
increasingly common in Australia. This
one operates out of a gorgeous stone
building that housed the Enterprise
Brewery until 1916 and, more recently,
has been headquarters for Knappstein
winery. Their sole brand is a full-bodied
lager, which is the beer equivalent of
a good Clare Valley Riesling.

LITTLE CREATURES

40 Mews Road, Fremantle,
Western Australia, 6160
www.littlecreatures.com.au

Based in an enormous hangarlike
building on the water's edge at
Fremantle (close to where erstwhile
beer baron Alan Bond lost the
America's Cup yachting challenge in
1987), Little Creatures combines
a bar/restaurant within a busy
microbrewery. The flagship Pale Ale is
inspired by the likes of the US-based

BEER

FERAL WHITE
Belgian Witbier 4.5% ABV
Hazy, pale lemon; juggles delicate
citrus and clove characters, with
a crisp, tart finish.

HOLGATE ESB
English Bitter 5% ABV
Biscuity malt notes intertwined
with leafy hop flavors, rounded
off with a satisfying bitterness.

WINTER ALE
Robust Porter 6% ABV
Espresso and treacle aromatics;
palate shows coffee and cream, dark
chocolate, and blackcurrant hints.

KNAPPSTEIN RESERVE LAGER
Bavarian Lager 5.6% ABV
Lifted fruity aromatics; passionfruit
and melon notes married to rich
malt; fulsome bitterness.

LITTLE CREATURES PALE ALE
US Pale Ale 5.2% ABV
Citrus/grapefruit hop aromatics;
chewy malt and citrus-tinged,
robust bitterness.

LITTLE CREATURES BRIGHT ALE
Pale Ale 4.5% ABV
Bags of floral hops; juicy sweet
malt balanced with tropical
fruit-laced hop flavors.

Sierra Nevada, and, along with the venue, has been a runaway success. The company is currently gearing up production, and has announced bold plans for themed bars in Sydney and Melbourne, and a second brewery to be built in Victoria.

BREWING SECRET Little Creatures uses impressive quantities of fresh hop flowers to flavor the beer.

LORD NELSON

19 Kent Street, The Rocks, Sydney, New South Wales 2000, Australia
www.lordnelsonbrewery.com

Still going strong after 20-plus years, Sydney's original modern brewpub attracts ale lovers to this historic hotel, which claims to be the city's "oldest continuously licensed pub." The early brews were basic malt extract-based beers, but have evolved into tasty and complex ales, worthy of this gem of a watering hole.

MALT SHOVEL

99 Pyrmont Bridge Road, Camperdown, Sydney, New South Wales 2050, Australia
www.maltshovel.com.au

Positioned as Lion Nathan's craft brewing arm, the Malt Shovel Brewery has grown an impressive portfolio of beer styles under US-born brewmaster Dr. Charles "Chuck" Hahn. The brewery's first release in 1998 was Amber Ale, which found ready acceptance with traditional lager drinkers. Their James Squire brands are named after a former convict and highwayman, who became the colony's first successful hop grower and brewer. Malt Shovel consistently rolls out groundbreaking and true-to-style beers from within the Lion Nathan fold.

BREWING SECRET Adventurous limited edition releases have included a porter that was matured in rum barrels and a raspberry wheat beer.

ROGERS' BEER

AMBER ALE 3.8% ABV
Biscuity malt notes; caramel-laced mid-palate and spicy-citrus hoppiness; short finish.

LITTLE CREATURES PILSNER

PILSNER 4.6% ABV
Using Czech Saaz hops, Little Creatures Pilsner is classically European—crisp, clean, and fresh.

OLD ADMIRAL

STRONG ALE 6.1% ABV
Dense, malty palate, with plummy notes, lively bitterness, and a warming afterglow.

THREE SHEETS

PALE ALE 4.9% ABV
Malty, fruity aromatics; malt-accented, with citrus and apricot hints; well-rounded bitterness.

MALT SHOVEL INDIA PALE ALE

INDIA PALE ALE 5.6% ABV
Chewy, caramel-tinged maltiness balanced by robust (dry-hopped) hop flavor and lingering bitterness.

MALT SHOVEL PILSENER

CZECH PILSNER 5% ABV
Faintly spicy aromatics; rich, malty palate, with honey notes and fulsome bitterness.

JAMES SQUIRE PORTER

PORTER 5% ABV
Hints of coffee, dark chocolate, and dark fruit (plums); a sumptuous beer, with a smooth finish.

JAMES SQUIRE GOLDEN ALE

GOLDEN ALE 4.5% ABV
Easy-drinking summer ale, with passionfruit/citrus hop flavors; crisp, moderately bitter finish.

BREWERY

MATILDA BAY

130 Stirling Highway, North Fremantle, Western Australia 6159, Australia
www.matildabay.com.au

Australia's first modern craft brewery kicked off in Fremantle in 1984, was acquired by Foster's six years later, and has been revitalized in recent times. Original brews such as Redback (a hefeweizen) and Dogbolter (a dark lager) have been supplemented with a wide range of beer styles. Much of the new direction occurred under the watch of head brewer Brad Rogers, who has since left the Foster's fold after 15 years to embark on a new brewing venture.

BREWING SECRET The Matilda Bay output includes an experimental "out there" series, which features a *saison* (named Barking Duck) and Crema, which is a coffee-infused pale ale.

MOO BREW

655 Main Road, Berriedale, Hobart, Tasmania 7011, Australia
www.moobrew.com.au

A stunningly appointed microbrewery, with commanding views of Derwent River and Mount Wellington from the second-story, glass-fronted brewhouse. An off-shoot of Moorilla Estate winery, Moo Brew has set a new benchmark among Australian craft producers, with slick packaging, uncompromising beers, and premium pricing.

MOUNTAIN GOAT

Corner North and Clarke Streets, Richmond, Melbourne, Victoria 3121, Australia
www.goatbeer.com.au

Self-styled "goat guys" Cam Hines and Dave Bonighton have clocked up a decade in craft brewing and generously mentored dozens of aspiring players over the years. Open nights are staged every Friday at the brewery, and attract a mixed crowd of ale lovers and funky Melbourne types, with brewery tours on offer.

BEER

ALPHA PALE ALE
US Pale Ale 5.2% ABV
Rich, caramel-toffee malt character; resinous hop flavor; and finally a bold, bitter finish.

DOGBOLTER
Dark Lager 5.2% ABV
Roasty, dark chocolate notes; complex mid-palate; smooth, coffee-ish finish.

BOHEMIAN PILSNER
Czech Pilsner 5% ABV
A solid maltiness to the pilsner is well balanced with a generous hop bitterness.

REDBACK
Kristall Weizen 4.7% ABV
Pale straw; banana, vanilla, and clove hints; delicate complexity; crisp, refreshing finish.

MOO BREW PILSNER
Czech Pilsner 5% ABV
Bright, golden, with finely-beaded bubbles; honey-ish malt character balanced by herbal hop bitterness.

MOO BREW PALE ALE
US Pale Ale 4.9% ABV
Citrus aromatics; grapefruit notes dominate mid-palate, rounded out with substantial, tingling bitter finish.

HIGHTAIL ALE
English Pale Ale 5% ABV
Cloudy amber; chewy malt, with bristling hop flavor and after-bitterness.

SUREFOOT STOUT
Medium Stout 5% ABV
Attractive mocha aromatics; dusty, roasty characters with treacle hints; restrained bitterness.

MURRAY'S

Taylor's Arm Road, Taylor's Arm,
New South Wales 2447, Australia
www.pubwithnobeer.com.au

The ironically named Pub With No Beer takes its name from a popular song by late country singer Slim Dusty and is the rather unlikely base for an exciting new craft brewery.

BREWING SECRET Murray's has pushed the boundaries of traditional beer styles and rolled out a handful of flavor-packed, limited edition brews.

REDOAK

201 Clarence Street, Sydney,
New South Wales 2000, Australia
www.redoak.com.au

The Redoak Boutique Beer Café is the showcase for a staggering array of beer styles from David Hollyoak, one of Australia's most awarded brewers, despite the fact that he only launched his beer range in mid-2004. A fruit-infused ale, a Baltic porter, a hand-pumped English bitter, and a wood-aged barley wine are just a few on offer.

WIG & PEN

Canberra House Arcade, Civic,
Canberra, Australian Capital Territory
2601, Australia
www.wigandpen.com.au

Real ale diehards come for the hand-pumped house beers, but there's a beer style for every taste at this busy brewpub, situated in the center of the nation's capital. Seasonal brews might include an annual imperial stout, Berliner Weisse, and whatever takes brewer Richard Watkins' fancy. A haven of characterful beers.

DUX DE LUX

Cnr Hereford & Montreal Streets,
Christchurch, New Zealand
www.thedux.co.nz

One of South Island's most revered craft brewers, The Dux has brewpubs in Christchurch and Queenstown. A broad range of styles is produced under the watchful eye of brewmaster, winemaker, and chef Richard Fife.

BREWING SECRET Visitors to The Dux are likely to be rewarded with limited release seasonal specialties.

NIRVANA PALE ALE
PALE ALE 4.5% ABV
Complex palate with zingy spice and citrus notes; generously bittered finish.

SASSY BLONDE
BELGIAN ALE 4.5% ABV
Distinctly Belgian character with robust yeast notes, and a hint of fennel; dry, yeasty finish.

FRAMBOISE FROMENT
FRUIT-BASED BEER 5.2% ABV
Hazy and crimson in hue; tart raspberry notes on the palate and a super-dry finish.

REDOAK RAUCH
GERMAN RAUCHBIER 5.5% ABV
Hints of bacon, iodine, and driftwood smoke, held in balance with sweet-malt flavors.

BULLDOG BEST BITTER
ENGLISH BITTER 4% ABV
Soft, fruity nose; biscuity malt notes balanced by zingy hop flavors and a firm bitterness.

CREAMY STOUT
DRY STOUT 6% ABV
Silky body, with chocolate and caramel notes; distinctly smooth, satisfying finish.

NOR'WESTER
ENGLISH PALE ALE 6.5% ABV
Early grainy sweetness, then hints of nuts and smoke, fruity esters and a deep, lingering, hoppy finish.

BLACK SHAG STOUT
IRISH DRY STOUT 5.5% ABV
A dense, black brew with a persistent creamy head and a silky body. Appetizingly dry.

BREWERY

EMERSON'S BREWERY

14 Wickliffe Street, Dunedin,
New Zealand
www.emersons.co.nz

New Zealand's most awarded micro offers an enviable portfolio of year-round beers, as well as seasonal specialties such as Taieri George, a spiced dark ale, and a US pale ale featuring American hops.

BREWING SECRET Emerson's delightful session beer called Bookbinder Bitter is available only on tap.

GALBRAITH'S

2 Mt. Eden Road, Mt. Eden,
Auckland, New Zealand
www.alehouse.co.nz

Located in a former library, New Zealand's first real ale brewpub is best known for its home-brewed English style ales—all served by hand pump. Visitors can also enjoy an excellent Abbey-style ale and a couple of flavorsome lagers, as well as a fine range of imports and craft beers from other New Zealand brewers.

MAC'S

660 Main Road, Stoke,
Nelson, New Zealand
www.macs.co.nz

Eighteen years after opening the country's first microbrewery in an old cider factory in Nelson, former All Black rugby player Terry McCashin sold the Mac's brand to Lion Breweries in 1999. Since then the beer range has been extended and production split between Nelson and the Shed 22 brewery, on the Wellington waterfront.

MOA

Jacksons Rd, RD3 Blenheim, New Zealand
www.moabeer.co.nz

Nestled among vines in Marlborough's wine country is Moa's brewery and tasting room—the brainchild of winemaker Josh Scott, who wanted to make super premium beers with the winemaking techniques used for Champagne-style sparkling wines.

BREWING SECRET Moa's larger 750 ml bottles undergo the full *méthode traditionelle* production regime.

BEER

EMERSON'S OLD 95

BARLEY WINE 7% ABV
Robust bottle conditioned ale, with rich, toffeelike malt and resiny hops. Will reward careful cellaring.

EMERSON'S ORGANIC PILSNER

NEW WORLD PILSNER 4.9% ABV
Bursting with passion fruit and citrus. A showcase for New Zealand's Riwaka hop variety.

BELLRINGERS BITTER

ENGLISH BEST BITTER 4.5% ABV
Copper colored ale with a biscuity, toffeelike palate, plenty of earthy hops, and an appetizingly dry finish.

BOB HUDSON'S BITTER

ENGLISH BITTER 4% ABV
A full-flavored session bitter very much in the vein of the English pale ale Timothy Taylor's Landlord.

SASSY RED

NEW WORLD BEST BITTER 4.5% ABV
A sweetish amber brew with a leafy, hop-sack aroma and suggestions of toffee, nuts, chocolate, and toast.

BLACK MAC

DRY STOUT 4.8% ABV
A full-bodied, flavorsome, stoutlike dark lager, with roasted malt, dark chocolate, caramel, and liquorice.

MOA ORIGINAL

BOTTLE-CONDITIONED PILS 5.5% ABV
Extended yeast contact rewards this delightful dry, crisp pilsner with a savory toastiness.

MOA BLANC

BOTTLE-CONDITIONED
WHEAT BEER 5.5% ABV
Dry, crisp, hints of banana and vanilla; soft natural carbonation.

NEW ZEALAND'S BEST-KNOWN BEERS

New Zealand's best-known domestic beers are all made with a high proportion of sugar and are warm-fermented with lager yeasts.

As a result of this process, the beers tend to be sweet, light-bodied, and, by European lager standards, somewhat estery. The market leaders, Speight's, Tui, and Export Gold are made by the country's two dominant brewers, Lion and DB. There are three basic Kiwi beer styles. A bronze or amber-colored brew is confusingly termed "draught"—even when packaged in bottles and cans! Anything paler is usually identified as "lager" (the brand name often suffixed with the word "gold"). A deeper colored beer is known simply as "dark." In the case of New Zealand's "draughts" and "darks," the term ale is often erroneously appended.

In the last decade, there has been a strong swing away from traditional Kiwi styles in favor of paler, crisper, so-called premium lagers. These days, New Zealand's most famous international beer, Steinlager (which is now available in both Classic and Pure versions), competes with locally brewed-under-license lagers, such as Heineken, Stella Artois, and Carlsberg, as well as a plethora of imported brands from Europe, the Americas, Asia, and Australia.

SPEIGHT'S GOLD MEDAL ALE (LAGER 4% ABV)
TUI (LAGER 4% ABV) *left*
EXPORT GOLD (LAGER 4% ABV) *center*
STEINLAGER (LAGER 5% ABV) *right*

MONTEITH'S

Corner of Turamaha & Herbert Streets, Greymouth, New Zealand
www.monteiths.co.nz

Now one of four breweries operated by the DB group (which itself is indirectly overseen by Heineken), Monteith's can trace its roots back to 1868. Although many of Monteith's beers are produced elsewhere, the Greymouth brewery—with its rare coal-fired boilers and open fermenters—is well worth a visit.

THE MUSSEL INN

Onekaka, Takaka, Golden Bay, New Zealand
www.musselinn.co.nz

Quirky, rustic, and ecologically aware, The Mussel Inn brewpub-cum-café is located in one of the country's most remote and unspoilt regions. The famous Captain Cooker Manuka Beer is affectionately known as "The Pig," a reference to New Zealand's wild pigs, which were first released by Cook. It is also brewed under license by Belgium's Proefbrouwerij.

SHAKESPEARE BREWERY

61 Albert Street, Corner of Wyndham & Albert Streets, Auckland, New Zealand
www.shakespearehotel.co.nz

Owned by former All Black Ron Urlich, this well-known Victorian city center pub was New Zealand's first new-generation brewpub. Shoe-horned behind the bar, the cramped brewhouse is ably manned by long-serving brewer Barry Newman. The pub offers nine beers and occasional seasonal specialties in various styles.

MONTEITH'S PILSNER BEER
PILSNER 5% ABV
Mild for the style, this firm-bodied brew has a grassy hop note and lingering sweetish finish.

MONTEITH'S BLACK BEER
BLACK LAGER 5.2% ABV
Soft and sweetish, with coffee, chocolate, and nut flavours—and often a hint of banana too.

MONKEY PUZZLE
BELGIAN ABBEY-STYLE ALE 10% ABV
A copper-colored brew that's big, spicy, and warming, yet delicately balanced and remarkably suppable!

CAPTAIN COOKER
WOODY AMBER LAGER 4% ABV
Seasoned with leaves from native shrubs, this is a fairly sweet and perfumy brew.

KING LEAR OLD ALE
ENGLISH OLD ALE 8% ABV
Full-bodied ruby hued brew, with orange, toffee, and chocolate notes. Long, floral, hop-driven finish.

PUCK'S PIXIL(L)ATION
BELGIAN GRAND CRU STYLE 11.1% ABV
A rich, heady golden brew with typically Belgian clovelike phenolics, sweet malt, and floral hops.

BREWERY

STEAM BREWING

186 James Fletcher Drive,
Otahuhu, Auckland, New Zealand
www.cockandbull.co.nz

The brewery was set up in 1995 to produce beers exclusively for the Cock & Bull pub in Pakuranga. Nine years and five pubs later, the company acquired the much larger Auckland Breweries site, complete with a high-tech packaging line. In addition to the Cock & Bull beers, the company now produces several beers under license.

THREE BOYS BREWERY

Unit 10, Garlands Rd, Woolston, Christchurch, New Zealand
www.threeboysbrewery.co.nz

Microbiologist Ralph Bungard employs a broad range of yeasts to produce tasty Kiwi interpretations of classic beer styles. The senior "Boy"—the others are his sons Marek and Quinn.

BREWING SECRET The brewery's limited release seasonal brews include an excellent Oyster Stout in winter and a fragrant Golden Ale in summer.

TUATARA BREWING

183 Akatarawa Rd,
Waikanae, New Zealand

Named after an endangered native reptile, the brewery is located in hill country, about an hour's drive north of Wellington. Its beers are widely distributed in the lower North Island, and the brewery's success prompted the installation of a larger, German-designed brewhouse in 2007. Tuatara beers are often served on hand pump at The Malthouse pub in Wellington.

THE TWISTED HOP

6 Poplar Street, Cnr Poplar & Ash Streets, Christchurch, New Zealand
www.thetwistedhop.co.nz

Its ales may be English in style, but The Twisted Hop is no typical English pub. A former warehouse set in a quiet back street with a pleasant kerbside drinking area, "The Hop" is bright, airy, and modern, with internal windows offering views into the brewery. The beer is also available at The Prince Albert pub in Nelson.

BEER

EPIC PALE ALE

AMERICAN PALE ALE 5.4% ABV
Robust interpretation of the style, with an explosion of hop resins (US Cascade) and sweet malt.

MONK'S HABIT

AMERICAN AMBER ALE 7% ABV
Brewed exclusively for the Cock & Bull pub chain. Sweet malt, balanced by floral and resiny hop flavors.

THREE BOYS WHEAT

WITBIER 5% ABV
Plenty of zesty lemon and coriander notes, with a hint of ginger.
A spritzy and quenching brew.

THREE BOYS PORTER

ROBUST PORTER 5.2% ABV
Rich mocha notes dominate a silky palate, while heavily roasted grain and hops compete in the dry finish.

TUATARA PILSNER

NEW WORLD PILSNER 5% ABV
Generous late hopping (with locally grown Motueka hops) results in a fresh, hessianlike, hopsack character.

TUATARA INDIA PALE ALE

INDIA PALE ALE 5.5% ABV
Although there's some nutty malt sweetness, earthy hops dominate the aroma and palate—a tasty ale.

CHALLENGER

ENGLISH SPECIAL BITTER 5% ABV
Copper colored and full bodied, with a fragrant hop aroma, toffeeish palate, and a long, hop-driven finish.

GOLDING BITTER

ENGLISH BITTER 3.7% ABV
Light, crisp, and flavorsome golden colored session bitter, with a fresh, leafy hop character.

Little Creatures started up in 2000, and its bottle-conditioned, US-style Pale Ale has proved hugely popular in Australia.

GLOSSARY

abbey ale Belgian family of strong, fruity beers either produced or inspired by monastery brewers.

ABV Alcohol by volume, expressed as a percentage. A measure of the strength of a beer.

adjuncts Strictly speaking, anything added to the brewing process other than barley, hops, yeast, and water. More usually refers to unmalted grains such as rice, barley, oats, and corn, added to increase alcohol content and lighten flavor.

ale A beer made with *ale yeasts*. Styles include golden ale, brown ale, *mild*, and *bitter*.

ale yeasts Yeasts used in traditional *top-fermenting* ales, originating from recycled yeast skimmed from the surface of the last batch. They ferment at room temperature.

alt, altbier German style of beer similar to British *bitter* or *pale ale*, especially associated with Düsseldorf.

aromatic hops A term used to distinguish the floral and fruitier hops, such as Cascade and Goldings, that are used to impart additional flavors and aromas to beer. Aromatic hops are usually added later in the boil than *bittering hops* to maintain the subtlety of their attributes.

barley wine An extra-strong style of *ale*, originally English, but now produced by many US brewers.

Berliner Weisse A pale, *top-fermented wheat beer* from northern Germany.

bière de garde "Keeping beer" traditional to northern France. Brewed in winter and spring, then bottled and stored to be drunk later in the year by thirsty farmhands. The style is now brewed year-round in several brewing nations.

bitter, best bitter English beer style, usually designating a well-hopped *ale*. Best bitter usually refers to stronger variants of the beer.

bittering hops Hop varieties such as Chinook and Fuggles that are rich in chemical compounds that result in the bitter taste sensation in beer and are used to balance the sweetness of *malt*. As distinct from *aromatic hops*.

blonde, blond A mainly French and Belgian term for a golden beer.

bock A German term for a strong beer—formerly seasonal, but not any more. Several variations include the even-stronger doppelbock and urbock, made in the original 13th-century style. *See also eisbock.*

bottle-conditioning The process by which beers are bottled with live *yeast* and sometimes fermentable sugars, extending storage life and allowing flavor and effervescence to develop further over time.

bottom-fermenting Term used to describe *yeasts* of the *Saccharomyces carlsbergensis* strain that are used to make lager. During lagering (storage), the *yeast* sinks to the bottom of the brew, producing a clean-tasting beer.

brettanomyces A semi-wild genus of *yeast* used in *lambic* beers and some *porters* and *stouts*. Provides a distinctive aroma and flavor.

brew kettle The vessel in which the *wort* is boiled with *hops* to combine their flavors, usually for about 90 minutes.

brewpub A bar or restaurant with its own small brewery on the premises.

broyhan *Top-fermented* pale *wheat beer* created in Hanover, Germany in 1526.

burton union A system of fermentation in galleries of linked casks, in which a stable *yeast* culture develops over time. Introduced in the 19th century in the brewing town of Burton-on-Trent in England.

carbonation Carbonation is the cause of effervescence in beer, and is generated by the metabolic action of *yeast* or by the artificial introduction of pressurized gas.

cask conditioning, cask ale The practice of bringing draft beer to maturity in the cask, in the conditioning room of a brewery or in the cellar of a pub. Times range from a week to a year or more.

c-hops Term used for *hops* with a very high aromatic potential, which convey especially grapefruit and resiny flavors. They are known by this term because many have names beginning with C (Cascade, Chinook, Cluster, Centennial, for example), but it also encompasses Amarillo and Simcoe.

contract brewing Commercial arrangement in which the creator of a beer contracts to have it produced at a brewery with spare capacity.

copper Alternative name for the *brew kettle*. Many copper kettles survive, but today a greater number are made from stainless steel.

craft brewer Term referring to breweries opened since the late 1970s that produce specialist beers.

curaçao A small, bitter orange grown in the former Dutch colony of Curaçao in the Caribbean. The dried peel is used in some Belgian *wheat beers*, most notably Hoegaarden.

decoction A process in which some of the wort is removed from the mash tun, heated to a higher temperature, then returned to the brew. It helps produce complex caramel flavors and clearer beers.

doppelbock *see bock*

dortmunder Pale golden, full-bodied, bottom-fermented beer from Dortmund in Germany.

double, dubbel A Belgian *abbey ale*, stronger than a pilsner but less so than a triple or trippel.

dry hopping The addition of *hops* to the finished brew to enhance its aroma and flavor.

dunkel, dunkler bock Dunkel means "dark" in German, and the term most readily applies to dark lagers, though it can also be applied to dark *wheat beers*. A dunkler bock is a *bock*-strength dark lager.

eisbock The strongest type of *bock*, lagered in ice-cold cellars, with frozen water crystals filtered off to increase the strength of the beer.

ester, estery An ester is a natural chemical compound that imparts fruity and spicy flavors (banana, strawberry, clove). Consequently, estery is a tasting note associated with some beers.

export Term often used for a premium beer, except in Germany, however, where it indicates a *Dortmunder*-style beer.

extreme beers Term originating in the US to describe a wide range of beer styles that are extraordinary in some way. Unusual ingredients, wild *yeast* fermentation, bourbon-keg

ageing, or very high alcohol content might earn a beer the title "extreme."

fermentation The conversion of malt sugars to alcohol and CO_2 by the action of *yeast*.

feistbeer German term for any beer that is traditionally brewed for a festival. Sometimes it refers to *märzen* and *Oktoberfest* styles, both strong variants of *Vienna lager*.

gose Distinctively salty style of *wheat beer* native to Leipzig.

grist Ground *malt* (or other grains) which, along with warm water, forms the basis of *wort*.

gueuze, geuze A blend of young and old *lambic* beers, blended to produce a sparkling, refreshing beer.

head The foam that forms on top of a beer when it is poured.

hefeweizen German term for *wheat beer* with yeast sediment. "Hefe" is a German word for yeast.

hell, helles German term designating a pale-colored beer.

hops Hop flowers—in dried, pellet, or resinous form—are added to beer to give flavor, aroma, and a bitterness to complement the sweetness of *malt*. See also *aromatic hops*, *bittering hops*, and *noble hops*.

hop back A sievelike vessel through which a brew is filtered. Its purpose is either to remove hop petals, or, when pre-filled with fresh hops, to add more flavor to the brew.

imperial stout Extra-strong stout made for export; the name stems from the beer's popularity with the Russian Imperial court.

IPA India pale ale; a robust and heavily hopped beer that was originally made to withstand the rigors of export by sea to India from Britain. Now also produced by several other brewing nations.

kellerbier "Cellar beer" in German; usually an unfiltered *lager*, hoppy and only lightly carbonated.

kölsch Light style of top-fermenting golden *ale* first brewed in and around the city of Cologne (Köln).

krieken A Belgian *lambic* in which macerated cherries are fermented, giving a tart, fruity flavor.

lace Pattern of foam left clinging to the sides of the glass.

lactic, lactic acid An acid that imparts a sour flavor to beer, produced when *lactobacilli* metabolize sugars. A tasting note for some beers.

lactobacillus A family of bacteria, usually benign, that convert sugars to lactic acid. The resulting sourness defines certain styles, such as *Berliner weisse*.

lager Family of bottom-fermented beer styles. Examples range from black beers such as *schwarzbier* to the more familiar golden pilsner.

lambic Designates beers fermented by wild, airborne *yeasts* in small, rural breweries in the Payottenland region of Belgium.

late-hopping The technique of adding *hops* to the brew kettle in the final minutes of boiling, so imparting pronounced hop flavors.

lees *Yeast* deposits resulting from secondary fermentation in the bottle.

malt Barley or other grains that have undergone a process of controlled germination, which is arrested at a point when the seed contains high concentrations of starches. After drying, kilning, or roasting, the malt may be made into *grist* for brewing.

maltings A facility in which the grain is steeped in water, allowed partially to germinate, and then dried.

märzen Originally a German style of medium-strong beer brewed in March (März in German) and matured until September or October. These days, the style of beer may be brewed and drunk year-round.

mash The mixture created when the *grist* is steeped in hot water. The mashing process breaks down grain starches into fermentable sugars.

mash bill A north American term for the proportion of different grains used in the mash.

méthode champenoise, méthode traditionelle A form of bottle conditioning that follows the method for creating Champagne. A secondary fermentation is achieved in the bottle by adding yeast and fermentable sugars. Beers made with this method are usually produced in Champagne-style bottles and the beer can usually mature for several years.

microbrewery Generic term for small breweries founded from the 1970s onwards producing relatively small quantities of beer. The US Brewers Association defines the term as a brewery that produces less that 15,000 barrels of beer per year.

mild A lightly hopped and thus mild-tasting ale, usually of modest alcoholic strength. Traditionally associated with the industrial regions of Wales and the English midlands.

milk stout A sweet *stout* made with unfermentable lactose sugars, derived from milk, that sweeten the beer's final taste.

münchner (munich dunkel) A German style of dark *lager* that was developed in Munich.

noble hops Term used specifically for a group of four traditional aromatic varieties of hops that are low in bitterness: Hallertau, Žatec (or Saaz), Tettnanger, and Spalter.

nonic glass A classic style of smooth-sided beer glass, typically made in half-pint and pint sizes. It is characterized by a bulge in its profile that aids grip.

northwest hops Refers to the Pacific Northwest—the country's main hop-growing region. Cluster hops were traditionally grown here, but now many other, especially aromatic, varieties are grown too.

oatmeal stout A revived style, popular in the US, brewed with up to 5 percent oats.

Oktoberfest A two-week beer festival held in the Bavarian city of Munich in Germany.

original gravity A measure of density of wort. High density indicates abundant fermentable sugars. The more sugar is present, the stronger the resulting beer will be.

oud bruin "Old brown;" a Flanders-style beer with a lengthy ageing period of up to a year.

pale ale A style of beer that originated in Britain, characterized by the use of pale *malts*. It mostly applies to bottled beers.

pasteurization Heat treatment process applied to beer to maintain its stability during storage. Arguably, pasteurization deadens the flavor of beer marginally.

pilsner, pils A popular style of golden *lager* pioneered in the Czech town of Plzeň, or Pilsen.

porter A family of very dark beers characterized by dark chocolate *malt* flavors and assertive hop bitterness.

priming The addition of sugar to a beer before it is bottled to encourage *carbonation*.

rauchbier A German style of *lager* made from *malt* that has been smoked over beechwood fires. The beer is a Franconian specialty.

reinheitsgebot The German beer purity law of 1516; now superceded by updated legislation but still a guiding principle in German beer making. Under its ruling, beers must not contain anything but water, yeast, malt, and hops.

saison Originally a Belgian beer style; a dry, strongish *ale*, traditionally brewed in winter for drinking in summer. These days, the style can be produced year-round, and it is usually *bottle-conditioned*.

schwarzbier "Black beer" in German. A dark, opaque style of *lager*.

seasonal beers Beers made for limited periods of sale, usually to suit climatic conditions at a given point of the year (such as *märzens* and *saisons*), or to celebrate a holiday or commemorate a historical event— a festbier for *Oktoberfest*, for example.

session beer Term describing an easy-drinking beer that is relatively low in alcohol and thus suitable for drinking in quantity.

sour ales, sour beer Originating in Flanders, these *ales* typically undergo ageing for between 18 months and two years in oak tuns, during which they gain a sharply thirst-quenching acetic character.

stein A traditional German tankard, made either of glass or ceramic (stein translates as "stone").

stout A dark style of beer, usually *top-fermenting*, that is made with highly roasted grain.

tap, taproom On-site bar or pub that serves a brewery's products direct to visiting drinkers.

top-fermenting Descriptive of all ale *yeasts* of the *Saccharomyces cerevisiae* strain, which produce a

thick foam at the top of the *fermentation* tank.

tun A vessel in which mash is steeped.

triple, tripel, trippel Traditionally the strongest Belgian *abbey ale*; though there are now quadruples to exceed them. In more general use, it denotes a very strong *ale*.

urbock see *bock*

urtype "Original type" in German; term used to emphasize that a beer is an authentic example of an established style.

Vienna lager Bronze-to-red *lager* with a sweetish *malt* aroma and flavor. Pioneered by Austrian brewer Anton Dreher.

weiss, weisse "White" in German, denoting a *wheat beer*.

weizenbier German generic term for *wheat beer*.

wheat beer Beer containing a high level of malted wheat. Usually *top-fermented* and often *bottle-conditioned*. Pale and cloudy with suspended *yeast* particles, creamy-textured and sweetish.

wild beer Beer that has been spontaneously *fermented* by wild *yeasts*, through being left exposed to the elements for a period of time. The classic example is Belgian *lambic*.

wit, witbier "White," "white beer" in Belgian: *wheat beer*.

wort An infusion containing fermentable sugars that is produced by the *mashing* process. The wort is filtered, boiled, and cooled before *yeast* is added to initiate the process of *fermentation*.

yeast A large family of unicellular fungal organisms, certain species of which are active agents in brewing and baking.

Yorkshire squares Square *fermenting* vessels associated with traditional brewing in the English county of Yorkshire. Still in use at Samuel Smith's Brewery and at Black Sheep. It is said to produce a remarkably well-balanced beer between sweet maltiness and yeasty sourness.

YOUR TASTING NOTES

You can use these pages to make your own notes about the appearance, aroma, flavor, and finish of different individual beers that you have the opportunity to sample. For more guidance about tasting beer, see pp36–7.

BEER	STYLE	BREWERY	CITY	STRENGTH

COLOR	AROMA	TASTE	FINISH	VERDICT	
				SAME AGAIN TRY AGAIN NEVER AGAIN	
				SAME AGAIN TRY AGAIN NEVER AGAIN	
				SAME AGAIN TRY AGAIN NEVER AGAIN	
				SAME AGAIN TRY AGAIN NEVER AGAIN	
				SAME AGAIN TRY AGAIN NEVER AGAIN	
				SAME AGAIN TRY AGAIN NEVER AGAIN	
				SAME AGAIN TRY AGAIN NEVER AGAIN	
				SAME AGAIN TRY AGAIN NEVER AGAIN	
				SAME AGAIN TRY AGAIN NEVER AGAIN	
				SAME AGAIN TRY AGAIN NEVER AGAIN	
				SAME AGAIN TRY AGAIN NEVER AGAIN	
				SAME AGAIN TRY AGAIN NEVER AGAIN	
				SAME AGAIN TRY AGAIN NEVER AGAIN	
				SAME AGAIN TRY AGAIN NEVER AGAIN	

YOUR TASTING NOTES CONT.

BEER	STYLE	BREWERY	CITY	STRENGTH

COLOR	AROMA	TASTE	FINISH	VERDICT	
				SAME AGAIN	
				TRY AGAIN	
				NEVER AGAIN	
				SAME AGAIN	
				TRY AGAIN	
				NEVER AGAIN	
				SAME AGAIN	
				TRY AGAIN	
				NEVER AGAIN	
				SAME AGAIN	
				TRY AGAIN	
				NEVER AGAIN	
				SAME AGAIN	
				TRY AGAIN	
				NEVER AGAIN	
				SAME AGAIN	
				TRY AGAIN	
				NEVER AGAIN	
				SAME AGAIN	
				TRY AGAIN	
				NEVER AGAIN	
				SAME AGAIN	
				TRY AGAIN	
				NEVER AGAIN	
				SAME AGAIN	
				TRY AGAIN	
				NEVER AGAIN	
				SAME AGAIN	
				TRY AGAIN	
				NEVER AGAIN	
				SAME AGAIN	
				TRY AGAIN	
				NEVER AGAIN	
				SAME AGAIN	
				TRY AGAIN	
				NEVER AGAIN	
				SAME AGAIN	
				TRY AGAIN	
				NEVER AGAIN	
				SAME AGAIN	
				TRY AGAIN	
				NEVER AGAIN	
				SAME AGAIN	
				TRY AGAIN	
				NEVER AGAIN	

YOUR TASTING NOTES CONT.

BEER	STYLE	BREWERY	CITY	STRENGTH

COLOR	AROMA	TASTE	FINISH	VERDICT	
				SAME AGAIN	
				TRY AGAIN	
				NEVER AGAIN	
				SAME AGAIN	
				TRY AGAIN	
				NEVER AGAIN	
				SAME AGAIN	
				TRY AGAIN	
				NEVER AGAIN	
				SAME AGAIN	
				TRY AGAIN	
				NEVER AGAIN	
				SAME AGAIN	
				TRY AGAIN	
				NEVER AGAIN	
				SAME AGAIN	
				TRY AGAIN	
				NEVER AGAIN	
				SAME AGAIN	
				TRY AGAIN	
				NEVER AGAIN	
				SAME AGAIN	
				TRY AGAIN	
				NEVER AGAIN	
				SAME AGAIN	
				TRY AGAIN	
				NEVER AGAIN	
				SAME AGAIN	
				TRY AGAIN	
				NEVER AGAIN	
				SAME AGAIN	
				TRY AGAIN	
				NEVER AGAIN	
				SAME AGAIN	
				TRY AGAIN	
				NEVER AGAIN	
				SAME AGAIN	
				TRY AGAIN	
				NEVER AGAIN	
				SAME AGAIN	
				TRY AGAIN	
				NEVER AGAIN	
				SAME AGAIN	
				TRY AGAIN	
				NEVER AGAIN	

INDEX

The Contributors

Tim Hampson, Editor-in-Chief of this book, reckons he has one of the best jobs in the world—he is paid to drink beer for a living. A regular broadcaster and writer on beer for many years, he has traveled the world in pursuit of the perfect drink. Chairman of the British Guild of Beer Writers, he wants more people to understand that beer has far greater complexity than wine can ever have. And it is harder to make too. His work appears in *The Telegraph*, *Food & Travel* magazine, *What's Brewing*, *Drinks International*, *Beers of the World*, *American Brewer*, *Brewers Guardian*, and *Morning Advertiser*; he has also appeared on BBC Good Food Live and Sky TV. He is author of *Room at the Inn*. In his writing for this book, he was assisted by **Adrian Tierney-Jones**.

Stan Hieronymus is a lifelong journalist who has made beer his "beat" since 1993, authoring four beer-related books, contributing to several others, writing hundreds of articles for scores of periodicals, and founding the Beer Oral History Institute. His work has won scores of awards and he was the US Beer Writer of the Year in 1999. Since 1998 he has been editor at Realbeer.com, taking a leave of absence in 2008 to spend 15 months traveling —and more than occasionally visiting breweries—with his wife, Daria Labinsky, and their daughter, Sierra. For this book, Stan wrote the section on beers of the US.

Werner Obalski has been a journalist for 30 years, specializing in spirits, wine, and of course beer. He also reviews bars and restaurants for several guides. Among his books are *365 Wine Tips* (Dumont Verlag, Köln), *Sherry* (Haedecke Verlag, Weil der Stadt), and *Tequila* (Haedecke Verlag Weil der Stadt). Werner is a member of the organization Food Editor's Club, Germany, and he is also judge and member of the ISW (the International Spirits Competition in Neustadt, Germany). Werner lives and writes in Munich, and here contributed the section on Germany's beers.

Alastair Gilmour is one of Britain's leading regional journalists. He is Features Editor of *The Journal*, the daily newspaper for the northeast of England, where his specialist work on beer has an extensive and enthusiastic following. He was Glenfiddich Food & Drink Awards regional writer, 2004 and 2007, and has been the British Guild of Beer Writers' "Writer of the Year" on four occasions between 1998 and 2007. He has been a judge at several international beer competitions, including The Great British Beer Festival in London and the International Master Bartender Awards in New York and Prague. Alastair wrote the sections on beer in the British Isles and in the Czech Republic.

Joris Pattyn was a founding member of Objectieve Bierproevers (OBP) in the mid-1980s, since when he has helped organize and spoken at many beer festivals, seminars, and competitions. He has also been a judge at several international competitions, including, most recently, the World Beer Cup, 2008, in San Diego. He has written for publications in the UK and US, and coauthored *Lambic/Kland* with Tim Webb and Chris Pollard. He is also soon to publish *100 Belgian Beers to Try Before You Die*. Joris is a member of Zythos in Belgium, PINT in the Netherlands, CAMRA in the UK, Les Amis de la Bière in France, and ABO in the Czech Republic. For this book, he wrote about Belgian beer.

Lorenzo Dabove was born in Liguria, though today he lives and works in Milan and Genoa as the Cultural Director of Unionbirrai. He is the foremost expert on Italian craft beer, and is internationally recognized for his efforts to promote Italian beer and traditional lambic brewing as well. He has judged in such prestigious contests as the World Beer Cup in 2004, 2006, and 2008, and the European Beer Star in Gräfelfing, Bavaria, in 2006 and 2007. He wrote the book *Le Birre*, published in 2005 by Gribaudo Editore, Savigliano. Lorenzo contributed the section on Italian beer.

Gilbert Delos is a French journalist and beerologist. For more than 20 years, he has tasted the beers of Europe—especially those of his native France. Among the books he has written on the subject are *Beers of the World* (Tiger Books, 1994) and *The Master Chefs and Beer* (Somogy, Paris, 2003). He is also President of The Friends of Beer in Ile-de-France—an organization of beer lovers located in Paris and its environs. He regularly leads tastings of beers. Gilbert wrote on French beer for this book.

Conrad Seidl was born in Vienna, where he lives as staff writer and political commentator for the daily newspaper *Der Standard*. For his beer writing he uses the "Bierpapst" moniker. His columns appear regularly in the gourmet magazine *Falstaff* and in the trade magazine *Der Getränkefachgroßhandel*. He has a monthly TV show, which can also be seen on the Internet (www.bierpapst.tv). His career as a beer writer started with a guide to Austrian beer

(*Hurra Bier!*) in 1990, and he has now published more than 25 books. He is a member of the British Guild of Beer Writers in London, the Gesellschaft für Geschichte und Bibliographie des Brauwesens in Berlin, the Confrérie Gambrinus in Luxembourg, and the Bier Convent International in Munich. Conrad wrote about Austrian and Swiss beer for this book.

Ron Pattinson is a member of the British Guild of Beer Writers, and has written extensively about European beer. His pub guides, written in a gloriously chatty style, have been used by thousands of beer lovers. Bad jokes, a superfluity of statistics, and an obsession with Barclay Perkins, Dark Mild, and Leipziger Gose litter his many writings on the history of beer. He lives in Amsterdam. Ron contributed the section on beers of the Netherlands.

Laura Stadler-Jensen is an American freelance journalist based in Copenhagen, Denmark. She specializes in Scandinavian culture and writes on topics that include gastronomy, travel, and design. She is married to Lasse Fredrik Jensen, an accomplished Danish chef, who provides insight into exciting culinary trends such as beer pairing and molecular gastronomy. Laura wrote the sections on Denmark and Scandinavian beer.

Bryan Harrell is Californian by birth, but has lived in Japan since 1977. He has been a writer and correspondent for several US magazines, and has also extensively researched the beer scene in Japan for the late, eminent drinks writer Michael Jackson, contributing to several of Jackson's books. Bryan has written books on cycling and home brewing, currently publishes the monthly *Brews News* (www.bento.com/brews.html), and writes a regular beer column in Tokyo's *Metropolis* magazine (www.metropolis.co.jp/tokyo/recent/beer.asp). Bryan wrote the Japan section.

Willie Simpson lives in a one-pub town in northwest Tasmania and is regarded as Australia's foremost beer writer; he has been commentating on the amber nectar and other alcoholic beverages for the past 20 years. His writing appears regularly in the *Sydney Morning Herald* and *The Age* (Melbourne), and he is the author of three books: *Amber & Black* (New Holland Publishing, 2001), *The Beer Bible* (Fairfax Publishing, 2006) and *Home Brew* (Penguin, 2007). More recently, he has become a craft brewery operator, with the opening of Seven Sheds—a brewery, meadery, and hop garden. Here he has written about Australian beer.

Geoff Griggs is New Zealand's only full-time specialist beer writer, commentator, judge, and educator. He has written for many magazines, and, in addition to writing a weekly beer column in his local regional newspaper, Geoff reviews beers for the country's largest supermarket group. Having judged at New Zealand-based international beer competitions for the last decade, Geoff was invited to join the judging panel at the world's largest beer competition, the World Beer Cup, in 2008.

PICTURE CREDITS
The publishers would like to thank all the breweries that provided their kind assistance in sending bottles or bottle images to be used within this book and related works.

Thank you to the following picture agencies and companies for their kind permission to reproduce images for features within this book:

Key: a=above, b=below/bottom, c=center, l=left, r=right, t=top

Alamy 20 (t/l, t/c, c), 158 (t/c, b), 159 (t/r, b/r), 204 (l/c), 241, 271, 304–5, 312, 316, 322; Anheuser-Busch 49 (b, b/r); Carlsberg 50–51 (b, c, b/r); Corbis 20–21 (b/l, c, c/r, b/r), 66–7, 88–9; Gotty 96–7; Gulden Valley Brewery 65 (t/l); Heineken 50 (t, t/r); InBev 49 (t/l, t/c), 204 (t/l, b/c), 205 (t/r, b/r); Orval 218–19; Pelican 64 (b); Pilsner Urquell 236–7; Rogue Brewery 64 (t/r, c); SABMiller 48 Sierra Nevada Brewery 11(b).

Additional studio and location photography by Thameside Media, Quentin Bacon, Joe Giacomet, Tim Hampson, Catherine Harries, Michael Jackson © DK/Michael Jackson, Roger Mapp © Rough Guides, Ian O'Leary © DK, Michael Schönwälder, Mark Thomas © Rough Guides.

Jacket: (on spine) Berg Brauerei Ulrichsbier; (on back) Kinshachi Red Miso Lager, Sierra Nevada Anniversary Ale, Hogs Back Brewery TEA, Žatec Pivovar Blue Label, Butte Creek Brewing Pilsner, Heineken Premium Lager, Diageo/Guinness ® brand, La Trappe Quadrupel, Little Creatures Pale Ale.

Maps: Casper Morris, Paul Eames, David Roberts.

The publishers would also like to thank the following people and organisations for their help in the preparation of this book: Beers of Europe, Finn at Utobeer, Jeff at Cracked Kettle, Lithuanian Beer, Belgian Beer Shop, The Grove Tavern, Karen Heptonstall, Malini McCauley, Jennifer Crake at Tourmaline Editions, Florian Bucher, Dorothee Whittaker, Tina Gehrrig, Monika Schlitzer, Ina Melzer at DK Verlag, Dirk Kaufman at DK Inc, Rebecca Carman, Shawn Christopher, Katerina Cerna, Wojciech Kozlowski, Agnes Ordog, Jürgen Scheunemann, Yumi Shigematsu, Diggory Williams, Nora Zimerman